Sons of Francis

SONS OF FRANCIS

National Gallery London.   Botticelli.

The Nativity.

M.

SONS OF FRANCIS

BY

ANNE MACDONELL

WITH PHOTOGRAVURE FRONTISPIECE
AND EIGHT ILLUSTRATIONS

" Ritter von dem heil'gen Geist"

1902
LONDON
J. M. DENT & CO.
NEW YORK: G. P. PUTNAM'S SONS

Printed by BALLANTYNE, HANSON & CO.
At the Ballantyne Press

CONTENTS

LIST OF ILLUSTRATIONS

SONS OF FRANCIS

INTRODUCTION

" Cristiani del terzodecimo centinaio."
—Vita Nuova, xxx.

By a rare chance the spirit of the early Franciscan movement, ere yet the movement had grown old, was accurately reflected not only in sober lives of the Founder and in pious tracts, but also in a book of stories, which after delighting many generations of friars, made its way outside convent walls, and found the widest welcome. The other Orders have their legends, full of worthy heroes too, but neither by their matter nor their form have they touched the popular heart to the same degree. They have their great literature, but it is a literature of the cloister and the cell. In the *Fioretti* the tales of the heroic age of the Minorite brotherhood took a shape which to this day makes equal appeal to men of the world and peasants, to religious thinkers and children.

To read the *Fioretti* without a running commentary of history is to be transported into a kind of fairyland of the spirit. These knights of the Franciscan Round Table seem just as near and just as remote as Arthur's, that is, their reality is surely the reality of forcible poetic legend. And to a reader with this idea in his mind it seems natural to divide the early Minorites into two classes—on the one hand, those who appear in serious ecclesiastical history, well authenticated by the Church, such as Saint Anthony of Padua and Saint Bonaventura :

A

on the other, the heroes of the *Fioretti*, legendary "knights of the Holy Ghost," nearer to our hearts, but dwelling in a land of exquisite fancy. Yet if there be a division, its line does not mark off a greater reality on this side, a lesser on that. Let Bernard, Leo, Giles, and the rest remain in their poetic atmosphere, but only because it was about them when, as real men, they lived in our common world. If they seem extravagantly romantic beyond the usage of our world, the better did they fulfil the soberest intentions of the Founder. The tales in the *Fioretti* owe much, doubtless, to their author Ugolino's imaginative sympathy, but probably little to his invention. The actual facts were as shining as any embellishments of his.

Francis drew to his banner many saints, and poets not a few, with whom his Idea was in safe keeping. But when his own band of brothers grew into a great Order his Idea became modified and even distorted. Then the brethren of his spirit fought for its integrity in knightly fashion. You need go no further than the *Fioretti* to learn this: read between the lines there, and you will see the traces of a sharp struggle. The pæans of Joy in the book cannot all shut out the rumours of war. In presenting, therefore, some of the *Fioretti* heroes and their successors in the second and third Franciscan generations in the arena of the actual world, I am bound to tell of strife; for they were no quietist order of monks, but an order of chivalry—*ritter von dem heil'gen Geist*— and as such active combat was the reason of their being. The fault will be mine if the smoke of battle hide the heroes' continued joy in their share of the discovery which Francis had made, and the peace from his dream which visited them even in the thick of the fight. But the main theme must be struggle. And though they did much for early Italian art and poetry, yet the chief interest of the Sons of Francis seems to me not their dreams and imaginings, but their strenuous attempts at translating dreams into life and action. Infinitely finer and rarer are such attempts than art and poetry, however fine and rare these be.

II. I make no claim to have written a book without bias. The whole subject is prickly with controversy. The early Franciscan movement, as I have said, was a continuous warfare, and not only with the world of sin. There was war to the knife among its own adherents. The strife has lasted to this very hour, and seems to grow in intensity. I know no question of social economy or of politics which divides, as does this one, its students to-day. It rouses heated passions, calls out abusive and scornful language, provokes withering attacks. Those who write coolly are, in the main, mere mechanical compilers. A lively interest involves ranging yourself definitely on one side or the other; for the questions at issue are as big with import to-day as when they were first mooted, and that was long before Saint Francis appeared in the world. Scholars may think themselves quite detached from the concerns of the present, and when they wax hot over the religious history of more than six hundred years ago, may congratulate themselves on the intensity of their intellectual interest. But, consciously or not, they are partisans in a struggle of their own hour. It is not the question of the supreme authority of the Catholic Church that divides them, any more than it divided the men over whom they quarrel now. The separation lies far deeper, springs from an ideal half concealed, half revealed, as much social as religious, never realised, yet always dimly felt, an ideal that has divided, that will eternally divide the world till the millennium.

Some readers to whom the figures in this book may have a pious interest will only be wearied by the insistence on controversies; yet constant reference to these is essential if the histories I have to tell be given their right significance. Certain energetic but ill-founded attempts to trace Protestantism to the free spirit of Francis have received so much credit that many readers will expect the assurance that the frankest, deepest searchers on the subject are Protestant historians. But with the sole exception of that profound student of the movement, M. Sabatier, the most thorough, the most learned investigators have been members of the Catholic Church. I believe it is to go widely astray to trace the Protestant Reformation to the influence of the Sons of Francis. Francis himself and his companions loved their own Church with a fervour that cannot be exaggerated. Rome was their mother, whom they venerated, believed in, and hoped all things from. Even among the extreme Joachimites of the Order it was not Protestantism that was germinating, but something far more revolutionary, which was more likely, while it clung to any definite dogmas and ceremonies at all, to cling to those of Rome than to adopt the tenets and forms of Geneva, or any forecast of these. So far as the movement of the Spiritual Franciscans was disintegrating, its attack was directed towards something more fundamental than the authority of the Pope.

On the other hand, while some learned Catholic historians have displayed an exemplary frankness and thoroughness in investigating, others, not less learned, have made their researches valueless, for themselves, by striving to reconcile the records and the workings of a free and independent spirit with the very conventional traditions which that spirit had sought to destroy. There are ancient formulæ for hagiography which render that department of literature a curious and sadly instructive subject of study, but touching actual human life at fewer points than, say, conchology. Even some who have freed themselves from the formulæ dare not trust themselves to make inferences from their patiently, honestly acquired knowledge. They dare not apply to personages blessed by the Church, or banned by the Church, or misunderstood by the Church, the tests of character and of work they would employ towards men and women to-day, on whom the Church has pronounced no judgment. They fear psychology. The learned modern Bollandists—and I pay all honour to their learning and their patience—are typical sinners in this respect. Their own excellent purpose is to collect facts and documents, to sift them, and pronounce, by the aid of ripe scholarship, on their authenticity. They need no justification for adhering narrowly to this task. But watch their reception of the works that venture to understand facts, to combine them intelligently, to make them live, to test them by common sense, or by the light of poetic instinct, or by a general knowledge of human nature. These are almost invariably dubbed wanting in erudition, hasty, superficial, misled by sentiment. It is good to be learned and industrious in document-reading ; but documents are dead dust and ashes without an open and experienced mind to read them by. The present day Bollandists, however, have done too much excellent work to deserve to be pilloried alone. Take nine-tenths of the historians who have touched on the history of Brother Elias, and surely candour will force the cry that the extraordinary ingenuity used in shirking facts had been turned into the courage and capacity for facing and understanding human nature.

III. But as I have said, my own book is biassed. In reading the old chronicles I have felt strong preferences. Of the men and women they reveal, some have touched and kindled me, and others have left me very cold. In the struggles between the two chief parties in the Order I have ranged myself definitely on one side, and my reason is—Francis. Not that the other side was wanting in virtue, or talent, or interest, or in great personalities. It illustrated many excellent things—but it did not particularly illustrate Francis·; and my interest in Franciscanism derives solely from its Founder, and follows only where I see the traces of his spirit. But perhaps I may plead guiltless of the monotony of showing only one type of Minorite, since among my portraits are those of two brothers with feet so well planted in our common earth as Frate Elias of Cortona and Fra Salimbene of Parma.

Francis works miracles still in Assisi. He worked one on a June evening not long ago. The morning had been spent in listening to a garrulous young *frate* up at the Carceri, whose cheerfulness in the mountain solitude showed him of the true breed, and who told his tales from the *Fioretti* with a simple glee, and the dramatic instinct of the early times. It was charming, it was stimulating; and Francis was a wonder and a lovely thing. But, out of Umbria, what would Francis be to us, save one more object of dilettante interest? In the evening we lay on our balcony at the *Subasio*, when the moon was up, and yet there was daylight in the sky. The olives were a tender mist upon the hillside, and the fire-flies raining about. A touch of gold on this hill-top, of white on that, marked Perugia and the other high-set towns. The line of the mountains carried one's eye along, and back it came by the blessed valley below, where colour and sound were linked in softness and in calm. An exquisite harmony, unforgetable—but only landscape after all, to stir the artist within us. Then a turn of the eye showed us the gate, and the winding of the road down to St. Mary of the Angels. Suddenly before us came the old scene—the litter carried gently by grey-frocked brothers, the poor haggard man in it, lifting his face and bidding them halt, bidding them turn him round again towards the town he had left, and saying while they stood, "'Blessed be thou of God, O holy city, seeing that through thee shall many souls be saved, and in thee shall dwell many servants of the Lord : and out of thee shall many be chosen for the kingdom of eternal life.' And said these words, he let them carry him on to St. Mary of the Angels." We heard their steps down the road in the quiet evening, went with them, of them, grieving as they.

A scene realised with rare intensity, we should have said, had we spoken. For we still knew we were lying up there above. But we seemed also to know when they reached the Porziuncola, and laid the dying man in the infirmary. And suddenly it was no "scene." The valley rocked with fresh grief, and our hearts were wrung. The joy and pleasantness that followed were as great, filling the whole of the soft valley, speaking in the tender speech of the leaves, in the shining of the fire-flies, in the far reach of the ranges, and the lights upon the hill-tops. Francis was there, the living man, and the eyes of strangers from another land of thought and feeling were rendered less gross that they might see him. He was never one to keep himself among the elect and the worthy. Since then he has been something to the strangers outside Umbria. And so, in gratitude, this book, which every good lover of his must think poor homage, is yet laid on his shrine in confidence.

IV. The life of Francis was a romance, and could have been nothing else. Even had he stopped in Assisi measuring bales of stuff in his father's warehouse, he would have set the town agog with some great enterprise. He turned back from the adventure with Walter de Brienne because a greater was germinating in his soul. The romances of chivalry he pored over as a boy ; the troubadour songs he sang along the streets, leading his band of golden youth, were his natural food. His nature dominated his career inevitably, and to the very end. He was always knight-errant, ever tilting, ever dashing into the midst of danger, and espousing lost causes. Poet, he loved and glorified the common things, and scorned the commonplace. He is the great adventurer, not of religious thought, but of religious life. Eminently practical, his dreams were always spurs to action. He and his first brothers were like boys daring each other to feats, he the most impulsive, headstrong, and audacious. There was nothing reasonable or sensible about him. He never learned to grow old, or even middle-aged, though bitter disappointment fell to his lot as well as terrible hardships. The sign mark of true vocation in his company was *joie de vivre*. The foundation of this in Francis was his own lusty nature; but if a man had to be persuaded to rejoice, there were excellent reasons to be given. The one of his choice was common enough in theory, but belief in it was the breath of his being. The world groaned because it forgot that it had been redeemed, and that there was a good chance for it yet. Believe that, and live a courteously thankful life, and all should be well. Tell everybody the good news. The world showed him miseries that mocked at his hope. He never grew incredulous, but took his sword in one hand and the balm of healing in the other. As a born adventurer he attacked the hardest foes. The loathsomest diseases had the most tender care from him who had been a fastidious young elegant. Lepers and criminals he made verily his brothers. And he cheered his followers on, never sparing them. They had always to be in the thickest of the fight with him. Where there was safety there could be no adventure. The popular idea of Francis as the most feminine of the saints, manifesting only the gentle, patient virtues, is totally wrong. He is the young restless hero among them, most gentle, indeed, but virile.

The world showed him heavy burdens, crushing the able-bodied, the rich, the noble, the powerful. Well, what wonder? They were in prison. They were shut out from everything that was worth having by the consciousness of possessions, of the difficulty of keeping them safe against robbers, or insinuating friends, or designing relatives, by the desire of making them more. What a life! In their high place they forgot all men were brothers, and lost the joy of friendship. Shake yourself free of the world's trammels if you would have joy. Francis was quite convinced of the deceitfulness of riches; but he did not war against rich men. He was all the more a social solvent that he made no cut and dried scheme of social reform. His intellect was not speculative. Riches might be used well. He did not set up to be the judges of their possessors, and especially enjoined his brothers not to do so. But there was a royal road to freedom of spirit, and that was to have none of them. As for the adventurer, the knight-errant, he must have no such burden. He needed his hands, his heart, his soul free. The scaler of the celestial city might never win in, if he had a thought of his money bags. To make the whole world Franciscan was not in Francis's mind. He was but concerned to train his own little army for the service of the world.

In no proper sense of the word was his system ascetic. His end was joy as much as that of any epicurean. Cheerfulness was blessed, and sadness damned by him. "Indeed, if I were at any time tempted or sad, when I look at my companion's cheerfulness straightway am I turned from temptation and depression towards inward and outward joy." And so the father sharply reproved those who showed their sadness outwardly. "Why," he would say, "dost thou show outwardly the grief and sadness of thy sins? Let thy sadness be between God and thee, and pray Him that of His mercy He spare thee and give back to thy soul the wholesome joy of which it is deprived because of thy sin." It was by a Franciscan inspiration Dante assigned a bad place in hell to those who were sad in the sunshine.

When I say his system was not ascetic, I do not deny the asceticism of his own life. He was by no means free from the cruel traditions of an earlier time which delighted in the mauling of the body. And though for Brother Body he demanded justice, he owned in the end he had overtasked it himself. But let us remember he was a spiritual athlete—his end, complete freedom of the soul through the body's obedience. The obstinate body had to be mastered that it might become a perfect instrument. Eager and keen he spurred it, and flogged it, and ran it up and down rough roads, and fed it sparely and seldom, ever uncontent till it was willing and swift and hardy. It was a knightly exercise, a trial of strength and skill, and the Bride looked down, and you carried yourself with a high heart. Emulation did wonders, no doubt, and Francis had to cry halt sometimes and feast poor Brother Body, that some failing companion by his side might not faint for shame of halting first. They were very extravagant in their feats of endurance. As I have said, there was nothing reasonable about them. And it was not the Body alone they would dominate, but the will, the mind, till every faculty should be at the bidding of the soul. They took an intense joy in these exercises. Brother Masseo, a lusty, well-favoured fellow, ready of speech, whom people flattered instinctively, becomes enamoured of the virtue of humility with which nature had perhaps poorly endowed him. He has no rest till he acquires it. He vows the eyes out of his head if it may be his. He contemplates all the errors of his life. He contemplates the vast difference between himself and goodness, accepts reproof, menial tasks, degradation. It is a long struggle. He might have learned, say, geometry, a few languages, much skill in the game of chess, in half the time. And it is revealed to him in the end, as the ultimate lesson in the virtue, that he cannot ever win it of himself, but that it will be given to him as a grace. Morbid? Well, but humility is a good thing for some to learn, and tremendously difficult, and quite as useful in the advancement of character and in social intercourse as many accomplishments to which strenuous years are cheerfully given.

They flew at their vices as at an enemy's citadel between them and the country of their desire. This is the secret of their love of being shamed. Nothing, Francis had discovered, hindered a man's mastery of his soul as the fear of ridicule. After that, he and his courted ridicule. When a respectable brother, who had been a grave signor in the world, went through the streets, and naughty boys hung on to his capuchon, he had to learn to be glad and not angry, for it was but one little test in the exercise-ground, where he was learning to be a champion. Read, in its own place, how Brother Rufino, with the hermit's terror of men, had to defy his shamefacedness; and how great a ring-master was Francis. Juniper is the typical brother who gloried in making a fool of himself for the Lord. I need not repeat the well-known stories of him going naked for the urchins of Viterbo to fling mud at, or playing see-saw to abase himself before the serious Romans come out to do him honour. Fra Jacopone is his rival—but I speak of him elsewhere. Indeed, a brother was but a poor athlete, and at the beginning of the race, if scorn or ridicule perturbed him. Begging itself was a severe enough discipline for some of the less zealous. But it was involved in that part of their system which decreed they should have no privileges. The lot of the poorest was theirs: they were even jealous of greater hardships than their own. By such labours as they were fit for must they earn their living. If they knew no honest trade or calling, for the exercise of which men would give them bread to eat— and the brothers were largely drawn from the richer classes and the nobles—they must learn one. If they worked and still went hungry, they need feel no more shame in begging than children who accept their meat from their parents. No man among them, however highly born, however learned, but must know the primitive needs, and practise the common duties of life, as servant, doorkeeper, cook, or nurse.

They were almost proud, you would say, to be assailed by their vices; had even a grim joy in their despair when the Lord withdrew His face from them, for then they knew they were in the training-ground. "I have never been Brother Minor save in my temptations," said the dying Bernard of Quintavalle. Read Francis's ecstatic pæan to Brother Leo on perfect joy. His discourses were all pictures or dramas. He imagines them both arriving at their own St. Mary of the Angels, hungry and weary and cold. They knock and knock and knock, but are refused entrance, for all their weeping and beseeching. The enraged porter says, "These be importunate knaves. I will pay them well as they deserve," and rushes out with a knotty stick and sends them rolling in the snow, and beats them with the knots of the stick. "If with patience and with gladness we suffer all those things for the love of Him, thinking on the pains of the Blessed Christ, the which we ought to suffer for the love of Him, O brother Leo, write that here and herein is perfect joy." There is too much quick-blooded eagerness in this for it to be called morbidity. It is the very lust of fight and adventure.

V. What was all this training meant to end in? For the rank and file, it was to make them ready, obedient, hardy, untiring servants of God and their fellow-men. And, indeed, the Franciscan training, even in the degenerate times of the Order, made the Brothers Minor redoubtable helpers in any enterprise, sacred or secular, redoubtable fighters, redoubtable foes. But there was another end in view. The supreme type of the more sober Franciscan is John of Parma, a man of fine brain, of learning and eloquence, before whose purity and dignity kings were proud to be humble.

He rose to the highest rank in the Order, yet remained to the end a hardy, frugal brother, tirelessly tramping the roads, sharing the burdens of the most insignificant, as fearless as he was humble, a man of great strength of purpose, of miraculous endurance, and with the resignation of a sweet-natured child. When the Pope said he must no longer govern the Order, he retired with perfect dignity, not to fret, nor to plot, but to the life of a sage. There is no better example anywhere of the perfect soldier. And in him are manifest the various purposed results of the training. The victory over will, over appetite, over habits and desires, produced in the *élite* special faculties, the highest of all, ecstatic contemplation, when the body gave way before the might of the soul, which, free, entered into that City of God, which was no hazy poetic dream, but, to the Franciscans, an actual reality in the world that is the world of all of us.

It is an easy thing to recommend the early Minorites to modern men as brothers of the poor, partisans of the weak, pioneers of popular movements, nearly concerned with the bettering of the world around them. It is true for many of them, and true for the movement as a whole. They did very ardently, and in a very human way, love their fellow-men. But it is only part of the truth; and at the risk of alienating them from modern sympathies, the rest of the truth should always be boldly stated. They cared a great deal for this world, but first as a tilting-ground for champions of the heavenly kingdom, and, ultimately, as it manifested another. By service in menial things to be accounted worthy of hours when they should lose themselves in something far better and vaster—that was their supreme desire. Their ideal of contemplation was as complete as that of any Eastern sage. If on their return they told very haltingly what they had seen, at least they could tell their joy, and how hard it was to come back. "Give me thy wings," cried Conrad to the dead Giles, "that I may fly with them

to where thou enteredst in." But in the record of every
one of the ecstatics we read the tale of long and humble
toil. They paid the common tolls of humanity to the
uttermost farthing ere they crossed the misty river to
the country where human feet tread not.

Francis himself was more than a mere visitor to the
City. His raptures were not detached incidents, but
symptoms of his mystery. To him the scheme of the
universe was Love; but men had ruined it by sin. Love
then made itself manifest in the Passion of Christ to save
the world. In gratitude, but also instinctively, by his
own happy nature, Francis loved all things, birds and
reptiles, and ravening wolves, and stones and trees, and
robber-men, and lepers, and his own brothers, and
Lazarus, and the rich man, with a serviceable love. But
with every step of love pain keeps pace : such is the eternal
law. And ere on Mount Alverna his was made one with
the Universal, he had known the pain of the Passion of
Christ.

VI. These great rewards, these lonely triumphant
experiences were for the chosen, and for chosen moments.
But the secret of the commoner joys was still emanci-
pation from petty cares, from cumbering possessions.
They were sent back to Nature for their comfort and
their joys, and she did not send them empty away.
The House of Nature is continually being rediscovered
by her children. Francis made the discovery for his
time. Because he had eyes, other men saw the fairness
of the world. Because he had ears, other men heard
harmonies. Because he became himself a part of the
love of the world, and heard living hearts beat in beast
and bird and tree and stone, other men grew tenderer,
and counted common things not vile.

"He went honourably upon the stones," says
Voragine, in the *Golden Legend*, "for the worship of
Hym that was called stone. He gadryd the small

wormes out of the wayes, by cause they should not be troden with the feete of them that passyd by. He commanded in winter to gyve honey unto bees that they should not perysshe for hungre. He called alle beestes his Bretheren. He was replenysshed of merveylous joye for the love of his creatoure. He behelde the Sunne, the Mone, and the Sterres, and somoned them to the love of theyre Maker."

When at Rieti the leech was about to cauterise his eyes, Francis said unto the fire, "'Brother Fire, noble and useful amongst all the creatures, be gentle to me in this hour, for I have always held thee in love, and shall ever do so for love of Him who created thee.' . . . And his prayer made, he signed the fire with the sign of the cross. . . . Nor is it wonderful if fire and other creatures would obey him and do him reverence, for, as we who were with him saw very frequently, he so loved them and delighted in them, and his spirit was moved by so much piety and pity towards them that he would not see them churlishly treated, and so would speak with them, manifesting an inward and an outward joy, as if they had been reasonable beings, for which cause he was often rapt unto God."

So great was his love for the beauty of fire that he would never hinder it in its function. Once when a part of his clothing was alight, he would not put it out. Some one rushed to him, but he said, "Nay, dearest brother, harm not the fire;" and they had to use force before he would suffer them to extinguish it. So with a lamp or a candle. "Nor would he that any brother should throw away fire or move a smoking log from place to place, but should just put it on the ground, for reverence of Him whose creature it is." Once when he had saved a fur rug, his covering for the night, from being burnt, so disgusted was he with his avarice he said he would never use it again because he had grudged Brother Fire's eating it.

"After fire, he loved with a special love Water, by
which is figured holy penitence . . . and for the first
washing of the soul is made in the water of baptism.
Thus, when he washed his hands he chose a place so
that his feet should not tread the water which fell. . . .
Likewise to the brother who prepared the logs for
burning, he would say never to cut up a whole tree,
but that some part of it should always remain for love
of Him who worked our salvation on the wood of the
cross.   And so to the brother who was the gardener,
he used to say not to till the whole ground only for
vegetables, but to leave some part for green herbs which
in their season should produce our brothers the flowers,
for the love of Him who is called a flower of the field,
and a lily of the valley. . . . Whence we who were
with him saw him rejoice so greatly, with inward and
outward joy, in all created things that, touching them
or seeing them, his spirit seemed to be not on our earth
but in heaven.   And for the many consolations which
he had so often had in created things, a little time
before his death he made certain Lauds of the Lord
concerning His Creatures, to incite the hearts of the
hearers to the praise of God, and that the Lord should
be praised of men in His creatures."

True Pantheist, however good a Catholic — and,
indeed, where's the contradiction?—he made the men
of his time heirs again of the common benefits and
beauties, and hastened that return to Nature which was
the dawn of Italian art.

What, then, of his attitude to art and to intellectual
matters? He cannot be said to have had any attitude at
all.   He was a poet himself, and in youth he had fed on
the romances of chivalry, and on troubadour verse.   He
never seems to have condemned these, and, outside his
Bible, they were probably all the literature he knew.
If he could spell out the Latin of his mass book, he
could do little more.   Music was a delight to him,

though very likely he heard only the brothers' rough voices and Giles's flute. But then he could call angels from heaven with their viols, to wile away his nights of pain. At the end he had a plan—even then he was full of eager plans—to send a company of singing brothers through the land to be the Jongleurs of the Lord. With an ear and eye so attuned to the beauty of the world, it is safe to say he had the instincts of his race for art. But as to erudition, he had none himself, and it is not to his discredit that he distrusted the scholastic learning of his day. Sometimes he speaks respectfully of theology, but he did not mean the fine-spun theories of the schools, mere webs of vanity. His Knights of the Round Table had no use for these. With the love of God in their hearts, and the gospels on their tongues, he held them well enough equipped for their humble mission. When the brothers clamoured for the theological training obtainable in other Orders, he gave reluctant leave to Anthony of Padua to be a teacher. Both the poet in him, and the practical man, and the man of the new time, were concerned in his distrust of the learning of his day. When the brothers of his spirit betook themselves in earnest to theology, they brought to it so much of their own that the old scholasticism did not survive their studies of it.

VII. The aims of Francis are not so much a matter of surmise as might be expected, seeing he did not expound his doctrine in lengthy volumes. All his doctrine was in his life. His authentic writings are very few. Wadding was too profuse in his attribution of Franciscan works and fragments to the Founder. But he inspired the men around him in an almost un-exampled way—if we consider the age—to record his sayings and their memories of him. Of all the saints, not excepting those who have written autobiographically, him we know with most intimacy, from contemporary documents and from the writings of the next generation. A few of these have long been known to all Franciscan students. The rest are one by one being published. Whenever it has been in my power, I have consulted originals—my guide in the first place being M. Sabatier, to whom every student of mediæval religious history owes the deepest debt of gratitude. In Celano's two Lives, in the *Speculum Perfectionis*, in the *Legend of the Three Companions*, is to be found a wealth of vivid memories set down by men who lived near him or with him. Some account of the controversies concerning these will be given later. In the *Sacrum Commercium* a man of his time, or of the next generation, expanded Francis's own tale of his mystic espousal of Poverty. Reflections of the legends of him and his first followers, are to be found in the *Actus Sancti Francisci et Sociorum Ejus*, in that entertaining body of narratives, the *Chronicle of the Twenty-four Generals*, and, in delightful and popular form, in the *Fioretti*. The Spirituals' point of view is, without too much exaggeration, to be read in the *Epistles* and the *Tribulations* of Angelo Clareno, who lived near enough to Francis's time to hold direct communication with friends of the master's immediate followers ; while the essence of Franciscanism can be extracted, though with much difficulty, from the later hopelessly diffuse, not always dependable, yet very remarkable book, the *Conformities* of Bartholomew of Pisa. Among later historians that have either industriously collected material, or have shown critical ability in dealing with it, may be mentioned the faithful and zealous Luke Wadding, Affò, the eighteenth century student of the literature of the Order, patient and able, but with a rather shifty point of view ; Papini, a clear-headed searcher in Franciscan records, with an unscientific contempt for legend ; and, in our own day, M. Sabatier, the most philosophical of them all, and by no means the least pious.

But I hold that the ultimate meaning of a movement will always be best expressed, not in the narratives of its history, not in its doctrinal treatises, but in its poetry. One laud remains of the many Francis made. And he made no poem so great as his own life. Yet to judge his system by himself is hardly fair. He fascinates too much. And Fra Pacifico's lauds are lost or sunk into the vague sea of Franciscan anonymity. Deep as was the Minorite influence on Dante, his great mind held the whole ancient and mediæval world in fee. But there is Jacopone—and to him and the tale of his life, I would send such new students of the movement as the *Fioretti* and any other early chronicles they may have read—frank enough most of them in their revelation of Minorite crudities when frankly studied—have still left inclined to sentimentalise over the ideals and the doings of the *frati*. He, too, has been sentimentalised over, but only by those who have skimmed his surface. Nearly all his students have either haltingly apologised for, or straightforwardly condemned his work. He is a strong dose— a real test of the power of a modern constitution to assimilate, even to tolerate, what was meant by pure Franciscanism. Its ultimate possibilities are expressed in him, and some of them are entirely shocking to modern minds. And he is all Franciscan. If he drank at other sources, it was only at such as were similar in effect. The draught made him drunk, but the truth of its spirit spake in his intoxication. The folly of the cross, the deep scorn of worldly opinion, the contempt beyond telling of material possessions, the persistent and grotesque abasement of the body, the audacious ambition of the spirit, the complete indifference to final damnation or salvation, are all in Jacopone, and make disturbing reading. We may turn for relief to his lauds of the Christ Child, more tender than any in northern tongue. But in his spiritual love songs we are shaken, even shocked, by the vehemence of his passion, and borne to regions where we have not learnt to breathe. Once a learned Bologna doctor, and lapped in the world's luxuries, his later life, judged by even moderate standards of comfort and decency, was hardly higher than that of the beasts of the field. And Jacopone died in very truth of a spasm of intimate love for things too high for the dreams of most of us. Not a comfortable poet for quiet Sabbath reading, but a great force, his spirit one of the generating wombs of a new world—yet not of our world, and not of any world even distantly resembling it. Translated into modern action, his spirit would be the denial of all our civilisation. Supreme type of the Franciscan mysticism —and awful warning! A serious estimate must condemn his spirit as criminally presumptuous, stultifying to human energies, or boldly acknowledge the mad *frate's* rocky path the way of eternal truth.

VIII. There is a determined theory that Francis formed the Franciscan Order. He may be called its Founder. He was responsible for its main features, and its mighty impulse came from him. But that he formed it, such as it has ever been at any day after it could be called an organisation at all, is far from the truth. At some kind of organisation he aimed, of course; but he was quite incapable of forming the complicated machine the Minorite body became. Not that he was wanting in will, or clearness of aim, or a sense of the value of discipline. His pertinacity was unexampled; there was not a hazy spot in all his mind; and the obedience he demanded from his recruits was that of a commander in time of war. But see him fumbling over all the Rules, save the few verses from the Gospels that made the first. He never saw the use of any other. He had the deepest horror of formality and pedantry; and, with all his shrewdness, an almost unbounded trust in men.

See him before Honorius at Perugia, begging the Indulgence of the Porziuncola, by his simple confidence gain-
ing it, in the face of unwilling Cardinals, and turning
away happy and triumphant with the mere word of the
Pope, who calls after him, *O Simplicone, quo vadis?* So
with his army. By the Rule, which was the Gospel, and
not of him, they were bound. He was not their jailor.
Every Rule he made, every direction he gave, was for
spiritual incitement. He would fain have had them free
men. He could not, but also he would not, organise
and administer even a large body of men by complicated
rules. He could command an army and endow it with his
spirit, so long as he had the enlistment in his own hands.
Had there been no Elias, no Cardinal Ugolino, there
would have been no Franciscan Order; but a loose company of spiritual men in many lands would have looked
to him as their father. His spiritual following would
have been the same, his substantial work perhaps the
same. But he would have had no *réclame*, and saint as
he was, he might not have been canonised—though to
the Umbrians he must ever have been *beato*.

It is not my purpose to trace in detail, as has too
often been done, the degradation of the Order. Its own
early success was of course a terrible danger. Francis
saw that himself: witness his dream of the little black
hen, given by the Three Companions. The little black
hen was sad and anxious because, do what she would,
she could not shelter all her brood under her wings.
In Francis's fear lest he should neglect the well-being of
the brothers who trusted themselves to him, he ran to
Orvieto to the Pope, to ask for a Protector for his Order,
and he was given that very able man, Ugolino, the Cardinal Bishop of Ostia.

If only the little black hen had trusted a little longer
to her own motherly care! But what use to open up
the question of Organisation? The very word is sacro-
sanct among us to-day.

Francis, with all his trust in men, was too shrewd to enlist them recklessly. A story in the *Speculum Perfectionis* tells of a recruit, a nobleman from Lucca, coming to him and begging him with tears to admit him as a brother, and how Francis was not touched by his tears at all. "O miserable and carnal man," he said, "why dost thou lie to the Holy Ghost and to me? Thou art weeping carnally, not spiritually." Just then came his kinsmen with intent to take him away. Whereupon, hearing the neighing of the horses, he looked through the windows, saw his kinsmen, went down to them, and returned with them to the world.

But with Ugolino and Elias numbers counted for much. They refused no recruits, and were quick to see the splendid instrument for the Church Francis was training. It was Ugolino's business to see it, to use it. Gradually, very partially in the lifetime of the Founder, he attached the Minorites close to the Roman Curia. Very loosely associated with special localities and offices, they were the better servants of the central power in Rome, could be sent out as missionaries, secret messengers, ambassadors, inquisitors, and spies. Men so powerful, active, and popular, it seemed absurd to keep out of the high offices of the Church. Favour brought them all the wealth they desired to have., The purpose of mendicancy was degraded. But every one knows the story. Was it inevitable? The history of every great organisation would seem to answer yes. But though I distinguish Francis and the Sons of Francis from the Franciscan Order, I own the Order has had a great history, and in every age many of its members have been worthy to be of the little circle, *Nos qui cum eo fuimus.*

IX. Only a few great ideas fit for translation into a plan of life have been conceived by the human mind, and these are stronger than any corporate manifestation of them, however potent. The ultimate test of such a great idea is not its power to seize on an age or a great mass of men, till the age and the mass are called by its name. It is tested rather by its strength in resisting the wear of the blundering hands of men, and all the ruin of change and circumstance. A mediocre idea can produce a splendid organisation in its day and generation. The greatest idea may just possibly miss adaptation to a special epoch. But it will filter through the ages, nor ever lose its early force. The Idea of Francis almost forbids definition, since his originality consisted in there being no separation between it and the conduct of his life. At first sight, therefore, he seems much more limited than some hermit writer of a book of pious maxims, because his notion of expression was action, suffering in his own body what he conceived in his heart and mind. What he did not experiment with thus, may be left out of count. Is his Idea only an interesting historic fact, dead, save as a stimulator of intellectual inquiry?

Curiously modern, the most modern of all the saints, yet the thought of him amongst us scatters our complacency. Brother of all men was he ; nevertheless, we cannot think of him as patron of our democracy, which is mainly intent on getting what he thought not worth while troubling about. The aristocrat in the little rough-clad, barefooted Umbrian might rise in disdain of our civilisation. But he would not cry Woe! Woe!—for that was never his way—and if he should go to his brother in Russia, he would leave him more cheerful, and bid him let folks sing in their own fashion, even if their songs were shaped a little more elaborately than befitted *moujiks'* voices—since singing is mostly good. Or he might think more hopefully of us than we deserve, but when he took the road again we should be left with our piled-up furniture and possessions, feeling vulgarians and very poor, and wondering through what ages of striving we should have to pass before we reached his rich simplicity. That he could raise a band of young athletes, I make no doubt. But supposing he were to come back with his fresh spirit, and, in his travel through the ages, had forgotten his motive, could he find one again, as he found one before, wandering through the olive groves of Assisi? We should explain to him elaborately the complicated problems of our social and industrial life, and ask him to thread a way for us out of the difficulties. He couldn't —even if he could be got to understand the problems. There are no solutions, he might say, though with a good will we could cut a knot or two. He could only make the problems non-existent for those whose minds he could divert out of the press and struggle.

Yet consider for an idle moment what could be done to-day by a band like his, athletes filled with no mere pious opinion about the mastery of vices, but vowed to their overcoming by the energy we see displayed in champions of the cricket-field or the billiard-room, so hardy of body that half the products about which the modern world busies itself would have no meaning for them at all; pledged to accept no privileges of rank, or fortune, or deference; trained to obedience so that material humiliation would be impossible; civilised by bye-laws that made courtesy the plainest duty, and gloom a malady to be hidden like a festering sore; spurred by a sense of adventure that should make frontier-crossing like the stepping from the causeway to the street, and give the world for a tilting-field. What could not such a band do, led by a motive, captured by a movement, for good, or, some may not unreasonably ask, for evil? Let the age be tranquil. The latent energy is here. But the motive? And where is the Bride of the new chivalry, so fair that once dreamed of she must be sought, in however far a court, beyond whatever seas, in whatever inaccessible mountain citadel?

X. It would be an interesting speculation to trace the possible progress of Franciscanism as a political economy, to guess how it might revolutionise society, and what would remain of modern triumphs after its reign; or to compare it with modern communism, and mark the meeting places and the parting of the ways of two systems, each demanding the means of material subsistence as an elementary right, but one condemning individual possessions as an injustice, the other conceiving them as a hindrance to spiritual well-being and to everything worth possession. But Francis must be left out of this inquiry. He never undertook a plan of the world's salvation, never recommended panaceas. He only inspired and trained a wandering chivalry.

Yet the most serious and strenuous among the typical thinkers of the present hour will not for that exonerate him. They can scent in him the Enemy, and if challenged to more than a chill admiration for a dead man pictured in an altar-piece, will cry out that his spirit is a calamity. What distracts men's minds from material things is dangerous, they say. Such distraction ends in the exploiting of the weak. Ware, ware, workers of the world! Materialism is the safeguard of the poor—idealism a conspiracy of the churches in the exploiters' pay.

This is a conceivable position, hardly to be captured by the fact that the Franciscans played a prominent part in the popular movements of the thirteenth and fourteenth centuries. The contemplatives, the ecstatics, we are told, are breaking a compromise of world-wide obligation till Time shall be no more. To scale the ladder of the skies, to endeavour to realise truth in its entirety, to condemn alloy in the common conduct of life, is presumptuous, and towards humanity as treasonable and as dangerous on earth as was Lucifer's revolt in Heaven. Man is mortal and incomplete, and should behave as such. Keep to the rules of the earthly game.

Alloy is like gravitation, it keeps humanity from being scattered in space. Have ideals by all means for Sabbath hours. Have we not poetry on our bookshelves, and do we not give it to youth?

Well, in the very movement of whose history I recount some incidents there is an echo of these sentiments. Brother Elias, who organised it even in the Founder's lifetime, was an accomplished man of the world. But Francis, and most of the men whose tales I tell, were romantics, adventurers in life; and if the compact be ·indeed sacred, they were in truth very dangerous, those "Christians of the thirteenth century."

NOS QUI CUM EO FUIMUS

Francesco e Povertà per questi amanti
Prendi oramai nel mio parlar diffuso.
La lor concordia e i lor lieti sembianti,
Amore e maraviglia e dolce sguardo
Facean esser cagion di pensier santi;
Tanto che il venerabile Bernardo
Si scalzò prima, e dietro a tanta pace
Corse, e correndo gli parv' esser tardo.
O ignota ricchezza, o ben ferace!
Scalzasi Egidio, scalzasi Silvestro,
Dietro allo sposo; si la sposa piace.

PARADISO, xi. 74–84.

Nos qui cum eo fuimus — the words are a refrain in the mouths of Brother Leo and his companions, a refrain to many songs in various keys. There is exaltation at their own privilege, and joy in the great days when Francis was alive and they lived by his side. There is a pathetic remembrance in them of a vanished presence, and an ardent purpose to keep his spirit alive; a calm conviction that whatever may be ordered, in the name of their friend, by the great ones who wield the power, they knew best what had been his plan; a gentle defiance of all the authorities that would give them a less heroic task than he did; an appeal to all his lovers not to be content with a mere tasting of the spring he released for them. They, his companions, had drunk the full cup from his hands, and their lives had been glorified ever since.

Three of them wrote later the tale of their happy community in the early days.

"Eager were they all each day to pray and to work with their hands, that they might put far from them all indolence, that enemy of the soul. In the night time they rose and prayed most devoutly with profound sighs and tears. They loved each other with a cordial love, and served each other; and one man gave his brother bread as a mother feeds her only and well-beloved son.

"Such love burned in them that it seemed a light thing to them to give their bodies up to death, not only for the love of Christ, but for the saving of the souls or the bodies of their brethren. . . . They were so founded and rooted in humility and charity that one revered another as his father and lord, and those who rose to the office of prelate, or had other favour of rank, seemed lowlier than the rest. Ever prepared for obedience in all things they gave themselves up continually to the will of him that had command over them, making no nice distinctions between just and unjust commands; for whatever was ordered they held to be God's will, and to do His will was easy and sweet to them. . . ." An anxious judge was each man of himself, careful in nowise to offend his neighbour. "And if it happened that one said to another a vexing word, his conscience gnawed, so that he could not rest till he had said his fault, throwing himself on the ground and making his brother place his foot upon his mouth. . . .

"No one kept anything for himself; but the books and other things given to them they used in common, according to the rule observed and handed down by the apostles. And for true poverty was to be seen in them, liberal and open-handed were they with all things given them by the Lord, giving freely, for His love, to all that asked of them. And when they went along the road and found poor folks that begged alms for the love of God, if they had nothing else, they gave them some part of their raiment, poor and spare though it was. Sometimes it would be the hood they would give, tearing it apart from the tunic, or perhaps a sleeve or some other part. . . .

"In their poverty they were gay, for they had no desire after riches, but despised all worldly things that are dear to the lovers of this world; especially money, which to them was as dust to be trampled under their feet. . . . And ever they rejoiced in the Lord, not having among themselves anything to be sad about. So far as they were parted from the world, so much nearer were they joined to God, walking in the way of the Cross and in the paths of His justice."

Such were the knights of Francis's Round Table; such their life in the first days at Rivo Torto and the Porziuncola. They kept their vigils, trained themselves in chivalry, and for privilege had a place at his side, where they suffered more hardships than other men, and knew his heart. They were looked on as an aristocracy even in the later days when persecution was the reward of their inconvenient memories and their stubborn adherence to the ideal of the early times. But it was an aristocracy entirely Franciscan, and by its nature precluded all ruling over their brethren save by the spirit. It was not they became the administrators and governors in the Order. Rome did not appoint them princes of the Church. They were always Brothers Minor, the servants of the servants of God, who were subject to other men without shame, who for all relaxation and reward hoped, but did not claim, some quiet contemplation in the hills and desert places. The parallel between this company and Merlin's is not idle. "And when they are chosen to be of the fellowship of the Round Table," we read in the Book of Sir Percivale, "they think them more blessed, and more in worship than if they had gotten half the world, and ye have seen that they have lost . . . all their kin and their wives and their children for to be of your fellowship." Said

Merlin, " By them that should be fellows of the Round
Table the truth of the Sancgreal shall be known."

The intimate friends of Francis were not all among
the traditional first twelve that set out for Rome in
1210. He had a genius for coming near men's souls,
and they were not few who could have said in after days,
nos qui cum eo fuimus. But we know his dearest, for
popular legend and authentic history have kept their
names and their memories alive—sometimes in defiance
of official biography. In telling of his closest circle one
might limit one's self to the friends who went up to
dwell with him on Alverna—Masseo, Angelo, Rufino,
Leo, and probably Silvestro and Illuminato. But that
list would omit two commanding figures. A more representative one is contained in the prefatory letter to
the Minister General Crescentius, which introduces the
Legend of the Three Companions—the authors, Leo, Angelo,
and Rufino, and their witnesses, Philip, Illuminato,
Masseo, and John the companion of Giles and of Bernard.
Concerning Philip a few facts are known, chiefly in connection with the administration of the Clares ; but his
personality has not stamped itself clearly on the history
of the brotherhood. Of John there is no record save of
his friendships ; but his friends are in the first rank
of the Companions ; and Illuminato I shall deal with
in the chapter on " Dante and the Franciscans." This
list is, of course, lamentably incomplete, since it does
not contain the ever delightful Juniper, the divine clown,
the *egregius joculator Domini.* But there is little to be
added to the tales of him in the *Fioretti*, where his
portrait stands unforgetable for ever. Indeed, for the
others, save Giles and Leo, I must depend greatly on the
Fioretti, whose familiars will forgive me when I lead them
again along well-known paths, since they are beloved ;
and may welcome the little I can add by way of authen-
tication and supplement to the legends of the men that
walked with Francis, full of cheer along hard roads.

I. BERNARD OF QUINTAVALLE

Lo secol primo quant' oro fu bello ;
Fe' saporose con fame le ghiande,
E nettare con sete ogni ruscello.
                          —Purgatorio, xxii. 148–150.

WHEN Bernard of Quintavalle—the first companion,
according to tradition—joined Francis, he was a man of
weight and substance in Assisi, one with what the solid
people call "a stake in the country," looked up to by
his fellow-townsmen. By his counsel, says an old
chronicle, all that city was ruled. For two years he
had been watching Bernardone's son playing his holy
antics, a byword among the stable families of the
place, renouncing his business and his respectable father ;
had seen him a ragged beggar mocked by the children in
the streets, as a year ago before he had been followed by
all the golden youth, their prince, the gayest, the most
finely feathered of them all. Perhaps he had never seen
Francis save as an eccentric, a fantastic ; and he was one
of the grave fathers of the city, with every motive
for despising the young man. Yet the fool of Assisi
became for this grave councillor the most considerable
person among his acquaintance. They point out to you
yet the old Palazzo Sbaraglini, not far from the Teatro
Metastasio, as the house of Bernard, where he invited
the homeless young man to sup and lodge with him one
night. The host deliberately set about a close scrutiny
of his visitor. You know the story in the *Fioretti*, how
he made a bed for him in his own room, and how Francis
feigned to be a ready and sound sleeper ; but how the
host fought against sleep, also feigning unconsciousness,

watched and saw his guest rise and spend the night in
prayer, and heard the fervent cry of triumph in the riches
found, *Deus mi et omnia, Deus mi et omnia*—" My God,
my all "—till morning broke. By the light of the little
chamber lamp he had seen the fool transfigured. Bernard that night left all his former life behind him.
Francis never quenched the fresh ardour of his friends,
and there was only one step between the complete acceptance of the offer of his new disciple and Bernard's
renunciation of his honours, dignities, and riches. They
went to the Church of St. Nicholas, heard mass, with
childlike confidence opened the Gospel, and read the
several verses that were to form the essential part of
the first Rule :—

*If thou wilt be perfect, go and sell that thou hast and
give to the poor, and thou shalt have treasure in heaven.*

*And he sent them to preach the kingdom of God, and to
heal the sick. And he said unto them, Take nothing for your
journey, nor staves nor scrip, neither bread, neither money,
neither have two coats apiece.*

*If any man will come after me, let him deny himself and
take up his cross and follow me. For whoever will save his
life shall lose it ; and whoever will lose his life for my sake,
shall find it. For what is a man profited, if he shall gain
the whole world, and lose his own soul ?*

That was the formula of enlistment. There was no
pause to reconcile it with comfort, with common sense,
or with public opinion. Bernard gave all his wealth away
at once to the poor, the sick, the unfortunate, and along
with another citizen of Assisi, Peter by name—probably
Peter of Catania, the first Vicar-General—who had been
fired by Bernard's example, went to live, as Francis had
been living, down below the town, among the woods, at
the Porziuncola, leaving Assisi buzzing with the noise and
the scandal of their strange determination. Soon after,
they were joined by Giles, who had returned after an
absence from home to find the town ringing with the

story. As soon as Giles heard of the ridiculous persons down at St. Mary of the Angels, he went off straightway and joined them.

M. Sabatier does not find in Bernard the true Franciscan flavour, seems to think he was too old, too " set " for Francis to form. To me, on the contrary, no other brother shows more strikingly the releasing spirit of the new movement than this grave and weighty magistrate, quitting deliberately his house, his possessions, his dignities, to find a better fulfilment of himself in serving the humble and the sick, in working with his own hands, in begging his bread and the bread of the needy, not in some distant mission field but within sight of his old neighbours. The brothers lived in huts or in the open air, but not hidden away in contemplation. Every other day they would be taking the hill, pacing the streets of the town amid the stares and the mocking of those who had been wont to do them reverence.

The idea of an Order at this time cannot be too far banished from our minds. Bernard chose to be the friend of Francis, and to do as he did. Bernard drew Peter after him, and Giles felt the adventurous flavour of the enterprise and joined on too. They were good comrades, and life with Francis, though he made sin and suffering hourly realities to them, and penitence and discipline were conditions of their existence, was yet buoyant and exhilarating. Their master's fellowship in serving they counted a great gain. They waited no longer on the fickle favour of men. Bernard probably remained begging and working and nursing the lepers all the summer and autumn of 1209. Then they could not keep the good news of their discovered liberty within narrow limits. It was perhaps during the next winter that he with some other brothers undertook the mission to Florence. No friends were there to receive them. When they begged shelter they got it grudgingly in a porch, and though the weather was bitter, they were

c

driven from the porch to the shelter of a church, where
they tried to forget their sufferings in prayer. A charitable man, Guido by name, seeing their devoutness and
their poverty, offered them money, and was astonished at
their refusal. "And yet you are poor?" "Yea, but
poverty is no ill to us. We have chosen it." "Do you
know what it is to be other than poor?" And Bernard
said the goods of this world had been theirs in abundance,
but they did not regret them. Shelter was not wanting
to them after that, and they had need of all Guido's
protection. In the streets of Bologna they were mocked
and maltreated. At the grave Bernard, with his honourable estate in Assisi only a few months behind him, mud
was thrown. Mischievous boys took hold of his capuchon
and hung on behind. Their wretched garments were
stolen, and they might not retort or grumble. If
their joy was not enough to make such mean persecution seem as nothing, they had not been worth recruiting.
In reading of the relations of Francis with his first
brothers one realises constantly how rigid was his discipline, and remembers he had been a soldier. So often
is he represented as the feminine type of sainthood, all
smiles and tears and ecstasy, that we are apt to overlook
the virile character of his brotherhood, with its conditions
of strict obedience and unending endurance. But no
man was called to the brotherhood in those early days
merely because he could obey and endure. A recruit
brought obedience as a matter of course, as he brought
hands to serve and feet to walk the roads of a needy world.
With all its republican spirit of mutual obligation, the
early brotherhood was an aristocracy. The brothers,
from whatever social ranks enlisted, must be well born,
that is, endowed with the royal gifts of joy and fervour.
If the Franciscans were quickly successful, they bought
success with these rare and priceless qualities.

Meanwhile, they were growing in numbers. Tradition says they were twelve when Francis, a most loving

and loyal son of Rome, burned to show the Holy Father
what he was doing, and win his approval.   Among the
naïf company—they called themselves the Penitents of
Assisi—that set out so confidently for the City, it is
possible Silvester may have been one—for the lists vary,
and none of the complete ones were compiled till many
years later.   At least, he was an early brother, and may
be mentioned here.   Silvester was a notable churchman
of Assisi, and belonged to one of the chief families of
the place.   A little time before he had shown himself
greedy for money in his dealings with Francis.   Francis
had retorted in his own grand manner by shovelling piles
of money into his hands—part of Bernard's renounced
treasures deposited with him for distribution among the
poor ; and Silvester, who knew the world as a place of
haggling, stood open-mouthed, and went home to think.
Since then he had had visions which drove him to join the
brothers.   He had a great career before him, and his fame
was that he spoke with God as one friend with another.

Francis, with much to think of on the way to the
City, and ever ready for obedience, said one of the others
must be chosen as leader and guide, whom all should
obey.   At his word they should stop, at his word go
on their way again.   Bernard was chosen.   They found
friends on the journey, also a new recruit, Angelo
Tancredi, and they reached Rome in safety.   The great
ones there looked at them as at some brave wandering
children, gave them sensible advice, sweetly welcomed
and not taken.   Would they not enter this Order or
the other, where this and the other privilege would be
theirs ?   They wished for no privilege.   But the life
they planned was hard.   They found it joyous.   Their
gentle obstinacy had its way at last, and the Pope saw
them.   Innocent III. did not know what to make of men
who only desired, under the favour of the Church, to
give the whole of themselves, and to live in all things
according to the Gospel.   The Cardinals were mostly

irritated or scornful, and called the enterprise presumptuous. The Pope was inclined to think it beyond their
power, till the friendly Cardinal John of St. Paul reminded him it would be imprudent for the Church to
declare the evangelic life impossible. So Innocent, much
wondering, doubtful, but touched, gave the permission
to continue to live as they had lived, ordered them to
appoint a head, and to work with the approbation of the
clergy. There could be no serious question of approv-
ing their Rule. Two or three verses from the Gospels
couldn't be looked on as a Rule—though they contained
the whole law and spirit for the ordering of the lives of
the sons of Francis. Save Silvester—if he were among
them—they were all laymen, and a brotherhood of priests
had never been contemplated. But before they left Rome
the authority of the Holy See made them submit to the
tonsure at least. Their return home was full of hardship
and full of joy.

The old legends tell of Bernard's setting off with
Francis on a pilgrimage to St. Iago ; also that Francis
never reached there because of illness, and that he
stopped Bernard's journey, too, finding some poor sick
folks needing care in the place where they had halted.
He was to wait till he had nursed the sick folks well
before he paid homage at St. Iago's shrine. He did the
bidding of Francis, and on his way back to the brothers,
halting by the side of a river he dared not cross, was led
over safely by a beautiful shining youth—the very angel,
according to the *zelanti* story in the *Fioretti*, that had
been dealt with so cavalierly the same day by Elias.
But the other *Fioretti* tale of Bernard being rewarded by
the admiring Bologna doctor for his patience in persecution by a gift of a house for the brothers, and Francis's
joy over the same, needs modification. The place was
only lent. From the first house built for the brothers
in Bologna some years later, the very sick had to turn
out at the coming of Francis, who repudiated all posses-

sions, and would in the end only accept a loan of it at the eager persuasion of Cardinal Ugolino.

What were the demons that assailed Bernard so sore that the brothers wondered and Francis prayed fervently for his friend? Was the new world very hard to one who had lain soft in the old one? There is no trace of his ever looking back once he had put his hand to the plough. But he was a doughty fighter against invisible foes, and it was revealed to Francis there was no shame in the struggles, and that Bernard was "one of the guests in the kingdom of Heaven." He was specially grateful to the man who had first joined him, and made of him a particular friend, counting so on his sympathy that to have it not was unendurable. Bernard had been staying up at the Carceri in an interval for rest and contemplation. It was towards the end of Francis's life, when he was very ill, very weak, nearly blind, and in sore need of human comfort. Along the hard rocky path he had toiled from Assisi, dragging his weary feet, but saying to himself, "Bernard will be there. When I reach there, I shall find Bernard." But Bernard was in the wood, with no eyes or ears for him, far from him, rapt in ecstasy. "Brother Bernard, come. Speak to the poor blind man." There was no answer. Again and again he called, "Bernard, come, speak to me. I am blind. I need you." But not a word came in reply. Then poor Francis, sore, weary, and hurt, went away murmuring. But a divine voice came to him, "What art thou grieving at, miserable little man? Shall a man send God away for some creature guest?" And as Francis repented of his murmuring, Bernard came back to earth, and seeing his master for the first time, ran to meet him. But Francis, throwing himself on the ground ordered him, by obedience, to trample on him three times, and say, "Lie there, thou boorish son of Bernardone! Vilest of creatures, whence thy pride?" And Bernard had to do it, hoping humbly when next he did wrong himself, his master might be there to be the executor of justice.

At the death of Francis, on Bernard fell the blessing of the first born. It is surely not necessary to repudiate any more the version of Thomas of Celano in his First Life, whereby the special blessing of the Poverello fell on Elias, a version he did not repeat in his Second Life, which has no other authority to back it up, and which is outside the bounds of probability. That Francis blessed Elias I am sure, but he reserved his most tender blessing for the earliest brother ; and this is how the story is told in the *Speculum Perfectionis*.

"When about the time of his death a delicate dish was being prepared for him, he remembered Brother Bernard, the first brother he had, and said to his companions, 'This food is good for Brother Bernard.' And straightway Francis called him to him. And when he had come he sat by the bed where the saint was lying, and said Brother Bernard, 'Father, I beg that thou wilt give me thy blessing and show unto me thy love for me, for if thou showest thy fatherly affection, I think that God Himself and all the brothers will love me more.'

"The blessed Francis could not see him, because for many days he had lost the sight of his eyes ; but stretching out his right hand he placed it on the head of Brother Giles, who was the third companion, thinking he had put it on the head of Bernard, who sat by him. And immediately knowing by the Holy Spirit, he said, 'This is not the head of my brother Bernard.' Then Bernard came nearer, and the blessed Francis placing his hand on his head, blessed him, saying to one of his companions [his secretary, Leo, probably, and the writer of the account], 'Write what I shall say unto thee— The first brother that God gave me was Brother Bernard, who first began with me and fulfilled entirely the perfection of the Holy Gospel, distributing to the poor all his goods. For that and for many other reasons I am more bound to love him than any other brother of the whole Order. Therefore, I will and I order as I can,

that whoever be Minister General love him and honour
him as he would me. Let the ministers and all the
brothers of the Order look on him as they would look
on me.'" If Elias was present when these words were
uttered they must have rung reproaches in his ears
in after days. But, doubtless, he consoled himself by
saying Francis had not realised how stiff-necked was
Brother Bernard. And indeed Bernard permitted himself
an attitude of frank criticism towards Elias which the
ambitious Minister General found particularly galling.

Till now I have only shown him as a humble
disciple. But he had been a man of the world, and
he retained some of the qualities of such after he
embraced the religious life. There are tales of his
extraordinary endurance and abstinence, but not of any
determined asceticism. He ate what was set before
him, finding the Rule to be better kept by little consideration about food than by too much attention given
to fasts. He ate little because he was thinking of other
things, and he was not inclined to give credit for abstinence to a man refraining from wine who had never
tasted the juice of the grape. Elias, raised to the
Minister Generalship, found Bernard, who had been a
great man when he was a poor youth in Assisi, an
embarrassing subordinate, who poked fun at his fine
horse and made him supremely uncomfortable. When
he was dining in his own room, suitably to his station
and the delicacy of his appetite, Bernard would come
in genially and sit down at table with him, "to share
the good things God had sent." But Elias and Bernard
had more serious disputes than such as respected the
quality of a horse a Brother Minor might ride, or
the length of his menu. When the exactions for the
great Basilica became importunate, so that the brothers
in every province were diverted from their own work to
find, by any means and immediately, funds for the
building, Bernard was one of the strongest protestors.

Outspoken as usual, he incurred the wrath of Elias and had to flee out of the reach of his vindictive arm. On the side of Monte Sefro, in a lonely spot, he built himself a poor little hut, and there he lived contented for two years, till, in 1239, Frate Elias was deposed from his office. A poor carpenter who used to go up the hill to cut wood found him there and marvelled at his isolation. This exile was no hardship to his spirit, for there was nothing cheering in the state of the Order, and Bernard was used to loneliness. But his body suffered if his mind did not. He was an old man, and he probably did not long survive the trial. Fra Salimbene as a young brother in Siena, in 1241, found him in the convent there, gentle and venerable, full of kindness to the young brethren, and with wonderful stories to tell them of Francis.

It is to be remarked of the disciples found by Francis himself, that they by no means all, indeed, that they rarely follow the track they had followed in the world. He did not, with mere shortsighted intelligence, set one of the ruling classes, as a matter of course, to the work of government, or a soldier necessarily to difficult enterprises in distant and unfriendly lands. His mission was the release of souls. They could take up such former occupations as were compatible with their vows, if instinct and temperament directed them. But Bernard, though a city had depended on him for its ruling, was not set to administration. He served humbly as a nursing, begging missionary, and his leisure was given to contemplation. One of the most beautiful of all the chapters in the *Fioretti* is devoted to the description of his temperament. "For this excellent grace," it tells, "Saint Francis right willingly spake with him by day and night : whereby were they sometimes found together rapt in God the whole night long in the wood, wherein they twain had met to speak of God together." He shrank from no duty, and the duties imposed on the companions meant the serving of a crowd of quite ordinary and

sometimes very loathsome mortals. But when leisure came
his refuge was ready.   Bernard has not the great repute of
Giles as an ecstatic, but it would seem as if he more quickly
gained the skill of entering the kingdom of ecstasy.

"Frequently," says his legend in the *Chronicle of the
Twenty-four Generals*, "after temptation and other labours
of the active life, he was translated to the rest of the
life contemplative, was rapt as if to the kisses of a
Rachel, for whom he had served many years." He
hardly needed isolation. The mood would come on
him as he walked with a brother, who, seeing him cling
to a tree for earthly support, could guess the wanderings
of his spirit in the drunkenness of ecstasy. On any
errand he could make his celestial journeys. He fed
flying, as the swallows, said Giles of him. But too
much of the world made him lonely. Eight days when
he might not give himself up to spiritual delights
seemed eight years. Free, he went at once to the desert,
to the hills, the woods. In one such escape there
suddenly appeared to him a hand in the air, holding
a viola. One drawing of the bow towards earth filled
him with such ecstasy of melody that, if the bow had
been drawn yet again towards heaven, he believed his
spirit would have departed.

Francis loved him not least for his royal recklessness
of generosity, because he gave away all his riches for
the joy of the act. There is something finely Franciscan
in his grand manner of giving alms. One day he was
grumblingly asked why he gave so much food to a
sick man he was tending, and he answered, "I do that
because it is for me to give, and Charity commands
it. Our sick brother will eat of it according to his
needs." This is the manner of giving sung of Jacopone—

"Povertade non guadagna ;
D'ogni tempo e tanto larga ;
Nulla cosa non sparagna
Per la sera o pel dimane."

In his last illness he would fain have been as strenuous in spiritual fervour as ever. Remedies he would have none—they disturbed him. A kind brother put rose-water under his nostrils, but he waved it gently away. It interrupted his thoughts. When his mind was growing hazy he struck his head to call back his brain to its functions. And he had a visitor able to make his fleeting spirit speak once more. The lusty Giles came in and cried to the dying man, "Sursum corda, frater Bernarde, sursum corda!" Bernard kindled at the greeting, his heart was lifted, and his soul revived. He was fain to bid a last farewell to the brothers, and in the cheerful Franciscan way. Death was freedom. His going should be a feast. The doctor consenting, he ordered a dish of cherries to be brought, and sent to ask all the brothers of the place to eat with him. "I beg that you will all eat with me my last supper." There were many at that feast of cherries, for word had gone to neighbouring houses that their eldest brother was passing away. I wish Giotto had known that legend of the dying Bernard, and painted him, out-of-doors, giving good cheer to his brothers, strong of spirit, high-hearted to the end. When they had eaten, he spoke words of warning, but still more words of triumph. "I was never Brother Minor," he said to them, "save in my temptations. . . . I feel in my soul that for a thousand worlds I would not have been other than a servant of Christ. Hear my prayer that ye love one another." Then, leaning back, his face became joyful and shining, and so his blessed soul flew away to the Lord. His body remained white and soft, and on his face there was a smile.

They buried Brother Bernard in San Francesco, under the Altar of the Conception; but in later days his precious relics were scattered.

ST. FRANCIS AND ST. CLARA

TIBERIO D'ASSISI.   Assisi, S. DAMIANO.

To face p. 43.

II. RUFINO OF THE SCIFI

"Quasi arcus refulgens inter divinæ contemplationis nebulas varietate virtutum picturatus in civitate Assisi frater Rufinus Cipii exemplari vita resplenduit et inter alios beati Francisci primos discipulos caritatis rubore, liliali puritatis candore enituit ac generalis fragravit redolentia sanctitatis."— VITA FR. RUFINI, "CHRONICLE OF THE TWENTY-FOUR GENERALS."

THE first companions were not largely recruited from men instinctively drawn to the monastic life. But in Rufino we meet one saved by Francis, I think, from the perpetual cloister, and from a narrow solicitude for his own soul. In youth he had the world at his feet—at least, all the chances of his time and country; and should have been a gay young fighting gallant, with a becoming scorn of beggars and hermits, and a magnificent wonder at penitents. But legend never hints at any time when Rufino loved the world or its treasures or its strifes. He was of the noble Assisi family of the Scifi, son of Berarduccio Scifi, and therefore related to Silvester and to St. Clara. Silvester, his clerical cousin, may have had influence with the pious thoughtful young man, and to his tales of Francis was probably owing the fact that Rufino was not drawn to one of the older monastic orders. In 1210, the year he is said to have been received, Clara, a girl of sixteen, was listening, with open ears and heart on fire, to the preaching of Francis in the cathedral, and in her home to the tales of his egregious folly. Her cousin Rufino's decision, doubtless, helped her to make her choice; and two years later she fled from the house of the Scifi to the Porziuncola, to take Francis for her guide.

Rufino had none of his master's buoyant nature; was

like him only in his virginal purity and his indifference
to worldly comforts and estimation. Francis had run
to the world with open arms, and found it wanting;
but his gay spirit was not quenched thereby. Joy dwelt
elsewhere, and he would find it. Rufino, born in conditions that offered him more than could fall to the lot of
a merchant's son, had probably never believed the world
had anything to give him at all. He had always known
his treasure was elsewhere. His leader, ever touchingly
appreciative of the gifts of his comrades, said to the
brothers one day, "Tell me whose is the holiest soul
in the world." "Thine, Francis," they answered. But
he would not have it so, and told them of his vileness.
To himself he was always the poor blundering, sinning
son of Bernardone. "Nay," he said, "I will show you.
Look there at our brother Rufino coming out of the
wood. His is one of the holiest souls God has in all
the earth. God has revealed this to me. And I do
not hesitate to call him Saint Rufino, while still he lives
here in the body."

Modest, diffident, lofty-minded, and of an exquisite
refinement, the man had the defects and the limitations
of such a character; and Francis dealt with him strenu-
ously. Of a highwayman's repentance and future service he would have had no doubt. But then, too, had
an angel, undisguised, come as a recruit, Francis would
have wished to know how he was to serve the poor
sons of men. Up at the Carceri, among the woods
there, or in the rocky gorge, or climbing the sides of
Monte Subasio, or watching in the lonely cells, Rufino
felt a great release from the bonds of the world. Here
God spoke to him in the stillness; and what better
could he do than listen? But there were weeks without
this peace. Francis would call for him. Poor folks
down in the town had to be relieved, or an extra hand
was wanted to tend the lepers. He had to trudge down
to Assisi, and toil among those to whom God never

spoke at all. One night in a vision an angel appeared to him, very beautiful and resplendent, and in a clear and welcome voice told him he had been right in thinking it unsafe to follow in all things that simple and ignorant brother Francis. A better guide would be St. Anthony and the other anchorites, who from solitary places had put up their prayers to God all the day.

Rufino obeyed the vision. He came no more to the table of the brothers, and saw no one save when he begged his morsel of bread about Assisi. They respected his solitude for a time, for his great sanctity. But on Holy Thursday Francis called the scattered brothers together for the Feast of the Lord's Supper. Rufino sent back word he would not be there. Francis received the answer in sadness, but sent again, with a like result. Before the elevation of the host, once more a messenger was sent to persuade the recluse, but in vain. Then Francis wept; and in a solitary place asked, "Why, Lord, hast thou let my sheep so wander from me?" Rising, he went himself, would not take the silence for an answer, and at last prevailed. Rufino went back with him and ate with the others. After meat Francis spoke with him, and Rufino was fain to give in. But then that vision? Could it lie? "I will show you your beautiful angel," said Francis. "Wait." He prayed. And, lo! there it was again, wonderful and radiant, so that all were amazed. "Yes, yes," cried Rufino, "it is he." Then Francis commanded the angel to declare who he was. And straightway the vision was transformed into a thing so horrible, that Rufino never lost the terror of it till his dying day. He fell, and lay like one dead till Francis lifted and comforted him. He was reclaimed for the life of the world again.

But such evil spirits are not laid by one exorcism. Rufino was of the race of the Puritans, as such saved from many temptations, but a prey to many terrors.

There were nights he lay awake, days he went sorrowing, without spiritual consolation or joy, the prerogatives of the brothers. He felt convinced he was not among the elect. The Crucified appeared to him and said, "O brother Rufino, why all these prayers and penances, since heaven is not for thee? Believe me, for I know whom I have chosen. Put not thy trust in the son of Bernardone, whatever he says. For thy name is not written in the Book of Life. Nor is that of Francis there, nor are his brethren's." Rufino fell out of love with his leader and his comrades. Their gaiety—was it not recklessness? Their labours—what did they profit the soul? And their prayers even—of what use save to mock at their damnation? But the silent, self-torturing man, morose in his depression, said not a word. Francis, the diviner, sent the genial Masseo to him. But Rufino repelled him, and finding utterance, denounced them all. Masseo, however, persuaded him to come back with him to Francis, and when he met the master he had no need to say anything. "It was the devil that spoke to you. When that Crucified appears to you again, flout him." He gave him words of deepest insult to be used on the occasion. "If it had been Another, He would not have made your heart hard against us, your friends." Rufino's dark mood was shaken by the frank audacity. But when he went apart to pray in a wood, the ancient enemy came once more, and in the same lofty shape. For the tormenting demons were shrewd enough to know nothing base in semblance would ever tempt Rufino. Again the doubt and bitterness of heart. But, in despair, the audacious words Francis had taught him he flung at the apparition, with tremendous effect. Monte Subasio was convulsed. Its rocks and stones flew about in the most terrifying way, hurling themselves down to the valley, and spitting fire as they collided. Francis and the brothers came out to see, and to meet the exultant Rufino. To him the real Crucified appeared, and filled his soul with love, and promised an end to all his sadness.

I know not where to place in his career the best story of the shy, diffident brother of few words, who shunned men when he was not serving them. Speech was difficult to him, and preaching a terror. In those early years, ere he knew the world, he was ever on the brink of the hermit's life. Francis put out a rough and vigorous hand to tear him from the edge. "Go up to Assisi, Rufino, and preach to the people as God inspires you." Rufino excuses himself. Anything else he will do. But his father knows he is not gifted with words. Then Francis, putting on his tone of authority, commanded him by holy obedience to go off at once to the task. Nay more, he was to strip himself of all his garments save his breeches, and then to enter a church and preach. And the son of the Scifi went half naked through the streets of the town where his family was honoured, on his way to fulfil his master's bidding.

No sooner was his back turned than Francis began to abuse himself soundly for his presumption. He, the vile little man, son of Peter Bernardone, to bid one of the nobles of the place go and appear before the people like a madman! Thereupon he threw off his own tunic and followed hard on Rufino's steps. Leo hurried along with him, bearing on his arm the tunics of the two. Rufino they found in a church, obediently doing his best. From the pulpit he was preaching repentance to a ribald crew, who were jeering at his naked body, and at the folly of the brothers. Then Francis mounted after him, and they laughed the more to see another madman. But he held them by his power. The jesters remained to weep and pray, for never had they known before how beautiful were repentance and poverty, and the hope of the heavenly kingdom, or how terribly sore had been the Passion of Christ. The two preachers left Assisi forgetting itself, in the pain of the Passion. With his own hands Francis clothed Rufino, proud for him, humble himself; and as they went down the hill to the Porziuncola the jeerers were fain to kiss the hem of the tunics that had been cast off only to show the wearers' dignity the more brightly.

Perhaps Rufino never gained great power with men. He did not hold them bound like Francis by his simple presence; he did not speak the tongue of the people like Giles; nor had he the winning ways of Masseo. But the silent man was reputed to wield a tremendous power over demons. He was the strongest wrestler of all the brothers against the dark foes of men. Demons loathed and feared him. They could not abide his purity. They had tried to assail him in lovely guise, but he had learned their arts and could not be overcome. Once when he was begging about the streets of Assisi a certain man possessed of a devil looked and looked at him trembling. Some persons brought the demoniac to Francis, but the possessed one broke loose and fled. Caught again and asked what he feared, he said, "Brother Rufino with his goodness tortures and burns me." This testimony to the source of Rufino's power was enough, and the demon straightway left him. Another day ten poor demoniacs were together at the meeting of three roads. A soldier on a horse came along one and was fleeing in terror at the sight. Rufino, in his rough tunic, came up by another, and the demoniacs scattered at once; but in fleeing they cried to the soldier, "See that man there. By his prayers he so tortures the devils in Hell that they are squeezed as the grapes in the wine-press."

He was called on to exorcise the most obstinate demons. When Francis, praying on Mount Alverna, was disturbed by the dark enemy, Rufino had only to come by and call out, "*Laus et benedictio sit Domino Deo nostro !*" and they vanished.

After the first years of doubt and of longing for a perpetual hermitage, Rufino was a worker; but while he worked his spirit dwelt beyond human things, and it was said of him that while he slept he prayed. None of the other early companions had doubted Francis as had he, nor so far revolted from his influence. And none was more loyal. He was with Francis on Mount Alverna; but of that mystery he would never speak till long after the Founder's death. "It is right," he said, "to hide the secret of the king." Though he is one of those of whom the common story is told of seeing the stigmata, even the wounds in the side, by a trick, it is so entirely out of keeping with what we know of this modest, diffident disciple, that it may be put aside as incredible.

One of the tender nurses of Francis, he was with him at the end. After that we hear of him only at long intervals. The new time was not favourable to the first companions, good to be the nurses of a dying saint, but out of place in what had grown to be a large and most business-like Order. Francis had been his inciter to the active life. Perhaps having served his hard service to the sick and the poor, he may have given himself, as did Giles, to the life contemplative. In 1247 he was at the little convent of Greccio. A year before had come the summons of the Minister General, Crescentius of Jesi, to all those brothers who had been the intimates of Francis, to write their recollections. Leo, Angelo, and Rufino answered the call. Together at Greccio they lived over again the old life, lovingly set down their memories, and called on Masseo, and Illuminato, and Philip, and John the friend of Giles, to help them too; and sent their book, the *Legend of the Three Companions*, to Crescentius to do what he liked with.

Later, Rufino may have wandered on some mission, for he is not among the brothers of the early days who stood round the dying bed of Clara. Yet Leo would surely have summoned him, had he been near, to the passing of the saint, his kinswoman.   Wherever he lived, he lived long, through the strenuous hopes of John of Parma's days, and nearly through the somewhat chilly peace of the reign of Bonaventura.   No doubt pilgrims came to him, as to Leo, to drink of the old vintage, though he is not named.   But he and Leo were together in their last days, two old men waiting for death at the Porziuncola, in 1271.   One night their long dead brother, Bernard of Quintavalle, came to both of them.   Each felt with joy his summons had come.   Leo told Rufino in the morning of his vision.   But Rufino said, "Mine the summons, Leo.   You saw Bernard in sleep, I with my waking eyes.   And Francis came to me and said I was about to go to God with the brother whom thou sawest.   Then Francis kissed me."   And Leo felt the fragrance on the lips of his dying friend, whose soul soon after took its flight.   They bore his body up to Assisi, and buried it in San Francesco.

Rufino is a pale shadow by the side of the sturdy Giles or the vital Masseo, not one of the more imposing figures of the company.   Yet unforgetable is the pure ascetic creature, whose soul could harbour nothing gross ; sensitive and shrinking from the rude contact of the world, yet bearing ridicule, making himself grotesque at the bidding of him who reminded him of his kinship with the roughest.   A timid, brooding soul, but one who, having overcome the terrors of Hell, made Hell itself tremble, from whom all things evil fled.   The Church never canonised him, in spite of the word of Francis.   But his memory is like that of some pale, white flower, slender and erect.   The lily was ever the emblem of Rufino.

BROTHER BERNARD OF QUINTAVALLE AND
BROTHER GILES

BENOZZO GOZZOLI. Montefalco, S. Francesco.

To face p.

III. GILES THE ECSTATIC

" Frate, il tuo alto disio
S' adempierà in sull' ultima spera,
Dove s' adempion tutti gli altri e il mio.
Ivi è perfetta, matura ed intera
Ciascuna disianza ; in quella sola
È ogni parte là dove sempr' era ;
Perchè non è in loco, e non s' impola,
E nostra scala infino ad essa varca.

Ma per salirla mo nessun diparte
Da terra i piedi."
  —Paradiso, xxii. 61–68 ; 73–74.

THERE is a marked discrepancy between the contemporaneous records of the life of the Blessed Giles and contemporaneous estimates of his character. The records, copious enough, reveal a career of many phases, a nature where currents cross and impulses war, complex even to contradictoriness, whose elements were reconciled obscurely, against odds, if ever they were reconciled at all. The estimates, numerous too, invariably summarise him, and to his praise, as a very simple man. But then a clash between difficult knowledge of a personality and popular judgment is an everyday happening among ourselves. If a man have few material wants, still more if he have few material possessions, he is ranged among the simple-minded folks. An inhabitant of Mayfair, living among complicated upholstery, and in a whirl of social engagements, smiles benignly as he speaks of the charming simplicity of a Highland peasant. The simplicity is probably all on the side of the kindly, hasty judge, who would be fatigued more than he knows, were he to attempt to thread the labyrinth of the mind housed in the spare-fed body, a mind untouched by all the winds that spin Mayfair round so busily. They were sober ascetic persons that spoke or wrote the estimates of Giles, but not perhaps uninfluenced by his scorn, beyond even theirs, of material possessions—though a careful reading of his life leads one to believe that their judgment was based on a confusion of the occasional recklessness of his character with a want of knowledge of the world. At all events, the discrepancy forces one to close examination.

In his friend Leo, from whom we draw the main part of our knowledge of him, Giles had a rare and admirable biographer, one who leaves us to find our own way about his gathered matter, but who never misleads. There is no design at all in the work. There is no art. Great things and little he narrates with equal patience. But a fine instinct has preserved him from recording the non-significant. Unknown save to diggers in Franciscan lore, the life of Giles in the *Chronicle of the Twenty-four Generals*, published with variations in the *Acta Sanctorum*, stands one of the most curious studies of mediæval human nature, one of the most noteworthy chapters of the religious history of any time. When Leo found contradictory facts he humbly set them down, attempting no reconciliation, and still faithful to his conviction that Giles was a simple man. We can but use such light as we possess, and pray that in the difficult task some of Leo's humility be vouchsafed us that we may not misread.

"Knight of my Round Table," Francis called him. Watchers of the later years of Giles are puzzled by the phrase. But Francis knew him well; and not merely for the first part of his career is the name supremely fitting. His life was all one divine adventure—though his knight-errantry was in the end on obscure roads, his joustings on mystic fields. An eager knight he was,

that made the heart of Francis beat with joy from the
first hour of his enrolment in the new chivalry. We
know nothing of him till we learn that, after an absence
from Assisi, he returned—the year was 1209—to find
his friends Bernard of Quintavalle and Peter of Catania
had joined that unaccountable son of Bernardone in his
new, strange, and quite beggarly enterprise, about which
there was much talk in the little town. The news did
not fall on unprepared ears, and—*velociter currit sermo
divinus*—Giles knew swiftly that his path lay with theirs.
Next morning, St. George's Day, he vowed himself to
the new service in the Church of St. George (now
St. Clara), and then fared down the hill to seek the
brothers at Rivo Torto, where he heard they were staying. Their hut was not easy to find, and in a maze of
paths and trees he stopped to pray for guidance. Just
then Francis came out of the wood. Giles threw himself at his feet, and begged he might join whatever
enterprise was forward. Francis, the humblest of men,
always used high words when he spoke in the name of
the Great King. "Dearest," he said, "God is wondrous
kind to thee. If the emperor came to Assisi and asked
one of the townsfolk to be his chamberlain, or his
familiar friend, would not his heart be glad? Far
greater then should be thy gladness, God choosing thee
to serve in His own chivalry." Calling the others, he
said, "God has sent us a good brother," and Bernard
and Peter embraced him, and they all sat down to food
together with joy. The conditions of service were
spoken of with cheerful frankness. The new recruit
was not afraid, and set off up the hill to Assisi with his
captain, one as eager as the other, to procure the rough
grey tunic the brothers had adopted to mark their union
with all the poor and lowly of the world. A woman
begged from them on the road. Francis had nothing
to give her, but on his new comrade's shoulders there
hung a fine mantle. "Give her that," he said, "in

God's name." Giles gave it instantly, and straightway felt his soul very joyful. He pierced through some layers of the earthly sky at that moment. In the town he cast off the garments of the world for ever. How much he sacrificed is unrecorded—but it was his all. It has been said he was noble. Papini calls him *galantuomo*—I know not on what authority.

Glad haste was the note of all the early Brothers Minor. It is the trait in them Dante commemorates :—

> " il venerabile Bernardo
> Si scalzò prima, e dietro a tanta pace
> Corse, e correndo gli parv' esser tardo.
> O ignota ricchezza, o ben ferace !
> Scalzasi Egidio, scalzasi Silvestro,
> Dietro allo sposo ; si la sposa piace."

Bernard and Peter were setting off for a mission into Emilia. Francis, bound for the Marches of Ancona, took with him the new recruit. There was not a happier pair of comrades in all Italy. They sang divine lauds all the way. Men who saw the hardships they endured wondered at their high spirits. They were laughed at, suspected, stoned, treated as rogues and vagabonds ; and their patience and cheerfulness grew with abuse. When gentler souls pitied or praised them Giles was uneasy. " Father," he said, " already our glory is waning." The heart of Francis was glad the while he assured his companion that the hour of trial would never be lacking. He preached everywhere, his sermons brief informal talks, breathing happiness, telling suffering men the world was less dreary than it seemed, since God was always good.

It was the part of Giles to gather the people to tell them this man was worth listening to. It seemed the best of holidays he had begun, freed from all the burden of possessions and of self. Just so would he like to wander for ever, Francis's squire, the comrade in arms of Bernard and Peter in the war against misery and despair. The longer vision of his captain made him wonder. So poor and small their little band, and yet Francis saw it reaching far and growing into a great chivalry. "We are like fishers," he said. "We let down our net into the water. We catch many fish. We keep the big ones in our vessel, and throw the little ones back." If only they had not multiplied the vessels, if only they had thrown the little fishes back, the Order would have had a serener history! But Francis measured the strength and endurance of no man by narrow, grudging eyes.

The world seemed to Giles to grow very big. There were calls from many sides—and it was so easy for a poor man to answer. In those days he was what Francis never seems to have been, what he himself ceased to be, an eager votary of the saints; and he had full leave to go to any shrine, if he went as knight-errant along the roads, not all absorbed in the thought of his own salvation. So he set off to Spain, to St. James of Compostella. The road was long. He was nearly always hungry, and hardly ever knew it, being more struck by the fact that bread came to him at unexpected times and in unlikely places, and that the number of bean fields where a healthy man could stay his appetite was really very great. What with the company on the road of folks who needed help, to whom he had something to say, and the fields and woods for praying and dreaming, the life was a fine one—though its darker sides were not hidden from him. There were so many poorer than himself. Twenty days he went bare-headed, having given his *capitium* to some one who minded cold more than he. Of course, he was often taken for a vagrant rogue or madman, once for a gamester. At Ficarolo on the Po, between Mantua and Ferrara, a certain man sent for him. Giles went eagerly, looking for an alms. No alms, but dice, were put into his hand, and his pious horror caused much wonderment.

Later, he wandered off again, and far, to pay his vows at the Holy Sepulchre, going by way of Brindisi. But bean fields do not grow in great towns, and Giles was no mere beggar from "the table of the Lord." While waiting for a ship, he earned his living as a water-carrier. *Quis vult aquam?* ran the cry of the stalwart brother every day along the streets. On his way back from the Holy Land he sojourned for a space at Ancona, and lived, still by the labour of his hands, as a water-carrier, or by burying the dead, or weaving osier baskets. And when no man wanted his services, he took the bread kind folks gave him with a good grace. It was probably on his return from Jerusalem that he visited the shrines of St. Nicholas of Bari and St. Angelo—that is, the sanctuary of St. Michael on Mount Gargano in Apulia. The plan of his life in these wanderings was ever the same, ready service and teaching on the roads, and for all luxury, some leisure for communion in lonely places. He saw many cities and much people in those days, and sharpened his naturally shrewd mind with the various human contact. Then he came back to St. Mary of the Angels, to refresh himself with the company of Francis.

But he had a relentless zeal for asceticism, and it seems he grew frightened by his love for this free, wandering life that suited him so well. Giles had a restless spirit, as had Brother Lucido, of whom it was written, "He never would stay in one place more than a month or so, and when he liked a place would straightway depart from it, saying, 'Not here our home, but in Heaven.'" Neither was of the stuff of which good householders are made; but while the asceticism of the one made him still wander, that of Giles made him afraid of the liberty Francis gave him. "Go wherever you will," said the trustful captain. But he begged for orders. "Father, in such free obedience I cannot find rest." And Francis sent him to the hermitage of Fabriani in the county of Perugia. He set off at once in a time of great cold. His shelter was wretched, and the folks of the neighbourhood shrugged their shoulders, and wondered whether Paradise was worth all it cost him. Giles, considering, thought it was, as he grew warmer with pitying love for Jesus who had trodden rougher roads, barefoot and hungry. He alternated his prayers with hard work. A handy man was Giles. Now he made cases for vessels, which found buyers in Perugia, and procured food and clothing for himself and others. The eager soul, so exaggeratedly humble when he was humble at all, fain hoped that his alms would pray for him while he rested or slept. From this time forward he must have been a familiar figure in the streets of Perugia.

His wanderings were not over. At Rome, as elsewhere, he lived by the labours of his hands. After hearing mass in the morning he went to a wood outside the city, gathered fuel, and sold it for what would buy him bread. When a woman wished to give him more than he asked, he refused. Then, too, he gathered grapes, and trod them in the wine-press. A man who owned many nut-trees could find no one to help him in gathering the fruit, for his gardens were distant, and the trees were very high. Giles climbed the trees blithely and reaped the nut harvest. The owner gave him a good share, and Giles had enough for others besides himself. So, at wheat harvest time he gleaned with the other poor folks, and shared his gleanings with the rest. At the monastery of Quattrosanti, near the Lateran, he sifted corn, carried water, baked bread. An excellent day-labourer, yet he was no drudge, for he found time to feed and tend the guest within. Even while he lived with the Cardinal Nicholas Claramontana, when the Pope's court was at Rieti, he was no charge to the household; and one day, when it rained, and he could find no outside work, he made a cheery helper to the cook in the kitchen, and cleaned the knives and sharpened them; nor, I am sure, were they ever brighter or keener. Here was Francis's plan literally in action: between big enterprises fill up the time with little ones.

But from the first he had needed solitude; and when he was staying with the Cardinal at Rieti, he craved to get away during Lent into quiet, with one companion, perhaps the beloved John, always mentioned as Giles's friend. The Cardinal allowed them to go, but with pitying wonder about the fate of the nestless birds. The two made their way to the Church of St. Lawrence, on a hill above Deruta. In very truth they had got their desire for solitude. The place was desolate and remote. The few inhabitants were not friendly. A great snowstorm came on. They could not work. There was no one to beg from. But they had come for prayer, and they prayed while they waited for food. And God put it into the head of a man of these parts, Benincasa by name, to go to the Church of St. Lawrence. He brought them bread and wine, and spoke of them so persuasively to his rough neighbours that the brothers never lacked again for food during all their stay there.

Giles was fit and willing for any service. The inconvenient hours were missed out of his day. But, of course, a man of his temperament and of his time longed for martyrdom. He had never yet been asked to give enough. He might be a cheerful scullion, but he had a high mind, and desired to die the glorious death. The conversion of Mahometan Africa was a dear wish of Francis's heart, and when the mission there was planned, he passed the word of order to Giles, Knight of his Round Table. Giles ran to the perilous enterprise as to a feast. The brothers reached Tunis, and began a vigorous mission. But a fanatic, who marvellously found speech after a long silence, lit the flame of hatred and persecution against them. The town was in a ferment; and they preached peace with knives at their throats. At last, whether they would or no, the Genoese,

Pisan and Marseilles merchants drove the brothers by main force to the safety of the ships, and prevented their relanding. Even from the deck the voice of Giles and his comrades rang across the harbour prayers and protests and the undelivered messages of peace. The failure was a bitter blow. He went back humbled he had not been deemed worthy of a martyr's death, and lived to be glad of his survival.

This probably ended Giles's wanderings far afield. His feet still trod the roads of Central Italy, but the circle of his travel was henceforth not a large one—Perugia, Assisi, Cortona, Chiusi, Cetona, Spoleto, Fallerone, Viterbo, almost mark its confines.

The later phase of his life, the period of ecstasy and contemplation, is spoken of as if it had been deliberately planned—which is most unlikely—at least, as if it had been sharply divided from the rest, which is not the case. A man of active body and restless physical energy does not suddenly say to himself, "Lo, now, from this time I will be contemplative." There seems to have been a long transition stage, and I doubt if anything save death entirely cut the links between him and this world's interests. There were causes enough for the gradual change besides the passing of youth. Troubles in the Order drew Francis home from the East about the time Giles came back from Tunis. The little band of stalwarts, zealous for the integrity of the idea of the Founder, drew instinctively together. In his last years Francis suffered grievously in soul and body. If Giles had been the simpleton he was thought to be, he might have gone on tramping the roads of the world, an exalted vagabond, till age overtook him, hearing only his own call, heedless he belonged to an Order, and that the Order was making history, as history is made, in travail and pain. The troubles of Francis made his friends think. The growing ambition and discontent among the *frati* made them wonder and be on the defensive. Then Francis died, in 1226. They woke out of their grief to find Elias's masterful hand over the Order, in defiance of the appointment of John Parenti, guiding it where he would, far from the Founder's plan. Protests were vain. The current was setting away from them. What could they do but watch apart sorrowfully? To them it must have seemed the Order was dead, just when it was becoming a reality to the vulgar world outside. As Giles said, later: "*Navis fracta est et conflictus factus est; fugiat qui fugere potest, et evadat si potest.*"

Giles kept apart more than most. He felt not only sorrow and indignation, but utter scorn, of which he was abundantly capable. The gentler Leo fumed much more. Gentle, tender souls do not always keep outside strife and controversy, but rush on bare knives in defence of what they love. Leo could not be still. So he ran to Giles at Perugia, crying, "There is a marble vase set up at Assisi; and they throw money into it by order of Elias, to build a great rich convent for the brothers, who yet have vowed to be poor like Francis!" "Let them build a convent as long as from here to Assisi," said Giles; "my little nook is enough for me. If thou art dead, brother Leo, go and break that marble vase to atoms which sins against holy poverty. But if thou still livest in the world, refrain, for the hand of Elias is heavy." Leo, with some others, ran impulsively and smashed the vase; and was beaten with rods, and exiled from Assisi.

Probably Giles was on better terms than some of his friends with the *mitigati*. He never flattered them. He was the poles apart from them in life and ideal. He had a rough tongue, and he let it loose on them. They feared his sarcasm, his power of retort. Plainly he was not a man to be bullied. But he was neither sullen nor over-sensitive, and a man who can laugh while he keeps his own ground is more at ease with his opponents than a gentler, oftener tortured soul like Leo. Some years later Giles consented to visit the Sacro Convento. It was after the basilica was built—and a church for the glory of God and the honour of Francis was a more tolerable thing than a fine convent. He had gone to visit the Founder's tomb; but the brothers were proud to show him also their dwelling. They felt sure the contrast with his hermit's cell would impress him mightily. And it did. One can see him nodding his rough head in their sleek faces, as he says, "Splendid! splendid! And so complete! Only one thing is lacking now, my brothers. You want wives!" They were terribly shocked.

Up there at Perugia, looking at the great hills and over the plain, he was by no means out of the world. Hermit and contemplative by hours, and learning the sweetness of these hours, at other times he was missionary, street-preacher, and enthusiastic gardener. Giles found much of his rough wisdom in digging, and flowers loved his care. An ascetic he was, even to the point of cruelty towards himself: his wattle hut, his single tunic, his one meal a day are amply attested. But he had the strong Franciscan bent against mere otherworldliness, and he had enormous belief in the healthfulness of good works, if not in their merit. His scorn for the idle prayerful man was deep and constant. A brother complained to him that in the convent he was made to work so much he could not pray. Said Giles to him, "If you were to ask the king of France for a thousand marks, would he not just laugh in your face? He would bid you earn them first. So, if you would beg from the Lord, first work for Him. It will be counted for more virtue to you to do one thing for another than two for yourself, though the two were prayers." To another he said, with a wholesome sneer, "Do you think in doing nothing you are being spiritual?"

Once he heard a tree-hopper, and he cried out,

"O Lady Cicala, I would fain hear from you the praises
of the Lord. For thou dost not say, 'La, la,' but
'Ca, ca (qua, qua).' Not in another life, but here, here,
thou strivest to do well."

A pithy preacher he was of a certainty, unconventional, and with the brief pointed style liked of the
people. But sermons were only tolerable in the mouths
of workers. A wordy brother who was going to preach
in the Piazza at Perugia, came solemnly to Giles for
advice. Giles paused in his digging, and threw over
his shoulder, "Bo, bo, molto dico e poco fo."

His converts were many, but he had his own ways
of dealing with them. He brought a noble knight to
religion. Once in the Order, and thus of equal rank,
his convert was left alone. It is significant that the
only two women whom we hear definitely of his having
any intercourse with were both of great and exceptional
character — Clara and Jacoba of Settisoli. The *petits
soins* of the tactful confessor to penitent ladies were
not in Giles's way. But tempted men cried for him,
ran to him, to draw strength from his warm vitality.
He interested; he made people listen. He was a
character. Once at St. Damian a learned theologian, an
Englishman, was preaching. Giles was there with Clara
and her *povere donne*. In the middle of the doctor's
discourse Giles had a burning thought, and burst in,
"Stop, sir, stop. Now *I* want to preach." The meek
and astonished Englishman obeyed. Giles took his
place, and justified his interruption. Then having
said his say, he broke off with "There, brother, I have
done. Finish your sermon." And again the Englishman obeyed, wondering a little perhaps at southern
impulsiveness. Clara was delighted at the scene. Clara
had a sense of humour. But she was edified, too. Now
was the desire of Francis's heart fulfilled, for he had
wished priest brothers to be so truly humble that they
would willingly stop preaching to hear a layman. And

Giles was always of the laity. The meek Englishman filled her with admiration more than if she had seen him raising the dead to life.

Giles was a hot-tempered man, as the treacherous friend who annoyed him by ravaging the flowers in his beloved garden at Cetona found to his cost. But if he did not always wear his armour of mildness, he cooled quickly for any offence against himself. His scorn for idle speaking, for idle sentiment, never cooled. It runs through half the tales of him. A solemn man comes to him one day, and says he has made up his mind to enter the Order. "All right," says Giles. "Now go and kill your parents." The solemn man is stupefied, and Giles calls him a blockhead. Says a priest in a lachrymose voice to him, "Pray for me, Giles." "Pray for yourself," retorts Giles. When the two fine Cardinals come to him, and after hearing wisdom from his lips, ask for his prayers, he says, "Oh, I needn't pray for you. You have greater hope than I." "How?" they ask. "Why," answers Giles, "you, with all your riches and honours and friends, hope to be saved. I, with all my calamities, miseries, and enemies, fear to be damned."

Do not look in Giles, especially in the Giles of this period, for the calm tolerance, the sweet reasonableness of Francis, who felt all men, rich as well as poor, to be his brothers. Indeed, his pungency, wholesome in the main, was sometimes bitter enough. The experiences of his life were turned up by his tongue, and he lived to see the Brothers Minor petted in princely houses, waxing fat and sleek, mocking the poverty of Francis. One day, a brother comes in haste and in great joy, crying, "Good news! good news!" and Giles says, "Tell it, my son." "In a vision I was taken to Hell, and I saw there not a single brother of the Order." And Giles responds with a sigh and a strange smile. So the other goes on smugly, "Yes, there are none of our Order there. Or if there are, why did I not see them ?" "Because you didn't go deep enough!" was the brutal answer. Well, he had seen what had made his heart sore as he looked out from his cell and garden, and tramped to and fro between Perugia and Assisi. After the Founder's death he had to wait twenty years before John of Parma came to bring back the rule of Francis, and to give example from his high place to the brothers by his very gentle perfect life. "Welcome, brother," said Giles to him. "But, oh, you come late!" And he lived to see John deposed and exiled to Greccio by ministers who thought an apostolic example a very dangerous thing indeed.

Of his intellectual qualities we have clear evidence. They were certainly high and robust. His training was probably meagre, perhaps even less than that of Francis. I do not know if he could sign his name. It does not appear he had his master's troubadour culture, though he was, at least, something of a musician. *Idiota et simplex*, said of him Bonaventura, who had a sincere, though perhaps remote, admiration for Giles. There Paris spoke in its most cultivated tone of polite patronage. It sounds almost like an Oxford reference to a well-intentioned village lay-preacher. Ignorant, yes, and with a good deal of his master's distrust of science, that is, of the scholastic theology of the day. It was Giles that Jacopone da Todi was quoting, when he cried against Paris—

> "Mal vedemmo Parisi,
> Ch' n' ha destrutto Ascisi ;
> Con la lor lettoria
> L' han messo in mala via."

"*Parisius, parisius, quare distruis Ordinem Sancti Francisci ?*" cried Giles. But his natural gifts were great, and for his simpleness, well, I half suspect the humble Giles of laughing at that elegant, courtly doctor Bonaventura. Leo tells the story without a smile, and I may be wrong. "Father," said Giles one day to the Minister General, "God has shown you much favour. But we ignorant and foolish folks, who have received none, what can we do to be saved?" The Minister General replied suavely, "If God withholds gifts from a man, it is enough that he love Him." "But," asked Giles, "can an ignorant man love God as much as a lettered one? Could a poor widow love Him more than a master of theology?" The Minister General hauled his Christianity up to the surface, and replied fittingly. Then Giles ran out to the garden hanging over the town—the garden of the Sacro Convento, I suppose, unless he had been honoured by a visit at Perugia—and looking over the wall, called out to a woman passing, "Poor little widow, foolish and ignorant as you are, Love the Lord your God and you may be a greater person than Frate Bonaventura!" Was Bonaventura apostolic enough not to be disconcerted at hearing this kind of thing shouted over his garden wall, what time he was head of the Order?

But the *idiota et simplex* was a match for trained minds, and sometimes met them on their own ground. He was famed as a talker as well as a saint. One day he had a number of visitors in his garden at Perugia. Among them there came from Assisi the noble Roman lady, the friend of Francis, Jacoba of Settisoli. And a certain brother Gerardino was of the company, a very spiritual man. It has been suggested he was Gerard da Borgo San Donnino, afterwards the author of the notorious *Introduction to the Eternal Gospel*, who suffered long tortured years of imprisonment for his Joachimism. And the surmise is probably correct, not merely because of his being called *valde spiritualis*, but because the Gerard of this tale argued so stubbornly, a habit of the famous brother of the name. The conversation turned on the subject of human capabilities. Man does wonders sometimes against his desires, said Giles. *Propter illud quod homo potest, venit ad illud quod non vult.* Gerard, perhaps only to provoke Giles to more talk, disputed this, beginning, "I wonder now," and going on to pick Giles's words to pieces, with metaphysical quibbles. He used twelve arguments.

It was a little tedious, and Giles, doubtless to the relief of Jacoba and the other guests, didn't take the logician very seriously, but broke into his finest twelfthly disputation with, "Can you sing, brother Gerardino?" Gerard started. "Why, yes, but—" "Well, come sing with me." And Giles drew from his sleeve a little reed pipe, of the sort that boys make, and playing on the pipe dispersed the mist of wordy argument, and brought back the clear air again. Once more they were sitting in that garden at Perugia, looking at the hills and over the plain, and the twelve arguments of Paris seemed as a cloud that had passed. The teller of the tale—I think brother Leo was of the company that day, though Jacoba would have told him all on her return to Assisi—seems to say that every quaver of the reed pipe was a perfect syllogism—*incipiens a prima per verba rhythmica et procedendo per singulas citharae chordas annullavit et falsificavit omnes duodecim rationes illius*—and so it was.

Poor Gerard was vanquished. At least, he saw that the logic of the schools was wanting in something. And before he recovered his spirit, there was Giles speaking. The pipe was thrown aside, and he was reasoning, formally, weightily, too, though he had never been to Paris. But his resources were many, and he had those that were better than logic, which now in its turn was rejected. Giles was one of the thirteenth-century precursors of Dante. "Shall I show you really what a creature can do?" he cried. Then getting up in the midst of them, and mounting on a chest, he called in a loud and terrible voice to one lying in Hell. The damned one answered by the voice of Giles, but plaining piteously and horribly so that the hearers were sore afraid. "Ah, me !" it said, "ah, me !" Then Giles commanded him, "Tell us, poor wretch, why you went to Hell." And the sad answer came, "Because the good I knew I did not do, and the ill I might have avoided that I did." "What would you do," asked Giles, "if time for repentance were still given you?" And the answer came, as if from deepest Hell, "I would give the whole world, and bit by bit would I give myself to the flames. For that pain would have an end, but mine goes on for evermore."

Giles was possessed by the reality of his little drama. Turning to Gerardino, he said, "Do you hear, brother, what a creature can do?" It may seem a very poor argument read by us in cold blood, but if we had been of the company in the garden that day, we too should have heard the plaining voice from Hell, and been all convinced, as were Jacoba and Gerard and the rest. What chance has a reasoner against an actor of imagination? The play over, he changed his tone as he spoke of the strength of man, not measured by its own littleness, but drawing out of an immeasurable fund, and of human nature a mere drop in the great sea of the Divine. The mystery possessed him, and Giles was rapt before their eyes. Jacoba went back to Assisi, wondering and rejoicing over all she had seen and heard.

Doubtless Giles was growing eccentric, and at times he must have been an aggravating talker. The two Preaching Brothers were perhaps long-winded, and it may be their utterance was very inadequate when they spoke of John the Evangelist's words about God. But it must have been annoying to them, after all their efforts, to hear Giles's only comment, a very weary one, "Dearest brothers, the blessed John said *nothing* about God!" They were not very quick, and had to have it lengthily explained to them that the blessed John, being mortal, could not even begin to say anything worthy on so vast a subject. But people dared his rough wit, in expectation of hearing good things from him, and were generally rewarded, for his comments were rarely insipid or second-hand. Did they say, "Ah, well, flesh is weak: we must make allowances," Giles would turn on them with, "None, if you would win in the great battle. Our flesh is the champion of the enemy." Chastity, he held, was indispensable to victory. He himself had been tempted at Spoleto by a beautiful demon lady, but had fought and overcome. Said one self-satisfied man to him, "I abstain from all women save my own wife." "Can't a man get drunk on the wine of his own glass?" was Giles's retort. "How may I flee temptation?" he was asked. "Who flees temptation flees eternal life. 'And if a man also strive for mastery, yet he is not crowned, except he strive lawfully.'" But his wisdom was not cut-and-dried; it was always of individual application. If he would have a man face the world, he would not have him face its evil with bravado. To dodge the enemy was safer, he held, in carnal vices. Here is his saying concerning the union of the soul with God. The bridegroom before marriage sends to the bride jewels and dresses and purses and necklaces. But when he is married, he does this no more. He and his bride need no such links. So, good works adorn the soul as do gems and fine garments, but through prayer comes the true union. To persons fussily anxious about the fate of their souls, he would say, "Do your duty. What have you to do with Destiny or such high matters?"

He held steady before the brothers the hardy Franciscan ideal. Two of them, expelled from Sicily by Frederic II., came north to Umbria, and in Giles they made sure of finding a sympathiser. Not at all. He would not hear of their grievances. "Pray rather for the soul of the Emperor. What harm has he done to you? Expelled you from your country? If you are true Brothers Minor, you have no country."

But his rigour and roughness were not constant. Probably they did not grow after he learnt that whatever the evil fortunes of the Order, the Brother Minor could keep faithful against all hindrance, and dwell in a land where the spirit of the master was untampered with. The evil of the world seemed to weigh less. When it was spoken of, he would say, "I do not wish to hear of other men's sins." In real calamity he was a comforter, and there was a rare charity about him which overrode his theology. At Perugia there was a certain very unsatisfactory brother, a noble, who in a fit of repentance had entered the Order. But even after that he was dissolute, and most of the brothers frowned on him. They wondered, therefore, one day when, the prodigal William being absent, Giles said to them suddenly, just as he and the brothers were washing their hands before entering the refectory, "It is well with Brother William, and it shall be still better with him." Later, the news was brought to them that William had jumped into the water to save a boy, and been drowned. Giles, who was a fervent believer in the pains of Hell, had no fear for a brave man's soul.

His love increased. He had caught some of the fervour of Francis for the world and its beauty, and would embrace rocks and trees, the signs of God's goodness. And it is of Giles the legend is told concerning the visit of King Louis of France. St. Louis, on his way to the Crusade, visited the holy Giles in the convent at Perugia. The brothers were all excited; and, lo, the two saints embraced and embraced again, and never a word spoke they, and Louis departed. "That was the King of France," they said to Giles, "and not a word did you speak to him!" "Our spirits spoke," said he. "They understood each other like friends."

Giles, it will be noted, never accepted, perhaps

never was offered, any provincial charge, not even under
John of Parma. Unlettered sanctity was no disqualifi-
cation when the strict observance was in favour; but
frequent visions might have hindered the steady administration of a province or a convent. And some proof
that his attention was not to be counted on may be
found, I think, in the fact that the Three Companions
in their prefatory letter to their Legend, addressed to
the Minister-General Crescentius, in 1246, do not cite
him directly as a witness, but only at second-hand
through the evidence of his friend John — *fratrem
Joannem socium venerabilis patris fratris Aegidii, qui
plura de his habuit de eodem sancto fratre Aegidio.*

The world was loosening its hold on him. He had
often feared it while he had faced it so sturdily. Now it
was the wall between him and what he desired. The
curiosity of visitors spurred him less often to shrewd
comment or argument or retort. Eternal things came
as a veil between him and the little concerns of the day.
Brother Gratian, at Cetona, announced to him the
arrival of five Provincial Ministers, and—Giles had to be
" managed "—begged he would be kind and consoling
to them. But Giles, deep in the dream of the city not
made with hands, was hardly to be called back to present
realities, and all they got from him was an appeal—
" O mi fratello, o bel fratello, o amor fratello, fami un
castello che no abia pietra e ferro. O bel fratello, fami
una cittade che no abia pietra o legname." It was not
a bad discourse addressed to that audience in those
times, and the good Gratian's quite unnecessary explana-
tion was rather a poor one.

The transitions between his various phases—between
the hardy bohemian missionary, the scullion, water-
carrier, vintager, as need and chance appointed, and
the rough-spoken street preacher, the biting philosopher,
the shrewd critic, the rousing counsellor, and between
these again and the contemplative, ill at ease in our

world—were of course less abrupt than they seem in narrative. I do not think they coincide very accurately with separate periods of time. But if we cannot make his varied career all coherent, one link there is that joins the loose ends. Giles was no troubadour like Francis. There is something heavier in the rhythm of his soul. But Giles was poet. Amid all his austerities and asperities a sweet and fragrant poetry radiates from the brother who carried the pipe in his sleeve and piped away scholastic quibbles. Most certainly his fellows knew this side of him. All the visions, half the miracles recorded of him have this significance. They are not for nothing those tales of the miraculous flowers he called into being. When the brothers at Perugia lacked water, Giles struck the ground with his stick, and said, "Dig here." And to mark the place for the diggers a lovely violet sprang up. A Dominican, in trouble of soul, doubting the virginity of the Madonna, came to Giles with his doubt. " *O frater Praedicator*," cried Giles, " *virgo ante partum.*" He struck the ground with his stick, and lo, a fair lily was blooming there. Then he went on, " *O frater Praedicator, virgo in partum,*" and a second lily sprang up. And then, " *O frater Praedicator, virgo post partum !*" And behold, yet a third lily! Can you doubt that Giles was convincing?

Withdrawing himself then more and more from men, he drank frequent draughts of the wine that blotted out for him the world of sense. Ever since that day at Fallerone when he felt his soul slip out of the body and he saw secret things, he had looked back with gratitude on his escape from the martyr's death in Tunis, which at the time had humbled him greatly. Even when they quoted Francis as saying, "The martyr's death is best," he replied, "I do not wish to die better than as a contemplative." "Contemplation," he said, "is fire, unction, ecstasy, savour, rest, and glory." The good Bernard of Quintavalle, a near and dear friend, who feared this absorption in spiritual things, and may have thought it unfaithful to the plan of Francis, reproached him with a gentle jest. "You stay in your cell like a *domicella* in her chamber. Out with you to the roads among men. Have speech with them. Beg bread for yourself and others." But Giles answered, "It is not given to every man as to Bernard of Quintavalle to eat his food on the wing like the swallows." If Giles justified his retreat from the world by the long active years he had spent there, he never pleaded these. Contemplation, he knew, is a profession, and serious initiation in spiritual things demands a man's whole strength.

Soon he lost control over his comings and goings between the worlds of sense and vision. A certain spiritual sweetness that filled him gave him warning of the approach of the ecstasy; but even when prudence would have dictated his presence in the body, he could not command it. When Gregory IX. was at Perugia he called for Giles. Giles refused the audience at first, feeling the oncoming of the over-mastering force. But the reason of his refusal being mentioned, the Pope's curiosity grew imperative. And it was satisfied. Gregory was so struck by the wonder of the thing, that he said, "If you depart from this life before me, I shall want no other sign than this, but will enrol you in the catalogue of the saints." But Gregory had not the chance of keeping his word.

In these ecstasies he saw things sweet and strange and great. At Agello, near Trasimene, after supper one evening, he spoke to the brothers so as to move all hearts. Then he was rapt till the crowing of the cock. The brothers watched him go to his cell at last, the radiance about him so great that the moonlight was as nothing. But he hastened back; he had something to say; and it would always be worth saying to the end of time. "What would you do, my sons, if you saw the greater things ? Who never sees the greater things believes everything poor and small." He earned his rapture by pain. An old brother spoke to him of a certain ecstatic—Giles himself, but he loved not to make these secret journeys of his a matter of common talk— *Beatus homo qui scit conservare secreta Dei.* " It is hard for him, I have no doubt," said the old man, " to come back to us again." And Giles sighed as he said, " Ah, indeed, it is hard ! "

The scene of the greater number of his visions, Cetona, near Chiusi, was reckoned by him and others a very holy place. Demons, too, assailed him there. Sometimes the fight between the holy and the demoniac seemed nearly equal, and going to his cell at night, he would say, " Now I await my martyrdom." But the good spirits prevailed. As this faculty of abstraction grew, a word was enough to kindle it. To name Paradise in his hearing was to send him there. Rumour ran about the strange man, and teasing boys or ribald shepherds, meeting him on the road, would call, " Paradiso, frate Egidio, Paradiso ! "—and the gates would open. The brothers, who needed his shrewdness, his long experience of life and men, learned when to abstain from speaking to him of spiritual things, lest he should be rapt outside all their concerns. Sometimes the burden of the secrets and the sweetness was too great for him ; he was unworthy and weak. But little by little he was given more strength, whilst the joy did not lessen. In his earlier visions he is revealed as timid. In one of these, in the year of his master's death, 1226, at the hermitage of Cetona, on All Saints', Francis appeared to him. " Father," cried Giles impulsively, " I would we should speak together." " See first ye be worthy to speak with me," was the reply. I think that vision came not from the region where the friendly Francis dwelt, but from the depths of Giles's self, where, with some arrogance, much lusty self-confidence, there grew a timid flower of humility

never all uprooted, and now and then overrunning all the
garden of his soul. The hardy out-of-door labourer,
the shrewd common-sensible keeper of souls, had his
hours of morbidity. At Fabriano we find him practis-
ing an exaggerated humility, stripping himself of his
tunic, bidding a brother drag him by a rope along the
ground, for his great sins, and refusing to don the habit
again save at the brothers' insistence. When Elias fell,
Giles was seen crawling along the floor. "I want to get
so low," he said, "that I may be outside the danger of
the sin of pride." Giles knew his own perils. He is a
fruitful field for the study of religious psychology, and
especially of visionary psychology.

As the power increased he grew less distrustful. He
recognised his privileges. As God had breathed on the
Apostles, so now He was breathing on him, rude and
ignorant though he was. Three days before the feast
of the Nativity, Jesus Christ appeared to him. He saw
Him with his carnal eyes. He might not speak of these
things. With Francis he said, "*Secretum meum mihi.*"
But they oozed out. By night the intolerableness of
the visions would seize him, and he would cry aloud.
The brothers would run for his friend Gratian, with
the news that Giles was dying. And the great sights
came sometimes when they were by. A light would
strike between him and them. Startled, they would
cry out in inquiry. "Take no thought," he would
say, as he turned from them. Now there was a certain
holy man at Cetona, to whom God also, though in lesser
measure, revealed secrets. One night in his sleep he
saw above the cell of Giles a sun rise, then turn to set.
Giles, he knew, was changed, absent from them, wandering in strange regions; and full of love, of pity,
of wonder, and of wistful warning, his wise old voice
whispered to him, "Bear gently the Son of the Virgin."
Here we are on the threshold of a mystery. If we tread
softly, reverently, let no holy one resent it if we smile,

gazing from all our distance. The man Giles is never all lost in the contemplative saint. His story at Cetona is a very comedy of Divine Love.

Giles commended the place of Cetona above all others, because God had shown special grace to him and others there. God honoured it in sending not His saints to comfort them in visions, but in coming Himself. Therefore, he said, men should go to Cetona with greater reverence than to St. Angelo, to St. Nicholas of Bari, or to St. Peter's at Rome, for the Lord is greater than His vassals, Christ is greater than the saints. His companions would remind him of other shrines. "No creature is like the Christ," he would answer. Indeed, he was adhering to the early Franciscan spirit. Giles's own wanderings to St. Iago, to St. Angelo, to St. Nicholas, were in accordance rather with an earlier tradition. The one great shrine of the first Franciscans was the Holy Sepulchre in Jerusalem.

Some brother sitting by him would use all his skill of coaxing to make him talk. Giles would say darkly, "What thou seest, thou seest, and what thou hearest, thou hearest." But he would let a gleam of the glory shine out, gradually a little more, and a little more, then stop with, "If I glorify myself, my glory is naught. Let us speak no more of this matter." Brother Andrew of Burgundy would encourage him with, "I believe God wishes His favoured servants to tell these things for the good of others." Swelling with pride, and burning with the desire to show how God had blessed Cetona, then humbled to the dust, and again accepting his destiny frankly—"I have told God I am not worthy, but He is God and doeth what pleaseth Him,"—so, variously, pass his moods before us.

"God did great things in Mount Alverna," Andrew would say insinuatingly. "Yes, oh—yes," Giles would admit. But he, too, had looked naked glory in the face ; and no Alverna could pale the favour of Cetona.

If only he could tell all he had seen! Their questions
showed them so far from the reality. There was
Andrew asking, " Would it not seem a great thing if
an angel appeared to a man ? " An *Angel!* He *must*
at least tell, darkly, how God sometimes sends no messengers but comes Himself to sinful man ! " Oh," cries
Andrew, exalted at the thought, " Oh, for a beautiful
church where He might appear ! " " Yes, indeed," says
Giles, firing at the idea. " How should it be called ? "
asks Andrew. " The Church of Pentecost."

This is noteworthy. Giles was of the *zelanti*, who
read, if they read at all, the works of Joachim, or forgeries
of these. Gerard da Borgo San Donnino was probably
among his friends. But I doubt if any of the immediate
disciples of Francis were much influenced by the heresy.
Giles, least of all, would be touched by it, who read in
no books, save that of his own spirit. If, then, he has
reached Joachim's Third Stage, it is only as a true Franciscan of the early days, who, without thought of heresy
or schism, finds his love for the saints swallowed up by
his love for God. They and he are but drops in the
great sea of the Divine. So the church to be built for
the great visitation is not dedicate to St. Peter, nor St.
John, nor St. Francis, but is the church of the Holy
Spirit.

If there was some comedy in the demeanour of the
visionary, it was wistful and awesome. He must keep
loyal and reverent secrecy, yet he would have his privileges known. He was jealous of the shrines of St.
Nicholas, of Alverna, if you will. It is significant that
the tormenting demons tempted him to vainglory. One
guesses a double meaning in the gentle counsel of the
wise old man, *Porta suaviter filium Virginis.* But if self
played a part it did so naïvely. Love was the great
actor. He burned with love for God who had deigned
to visit him, the rude and lowly man. The ineffable
flame shone within him, yet to speak of it was betrayal,

for human words were so false when they dared tell of the highest.   Yet it would out.   So he stammered ; so he babbled ; so he kept silence.   But no one that dwelt with Giles denied the *magnalia*, the things that lie beyond the senses, or thought great things poor and small.

He was much loved, but he was an awesome old man, with his tales of his four births, in his mother's womb, in the sacrament of baptism, in his entry into the Order, and when God first rapt him from the earth at Fallerone.   He was a man, too, whom any other time or country would have teased and pursued into heresy, for he had risen beyond the latitudes, beyond the limits of creeds.

Says the anxious, pertinacious Andrew to him, " Once you told me that when Christ appeared to you, your faith was taken away.   Tell me now, have you hope ? "

" How can one have hope who has no faith ? "

" Do you not then hope for eternal life ? "

" God can give the reward of eternal life to whom He pleases," Giles answers with calm indifference—an indifference echoed later by Jacopone.

Andrew returns to the subject again.   " Having no faith, what would you do if you were a priest and had to say mass ?   How could you say, ' I believe in one God ? ' "

And Giles, with shining eyes, sang aloud, " I do not believe.   I *know*.   *Cognosco* unum Deum, Patrem omnipotentem."

And so, absent many times from the body, he drew on his way to death.   He was at Perugia, in the Romitorio del Monte outside the town, when he lay dying.   His heart desired that he should lie near Francis, but he made no peremptory demand, and his wish was set aside.   So he is not the Giles of Cappoccio that lies in the Lower Church at Assisi.

The fighting, quarrelsome, noisy, worldly, yet pietistic Perugians did not underestimate the relics of a saint. They were proud of Giles. They knew his commercial, or, at least, his honorific value to their city; and outside the convent they stationed a band of armed men to guard the place lest he should be taken elsewhere. When the holy man heard this he said, with some irony, some depression, much gentle resignation—I think, no bitterness—"Tell the Perugians that their bells shall never ring because I am canonised, or for any great miracle of mine." The brothers passed on the word to the citizens without. "Canonised or not, we will have him. He is ours," they replied. On the Eve of St. George, 1261, fifty-two years to a day after he had entered the Order, the brothers closed his eyes. The pain of returning from ecstasy was over at last. And Leo—a gentler soul than Giles, one who had suffered more, I think, because his talents, because duty and destiny had called him to dwell more and fight more in the world, without all Giles's holidays into clearer air—Leo cries aloud as he writes of his death, "O most holy father, our brother Aegidio . . . remember us whom thou hast left below in such peril and such misery!"

He was buried in Perugia. The citizens put a sculptured tomb over him, and did his remains much honour. Tradition says he did not disappoint them. He had prayed, in his humility, he might do no miracles after his death, says Salimbene. He had declared on his deathbed there was nothing to be gained in wonder-working from his relics; but the Perugians said his prayers and prophecy on this matter were not fulfilled. He was always venerated, though not till 1777 was he formally acknowledged as the "beato Egidio." Great and small had pilgrimed to him in life. His sayings stayed long in his hearers' memories; they were gathered by his friend Leo, and were re-published many times and conned in later ages. Some of them are in the *Fioretti*. At Cetona the Blessed a church commemorated his visions there.

This, so far as we can read him now, was Francis's " Chevalier of the Round Table "—no carpet knight, but no churl, one for wayside hourly combats, not for showy tournaments. By his boundless vitality and knowledge of men he was well fitted to live in the world. He left it in no puling mood, to adventure hardily on other roads.

What is the end of the life contemplative? The later ages ask the question in a voice full of morality, of a sense of duty, of the value of time and of the demands of positive science. What is the gain of vision—save to a poet with a publisher and a public? The friends of Giles answer timidly. Possibly he learned very few things in his ecstasies at Perugia and Cetona; and the sum of them, if they could be uttered, would pass the tongue in a flash. It is the road to learning that time is spent on. It is the means of getting it the world busies itself with. To make a doubtful guess, on which to build a shaky creed, a great man will spend a long, laborious life. Giles reached where there are no such things as creeds.

We cannot take any royal road or any short cut to knowledge, says the dutiful voice from the plain highway. But if you could?

IV. ANGELO TANCREDI OF RIETI

" He was a verray perfight gentil knight."

THIS is the story how Angelo the soldier became a
Brother Minor. Francis, in 1210, journeying to Rome,
on his first visit to the Pope, passed through the town
of Rieti, stopping two days. There he met a noble
knight of the place, by name Angelo Tancredi, to whom
the saint, ignorant even of his name, said, by Divine
instinct, " Lord Angelo, long time is it now since first
you girt on your sword, and donned all your warlike
armour. Now would it become you to gird you with
a rough rope like me; in place of the sword to take
the Cross of Christ, and for boots and spurs to shoe you
with the dust and mire of the streets. Follow me, then,
and I will make you a knight of Christ."

Angelo left all behind him, enrolled himself in the
little army, put on its uniform, and set off with it to
Rome. Francis understood soldiers. He had been a
fighting man himself, and had endured the fortunes
of war, in tough struggles and in a Perugian prison,
with gaiety of heart. It fitted his humour well to steal
a soldier from the battles of the world for his new
chivalry. Angelo kindled at his call, accepted his captain at once, learnt his new drill, the use of his new
weapons, and became the humble loyal squire of Francis.

He has little other history. His career from the
moment of his enlistment seems to have been sure and
serene; and he was of the very inner circle. He was
much with the saint in the early days, and to his witness,
or to Masseo's, we owe some of the most exquisite pages

in the history of Francis. After it had been revealed
to their perplexed father, by the prayers of Silvester
and Clara, that it was better to serve God in the world
than in secret places, Francis set off without delay
on a preaching mission. Angelo and Masseo were
of the company. "And setting forth with fervent zeal
of spirit, taking no thought for road or way, they came
unto a little town that was called Savurniano, and Saint
Francis set himself to preach, but first he bade the
swallows that were twittering keep silence till such time
as he had done the preaching; and the swallows were
obedient to his word." The men and women of the
town were so kindled by his words that they would all
have cast all behind them and followed too. But Francis
said, "'Make not ill haste nor leave your homes; and
I will ordain for you what ye should do for the salvation
of your souls;' and therewith he resolved to found
the Third Order, for the salvation of all the world."
(This last statement, I may say in passing, is at variance
with sober history.) Then, still with Masseo and Angelo,
he went on to a place between Cannaio and Bevagno.
"And as with great fervour he was going on his way,
he lifted his eyes and beheld some trees hard by the road,
whereon sat a great company of birds well-nigh without
number; whereat Saint Francis marvelled, and said to his
companions: 'Ye shall wait for me here upon the way,
and I will go to preach unto my little sisters, the birds.'
. . . And according to what Brother Masseo afterwards
related unto Brother Jacques da Massa, Saint Francis
went among them, touching them with his cloak, howbeit
none moved from out his place." Angelo heard the
saint's sermon to the birds, sharers with all created
things of the "Love that moves the world," and heard
the birds' glad response in song. Such was one day of
the campaign of the new knight of Christ in the conquest
of the new Kingdom of Joy.

There is little mention of him during the next years.

F

We can only guess his mission of good cheer, till in 1223 we meet him in Rome, where Francis had gone on the business of the Indulgence of the Porziuncola. That Angelo is there seen staying in the house of Cardinal Leo, instead of in a lazar house, or in some frugal lodging of the brothers, might seem to tell against his steadfastness, judged by our knowledge of the later history of the Order. But he was probably only a guest, as was Francis at the time. There is never a slur anywhere on Angelo's staunchness. It was he, when Francis feared the pomp and luxury of a cardinal's house, that sought out for him a lonely tower near by, where he and his companion could retire when they would. To this tower Angelo brought them food. But the demons haunted them. The Poverello trembled, and they passed a sleepless night till Francis faced the dark foes, and divined the reason of their troubling. They were the servants of God, *castalli Domini*, sent to punish one who had been lying in comfort in a Cardinal's court while his brothers walked the roads in weariness and want.

Next year he was of the little band, the special *nos qui cum eo fuimus*, who went to Alverna, there to be the witnesses of the awful union of Francis with Universal Love. And near the time of the saint's death, when his pains were sore, Francis sent for Leo and Angelo, minstrels both, that they might sing to him his own song of joy and triumph, *The Song of the Creatures*, he had made in Clara's garden at San Damiano. " When those two brothers came before him full of sadness and grief, with many tears they sang the song of Brother Sun and of the other creatures of the Lord, which the saint had made. And then before the last verse he added some verses concerning Sister Death."

Angelo lived for many years after, closely allied with Giles and Leo and Rufino. Perhaps it was because he was so little concerned with the public matters of the

Order, and more of an obedient, soldierlike worker than a protester, that he seems to have suffered little persecution under the régime of Elias. A few other appearances he makes in the Chronicles. He is one of the authors of the *Legend of the Three Companions;* and he is one of the brothers seen by the side of Clara at her death. He is joined with Leo, pious guardians both of the master's treasures, in giving the breviary of Francis to the Clares. Then he disappears. He died in 1258, it is said, and was buried in San Francesco in the Chapel of St. John the Evangelist, leaving a vague memory of staunchness and sweetness. A "verray perfight, gentil knight" was he, praised by his captain for his *benignità*, for his fine bearing and courtesy ; "for he was adorned with all courtesy and kindness." "And know, brother, that courtesy is one of the qualities of God Himself, who, of His courtesy, giveth His sun and rain to the just and the unjust ; and courtesy is the sister of charity, the which quencheth hate and keepeth love alive."

V. MASSEO DA MARIGNANO

" Noi volgendi ivi le nostre persone,
Beati pauperes spiritu, voci
Cantaron sì che nol diria sermone.

    .   .   .   .

Già montavam su per li scaglion santi,
Ed esser mi parea troppo più lieve,
Che per lo pian non mi parea davanti :
Ond' io : 'Maestro, di', qual cosa greve
Levata s'è da me, che nulla quasi
Per me fatica andando si riceve ? "
—PURGATORIO, xii. 109–120.

SOME of the most fervent, the most extravagant hours
of Francis were spent with Brother Masseo. Masseo
caught his intoxication readily, and probably fed it. He
is a favourite of the *Fioretti*, the author of which,
however, credits him with a discretion which was not
his. But he does not mean it—he contradicts himself
immediately, describing Masseo as teasing and mocking
his master. "Thou art not a man comely of form, thou
art not of much wisdom, thou art not noble of birth ;
whence comes it then that it is after thee that the whole
world doth run?" They were on the most intimate,
most informal terms, seem to have used the plainest
speech to each other, nor to have stopped at practical
jesting. The story of Francis making him turn and
spin like a dancing dervish at the meeting-place of roads
to Florence, Arezzo, and Siena, and choosing the road
towards which Masseo's face was turned when he stopped,
is told with seriousness, though the incident was probably no more than a joke, as light a thing as tossing
a penny when in doubt—and Minorites had no pennies.

But staid folks had passed by and frowned, and jesters had passed with a laugh. Masseo was proud, and did not forget he had been made fun of. They took the road to Siena, and Francis did good service as peace-maker there. They were lodged with honour in the Bishop's house. Francis, who was ill at ease in luxury, and who had done his work, was up and off betimes ; Masseo went with him, grumbling at his want of courtesy. Never a word of farewell and thanks to the great man ! Just like Francis ! There was bitterness in his heart for the event of yesterday. But his black mood did not last long. He was soon reproaching himself for thinking ill of a man who could heal a city's wounds, and telling himself he deserved Hell. And, of course, Francis knew what was in his mind, and revealed it to him.

Masseo was a big handsome fellow, well-endowed, ready of speech, with a personality written on his face ; and since, later, he had an overpowering ambition to be humble, he must at one time have thought a deal of himself. Francis's treatment of him was drastic. When they were living at the Carceri, he made him beggar for the brothers, cook, and doorkeeper, while the rest were given leisure for contemplation—till at last his companions protested and said they would share the hard offices. Francis consented, seeing Masseo had accepted his lot cheerfully. It is a testimony to the fine tempers of both that they became fast friends. When the Poverello set out for France—he never reached there, for Cardinal Ugolino called him back—Masseo was his companion. They were often hungry on the way, and they begged their bread. Masseo was the more success-ful beggar. So fine a fellow must want feeding, the people thought. It was but a poor meal they ate after all, said Masseo sometimes ; but one day Francis trans-figured it for him. "Here is nor cloth, nor knife, nor plate, nor porringer, nor house, nor table, nor man-servant, nor maid servant," the brother was thinking.

Quoth St. Francis, "And this it is that I account vast treasure, wherein is nothing at all prepared by human hands, but whatsoever we have is given by God's own providence, as manifestly doth appear in the bread that we have begged, in the table of stone so fine, and in the fount so clear." After their meal they entered a church, and there followed one of those strange moments of fervour, which had their climax on Mount Alverna. His companion was not one to hinder the ecstasy. "Ah, ah, ah! Brother Masseo, give thyself to me!" And Masseo gave himself and was lifted from the earth. "Afterwards he recounted to his companions how that, when as he was lifted and hurled along by the breath that St. Francis breathed on him, he tasted such sweetness in his soul, and consolation of the Holy Spirit, that in all his life he ne'er had felt the like."

Then from the mouth of Francis came a burning eulogy of Madonna Poverty, their Sovereign Lady, "whereby all hindrances are lifted from the soul, so that freely she may join herself to God Eternal." "Then let us go," he said impulsively, "to Rome, and beg the Holy Apostles to give us their gospel pearl." When it was the fervent, extravagant men ran to Rome on this errand, I do not know. Sober history does not tell the tale—which is very likely true none the less—nor that Peter and Paul appeared in great splendour to Francis and promised him his desire, and blessed his followers.

Masseo is the reputed witness of that strange interview of the Poverello and Honorius at Perugia, respecting the Indulgence of the Porziuncola. His nephew, Fra Marino of Assisi, heard the story often from his uncle's lips. I cannot give it better than in the words of Francesco Bartholi, who, in his *Tractatus de Indulgentia S. Mariae de Portiuncula*, written, in part, at least, in 1335, collects all the ecclesiastical information and popular legends on the subject.

"After the Blessed Francis had repaired the church

of St. Mary of the Angels, for the great love he had to
the Queen of the Angels, he dwelt there in deep devotion
and in continual prayer. One night when he was praying
God most fervently, it was revealed to him that our
Lord Jesus Christ and the Virgin Mary, His Mother,
were in the aforesaid church. Rising thereupon with
much devotion and spiritual joy and deep reverence,
he entered the church. And seeing the Lord Jesus
Christ with a multitude of angels, he prostrated himself
on the ground before the sight of Him and the glorious
Virgin. Then said the Lord to the Blessed Francis,
'Francis, ask what thou wilt for the saving of the
people to the honour and reverence of the Godhead, for
it is given to thee to save men and to repair the Church
on earth.' But he lay as in a trance.

"When he had come back to himself, he said, 'Our
most Holy Father, I beg Thee, poor miserable sinner
though I am, that Thou grant this grace to humankind;
give Thy pardon and indulgence to all and single that
may come to this place and enter this church, for each
and all their sins of which they make confession to a
priest.'" Then he begs the Blessed Virgin to intercede
for him, and is bidden go to Pope Honorius, at Perugia,
to state his wish in the name of God.

"Now the blessed Francis, rising betimes in the
morning, called to Brother Masseo, along with whom
he presented himself before the Pope, and said, 'Holy
Father, not long since I repaired a church for the
honour of the Virgin, Christ's Mother. I beg your
Holiness that you give to that church a free Indulgence
in memory of its consecration.'"

The Pope was astonished at the calm request of
the Poverello; but he asked, "For how many years
dost thou wish me to grant this Indulgence? For one
year? Well, for three years?" And Francis said,
"What is that?" And again the Lord Pope, "Dost
thou wish me to make it six?" Then they came to

seven. But the blessed Francis not content, still said,
"O my lord, what is that?" And the Pope, "What wilt
thou that I do?" "To whom Saint Francis answered,
'Holy Father, let it please your Holiness, give not years
but souls.' The Lord Pope said, 'Souls?' And the
saint answered, 'I will, if it please your Holiness, for
the benefits God does in that place that whoever shall
come to that church, confessed, and contrite, and shriven
by priest, shall be absolved from all penalty and fault
he has committed towards heaven or on earth from the
day of his baptism till the day and hour of his entry
into the aforesaid church.'"

"The Lord Pope answered, 'It is a great thing thou
askest, Francis, for it is not the custom of the Roman
Curia to give such indulgences.' But the Blessed
Francis answered, 'Lord, what I ask, I ask not of
myself, but in the name of Him that sent me, the Lord
Jesus Christ.' And the Lord Pope answered, 'I concede
it to thee.'" And he repeated his words with emphasis,
for Honorius was moved, "Placet mihi quod habeas.
Placet mihi quod habeas. Fiat in nomine Domini."

The cardinals were aghast. Such informality! Such
favour to a poor little obscure church! Besides, it
would prejudice the Indulgences of SS. Peter and Paul,
and of the Holy Land. Honorius must take it back.
But he was firm, and the sole concession he made to
the cardinals was to make the Indulgence last for only
one natural day, from the first vespers of one day to
the first vespers of the next.

"Then the Blessed Francis inclined his head, and
turned to go out of the palace. The Lord Pope, seeing
him go away, called to him and said, 'O simplicone, quo
vadis?' (O great simple one, where goest thou?)
'What dost thou carry away with thee to witness this Indulgence?' And the Blessed Francis answered, 'Enough
unto me is your word. If the work be of God, He
will make it manifest. I wish not for any document;

but let the Blessed Virgin Mary be the chart, the notary be Christ, and the witnesses the angels.'"

On their way back to Assisi, they stayed at the lazar house of Colle, and in the night time his faith was confirmed in a vision. He called to his companion, "Brother Masseo, I tell thee that the Indulgence given me by the Holy See is ratified in the heavens."

The rest of the legend concerns Masseo no more than the other companions. But it may be given here; and it will call up to some readers a few minutes spent in a poor little starveling garden in the precincts of St. Mary of the Angels, where yet they were fain to linger, and from which, maybe, they carried away a rose leaf or two, in memory of a naïf story told them by their brown-frocked guide.

"When the Blessed Francis was in his cell, which was in the garden behind the Church of St. Mary, in the month of January, praying and watching by night, behold Satan came to him, and said, 'O Francis, why dost thou die before thy time? Dost thou not know that sleep is the strongest meat of the body? Why dost thou watch thus? Did I not once before tell thee in the Church which is called Quattuor Capellæ in Todi, that thou art young, and that later thou mightst do penance for thy sins. Why, therefore, punish thyself with vigils and prayers?'

"Then the Blessed Francis went out of his cell naked, and entered a wood by a great thick hedge, tearing his body with the briars and thorns, and saying the while, 'Infinitely better is it for me that I know the suffering of our Lord than that I heed the blandishments of the Enemy.' Then when he was torn and bleeding, there shone round him a very great light, and red and white roses of wonderful odour and beautiful to look at in great plenty appeared about him, and with the light a multitude of angels in the church and near it. And the angels said to the Blessed Francis, 'Go in

haste to the Saviour and His Mother in the church.'
Quickly rose he, and behold he was clothed in white
raiment. And taking of those roses twelve white and
twelve red he went towards the church, and the path
was all strewn with silken raiments. Reverently entering,
he laid the flowers on the altar. Then saw he our
Lord Jesus Christ and His Mother, with a host of
angels." And Christ asked him why he did not bring
the due gifts to His Mother. Francis knew the souls to
be rescued by the promised Indulgence were meant. But
he had waited to learn what was the privileged day. Now
he heard it : and that is why so many pilgrims fare to
Assisi for the 1st of August. But said Francis, 'Most
Holy Father, how shall men be made to believe this?'
And he was bidden go to Rome to Honorius, and
receive the confirmation from his lips. 'But it may
be,' he said, 'Thy Vicar will not believe a sinner like
me.' And the Almighty Lord said to the Blessed
Francis, 'Take three of thy companions, who have
heard these things, and take the red roses and the white
thou didst cull in the month of January in the wood,
when thou went to chastise thy body. . . .

"These things were heard by Brother Peter of
Catania, Brother Rufino of the Scifi, Brother Bernard
of Quintavalle, and Brother Masseo of Marignano, and
the companions who were in the huts, that is, the cells
outside the church in the garden, where is the cell of
the Blessed Francis. . . .

"In the morning Francis put on his tunic, and going
to his three companions, Peter of Catania, Bernard, and
Angelo, said, 'Make ready to come with me to Rome.'"
And he went with them to the City to tell the High
Pope that the 1st of August was claimed for the Indulgence of the Porziuncola ; and all the evidence they
brought with them that such indeed was the will of the
Most High, was this strange tale, and the white roses
and the red culled in the snows of January.

There is some evidence that Masseo was a writer. If the following document be authentic, he was of the little band in Alverna. Leo, the scribe, was there also, but no account of the life they led has come to us directly from his pen—though his tales are doubtless the base of the accounts we have. And Masseo only wrote concerning the farewell of Francis to them all and to the mountain.

Jesu. Mary. My Hope.

"Brother Masseo, sinner, unworthy servant of Jesus Christ, companion of Brother Francis of Assisi, a man most dear to God, peace and health to all the brothers and sons of the great patriarch, Francis, ensign of Christ.

"The great patriarch having resolved to take a last farewell of this holy mountain on the 30th of September, 1224, the day of the feast of St. Jerome, Count Orlando of Chiusi sent him an ass that he might ride, since he could not put his feet to the ground—for they were wounded and pierced with nails. In the morning early, after having heard mass in St. Mary of the Angels, as was his wont, he called all the brothers into the oratory, and commanded them by obedience that they should always love one another, should watch and pray, and ever have care of this place and say an office in it day and night. Moreover, he commended to them the whole of this sacred mountain, exhorting all his brothers now and in the future, never to allow the place to be profaned, but to hold it ever in respect and reverence. And he gave his blessing to all those who should dwell there, and to all who should pay it reverence and respect. On the other hand, 'Let them be confounded,' he said, 'who will not reverence the place, and let them wait their due chastisement from God.' To me he said, 'Brother Masseo, my will is that in this mountain there dwell God-fearing brothers,

the best that are in my Order, and therefore it behoves
the superiors only to station here the best of the
brothers.   Ah! ah! ah! Brother Masseo.   I say no
more.'

"Then he commanded me, Brother Masseo, Brother
Angelo, Brother Silvestro, and Brother Illuminato to
have special care of the place where had come to pass
that great marvel of the impress of the Holy Stigmata.
And then, 'Adieu, adieu, adieu, Brother Masseo,' he
said; and turned to Brother Angelo, and said, 'Adieu,
adieu.'   And the like said he to Brother Silvester and
Brother Illuminato.   'Peace be with you, my dearest
sons.   Adieu! I go far from you in the body, but I
leave my heart with you.   I go away with Fra Pecorello
di Dio, to St. Mary of the Angels, and I come not
back again.   I go away.   Adieu! adieu! adieu to all!
adieu, holy Mountain! adieu, Mount Alverna! adieu,
mount of the Angels!   Adieu, dearest brother falcon!
I thank thee for the love thou borest towards me.
Adieu! adieu, Sasso Spicco!   Not again shall I come
to visit thee.   Adieu! adieu! adieu! rock that receivedst
me into thine entrails while thou mockedst the demon.
We shall never see each other again.   Adieu St. Mary
of the Angels!   To thee, Mother of the Eternal Word,
I commend these my sons.'

"While he said these words, our eyes were pouring
out floods of tears for him, our dear father, going from
us.   He, too, weeping, carried away with him our
hearts.   Truly orphaned were we by the departure of
such a father.

"I, Brother Masseo, have written this with tears.

"The blessing of God be on us."

Some phrases in the thirteenth chapter of the *Fioretti*
—already referred to—in praise of Lady Poverty, remind one of images in the *Sacrum Commercium*.   The
chapter in the *Fioretti* is probably based on traditional
reports of Masseo's own tales and language.   I do not

make the unfounded suggestion that Masseo was the
author of the treatise. But the connection of his name
with the discourse of Francis on Poverty, as popularly
reported and set down in the *Fioretti*, counts for something. He may conceivably have been the inspirer of
the author—if John of Parma were not he—the inter-
mediary between the author and Francis, from whose
own vivid images rose the legend of the Mystic Wooing.

They undertook strange enterprises those early
brothers. Masseo, the fine-looking, courtly man of
ready speech, whom the world found it easy to honour,
was all afire to be humble. He sought Humility as
his Bride, and the Bride kept far from him, and was
hard to win. He had intellectual difficulties about the
humility of a well-doing man. What wonder? He
touched there the crux of the Franciscan moral code,
that demanded perfection of the brothers, who were
yet to hold themselves of the vilest. It was a real
difficulty, and some solution of it was necessary, if
spiritual pride and self-righteousness were not to be
their bane. The solution was contained in the contemplation of the Divine Ideal, and in human love.
Masseo probably found the answer to his problem.
He vowed never to feel any joy until humility was his.
He vowed the eyes out of his head to obtain it. He
found it only when it was revealed to him that he could
never earn such grace; it should be given to him. After
that his joy was continual. He couldn't keep silent
about it, but must utter it. His joy could not find
articulate human speech, so he cooed with satisfaction
that he had seen his own vileness, and was not minded
any more to compare it with the beauty of holiness.
Brother James of Fallerone got tired of the note, and
suggested variety in his song. But Masseo was content.
" I feel it tells all ; so why change it ? "

Masseo is Giles's own brother, without his genius
for contemplation, but sharing the gift of speech that

went right to the heart of the people, and with much of his genial audacity of character and conversation. He was reputed a sayer of pithy things, but few of these have come down to us. Only two memorable ones have clung to his legend—that it is better to go to living men than dead saints; and that the best cure for conventual tattling over neighbours' sins and peccadilloes was to contemplate the deeds of the good and the holy. Strange, but faulty men would seem more tolerable in the light of these.

According to Wadding he lived beyond all the other early friends of Francis save Illuminato, dying in France in 1280. But this was probably another Masseo. The name of ours appears in a legal document in 1241, and in 1247 he was cited as a witness by the Three Companions. Papini is probably right in placing his death before 1265, when, had he been alive, he would surely have been interrogated concerning the Indulgence of the Porziuncola. Perhaps happily he died while yet there was hope that John of Parma's great experiment was to shape the Franciscan future.

VI. LEO

" *il dolce Maestro, che m'avea*
Da quella parte onde il core ha la gente."
—Purgatorio, x. 47–48.

The Leo of the *Fioretti* is an engaging personality. The *pecorello di Dio*, the little sheep of God, is seen constantly at his master's side, gentle, with no apparent vices to overcome, drinking in the words of Francis, eager to do his behests, answering him with dovelike simplicity. It is natural to think of him as a loving shadow, not a man likely to be a great influence in the Order, save as an example of sweet faithfulness. The author of the *Fioretti* has not been at pains to gather material for a complete picture of him, but, perhaps by accident, he has written something excellently characteristic in the ninth chapter. Francis and Leo were living up at the Carceri, and they had no prayer-books out of which to say the office, so Francis proposed a holy game. He felt, it appears, in need of the abuse and buffeting of the world. There on the quiet mountain side and among the woods, the world left him in languorous peace. So he commanded Leo to play the part of the world, and to echo his vigorous abuse of himself. Leo consented, with his dovelike simplicity, and Francis began to lash his poor innocent soul with angry words. The echo came back prompt, but strangely sweet, from the mouth of Brother Leo, little lamb. Francis tried again and again with the same result, till at last he charged Leo with disobedience in not answering as he had commanded. "Replied Brother Leo right humbly and reverently: 'God knows, my father, that each time I set it in my heart to answer as thou hadst bid me, but God makes me speak as it pleaseth Him and not as it pleaseth me.' . . . And thuswise in this humble strife, with many tears and much spiritual consolation they kept watch until the day." The story almost sums up the temper of Leo, gentle and obstinate. Only a little portion of his career was spent at his master's side. Readers of the *Fioretti* who may suppose the *pecorello* to have died of grief when Francis passed away, have yet to learn of another Leo, a wonderfully sturdy personage, who survived all the other intimate companions, save Illuminato, an eager purposeful man with a long memory. The little sheep, the man of dovelike simplicity, became a famous propagandist.

Leo was born, it has been generally stated, at Viterbo, but whether this is a mistake in fact, or whether out of devotion he chose to be counted a citizen of Francis's town, he calls himself a child of Assisi. Not one of the first twelve, he is said to have joined the Order in 1210, and perhaps was already a priest. In the course of time he became the confessor and the secretary of the Founder, and as such knew him with an intimacy that no other enjoyed. Whole-hearted, submissive, his entire being seemed submerged in the Lover of Francis. Living at the *poverello's* side, he listened, watched, and remembered. No one thought the little secretary at all formidable. But Francis was at ease with him, poured out his heart to him in the paean of Perfect Joy, and lived with him in many lonely places. Leo had one of the great rare chances of interpreting a human being of exceeding grace, which are so generally missed. He did not miss his. When Francis went to Monte Colombo to re-write his Rule at the bidding of Rome, Leo and Bonizio of Bologna were with him, witnesses of his struggle to keep to the early faith in the face of opposition, witnesses of the coming of the ministers with Elias as their spokesman, to say, "That Rule is not for us; make it for thyself." Leo heard the voice in the air confirming

Francis, and saw the ministers go away confused and
terrified from before the face of the *poverello*. He was
with Francis at Rome when Honorius examined the
new Rule; and heard the Pope's smooth words, his
insinuating suggestions, his bland curtailment of the
proposed sanction to the brothers to bind themselves
to the Rule only so far as their spiritual advancement
allowed them, provided they lived openly, and with a
striving after the best. He saw Francis's gentleness and
his failure. He was his companion on the road that
day they came to the Castle of Montefeltro, where a
great feasting was going on. The saint, who fled no joy,
went among the guests, and there saw the Knight Orlando
of Chiusi in the Casentino. Then Francis stood on a
parapet and preached, and as he was no death's head at a
feast, his preaching was of joy. The Knight Orlando
was so moved that he said, "O father, I would confer
with thee touching the salvation of my soul." Replied
Saint Francis, the ever courteous, "It pleaseth me right
well; but go this morning and do honour to thy friends
who have called thee to the feast, and dine with them ;
and after thou hast dined, we will speak together as much
as thou wilt." This was Orlando who gave to Francis
Mount Alverna, "very lonely, and right well fitted for
whoso may wish to do penance in a place remote from
men, or whoso may desire to live a solitary life." He
sent men-at-arms to protect the brothers in their explora-
tion of the mountain. In St. Michael's Lent, 1224, Leo
was of the company that climbed Alverna's side with
Francis, was witness of his terror of demons, his joy in
the wild birds, and in the silence of the lonely place.
His cell was apart, and it was Leo who brought him his
food. "Brother Leo, when it seemeth to him good,
shall bring to me a little bread and a little water ; and
do ye in no wise suffer any that be of the world to come
nigh me, but do ye answer them for me." The wonders
Leo saw on that mountain he never all told, but he

G

stammered some hint of them in later years to James of La Massa—how that the purity and the ecstasy of his master so touched him that he threw himself down, embraced his feet, and said, "My God, have mercy on me, a sinner!" It was Leo who helped him to find a still more secret place to keep the forty days' fast, so far from the others that no cry of his could be heard by them. Leo was to come once a day with food, and cry aloud. If he got no answer he was to go away. If Francis answered, they would say matins together. Leo might not be often with him. Only the falcon building her nest by his cell was suffered there. Yet the good, anxious, faithful soul did not always go away when he got no answer. He dared to see wonders, for which Francis but mildly reproached him, knowing the refinement of his soul. After the terrible vision of Mount Alverna was made manifest in his body, Francis chose out Leo to care for him, "as above the rest the most simple and pure." And it was with Leo alone that, feeble and driven by pain well-nigh out of this world, he went down the mountain on his way back to Assisi. Leo was witness of the strange triumphal progress of the *poverello* riding on the ass; and as they approached St. Mary of the Angels saw the cross go before the face of Francis, stopping where he stopped, going on as he went, and lighting all the way.

The famous blessing of Leo—the greatest treasure of the Sacro Convento—was written on Alverna. Doubtless he knew his master a dying man, and thinking of all the years without him, and of the hardness of life, he gave way to depression. Francis divined the cause, and, lover-like, gave him the sacred keepsake, afterwards looked on as a miracle-working charm. He dictated part—Leo himself the scribe—"The Lord bless thee and keep thee; the Lord make His face to shine upon thee, and be gracious unto thee; the Lord lift up His countenance upon thee, and give thee peace." The words that follow *Dominus*

THE STIGMATA

ANDREA DELLA ROBBIA.   Assisi, S. Maria degli Angel

benedicat f. Leo te are in the handwriting of Francis, the
cross in the shape of *Thau* being his usual signature.
That the autograph is authentic is beyond doubt.   Only
one other is known to exist, a letter also addressed to
Leo, in which we read again of the disciple's yearning
desire for the presence of Francis and his master's loving
response : " And if it be necessary for thy soul, to console
thee in any way, and if thou wishest, Leo, to come to
me, then come."   Leo, it is said, fell heir to the saint's
tunic, but the precious relic was sent to France to reward
some one's devotion, and was lost to sight.

After Alverna, Leo probably never left him for long.
He nursed him, he wrote down his words of warning and
counsel ; he listened to him and to all who visited him,
and he remembered.   It was his hand wrote the Song
of Love and Triumph which Francis made in the garden
hut of the Clares at St. Damian, the Song of the Creatures,
which is the human expression of Francis's union with
the universe, so awfully prefigured in the seraphic vision
of Alverna.   Soon he was bidden come and sing it with
Angelo by the poet's dying bed ; and when they had sung
all he had made concerning his love for the living world
of sun and moon and stars and birds and beasts, he
added the Welcome to Sister Death.   Leo wrote that
down too.

So far one reads of Leo, and then hopes he followed
his master ere long ; for surely he was of those whose
hearts must snap when they have lost what they have
spent themselves on.   Save to a few he can only have
seemed a meek shadow of Francis, and by him who stepped
into full authority as soon as the saint's breath left his
body, he was probably not regarded at all.   As the confessor and secretary, his presence had of course been
permitted till the end.   After that, obscurity was his
natural fate, since he had given no indication of talents for
administration or for " pushing " the affairs of the Order.
Elias was to learn what an observant eye looked out

from the *pecorello*, and what a faultless memory was lodged in his meek person. To Leo Francis was not dead; and to make manifest his living spirit was henceforth all his own life. He saw men stronger than himself, better spokesmen, go sadly apart, resigned, saying the day of Francis was over. Leo was never resigned. He was not one readily to accept facts. Such facts as he saw were a continual reproach. As the years went on, and the effort of his friends the Spirituals to regain the mastery of the Order signally failed, his attitude altered not at all. He was that rare and inconvenient person, the Idealist in Action, the only idealist worth considering.

Before his master was cold in the grave, Leo saw his fame exploited, his spirit betrayed. In the name of the *Poverello*, who had given his heart's blood to be the brother of the poor and the weak, who had made it the distinction of his fraternity that it should have no privileges at all, wealth and pomp and privilege were demanded and made to appear the things that mattered. Living, Francis had been, in the eyes of Elias and of Cardinal Ugolino, at once a hindrance and a great distinction; dead, he was a treasure and a source of treasure. They were collecting money already, Rome joyfully aiding and abetting, to raise a great church and convent, which should prove the Order to be, indeed, no hole and corner affair, but a great and powerful body, though it happened to have been founded by one who desired it should have no power at all save of the spirit. A marble vase for offerings was placed on the proposed site of the buildings, on the Colle d'Inferno, just outside the city on the west. Elias had many other ways of gathering money, but to Leo the marble vase was the symbol of a great change, nor was he deceived. He ran off at once to Giles at Perugia and told him. Giles had retired from the turmoil and the changes of Elias's energetic rule in lofty scorn. The great contemplative had far more experience

of the world and of men than Leo. He understood the
"facts" of the world, and withdrew beyond them. Leo
wished to fight them. "Let them build a convent as
long as from here to Assisi," said Giles; "enough for me
my little corner in peace. If thou art already a dead
man, Leo, go and break the vase to atoms as thou pro-
posest. But if thou art still alive to the world, refrain,
for thou wilt not be able to endure the persecution of
Elias." Leo was not a dead man. He had a great deal
to do in a very unsatisfactory world. But the brothers
needed to have the question put before them concretely.
So he risked Elias's vengeance, and smashed the vase.
The *pecorello* was not a man of speech. Whereupon
Elias, the Vicar-General, had Leo scourged and banished
from Assisi.

His friends would rally to him now. And even the
less intimate brothers did not soon forget the scourging
of the friend of Francis's heart. In the rally it was felt
and determined that the brotherhood must be saved
from the rule of the man of ambition. Whether or not
the *Speculum Perfectionis*, in whole or in part, was written
as a manifesto at this moment, is a matter of dispute.
In spite of the attacks on M. Sabatier's theory, that the
date on the Mazarin Codex, 1228, is the correct one, I
do not hold it has been seriously undermined. The
banished brother had either not gone far, or he had
crept back in secret to the Porziuncola, which indeed
was his usual dwelling-place. There, according to
M. Sabatier, he employed himself, probably several
brothers aiding him, in writing at least a substantial
portion of the *Speculum Perfectionis*, as a manifesto and
a protest against the proposed election of Elias at the
forthcoming Chapter General, in May 1228. It was
finished some weeks before the Chapter. If it be in truth
an election manifesto, it is a singularly magnanimous
one. True, according to some writers, the scourging
and the banishment did not take place till some years

later—though there is very strong evidence for placing them where I have done. But then no personal assault could influence so good a Minorite as Leo. Yet directed against one who was about to wreck the work of their Founder, it is wonderfully free from offence, and is a counterblast to Elias only because it is a reflection of Francis. Of the *Speculum* I shall speak more fully later. Enough to say now that, if it indeed belongs to this date, it was successful in its immediate object. For to Elias's great surprise he was not elected. A meek, good-living, learned Bologna doctor, John Parenti, became Minister-General instead.

To what obscure corner Leo retired, in what humble church did he serve mass, to what lazar house did he bring comfort, we have no knowledge. Of his private life, indeed, from this time till just before his death we have few glimpses. But he was venerated as the most faithful of all the sons of Francis, one whose glory was to be humble and helpful, and to live as he had lived in Francis's presence. His protest against the ambitious schemes of Elias had only for a moment seemed to triumph. Elias, the favourite of Rome, snapped his fingers at the Chapter General; and up in Assisi acted as if he were indeed head of the Order. Leo, the humble son of the Church, may well have been dazed and silenced at seeing the work of his master, whom he knew beyond any doubt to be a saint of God, wrecked by the aid of the Head of the Church, whom he quite willingly owned to be God's representative on earth. But in his heart the fire of hope never died. Under John Parenti's mild rule he could find some quiet place and wait till the world learnt that Elias and his allies, though their voice went throughout the world, did not speak the mind of Francis. Propagandist though he was, he was not a man for crowds, did not lead men in numbers. He was strongest with a pen in his hand, or when he found some pilgrim eager to hear of the

great days. In the deputations of complainants against
Elias he does not appear. He does not journey to Rome,
nor rise in the Chapter to protest. He is still the
Pecorello di Dio who lives apart, or with close friends.
After their first contest he is not named among those
zelanti on whom the hand of Elias fell heavy; and
though he may have been among the brothers scattered
by Elias or Crescentius, he never told of his own sufferings when in later years he related the tales of the
persecuted brethren. Elias had great confidence in his
own position. The little writer of tracts had threatened
to be troublesome; yet he had been proved insignificant
after all. The Minister's hand was heavy when he was
thwarted; but those who did not lead complaining bands
of brothers to Rome, and did not assail him in his fine
places at Assisi and Cortona, were probably left alone.
His attitude towards all the first companions, save
Bernard and Illuminato, seems to have been one of
scorn. Leo was never recognised as the leader of his
opponents: even to the *zelanti* Giles and Bernard had
more imposing personalities. And great men like Aymon
of Faversham probably thought of him as impractical
and useless for their campaign, if they thought of him
at all. But he was always there. His zeal never grew
chill. No hopeless waiting ever tired him out. His
influence was on one here, one there, and though his writings had perhaps no great vogue till late in his life, it
always seemed to him worth while to say the few things
he had to say again and yet again. So he lived somehow
through the days of Elias, of Albert of Pisa, of Aymon, of
Crescentius, was cheered by the coming of John of Parma,
and saddened by his fall. He may have been puzzled
by the saintly Bonaventura's harshness towards John, but
doubtless made the best of that highly respectable rule.

Leo, always on the alert to speak for Francis, found
a signal opportunity in the days of Crescentius. That
nondescript person, who figures now as a persecutor of

the *zelanti*, and again as a flatterer of their growing
influence, in 1246, in obedience to some spirit in the
air, sent out a command to all the brethren who were
of the first generation, or who had known any of
the first companions, to set down what they knew
of Francis. The official biography, Thomas of Celano's
First Life, was out of date, because of its eulogy of
Elias, now a disgraced man. Here was Leo's opportunity; and in lonely Greccio, a sacred place to them,
and ever a stronghold of the faithful observants, he,
Angelo, and Rufino, compiled the *Legend of the Three
Companions*—of which more hereafter.

In no one perhaps did Leo find such strength, such
loyalty to the first ideal as in Clara. At St. Damian he
found the spirit of Francis still living, narrowed and
hindered though the lives of the sisters were by regulations imposed on them, against their Founder's free
intention. Clara, most staunch and courageous of
women, had been formed in the school of the *Poverello*.
Leo saw her often, and trusted her in everything. He
was of the time when friendship between the brothers
and sisters was not only legitimate but a natural source
of mutual inspiration; and the after restrictions were
never enough to break their strong alliance. With his
own hands he wrote for her a breviary. He and Angelo
gave to the Clares, for their greatest treasure, the breviary
of Francis, authenticating it by an inscription — but
Clara was dead by that time. All he wrote he took to
San Damiano, after Clara's death to the new monastery
of Santa Chiara. His reason in the long run was, doubtless, that the treasury of the Clares was a safe place;
but probably the habit had its beginning in the fact
that Clara liked to know what he wrote, and desired
to fan her inner fire by the words of the man who had
loved as well as she. In 1253 we find him with Juniper,
the *egregius joculator Domini*, and with Angelo at Clara's
dying bed. It is Juniper, the holy jester, who is elo-

quent there. It is Angelo who weeps and consoles. Leo says no word, but kisses the little bed of his dying friend.

Perhaps we shall never know much more of the *Pecorello*, the faithful shadow of Francis while Francis lived, his faithful echo ever after. He sank his personality so completely in his master's that of himself we have only a picture of quiet untiring loyalty and endless persistence. This persistence had its reward. As the years went on he was more and more looked on as a treasury of Franciscan lore. They knew where to find him. Brothers from far and near came to talk to him and to hear him talk. Doubtless a good portion of his writings owed their existence to the desire of pilgrims to have some of his talk set down so that they could carry it away, and perhaps this also accounts for the confusion of after ages as to what he actually did write. He lived much at the Porziuncola, an obscure humble brother, a pathetic survival to the many; to the few no survival but a promise of life yet to be for the ideal of Francis. Conrad d'Offida and Angelo Clareno and their friends did not let Leo's testimony die. The torch was handed on.

But at last he felt it was time to go. He and Rufino were very old. He had done what he could, and he waited wistfully for the summons. One night, as I have already told, it seemed to him to come in the voice of Bernard. But Rufino said, "Nay, it was I that Bernard called." And so it was. But Leo had not to wait long. In 1271, five and forty years after the death of his master, he was released from a long watch. They buried him in San Francesco.

He has been called the Blessed Leo, though it is very doubtful if the Church gave its authority. The Umbrian folk arranged their own beatifications. Of course he was credited with miracles, and one, at least, his putting milk into the breasts of an old woman to succour a hungry infant, points to a kindly, serviceable nature. Leo was no great contemplative like Giles and Bernard, but he, too, had his rapt moments; and in one of these there flashes forth, in their manner, his understanding of his master's part in heaven and earth. He saw the Judgment Day. The angels sounded the trump, and all mankind were assembled in a vast meadow. He saw two ladders, one white, one red, reaching from earth to heaven. Christ was at the top of the red one, and near him, a little lower, was Saint Francis, who turned and called to his brothers confidently to come up—*Venite, fratres, venite, accedite ad Dominum, qui vos vocat. Confidete, ne timeatis.* And they all ran to climb the red ladder. But one fell from the third step, one from the fourth, one from the tenth, some from the middle, and so on. Francis encouraged them, pitied them, and looked to Christ to have mercy on them. Christ showed His wounds from which fresh blood was oozing. "Thus have thy brothers done to me." Francis still persevered: he must have his brothers with him; else he would be lonely in Heaven. So he went down the red ladder, and called his brothers to follow him to the white one. And behold the Blessed Virgin appeared at the top, and she received them, and they entered into the Kingdom without any more labour.

Of Leo the writer we know something more, though, indeed, he puzzles us sorely too. M. Sabatier was the first to give him the credit of the greater part of the *Speculum Perfectionis.* He claims that work to be, as regards its immediate purpose, a manifesto of the *zelanti* against the accession to full power of Elias; and, following the Mazarin Codex, asserted that it was finished at the Porziuncola the 11th of May, 1228, in time to influence the Chapter which met the same month. These assertions have been violently contested. The second has in its favour much probability. The first is, in the main, certainly accurate. The *Speculum Perfectionis*, as we possess it now in M. Sabatier's edition, was doubtless not what Leo wrote in the first instance. There are many quite evident interpolations by other hands in a later age. Leo himself added and altered again and again. He may have written a dozen versions of the same thing. Very likely he had collaborators—Angelo, Masseo, Rufino—though the pen was in his hand. The first version may have been a short affair, perhaps little longer—though this is improbable—than that recently published by P. Lemmens. But that he was the responsible author of a substantial portion of the book as M. Sabatier presents it is certain. The references to his work by Angelo Clareno and Ubertino da Casale coincide with portions of the *Speculum*. A great many of the *cedulæ* and *rotuli* of Brother Leo, pondered by Conrad d'Offida and quoted by Ubertino, were evidently only portions of the work detached from the rest, and written by himself, or transcribed by others, for particular needs. And the internal evidence of the preponderance of one man's work is clear to any one with a literary sense and with some skill in reading human nature and temperament. Unless he had a double among the Spirituals of the fourteenth century he wrote the main portion of it. And it is a great thing for him to have done, for it has hardly its equal in the religious biography of any time. It is a marvellous revelation of a man's soul, told in the simplest fashion, full of repetition and awkwardnesses, but with a rare unconscious skill, fruit of a clear eye, a fearless and a faithful heart. It is the tale of no saint in a niche, but of a man with whom he had walked the roads in gay humour and in sad, with whom he had kept vigil for nights together, whom he had known in the common intimate things of daily life and watched with awe on Mount Alverna. But of Alverna he does not speak.

Its attribution to Leo has called forth doubts concerning works that have all along been credited to him. One of the most notable of these is the "Life of Giles" —published in the *Chronicle of the Twenty-four Generals*, and, with variations, in the *Acta Sanctorum*. Very likely it has been added to, and probably he sought aid, say from Rufino, in writing the life of their old friend. But that Leo thought not and wrote not as did the other religious writers of his day would be evident if we were to accept as his only authentic works the *Scripta Fratris Leonis* as they have been published by Lemmens. However much collaboration he had, one commanding mind and purpose are visible in the *Speculum* and the *Vita Fratris Aegidii* at least. Till recently there has been no doubt cast on his joint authorship with Angelo and Rufino of the *Legend of the Three Companions*, which the Bollandist Fathers inserted among the Francis documents. M. Sabatier called attention to its fragmentary condition, and showed how little it answered to the promise of the authors in the prefatory letter to Crescentius. As it appears in the *Acta Sanctorum* it is a narrative of the youth and conversion of Francis, with a few chapters dealing with later episodes, but mostly belonging to the first days of the Order, ending with an account of the Stigmata and the canonisation, evidently by a later hand. It contains some charming pages, fresh, graceful, and spontaneous. But there is little in its matter that need have come from the first companions. There is no exclusive information—though such had been asked for, and though such is promised in the prefatory letter. In whatever shape it reached Crescentius it seems, at least as a separate work, to have had no vogue in the early days, and it was lost to sight for centuries.

Now amidst all the puzzling evidence on the subject, some things are clear. The Three Companions, judging from their letter, meant to write an ample account, if not a complete legend. They meant to tell not only of miracles—which they plainly looked on as of inferior interest and value—but of the saint's "holy conversation." And they did not mean to repeat what was to be found in other legends. Yet the fragment says nothing of miracles, very little of his "holy conversation," and it contains a great deal of what could be read in earlier legends. Also, Crescentius may have taken their permission to do what he liked with their book quite literally. He may not have given it circulation as theirs, but handed it to the official biographer, who was still Thomas of Celano, to use as he thought fit. But Celano's Second Life was not made only out of the fragment of the Legend we have. Is the fragment theirs? If so, what else did they send? Will the rest ever be found, or has it been found? The Padri da Civezza and Domenichelli say they have found it in an old Italian translation of the *Legend of the Three Companions*, which contains the version published by the Bollandists and much more, the much more being mainly chapters from the *Speculum Perfectionis*. This is the real *Legend of the Three Companions* they say, and their view has been accepted in many quarters. Melchiorri, by the way, had published this old Italian version in 1856; it had even been translated into French by the Père Latreiche, but nobody took any notice of either. Other critics declare it is a late compilation; and some assert that even the fragment is a forgery, or that it is wrongly tacked on to the Companions' Preface. The matter needs much further investigation, but in the meanwhile, whoever wrote it, and whether forgery or not, the Legend is well worth reading. Yet be it the whole or part of what the brothers sent from the hermitage of Greccio, I cannot feel convinced it is particularly the work of Leo. It may have been principally the compilation of the other two, and as his part Leo may have sent the whole or part of the *Speculum*, which had never had a vogue save among the *zelanti*, or he may have sent something we have lost. Is not the fragment from the pen of a better narrator than Brother Leo, who could tell the history of a soul, the inner history of a movement better than their external manifestations?

Leo was a famous tract writer, whose testimony long after he was dead played a great part in the struggles of the Order. His tracts were the weapons with which Conrad d'Offida, Angelo Clareno, Pier Jean d'Olivi, Ubertino da Casale, and the other Spirituals fought their fight. But he might have written the most serviceable of tracts, and these been dead centuries ago. Leo's words are still living, and can move hearts all unlearned in the struggles in which he bore his long and patient part. What keeps them alive? Not any literary qualities, in the narrower sense of the phrase. He wrote very bad Latin. He was utterly careless of form and every artistic effect. He repeats himself endlessly, and he has no thought of making his point neatly, or of epigram, or of climax. Beside Thomas of Celano and S. Bonaventura he is a bungler. But all the warmth of a singularly fervent nature is in his words. He gave the whole of himself to the only kind of work he could do. He had one thing to tell, his master's plan for the knighthood he had banded, his master's plan for the regeneration of human nature. Popes and Cardinals and Ministers General might deny that plan, distort it, and defeat it. Leo was convinced it was the right one, and that he, humble and obscure, knew the heart of Francis. He said it again and again. He had nothing else to say, and his lofty, single-minded persistence stamps his work with a rare individuality. But he could not tell that plan of his master's chivalry without telling of his master, whom he had known, well and ill, gay and in sore trouble, rising to the seventh heaven, and again beset by human fear and distress. Out of his love for speaking of his master's mind and moods rises the authentic portrait of Francis — Francis, genius, poet, saint, and most tender-hearted of men. With no skill save the humble lover's he has, in M. Sabatier's words, " saved his master's spiritual personality."

Leo takes a place that better writers of his time have no claim to. Perhaps no one in the Order had less interest in art and all such elegant matters. Maybe he would have thought his meddling with such things a sin. And yet in the history of the early Italian Renaissance he takes a much humbler, but as rightful place as Giotto. His work was the same as Giotto's, though his means and method and skill were infinitely less brilliant. He, too, in the track of his master's feet, went back to Nature. He had to tell of a saint, and he painted that saint as a man, with clearly recognisable human traits, with real hands that worked and consoled, real eyes that wept, a real voice that sang human melodies, a real heart that feared and hoped and loved. This little humble priest, bred on mediæval church lore, might, to judge from his work, never have read a single word of the life of a saint. What better can I say of him? Not of set purpose, and in no spirit of literary innovation, he ignored all the terrible art and science of hagiography and hagiology. I wish I could say he demolished them. Alas, they flourish to this day! Bonaventura, a writer of elegant style, a man to whom all the culture of Europe was open, Paris-bred, consorting with kings and the learned, was a hundred years behind Leo. His classic Life of Francis, for all its skill and beauty of phrasing, is but a sublimer specimen of the conventional saint's biography. He borrowed from the older lives, and had to tell unconventional stories of his hero; but in comment and arrangement and sentiment, in what he tells and what he omits, he does his best to keep in the saint's niche the man who was just a saint because he loved and felt with, and consorted with, his kind. The Seraphic Doctor's narrative of miracles is of the real old obscurantist order.   Leo tells of no miracles save the miracle of his master's marvellous love.   Except as a popular diffuser of the story of Francis—his position afforded him the means of being that—and as the author of the text to which Giotto gave life and colour on the walls of San Francesco, Bonaventura's Legend was no herald of the new time at all.   Leo was not Paris-bred, and the culture of Europe was closed to him.   But he had been at a fine school, for he had walked with Francis along the Umbrian roads, and lived in daily converse with the man who had left the schoolmen's folios all unopened, and read in the book of Nature.

BROTHER JACOBA

" Eam . . . pro virilitate virtutum fratrem Jacobam nominabat."
—DE LAUDIBUS, BERN. DE BESSA, viii.

To three women—besides his bride, the Lady Poverty—
Francis owed much love and consolation. But Pica his
mother, who had stood between him and his father's
wrath and scorn on the eve of his renunciation, nor
had ceased to love him when the family pride in him was
shaken, soon passed out of his life. Bernardone forced her
to disown the mad beggar, once their son. To be nothing
to him in the hard and glorious years that followed, the
one in all their town who might not openly pity him and
be proud of him—before that was a fact to her, I hope
she died.

To the strong-willed, high-hearted woman, St. Clara,
Clara of the Scifi, he owed most of all. Staunch to him
she was as were few of his brothers, facing the powers of
the Church in defence of his ideal, and with courage to
lend as well as kindness to give to the frail and sensitive
hero. The clouds on his spirit dispersed in her presence.
From the garden hut where she tended the weary, ailing
man arose the glad Song of the Sun. Truly, she had her
reward.

Yet who that has read of his last days but feels some
sorrow, nay even some jealousy—our feelings are so personal in reading these stories—that not Clara but another
was called for when the end was near? Clara was ill; and
doubtless the strictness of the Clare seclusion was growing
fast. But even had it been otherwise, and had she come
over from San Damiano to the Porziuncola, Francis
would still have remembered his Roman friend, to others

H

the noble Lady Giacoma di Settisoli, to him "Brother Jacoba."

"When he was in the place of St. Mary of the Angels," says the *Speculum Perfectionis*, "sick of the malady of which he died, he called his companions, and said to them, 'Ye know how the Lady Giacoma di Settisoli was and is most faithful and devoted to me and to our religion; and therefore I think she will hold it as a great grace and consolation if we let her know my state; and especially send her word that she send me some of that religious cloth of ash-like colour, and with the cloth some of that good thing to eat which she used to make for me in the City.' Now," adds the writer, "the Romans call that *mortariolum* [*mostacciolo*, marchpane], and it is made of almonds and sugar and other things."

The letter was written. And, lo, as a brother was about to set out with it, came a knocking at the door. There outside stood the Lady Giacoma, come from Rome in great haste, with her son and many others, to visit the dying man. The brother that opened to her was puzzled. A woman might not enter the cloister. But Francis said the rule was not for such as she, and bade him usher in the lady "whom such faith and devotion have brought hither from distant parts." And when she came into his presence and saw her holy friend signed by pain and death, her tears began to flow. The brothers discovered the wonder that she had brought with her all the things he had asked for, and incense as well. "And so it came about that He who inspired the kings to go with gifts for the honouring of His Son on the day of His Nativity, inspired likewise that noble and saintly lady to go with gifts for the honouring of His dear-loved servant as he drew near to death, nay, rather, to his true birth."

There were the comfits, but he could only please her with an effort to taste of them. He ordered many candles, however, to be made of the wax she had brought. His love of beauty survived in these last hours. For fire and light he had a particular love, and he could even now with joyous interest think of the flames that would burn about his bier, and make his Sister Death show something of her beauty to the companions left behind. Of the cloth the brothers made him the tunic in which he was buried. "And in that week in which came the Lady Giacoma our most holy father went his way to God."

This, so far as we know, is the earliest version of the story of her coming, written by one who was there at the time. It reappears later, with some developments and some slurring of circumstance. Bernard of Bessa, Bonaventura's secretary, in his *De Laudibus*, alludes to the goodly train she brought with her, and to the noise of horses and the serving-folk at the brothers' door. We hear her giving orders that part of her company should be dismissed, and Francis countermanding them, saying, "On Sabbath I shall pass away; on the day after you can return with all your company."

The *Fioretti* and Wadding give the letter :—

"To the Lady Giacoma, servant of the most High, brother Francis, the little poor one of Jesus Christ, greeting and the fellowship of the Holy Spirit in the Lord Jesus Christ.

"Know, dearest lady, that the blessed Christ of His grace has revealed to me that the end of my life is near. Wherefore, when thou hast seen this letter, if thou wouldst find me alive, hasten to St. Mary of the Angels. For, if thou comest after the Sabbath day, thou wilt not find me living; and bring with thee hair-cloth, in which to wrap my body, and wax for the burial. Also, I pray thee, bring me some of those things to eat thou usedst to give me when I was ill in Rome."

Wadding, drawing from the *Legenda Antiqua* (probably the *Speculum*), confesses what were the "things to eat" for which Francis asked—not so the *Fioretti*, timid on this occasion. Oh, the trouble which the letter, the comfits, the whole affair, has caused to the souls of good men! How indiscreet were those early biographers, save Celano sometimes, and Bonaventura always! Good Père Chalippe has taken such pains to tell us that really the letter was not too fervent—though lesser saints had much better not write to ladies—and, as for that request for the marchpane, well, he only wished for something to keep up his strength, so as not to distress his companions, and that he might be the fitter to receive spiritual consolation! "Pouvait-il agir plus sagement et par des motifs plus pur?" Imagine Leo's wonderment at the apology!

In the *Fioretti* she appears with her *two* sons. The account of her demeanour is more detailed, and is the one generally repeated by later historians. "The Lady Jacoba kneeled down at the feet of St. Francis, and took those most holy feet, marked and adorned with the wounds of Christ, and kissed them and bathed them with her tears in such a rapture of devotion, that to the brothers that stood round it seemed they saw the very Magdalen herself at the feet of Jesus Christ, and by no means could they draw her away. And at length after a long space they lifted her up thence and drew her aside." This account resembles that in the *Conformities*. Bartholomew of Pisa, who is somewhat given to forcing the emotion of a scene, as if he were writing for the peculiarly insensitive, always urges the Scriptural parallels. The picturesque reference to the Magdalen has proved misleading, suggesting to later writers the quite unfounded idea that the lady had once been a particular sinner. Chalippe is only quoting Wadding when he speaks of her employing "the gift of tears which she received from God, to weep without ceasing the negligence of her past life." There is not the slightest evidence that she had been a great sinner, or that she was very lachrymose. Bernard of Bessa speaks of "the virility of her virtues." But, indeed, she wept when she beheld the holy man, her own beloved friend, so near to death.

"So the said Lady Jacoba," continues the *Fioretti*, "abode there until such time as St. Francis passed away from this life and was buried; and she paid great honour unto his burying, she and all her company, and she bore the charges of whatsoever was needed." Did he see the face of his friend in this last visit? Very likely not. The *Speculum Perfectionis* says he was quite blind in those days before his death. But he had the comfort of her skilled hand and her kind voice while she kept watch. And she had the consolation of performing the last tender offices for his body when his soul had passed out of it. According to his desire, he was buried in the rough robe of "religious cloth"; but Fratini [*Storia della Basilica*] says Giacoma gave two cloths embroidered in gold with flowers and birds, and the body of Francis was covered with them in the funeral ceremony.

The chapter which tells of his call to her, her coming, her admission, her tending of him, is most precious in the history of the saint. And foolish persons have wished it away! Celano makes no mention of it. Bonaventura slurs it and makes it meagre. Later historians have tried to cast doubt on its truth, because nature speaks in it too clearly. The Bollandists grudge their references to the lady. Papini is inclined to deny her visit to Francis altogether, and speaks with pious anger of those writers who linger over the tale as "profaners of the glories of the Father." But sneer or fume as they may, Brother Jacoba is no myth. It was a real living woman to whom Francis bade farewell. Those "who were with him," to whom he was a friend and not a church image, were glad of the comfort she brought him, and told the story out of the simple gratitude of their hearts.

Who was Jacoba? The infinite labours that have gone to find out her history have had no great results, but have not been all unavailing. She was a noble Roman matron, a widow, and known as Giacoma di Settisoli. Wadding tells how he searched and searched in Rome till he learnt the reason why. It is generally agreed that the name Septisolium was given to a small district in Rome, between the Palatine Mount and the Scaurus, where had once been a temple of the sun and moon, a temple with seven rows of columns, or, according to another authority, with columns on which rested seven thrones. The name survived in Christian Rome. About 1145, the district was given, in perpetuity, by Pietro, Abbot of St. Gregory, to Cencio Frangipani and his heirs—*locamus tibi Trullum unum in idem quod vocatur Septisolia*. Now tradition has always declared her to have been the wife of one of the great family of the Frangipani. As to her own name, she has been said to be of the Orsini, of the Anquillara, and, more commonly, of the Ormanni or Nanni. The Bollandists believed her to have been the wife of Cencio Frangipani. So, she would have been a very ancient dame indeed when she visited Assisi. But, alas, for the *convenances*, the probability lies with those who say her husband was Graziano, very likely the son of the Cencio aforementioned.

The *Fioretti*, we have seen, mentions two sons. Tradition is quite sure on that point, and adds that they were Roman senators. Muratori (vol. iv., col. 493) records a *Jacoba uxor quondam Domini Gratiani Frangipani mater et tutrix Johannis et Gratiani filiorum meûm*. Her husband, Graziano Frangipani, died in 1217, when her son Giovanni was seven years old. The apparition of the noble Roman lady with her train of attendants, the costly honours she paid to Francis, caused much admiring excitement in the little town. Tales would be told of her wealth and grandeur, and the bearing of the two young Romans, seen afterwards in the streets of Assisi, would be foundation enough for the later report that they were both Roman senators. If they were not, then to look at them was to believe they should be. Diligent searchers have assured themselves that the Frangipani name does not occur among the senators. P. d'Alençon, to whose brief and precise study of Giacoma this article owes much, has found a Pietruccio di Settisoli a senator in 1214; but though possibly of the same family, he cannot have been her son.

When Francis was in Rome, in 1212, while the Order was still very young, Giacoma Frangipani heard of him, wondered at him, and became, so far as might a young married woman in a noble house, one of his disciples. Chalippe's statement that Francis consented unwillingly to the interviews, is a pure invention. He spoke willingly with all men and all women, great or small, young or old. The tale that she gave up henceforth her worldly cares into the hands of her sons, arises from a confusion of dates. Her sons were children at the time. And at all times she seems to have disposed most independently of her fortune—at least from 1217, when her husband died. To Francis and the brothers on their visits to Rome she was a Providence, or as they preferred to say, a mother. She devoted to their use a little church near the hospital of St. Biagio; and from the Benedictines of the Abbey of St. Cosmato she got for them a lodging within the precincts of the hospital. Later, in 1229, the whole place was given up to them, at the request of Gregory IX., and was the foundation of the convent of S. Francesco di Ripa, on the bank of the Tiber. She fed them, she housed them; when they were ill she nursed them. She was their constant, their staunch, their capable friend. There was nothing maudlin, nothing of the cringing penitent in her relations with them, and for the virility of her virtues (*pro virilitate virtutum*) Francis called her "frate Giacoma." Even Bonaventura thinks the story of her lamb worthy to be recorded in the life of a saint. Francis gave her the lamb—doubtless one of the poor animals he was constantly rescuing from unkind hands—and the little creature became her constant attendant. It was a pious little lamb, that went to church with her, and awoke her if she slept when she should have been at her prayers.

After the death of Francis, it appears she went back to Rome, to set her affairs in order, and then bade farewell to it for ever. Rome was too sumptuous, too noisy a place for tending memories; and among the Ghibelline Frangipani she can hardly have been at her ease. Well, Assisi in those days did not sleep and dream as it does to-day. Constant feuds kept the grass from growing in its streets. But between whiles it would be quiet enough, and now there was a hush on it. Just lately a quarrel between the Bishop and the Podestà had been healed by the dying Francis. And, for the moment, all the factions were joined in their tender pride in the dead saint. He belonged to all, to the Nepis as to the Fumis, or whoever were the thirteenth century equivalents of those turbulent families. So she took up her abode there, looking down from her dwelling in the town across the mist of olives to the forest in the plain, where nestled the hut in which he had died. And nearer, on the hill of Paradise, she watched the building of the stately convent and of the basilica, and mixed in the great throng of Pope and cardinals and *frati* and people that gathered in San Giorgio for the canonisation of the holy man who had been her friend.

I wonder the inventors of the ever-weeping Magdalen legend did not make her seek the shelter of the cloister. She never joined Clara at San Damiano, but lived alone, or with her sons, a life of great independence for her time—seeing she was young, rich, and a stranger. She was probably a tertiary, and she was devoted to

works of charity; but Brother Jacoba liked not over
strait bonds any more than did Francis and his other
first companions.   There is some evidence that her
loyal sons gave up their privileges of young Frangipani and abode with their mother in Assisi.   At least,
to some distinct connection with the town, or friendship
to the Order, they must have owed their place of burial
in the Lower Church.   It is not improbable that the
Gratianus romanus, Podestà of Assisi in 1233, was her
younger son.

The year of her death has been given variously as
1236 and 1239.   But M. Sabatier's recent researches
have upset both dates.   In the Archives of the Sacro
Convento he has found two documents which prove her
to have lived much beyond that time.   They are an
interesting addition to our knowledge of her, throwing
light on the particular kind of service to which she gave
her energies.   It appears she not only devoted her own
wealth to the Franciscan movement, but was one of
its almoners as well.   In a testament of 1258, three
pounds are bequeathed to Jacoba "for clothing."   In
another of as late a date as 1273, the Lady Marsibilia
bequeaths twenty soldi to the Lady Giacoma of Rome.
Other documents, found elsewhere, attest gifts of money
to her "for a refection to the brothers of the church
of San Francesco, and for one to the brothers of the
Porziuncola," and two pounds for a "tunic for Brother
Leo."   Of course, it will be remembered, the brothers
might not touch money, and Jacoba, the woman of
standing, wealth, and leisure, was an excellent inter-
mediary between charitable givers and the needs of the
frati and of their many poor friends.   As at Rome she had
been their stand-by, so now was she at Assisi, with greater
opportunity.   Her reward was their friendship.   Leo
recounts how she was of that company in Giles's hill
garden at Perugia, when Gerard wearied them all with
his Paris logic, and their host drove all their weariness

away by his piping, his acting, and his spiritual discourse.
She must have come young to Assisi, to shape her life
anew and more freely, far from the tumult of Rome
and the not improbable jeers of the Frangipani. She
lived there through many years of devoted service—too
long, perhaps, for she survived all her friends of the
first Franciscan inspiration. Clara had been dead at
least twenty years; Giles, Angelo, Rufino had passed
away. Leo, the last, the revealer of their souls, died in
1271; and we would fain share M. Sabatier's dream
that his eyes were closed by the friendly old hand
of " Brother Jacoba."

She was buried, of course, in the Lower Church, as
near Francis as might be. Where else should Brother
Jacoba have lain? Under the pulpit is her tomb. A
much-restored fresco on the wall represents her in the
robe of a tertiary, and a plaque of red marble bears the
inscription—

Hic jacet Jacoba sancta nobilisque romana.

A KING OF VERSES

" Qui vince la memoria mia lo ingegno ;
Che quella croce lampeggiava Cristo,
Sì ch'io non so trovare esemplo degno,
Ma chi prende sua croce e segue Cristo,
Ancor mi scuserà di quel ch'io lasso,
Vedendo in quell' albor balenar Cristo."
— PARADISO, xiv. 103–108.

KING of Verses is he called; but I cannot quote a line of his. Though there are some transcribed in my note-book, I will not wrong him by tagging to his memory a fragment that only a political chance and local pride have, indiscriminately, left recorded. An emperor crowned him, REX VERSUUM; and there are better reasons for calling him poet. Much of him has been forgotten besides his songs; but what remains is strangely significant. The few facts, surmises, stray traditions about him, are not disjointed, not incoherent. Reaching us from widely different sources, by their admirable unity they are proclaimed facts: they pierce the misty ages and flash upon us a personality. In telling of his life I may set down some things that are conjectural; but these things hardly at all concern the individuality of the man.

For this old obscure Italian poet of the twelfth and thirteenth centuries I make no appeal, as is the fashion of to-day, on the ground of his likeness to ourselves. He is a stranger—I think a fascinating stranger—a man very much of his own time and country, when men saw in pictures, when they thought through the eyes. Had he lived a century later, would he not have been a painter rather than a poet?

In the world—a world that honoured him and which he left for his greater glory—he was known as William of Lisciano. Lisciano, where he was born in the latter part of the twelfth century, is a village near Ascoli, in the Marches. Perhaps he was of the family of the Divini, but as of them we know nothing, the question is of no importance. Either because of family influence, or early proof of talent, he was already prominent when the Emperor Henry VI. came to Ascoli. Triumphal arches were set up; there were wreaths and flowers and banners—altogether a very fine scenic display. Helping to arrange the *mise en scène* our poet would have been in his natural place. He composed an ode in honour of Henry and recited it himself, but like most things of the kind, its value died with the occasion. Now its only possible interest is philological, for it was written in Italian, and is the earliest extant poem in the vernacular.

The Emperor, pleased with his reception, invited certain citizens of Ascoli to accompany him to Sicily. Among these were Berardo, afterwards the Archbishop of Palermo, and William of Lisciano. They both went and took up their abode at the court. William's fortune must have seemed made. Nor were they evidently subject to caprice: after the death of her husband, Costanza, in 1198, confirmed their privileges. The change from Ascoli was immeasurable. Sicily was the school of poets, and their home. There was not yet all the brilliance of Frederic's later days; but Frederic only polished, honoured, and enriched what he found at his mother's court. A new world this for the strangers—clear skies, kind sun, beauty of land and sea; a moving, various, luxurious company; men of many races; Normans with their tales and customs of chivalry, Greeks who had not forgotten all their old culture, Arabs with their subtle science and refinement, a constant mingling of East and West. Trouvères and musicians and singers found inspiration and reward, and the verse-maker from Ascoli blossomed in such an air. For a man with the lust of the eyes like William, the court of Sicily was a very Paradise; and every year of the youthful Frederic's life added to the interest and the stimulus. As yet the prince was a docile son of the Church that protected him, but restless, ambitious, precocious, trying his hand on a small scale and in a narrow sphere in preparation for the great empire in front. No court could have been dull where Frederic lived. The love of art is an early endowment, or comes not at all. Frederic was already a patron of the arts; and William, the ready singer of light song, who doubtless played a delightful part in all court festivities, would of course be singled out for honour.

A difficulty has been raised concerning his coronation by the Emperor. The year we do not know—only that it took place with great ceremony, *pomposissime*. Now our poet left the world of courts and princes behind him, it is said, in 1212. But Frederic was only eighteen then, and was not crowned Emperor till eight years after. Was 1212, it is suggested, the mistake of a copyist for 1221? There is no reason for altering the date: to do so only involves us in greater difficulties. 1212 seems a very good date. Frederic was Emperor in fact, if not in name, that very year; and his ambition had preceded his achievement. The lad who at eighteen crossed the Alps with little help or encouragement, and wrested back the German heritage of his fathers, the lad who had been nursed on politics, who had been tutored, warned, watched, and was already suspected by the Pope his guardian, was no fledgeling, but a full-grown monarch conscious of his power. Did the rite of crowning his *rex versuum* take place just before the great enterprise? It may well have been connected with this very real coming of age.

Of late years there had been other things besides
gay southern skies and troubadour gatherings to stir
the heart of the stranger. Struggle and strife were
looming. Restlessness was in the air. There was talk
of a crusade. Perhaps the light amorous songs seemed
now tamer to the singer. Besides, Frederic was going
—and the end of his mission who could tell? Did
the poet go on before, seeking something to which
his heart pointed vaguely? He must always have waited
the command of his eyes. Did he perhaps cross the
Alps with his master, or at least set out in the ambitious
company? Was he actually on the march with the
army when he saw what was better than the service
of the most splendid young prince?

At all events, in 1212, he had come north. At
his home in Ascoli, if not before, he would hear of
a new knightly enterprise. Francis had been at Ascoli
on his way to the East, and had gained thirty disciples.
Seeking him, or lighting on him by chance, the meeting
took place in the church of some poor nuns—*monasterium
pauperum inclusarum*, hardly the Clares at this date—in
San Severino. The court poet came along with his
train of followers. In the church he saw a company
of poor grey-robed friars. From the midst of his
knights William looked at them, and his eyes were
straightway drawn to one, meek and gentle of face,
miserably clad like his fellows. And, lo, he was not
as they were, but transfigured. Two great shining
swords were crossed on him. One stretched from his
head to his feet, the other over his breast reached
from hand to hand. And now the shining friar was
speaking. The knife of the spirit pierced the heart
of the listener; and the poet knew all the pain and
glory of the Cross of Christ. We never hear another
word of that band of knights that came with him.
Frederic and Sicily and the dreams of empire have all
vanished. William offers himself and all he has without

a moment's delay to Francis. It seems a poor offering. How withered the laurels of the King of Verses! But Francis will make them fresh again.

Here was an impulsive recruit. "Nay, I have heard enough—and seen. Take me from the world, and restore me to the service of the great King." What was the use of delay? He had but to look at the gentle friar, on whom was the symbol of authority—the Thau on his forehead. And others did not see it? But, lo, it was clear, shining, and in various colours, making beautiful the face of the herald of the Great King. Next day he had donned the grey robe.

Here was a man after Francis's own heart. They had a past with common joys and ambitions—troubadours both, loving light and music and singing. The poet had gone a little farther on the road of worldly adventure—had reached the splendours of which Francis had dreamed. But he had turned from them; and the holy man knew the offer was a good one. Now on this man of the world, "full of himself and ignorant of God, who had prostituted all to vanity, on this maker of carnal songs," had settled a great peace; and it abode with him. Francis, who knew men's hearts, and found them new names, called him Brother Pacifico. Between Pacifico and Francis the bond was instant and deep. They were much in each other's company; the recruit eager to give where he got so much, gave all his old skill to his new captain. Tradition is persistent that he put the songs of Francis into shape for him, and set them to music. Ozanam is probably right in his conjecture that some of the poems attributed to the saint may have been written by the *rex versuum*. In Sicily he seems to have been careless of his fame; and now he was too good a Franciscan to crave for personal glory.

Dates in his career are very uncertain, but it is not unlikely that the great vision at Bovara belongs to his earlier companionship with the saint, while the wonder of the height and of the lowliness of his master was still upon him. I will give it in the words of Leo, who wrote it in the *Speculum Perfectionis :*—

"On a certain day the blessed Francis went to the church of St. Peter of Bovara near the town of Trevi in the Valley of Spoleto, and with him went Fra Pacifico, who in the world was called the king of verses and the courtly doctor of singers. Now this church was all deserted. Then said Francis to Pacifico : 'Go back to the lepers' hospital, for this night I would stay here alone, and to-morrow early return to me.'

"Now, while he remained alone there, having said Complines and other prayers, he wished to rest and sleep, but he could not. And his spirit began to be afraid and to feel diabolical suggestions. And straightway he went out of the church, and making the sign of the cross, he said, 'I say to you, demons, in the name of God Almighty, exercise on my body whatever has been given you to do by the Lord Jesus Christ ; I am ready to bear all. For since the greatest enemy I have is my body, you revenge me on my adversary and my most terrible foe.' And thereupon the suggestions ceased altogether, and going back to the place where he had been lying, he slept in peace.

"Now the morrow having come, Fra Pacifico returned to him. And the blessed Francis was standing in the front of the altar in prayer. And Fra Pacifico waited for him outside the choir, praying also before a crucifix. And when he began to pray he was raised and rapt into heaven, whether in the body or out of the body God knows ; and he saw in heaven many seats, and among them one greater and more glorious than all ths rest, shining and adorned with all kinds of precious stones. And wondering at its beauty, he began to think within himself to whom this seat might belong. And straightway he heard a voice calling him—'This was the seat of Lucifer, and in his place shall sit the lowly Francis.'

"And when he had returned to himself the blessed Francis went out to him, and the brother threw himself at his feet, with his arms stretched out in the fashion of a cross; and thinking of him as already in heaven, and sitting in that seat, he cried, 'Father, forgive me, and ask God that He have pity and forgive my sins!' Then reaching out his hand the blessed Francis raised him, and knew straightway that he had seen something while he prayed. For he seemed all changed, and he spoke to his blessed master not as if he lived still in the flesh, but as if already Francis reigned in heaven. But after, for that he did not wish to tell Francis of his vision, he began to speak of it distantly, and among other things he said, 'What dost thou think of thyself, brother?' And the blessed Francis answered, 'It seems to me I am the greatest sinner that ever was in all the world.' And forthwith was it spoken to the soul of Fra Pacifico—'By this thou mayest know that the vision was true; for as Lucifer was thrown down from that seat for his pride, so Francis for his lowly mind shall merit to be raised to sit thereon.'"

But no companion of Francis could ever hope for perpetual comradeship. No hardship, no service with him could pay for that. Strangers and pilgrims, they must go where the work called them. In 1217 Francis had planned a mission into France, one of the fondest purposes of his heart without a doubt, for the country, its people, its language and legends were dear to him. The hard ways of the world he cheered with French lauds; he spoke out the choice things of his heart in that tongue. He had got as far as Florence—Masseo was with him—when Ugolino, the Cardinal Protector of the Order, stopped him. He was needed at home, said Ugolino. Francis meekly bowed his head, and sent Fra Pacifico in his place. To the country of the trouvères he sent a trouvère. To Paris, the centre of enlightenment, he sent the *nobilis et curialis doctor can-*

torum. His mission was the creation of a new and most important province. A band of brothers went with him. New work this for a courtly trouvère, and if they sang along the roads, they had need of all their holy joy. They begged their way through France, giving good return, however, for what stayed their hunger. By day they made the beds of lepers in hospitals or tended the sick. At night the churches where they prayed gave them some protection from the weather. And so they made their way to Paris. They owed the site of their first convent to the Benedictines; but while Pacifico was there, I doubt if they had more than bare shelter. From the first the Minorite settlement in Paris was associated with learning; but it is not easy to see traces of Sicilian trouvère inspiration in Hales and Scot. The Provincial did not stay in Paris very long. Under orders from his captain to extend the dominion of the Great King, he became a determined missionary. Leaving Angelo of Pisa as guardian, he continued his wandering life, enlisting men in the new knighthood of Lady Poverty, setting them to work in her service, and making friends for the Order. His propaganda, so far as we can trace it now, lay mostly in the Low Countries, then counted in the French Province. Joanna of Constantinople, Countess of Flanders, protected them, and the work prospered. Among the first houses built were those of Lens, Valenciennes, Arras, Ghent, Bruges, and Oudenarde, and some or all of these owe their origin to Fra Pacifico. It seems a far exile from sunny Italy to the misty flats of Belgium. But to a visionary of that time the journey of the spirit was not so long. In this soil the Béguines sprang up.

What brought him back? The Provincial in France in 1226 was Fra Gregorio Lombardo. And Pacifico was certainly in Italy with Francis the year before. Elias was Vicar then—a very energetic one, of course, who had much to say about the organisation of the

provinces. There was a tradition in the convent of
Lens that among the papers destroyed in the turmoils
of later times, were letters from Elias to Fra Pacifico.
Are these too slight foundations for saying that Elias
displaced him? I cannot believe the very simple,
though courtly, Pacifico would have pleased that excellent man of business as Minister of the Province
of France; and I am prepared to believe that the poet
was quite incapable of administration.

Or did he perhaps give up his post and hasten back,
hearing of the growing feebleness of Francis? What
little we know of him after his return from Belgium
is, at least, from the words of those who knew him
personally—Leo, the writer of the *Speculum*, and Thomas
of Tuscany. It seems he clung very close to the saint
in those latter days. He was his *pia mater*. Francis
called him so, and tracing him to Siena and Assisi while
Francis was gravely ill there, we learn the reason why.
Fra Pacifico was one of his tender nurses. He would
come over, we can imagine, from St. Mary of the Angels
to visit the sufferer in his hut in the garden of St.
Damian. How he came one day, being sent for, we
know; and how he found the sick man triumphant and
chanting his gratitude in the *Song of the Creatures*.
Pacifico was the visitor needed that day. Francis
had a plan in his head to form a new order, the
Minstrels of the Lord—*joculatores Domini*—whom
Pacifico should lead. "For what are the servants of
the Lord save His minstrels, who should lift up the
hearts of men and move them to joy of the spirit?"
Tradition has it that the King of Verses lent his skill
towards putting the *Song of the Creatures* into shape,
giving it music, and teaching the brothers to sing it—
though Leo says his master did everything. Was he
one of the twain sent by Francis to reconcile the Bishop
and the Podestà of Assisi by singing them the new
song?

He may have followed Francis to Rieti, where he was persuaded to consult a physician for a malady of the eyes. But he was certainly not the brother—as Papini blunderingly suggests—no king of verses he, but a lute-player in the world—who refused to sing and play to ease the suffering saint, for the scandal of the thing. Though, when the angels visited him in the night-time, I make no doubt they sang even better than our Pacifico.

But he was at Siena, in the old convent of Ravacciano there, in 1226, when Francis was very ill. And here we have a glimpse of what the good brother's temperament involved. A man who receives all his sensations and truths through the eyes has a very lust of seeing. If he is an ecstatic, he will divine images unguessed by others. But he will hunger for seeing out of his hours of ecstasy. The other and lower side of his faculty will be indiscretion. Fra Pacifico, it is said, was one of the very few, a much envied few, who saw the holy stigmata of Francis while the saint was yet alive. He saw them—at least, he showed them by trickery, amply justified, it would seem, in the eyes of the brethren. But with the echo of his master's reproach in our ears, we must wish Pacifico had restrained the curious hunger that outraged the sensitive reserve of the virginal soul. A brother of Brescia, who had heard whispers of the holy mystery, tempted him. Francis, who answered all curiosity by *secretum meum mihi*, was wont to keep his hands half-concealed in the long sleeves of his tunic. "But," said his own familiar friend to the inquisitive stranger, "when he is going out I shall beg to kiss his hands, and when he gives me them, I shall make a sign to you, and you shall see." And so it was done. But Francis suspected some pious fraud, and calling Pacifico back, he said, "God forgive thee, brother, for the pain thou givest me sometimes." Pacifico repentant, bowed, and asked humbly, "What

hurt have I done thee, dearest mother?" But Francis
answered not, and nothing more was said.

From Siena Elias took Francis to Cortona, thence
to Assisi and his last days. The *pia mater* did not
go with them. Elias no doubt strictly regulated the
company. Fra Pacifico stayed behind at Siena; for
next year, 1227, Pope Gregory IX. appointed him a
visitor of the Benedictine sisters of Santa Maria, whose
house was neighbour to the hermitage of the Minors on
the hill of Ravacciano. He was not with Francis when
he died. When Leo and Angelo were called to sing
the *Song of the Creatures* he might not join in. But
they sang it to his tune, and the saint's last days were
sweetened by his music.

The date of his death has been placed between 1230
and 1234; but he may have lived much longer. Papini
says he was alive in 1261. For a man who lived largely
by his affections life must have been an altered thing.
But he clung still to his fellow-creatures with that childlike warmth and ecstasy that Francis had proved. May
he not be the Pacifico of the *Fioretti?* I have no proof
of this—there were others of his name; and the question
has hardly been raised—but the story there is in keeping
with all we know of the poet brother. Here I come to
familiar ground, but for my own pleasure I will quote:—

"In the aforesaid Province of the March, after the
death of Saint Francis, there were two brothers in
the Order; the one named Brother Humble and the
other Peaceful, the which were men of exceeding great
sanctity and perfection; and the one, to wit, Brother
Humble, abode in the House of Soffiano, and there
died; and the other belonged to another community
at some distance therefrom. Now it pleased God that
as Brother Peaceful was at prayer one day in a lonely
place, he was rapt in ecstasy, and saw the soul of his
brother, Brother Humble, that had just then left the
body, going straight up into heaven without either let

or hindrance. It befell that, many years after, Brother Peaceful, being still alive, was sent to the community in the aforesaid House of Soffiano, where his brother had died. About this time the brothers, at the request of the lords of Bruforte, exchanged the said House for another; wherefore, among other things, they carried with them the relics of the holy brothers that had died in that House, and coming to the grave of Brother Humble, his brother, Brother Peaceful took up his bones, and washed them with good wine and wrapped them in a white napkin, and with great reverence and devotion kissed them and wept over them; whereat the other brothers marvelled, and deemed he set them no good example; in that it seemed that, albeit a man of so great sanctity, he mourned for his brother, with a carnal and a worldly love; and that he showed more devotion to his relics than to those of the other brothers that had been of no less sanctity than Brother Humble, and whose relics were worthy of as much reverence as his. And Brother Peaceful knowing the evil imaginings of the brothers humbly satisfied them thereof, and said unto them: 'My brothers most dear, marvel not that I have done for the bones of my brother what I have not done for the others; for, blessed be God, I was not moved thereto, as ye deem, by carnal love; but so have I done, for that, when my brother passed away from this life, I praying in a lonely place and distant from him, beheld his soul rise straight to heaven, whereby I am assured that his bones are holy and should be in Paradise. And if God had granted me such surety touching the other brothers, then would I have paid the self-same reverence unto their bones.' For the which cause, the brothers, seeing his holy and devout intent, were through him well edified, and gave praise unto God, that doeth such marvellous things unto His holy ones, the brothers."

So it may have been to his own country of the

Marches that he retired, for a time at least—that province "in olden time adorned, even as the sky with stars, with brothers that were patterns of holy life." Very likely he wandered. He was seen and known, after the death of Francis, by Thomas of Tuscany, from whom we have definite word of him. Pacifico, says Thomas, always carried about with him certain precious relics. One of these was a special treasure—a small wooden tablet, the section of the stem of a nut-tree that had grown up near the altar of a ruined church. On it was stamped, not in relief, but flat, the image of the Crucified. No corruptible hand had painted it, but the Divine hand itself. And, says Thomas, no great wonder is it he found the cross in the nut-tree, who was so passionate a lover of the Cross.

Now I have lighted on another mention of this miraculous nut-tree. Some dozen years or so after Pacifico was hugging this cutting of it, that good gossip Salimbene, beginning a tour through France, met with Fra Giovanni da Pian del Carpine the traveller. Fra Giovanni told and showed the brothers many wonders, and among them a wooden cup he had brought home as a present for the Pope, in the bottom of which was the picture of a beautiful queen, not painted but formed "by the influence of a constellation." The listeners seem to have been incredulous, whereupon Fra Giovanni, with the air of saying "Oh that's nothing," told them of another greater wonder of the kind. The Emperor Frederic, he said, had given to the Brothers Minor in Apulia a very old church, all ruined and deserted; and in the space where the altar had been, there had grown up a nut-tree of incredible size. Cut lengthwise, each section presented the face of Christ, and if you had cut it a hundred times, a hundred times would the image have appeared. "Which truly happened by a miracle, the tree having grown in that place where was wont to be renewed the Passion of the spotless Lamb

in the saving host and venerable sacrifice. Yet are there
some of the firm opinion that it may have been caused
by the influence of a constellation." It must have been
some years before this, 1247, that the Emperor showed
any civility to the Brothers Minor. So Pacifico's treasure may well have come from that nut-tree in the
ruined church in Apulia. Did any directer gift of his
old friend Frederic ever give him such joy?

Fra Pacifico found his rest at last in the Low Countries.
The accounts that state, severally, that his body lies in
Verona and in Venice, are evidently at fault. Perhaps
his old comrades in the convent he had founded at Lens
called him back as Guardian. There, at all events, he
died, and was buried in a marble tomb, near the high
altar, or as some say, without the choir. This inscription could once be read—*Sub hoc lapide recondita servantur
ossa sacra B. Pacifici Ordinis Minorum, qui ipse primus
fuit Provinciæ Franciæ Minister.* A very tombstone-
like epigraph, which omits all the essential. The church
was in later times wrecked and burnt. All its documents and treasures perished. Nothing remained save
dim memories of Brother Pacifico, among them that of
a mutilated statue that used to be carried about for
public veneration on his feast day, July 10th. The
old chronicles, at least, are quite sure about his beatification. A sweet odour exhaled from his tomb. Many
miracles were wrought there. His influence was specially
good against fever.

Crowned with high rites the King of Verses by an
emperor, singer of light love-songs, witness of splendour
and ambition and the pride of life, this was the fortunate
William of Lisciano—*nostro Vuillielmo*—Ascoli's pride.
Then his eyes beheld a greater glory, the gleaming Thau
on the brow of Francis, and he knew that visions are
even finer than sights; and they are best seen out of the
whirlwind of the world. Henceforth his joy was to
be forgotten, save by his *carissima mater*, to be near to

Francis, his fellow trouvère, to serve in the new chivalry and be its unnamed minstrel.

Near as he was to the person and the heart of Francis, he is not of that little stalwart band who grouped themselves together with the proud and tender words, *nos qui cum eo fuimus*, not of the Three Companions or their witnesses. Leo speaks respectfully, but not intimately of him. And certainly he was not of those against whom the whole lives of these faithful ones protested in grief and pain. Do men like Pacifico ever realise such strife? He was not made for controversy or protest. Something too much of the Sicilian sun was in his blood. And in mind he was too simple—probably simpler far than Leo, the little sheep of God. He may have been even a little blind to the enormities of Elias, and quite unanxious of the darkening future. This barefoot, rough-robed friar was no more ascetic than was his master—rich men both in the realm of vision—a man not of striving faith but of certain sight, who knew the beauty of humility, having seen the jewelled throne of Lucifer prepared for Francis, who did sweet honour to the relics of his beloved dead, of whose ascent to heaven his eyes were witnesses, a man to whom symbols were very real—a terrible idolater, as is every artist. He played no great part in the history of the Order. He was only Brother Pacifico, outside the turmoil and the arguments of the time. No wonder that at Lens his relics were held to be good for the allayment of fevers.

FRATE ELIAS

APOLOGIA PRO VITÂ SUÂ

" For hord hath hate, and climbing tikelnesse."
—Balade de Bon Conseyl.

A traveller is faring along the hard high road from
Perugia to Assisi. Fate has chosen well his hour, and at
a point where the trees by the roadside grow higher and
thicker and there are signs his journey is wearing to an end,
his ears are filled with sound, the sound of bells that come
from somewhere above‘ and fill the valley round him.
He can never afterwards know anything of those bells,
though founders and connoisseurs of tone do their best
to instruct him, save that they lifted his heart into a
sudden and inexplicable harmony with what he was
about to reach, and turned his spirit to reception. Bells
owe more than half their music to their placement.
(Remember that sound over the lagoons, and under the
lagoons, from Venice to Burano or to the Lido.) And
so the wise traveller, or the traveller guided by kind
chance, avoids convenience, comes along the highroad,
and is rung up into the surprise of Assisi. At first the
bells come from nowhere, then from the sky, then from
a half hidden hillside, till a turn and a gap show him
the rose-hued, many-columned, marvellous invention,
the Sacro Convento and the Church of San Francesco.
Now, if the traveller have a soul, he blesses somebody
as he climbs the path to the town. If he knows his
Franciscan history, he blesses Frate Elias. In those first
moments Elias needs no Apologia. The traveller's heart
is full of thanksgiving. From an artist, *pur sang*, he

never needs any Apologia at all; for was he not the
Master of the Works when that pile, perfect realisation
of the religious idea, rose as if by magic speed, a few
short years after Francis had died down in the valley
below, at St. Mary of the Angels?

But Elias cannot be left in peace to the eulogies of
the artist, for the reason that he himself was not content
to be only a patron and stimulator of the arts. He
played many other rôles. The great driving force of
his life was not Art. He rose by other means, and for
other ends; and when he fell it was not as Art's victim.

For six centuries and a half his bones have mouldered
up in high Cortona; and he is still the subject of
bitterest contention. Was ever any one so hated and
reviled by good men since Judas Iscariot? He has been,
indeed, to many faithful Observants the reincarnation of
Judas, all the more loathsome that it was his master's
spirit and not his body that he betrayed. And he has
had his warm defenders, who admit some degeneration
in his later years, but who point to the evidences of
his great mind, and to the marvellous stimulus given
to the Franciscan organisation under his rule. Indeed,
many have a rooted conviction, whatever they may say,
that it was Elias saved the Order from being a shabby,
low-down kind of thing, with no sort of standing in the
face of the Church and of the world. He has had
too much abuse, and too much praise. Both sides have
lied about him through the ages, and as "both sides"
represent an eternal difference of ideal and temperament,
it is not in the nature of things they should ever agree.

But they read his life ill who merely call him good
Franciscan, or bad Franciscan. Poor Elias! The tragedy
of his life was just that he was Franciscan at all. Why
am I not now writing the career of some great captain,
the mighty Bombarone, of some eminent cardinal, who
won triumphs for the Church, some chancellor in an
autocratic court, moulding his master and the State

to his will? Had he only found his way early enough to Frederic's court! But fate brought him into the world in the neighbourhood of Assisi, and gave him in youth a susceptible mind.

It is significant that not one of his detractors has denied his powers. Elias impressed all his contemporaries with a sense of his fine intelligence. The assertion that he had one of the greatest minds in the Europe of his day, is hardly proved; but he had that combination of strong will, self-reliance, mental energy, and agility in seizing an opportunity which marks the man who carves out his own career, and makes use of the hour and the men that are with him. He had a defect of vision; but in a score of other callings it would not have hindered his being a leader renowned and successful. What wonder if he called out on Fate?

To Fortune he owed nothing at all—for the tale of his being a scion of the noble house of the Coppi is a foolish invention. The facts of his humble birth are well authenticated. And, besides, *parvenu* is written all over the years of his success. His father was a poor man, a native of Castello de Britti, near Bologna, who married a woman of Assisi, and went to live in the neighbourhood of that town. Their son was born in the village of Beviglia, somewhere about the year 1180. They called him Bombarone. When he grew out of childhood he was taught the trade, probably his father's, of mattress-making. But the lad had aspirations, and already had picked up more learning than was usual in his station, for he joined to his mattress-making the profession of schoolmaster, in a humble way, teaching little boys in Assisi to read their psalter. Tradition has always said he was of, or about the same age as Francis. In fact, an old legend of the *zelanti* says he was born on the same day, as a contrast to the saint. But he can hardly have been of young Bernardone's companions. While Francis was roistering about the streets,

scattering his father's money in feasting and fine garments, light-hearted, open-handed, spendthrift troubadour,
Bombarone was leading a sober life of toil and poverty,
and probably struggling towards the learning which by
common rumour in later days he possessed.   But Francis
must have been known to him, as an object of distant admiration, or as an awful warning; and after his conversion
the rich merchant's son was the cynosure of all eyes.

M. Sabatier suggests that the grave, discreet companion, who took the place of his gay comrades when
he had gone apart from them in the trouble of his soul,
was the young Bombarone of Beviglia.   He it was
watched outside the grotto while Francis prayed within.
This surmise rests on the fact of the ample details concerning this period given by Thomas of Celano in his
"First Life," which was certainly inspired by Elias.
Who could have given the biographer the information save him who trudged the solitary woodlands
and hillsides with the troubled wrestler, and watched
his wrestling?   It is an imaginative surmise, not to be
lightly dismissed.   But it is almost certain he was not
among the first to join the Order.   The poor mattress-
maker's ambition at this time would seem to have been
rather towards law and learning.   While Francis and
the first brothers were casting the world from them with
joyous hearts, Bombarone was toiling as *scriptor*, and
probably picking up some science, at Bologna.   He was
on the right track.   He had risen already.   He might
hope to rise more.   As jurist, his clear mind would
be fittingly employed.   He might enter a noble house
as secretary, or even a princely court; and he would
grip hard his opportunities.   It is impossible to think
of him as a failure in any secular career.   But while
he was looking about, he seems to have fallen in with
Francis at Cortona, the town afterwards so closely associated with Elias's name.   If he had known him before
as a young man in doubt, he saw him now triumphant

in conviction. Bombarone was no dull dog. He knew
a great man when he saw him, at least if he were a
man of authority, and here was no longer the haggard
doubter haunting the woods of Assisi, but an enthusiast
of genius, who gripped men's hearts, who called them
to hardship and worldly disaster, and they followed.
There was a stir about the name of Francis. While
most men wondered, Elias saw with his keen intelligence
that here was the beginning of something great.

The finest of lines are needed to draw him at this
moment. He had the *flair* of opportunities, which
marks every man born to success. But to conceive him
now as a brutal time-server would be egregiously wrong.
He never became a priest; but he was never irreligious,
never even unorthodox in the most suspect portions of
his life. Excommunication tried him sorely. One can
think of him as a solid henchman of Dominic's in his
war against heresy. And though it is easy to imagine
him assimilating the secular learning that flourished at
the court of Sicily, he never seems to have come under
its influence. Besides, though the persistent theory of
the Conventuals, that Elias never erred from the strictest
path of loyalty and obedience to the Rule during the
lifetime of the Founder, is a senseless defiance of probability and of history, yet that he fell under, and remained under, the fascination of Francis, I hold to be
altogether certain. Very soon he learned to make use
of the master. But he loved him. Francis appeared to
him as the leader into a promised land of new opportunities, where the humblest might make his way. But
he drew him also, by moments, against the clamouring
whispers of self-interest. Even in his later, obviously
ambitious days, Francis was fast in his heart. Indeed,
there is no such admirer of saintliness as your real man
of the world, no one who subscribes so heartily towards
a fine pedestal for it, or a sanctuary where it will not be
defiled by common use.

But Bombarone, when he joined the Brothers Minor under the name of Elias, was no mature man of the world yet; only an eager, energetic young fellow, blind to the fact that he was taking a step in violation of his whole nature. Celano's tale that he was listened to by Francis, and thought much of, is certainly true. He was more articulate than the others; his intellect was subtler. He could not sing like them along the roads; but he could talk, and was quick to see his master's plans. Very early he seems to have been given responsibility. He was sent to the Tuscan mission, it is said; and Elias was well fitted to deal with the keen-witted Tuscans.

In 1217 there took place a more definite organisation of Franciscan missions; and the provinces were marked out. Almost simultaneously there was a revival of crusading zeal, and a band of brothers, with Elias at their head, set out for the Holy Land. When Syria became a Minorite province in 1219, he was appointed its provincial. Thus Francis never curbed his energy, and at once recognised his qualities, which were not those of Bernard, and Giles, and the others. His quick promotion—since he saw the first companions employed merely as wandering missionaries about Italy, or as sick nurses, or as common labourers—Elias probably misread, as any other young man of ability might, and he never seems to have discovered his mistake. Francis was his master, and a man of genius; but his humble followers were what they were, because they couldn't be anything else.

The most shining fact of his stay in Syria was his winning over to the Order a remarkable German who was travelling there. This Caesar of Spires became a zealous Minorite; and it is by a curious freak of fate that Elias introduced the Rule of Francis to the man who was afterwards his victim for adhering to it. On his way home from the East, Francis joined Elias and the new brother, and they all came back together in a

Venetian ship. This, of course, disposes of the tales of
later times that Elias took advantage of Francis's absence in the East to turn the Order upside down, and
to interfere to such an extent that the Founder had to
be called back. The Founder was called back, but not
for Elias's offences. Elias returned with his master to
find a ferment going on among the Brothers, everywhere
unrest, discontent, and the signs of the later cleavage.
And, remember, he was not like Bernard, or Leo, or the
others, joined to Francis by something profounder even
than affection, by the bonds of a kindred nature, so
strong that, even if the *Poverello* had not called them,
they would inevitably have carved out some life of sacrifice for themselves. Then, too, he was by this time a
man of some experience in administration. Probably in
Tuscany and in Syria he had met with the same discontent, the same difficulties, and had had to make deci-
sions. In a secular sense, things had prospered with him.
Out of his keen eyes he looked and saw the Order growing, an Order that had a place for a man of energy like
him. It was favoured at headquarters, as the older Orders
were not. And he understood a thousand times better
than did Francis the deeper meaning of the favour of
the Roman Curia. Elias was the equal in shrewdness
of any Pope or Cardinal, and perceived—I think, even
before Ugolino, who was more hampered by sentiment—
the engine for Rome that the Minorites might become.

When the party landed at Venice, the air was full of
complaints and contradictions. Elias heard both parties,
and he was not bound to the side of the strict observers
of the Rule by the instincts of his nature. Doubtless,
too, Francis's conduct at Bologna when they passed
through that town, astounded him. There is no mention of a protest from Elias, but it must have been an
object lesson as to what Francis meant by adhesion to
the Rule when he saw even the sick turned out of a
house because it was said to "belong to" the Brothers

Minor, to whom nothing belonged. Then Ugolino was
with Francis at certain points of that return journey—it
was he that stepped in to adjust things at Bologna—and
Elias was probably in their company. Here we may
place the beginning of the relations between these two men
so excellently fitted for collaboration. If Elias had ever
any need to be a pupil of the Cardinal's, it was now he
took his course of lessons. He would hear the gentle
and subtle complaints, "You see, Brother Francis, what
comes of trusting to a few verses of the Gospel for a
Rule. You turn your back, and each brother interprets
it in his own way. The brothers are growing fast.
They will become a danger to the Church; and then
who will regret it so much as you, so good a son of the
Church?" It is said that Ugolino isolated Francis
from all the rest at Camaldoli, and worked him into a
promise of a closer union of his Order with the Curia.
The first-fruits of this private intercourse was that Ugolino became the Protector of the Order. In the meanwhile, Elias was mingling with the struggling brothers,
all rejoiced at the return of the master, but of different
minds respecting the discipline and the policy of the
Religion. I can see Elias in every company defend-
ing Francis, holding him up as a shining light to
all the nations, but giving his mind judicially to this
man's query and the other man's plaint. The one great
politician of the Order was bound to the part he played.
More clearly than any other he saw what could be
made of the movement, if the Founder did but permit.
Francis's saintly rigour must give way, else what promised to be a thing of might and power—for the evangelisation of the world, of course—would turn into a
straggling band of despised fanatics, unworthy of the
great chance of having a genius and a saint for its head.

I am sure, in spite of vague traditions to the
contrary, Elias never said a hard word to Francis.
Even when he criticised him as organiser, it was with

K

the addition, "Ah, he is too good and lofty for the purpose!" When the malcontents came to him, doubtless he held the balance long. But being what he was, the cleverest, the readiest, the most articulate brother of them all, he became their spokesman. They were but emphasising Ugolino's demand for a more stereotyped pattern for the Order, and a rather more indulgent Rule. "Take nothing with you," was of too great practical inconvenience. Francis gave way in the end. He was forced to. He was never convinced. But he also gave the care of the practical matters of the Order into the hands of Peter of Catania, at the Chapter General, September 29, 1220. He did not go away, however, to live in solitude. The common sense of Elias alone would have been enough to have prevented that. They were nothing without him. Perhaps they could carry on the daily administration of the Order better in his absence. But he was their distinction. And humble as he was, his spirit even in his days of weakness, and from this time onward he was was always ailing, was too vital for suppression.

Francis was at the Porziuncola drawing up a new Rule, or rather a document in which he poured out his heart to the brothers, appealing to them to live by the spirit of their first foundation, which was the Gospel. The new recruit, that learned German, Cæsar of Spires, was helping him. Elias, no doubt, thought the saint well out of the bustle of administration, writing beautiful things. He himself would see much of the chief persons in the Order. Meanwhile he was getting to know his material; and he certainly had some intercourse with Ugolino. Think of the fervent talks these two arch-politicians had over the sanctity of Francis. "What a man!" "Verily a saint of God!" "Spare him, dear Brother Elias, all the worry you can. So frail he is! So sensitive!" "Yea, my Lord Cardinal, I would take all the burdens of common life from his shoulders." "Ah," the great man would continue, with an indulgent smile, "if men were but as he thinks them! Alas, you and I know what they are." Neither wished that Francis, the child of Heaven, should ever learn their earthly knowledge of men. His innocence, his hopefulness, his high expectations, drew souls as they could not. If only once drawn into the fold by Francis's high hopes for them, the souls might be left to men of the world to deal with!

If Elias was privileged to see the Rule of 1221 being prepared, he probably made no protest. It was fine literature; and he had taste and sentiment. Perhaps neither he nor Ugolino would have been much disturbed had they known of all the visits and letters to the saint at this time. Troubled souls cried to him, "Times are changing. The brothers are demanding liberty to live contrary to our Rule. Soon they will get it. When that day comes, then we shall be the rebels. Father, in that day let us go apart, and live as thou hast taught us." And he gave them authority to do so, and Angelo Clareno and his friends remembered it in the time to come.

But Rome was soon to learn that Francis, after his retirement for the compilation of "literature," remained the same clear-sighted, persistent, independent enthusiast as before. "Ah, how we want your sons, with their personal piety and their devotion to Rome, in the high places of the Church," had said the Pope to Francis and to Dominic. But Dominic would have no patronage for his Order, and Francis said, "My Brothers and I are *Minores*." Francis came back from Rome to find his Vicar, Peter of Catania, dead. Rome was expecting from his brotherhood duties he could not fulfil himself. He did not take up the burden again. And who could look after the growingly complicated machine so well as Brother Elias? Ugolino certainly suggested him, but everybody seems to have acquiesced, even Francis, who was perhaps powerless in the matter. He proved at once the most serviceable of vicars. Thousands came to the Chapter of Pentecost, 1221. They came to see Francis, of course. But Elias took from him the burden of presiding, arranged the business, and did the speaking. Jordan of Giano describes the scene. Elias sat in the President's chair. Francis was at his feet, and when he had something to say to the assembled brothers, he plucked his vicar by the tunic. The vicar would bend down, listen, and then standing up, would say, " Brothers, thus says Brother Francis." At this Chapter the evangelisation of Germany was the great subject. Germany was the hardest, wildest soil they had yet had to till. Some had come back with terrible tales of their treatment; but Francis plucked at Elias's tunic with words of hope and spirit, and Elias repeated them to the rest. Volunteers were numerous. Jordan himself, timid at first, was one of them; and they went off under the leadership of Elias's recruit, Cæsar of Spires.

From this point two roads are seen clearly to diverge. The appointment of Elias was followed by a great extension and increase in the Order, by the election of new officials, by the opening up of new sources of support. He kept things going. He "pushed" the affair. To many minds the Minorite Idea became now for the first time a substantial thing. The "places" of the brothers increased in numbers and in size, and churches began to be built. While they had the world for their cloister, the world hardly knew of their existence. But stone and lime convinced it.

Francis was probably little consulted, but that he did not openly protest means there were not many flagrant breaches of the letter of the Rule. As for the spirit—if you call a great mass of men together, and wish to organise them, that means, now and to all eternity, that you govern them by the law of the mediocre, to which all may strive without overstrain, and most may stoop without over condescension. Meanwhile, Francis was wandering about the hermitages of Umbria, seeing and consoling his friends, bewildered at the vanishing of the Idea as seen in the Order called by his name. He was following his old road, touching and encouraging individual souls. And so for ever after the ways are apart. The Founder is theoretically the head, and he is on friendly terms with the adminstrative government. But none the less he is an outcast, as he speaks to one here, one there, just as he had done in the beginning, as he does now. His vicar, speaking in the name of multitudes, claims their obedience, and forms the Franciscan Order.

In the two years, 1221 and 1222, comparatively little is known of Francis. He was more alone, and more with his own special disciples than either before or after, emerging now and then to try to come to some understanding with the ministers about the Rule that was to be. That of 1221 they rejected. In vain he told them not to talk to him of the Rules of St. Augustine, or St. Bernard, or St. Benedict—that he had meant no Order such as theirs, but a plan of good living for men in the world. Tradition and convention had their way. Ugolino had a great deal to say on the matter, and the subject probably formed a good part of the business of the Chapters of 1222 and 1223. Francis once more retired, with Bonizio of Bologna and Leo, to the hermitage of Monte Colombo, near Rieti. A Rule was it they wanted? Well, had they not had a Rule from the beginning? His Rule would always be the Evangel, sacrifice of self for the love of men. That was the essential; and he was a man, like all the great ones, to dwell on essentials. What did the other things matter? "Too vast!" they said. "How can we know we fulfil it?" "A man can always know if he is loving his neighbour, succouring the outcast, and if he have a humble heart. The Rule is nothing else." But Ugolino, lauding the sentiment of the *Poverello* with half his nature, clamoured with the other part for some test of instant and complete obedience to the Roman See.

Glassberger's account of the making of the Rule of 1223, confirmed by others, is that Francis came down from the hermitage on the hill and gave the Rule into the hands of Elias, who was probably at Rieti. A few days later Elias said to him, it was most unfortunate, but he had lost it. He probably counted on Francis's discouragement delaying the framing of a new one till a certain deputation he knew of should have an interview with the Founder. But Francis went straight up the hill again and wrote another, or rather rewrote the same. Meanwhile the ministers had appealed to Elias to use his influence with Francis. Leo, who was an eyewitness of the subsequent interview, says: " Brother Elias answered them that he would not go without them, and so they all went together. When Brother Elias was near the place where the Blessed Francis was sojourning he called to him. The Blessed Francis answering, and seeing the aforesaid ministers, said, 'What do these brothers want?' And Elias said, 'These are ministers, who hearing thou art making a new Rule, fear thou makest it too rigorous, and they say and protest, that they will not be bound by it, that thou makest it for thyself and not for them.' Then the Blessed Francis turned his face to heaven, and spoke thus to Christ, 'Lord, said I not truly unto Thee the truth, that they would not believe me?' Then all heard the voice of Christ answering in the air, 'Francis, there is nothing in the Rule of thine, but all that is there is Mine; and it is My will it should be kept to the letter, without gloss, without gloss, without gloss!' And He added, 'I know how much human weakness can do, and how much I wish to help poor men. Who will not observe it, then let him go out of the Order.' Then the Blessed Francis turned to the brothers and said, ' Do ye hear, do ye hear? Do ye wish that I should have it said to you again?' Then the ministers, conscience-stricken, confused and afraid, withdrew."

Elias was not confused, I am convinced. Was he not acting strictly in accordance with the democratic spirit of the Order, as delegate of an important mission? But he was certainly alarmed, for he, too, had discovered that the late Rules of Francis were not mere "literature," but most seriously intended for observance. Yet the protest, for all the confusion of the ministers in the master's presence, was not in vain. Ugolino saw to that when Francis went to Rome for the confirmation of the Rule.

Thus it is seen that in the story of the Founder's latest years Elias plays a prominent part. Francis was not unaware of the high-handed methods of his vicar, or of his spiritual limitations. But he could not have guessed how far out of the Minorite path ambition would lead him; and besides, it seems certain that Rome, or Ugolino at least, manifested its will that Elias should administer the Order in practical affairs. That he was blind to the harshness of Elias is disproved by the following letter addressed to him—a gentle, but quite definite command to exercise more loving kindness than he was wont to use with the brothers:—

"To Brother Elias, Minister.—The Lord bless thee. I speak to thee as I am able concerning the condition of thy soul. If there be persons, whether brothers or not, who are a hindrance to thee in loving the Lord God— even though some were to beat thee with stripes—yet shouldst thou count all such trials as favours. Such should be thy mind and not other. And let this be to thee for a command from the Lord and from me, for this I know surely to be true obedience. And love those that do such things to thee, and desire not anything else from them save what has been granted to thee. And in this thing love them, and do not desire that they be better Christians. [M. Sabatier explains that Francis is referring to ungrateful and recalcitrant lepers, whom he was wont to call 'Christians.' But the sentence—the epitome of his attitude towards suffering mankind—might surely be given a wider significance.] And let this be to thee more than a reward. And by this shall I know that thou lovest God and me His servant and thine,—that there be no brother in all the world—let him sin as deeply as he may—who shall go away from before thy face without thy mercy, if he would have mercy. And if he seek not mercy, then ask thou him if he desire it not. And if a thousand times he appear before thee, love him more than thou lovest me, so mayest thou draw him to love God. And on all his like have pity.

"And this shouldst thou say to the guardian when thou hast opportunity, that by thee he may be strengthened to do the same.

"Now of all the chapters that are in the Rule that speak of mortal sins, let us, at the Pentecost Chapter, God helping, and with the counsel of the brothers, make one to this effect:—If any brother, instigated by the Enemy, fall into mortal sin, let him be held bound to hasten to his guardian. And let none of the brothers who know him to have sinned, cause him shame or reproach him, but rather let them have great pity of him, and keep very secret that sin of their brother—for the hale need no physician but they that are sick. And so let them be bound to send him to his *custode* with a companion, and let that *custode* look on him pitifully, as he would that another should look on him if he were in a like case. And if he should fall into another venial sin, let him confess to his brother the priest, and if there be no priest there, let him confess to his brother till he find a priest, who shall absolve him canonically, as it is called. And let there be no power of ordering other penance than this —'Go, and sin no more.' This writing, that it may be the better observed, keep by thee till Pentecost. Thou wilt be there with thy brothers, and these things and others that are wanting in the Rule, thou shalt arrange to have put in."

Had Elias only kept this most precious document by him after Pentecost, kept it as a charm against temptation, as Leo did the scrap of his master's writing given him on Alverna! But if Elias did not take the advice, or if it did not influence him for long, he perhaps took the implied reproaches sweetly. He never was lacking in reverence for the little frail-bodied creature who couldn't make a Rule, but who was the distinction of their Order. Their distinction, also their danger, as such to be watched tenderly, insinuatingly guided. Business took him often away, but he kept as much as possible by his side.

About midsummer, 1224, they seem to have been together at Foligno. There, it appears, Elias was much exercised about the health of Francis, and doubtless wished him to say something of the future. With these preoccupations in his mind, he had a vision. "He saw in a dream a majestic old man, clad in white, who said, 'Rise, brother, and tell Brother Francis that eighteen years have gone by since he clave to Christ, abandoning the world. Tell him that two years yet shall pass, and then God shall call him to Himself.'"

Francis's response to the news was his journey to Alverna. His vicar had no time to spend in the mountains. But rumours of strange events came down with the returning company. It was an awesome thing to speak of, but its mere whisper was a mightier weapon for the spread of the Order than even anything that Rome could be made to do. Their treasure was now beyond price, and it was all in the shape of a frail, broken man. When, after a short rest, Francis set out again on a preaching mission, Elias clung to him. The saint's eyesight was almost gone, and his vicar insisted on their going to Rieti, where the papal court was at the time, to see an eye doctor. It was not easy to persuade him to go at once, and business carried Elias off. Francis had need of other care, and he got it, at Saint Damian's, from Clara. His soul was heavy and veiled till she and the gentle air of her garden brought relief, and it rose in triumph in the Song of the Creatures.

When they sojourned together as loving brothers, Elias may have been well aware of his limitations. He could lead the Order, but he could never feel he was leading the frail man, who yet had no will of his own. No will of his own—that was just it : he was led by the spirit into ways doubtful for the repute of a great Order. But perhaps it was hidden from him that he shared none of the great days of Francis. He was not at Greccio at the little humble feast of the Christ Child in the stable—and it was well. The Founder's voice imitating the bleating of the innocent lamb touched the Chevalier John, but it might have troubled his responsible vicar. Well, he presided at Chapters. Let Leo and Masseo and the others go into the wilderness, and up to Alverna. His voice sent out the orders to distant provinces. Let Leo and Angelo sing for the dying man the Song of the Creatures.

The pale, aching, yet radiant shadow went hither and thither on its holy work before it reached Rieti, and again after the unsuccessful operation there. At last, at Siena, he had a serious relapse, and Elias hastened to him. The end was near, and no one less than his vicar should have charge of him. Francis had a great desire to return to St. Mary of the Angels. Elias had strong belief in the air of Cortona, and took him there first. But in July they went along the roads, lined with anxious people, to Assisi, and he was installed in the Bishop's house. Elias would run to and fro between the Porziuncola and the palace, where the dying man lay. Angelo and Rufino and Leo were left as nurses—they were good for that. He would bring cheery news of an accession of brothers here and there, and what this and the other man thought of the Order. But from the intimate joy and some of the intimate sorrow he was shut out. "Father," the watchers

said, "thou wilt go beyond to the Lord, and this family
that followeth thee now must remain in the valley of
tears. Tell us, therefore, if thou knowest any one in the
Order on whom thy mind rests, and on whom the burden
of the Minister General may worthily be placed." And
the humble Francis did not point to Elias, toiling and
scheming for the Order. Sad of heart, he said he did not
know any one fit to lead so great, so scattered a flock. Then
he painted the picture of the good Minister General, and
his energetic vicar was certainly not the model. We may
cast aside as a slander the picturesque account, in the
Fioretti, of Elias's early pride and frowardness, and how
his master foretold he would die outside the Order. We
may refuse to believe the account given by Wadding of
Francis's dramatic reproof to Elias for the coquettishness
of his tunic—how he asked him to lend it him, how he
put it on, folded it, fitted it, smoothed it, straightened
his head, puffed out his chest, and walked pompously
along, saying to the astounded brothers, *Salvete gentes*,
salvete, with a delightful mimicry of Elias's most elegant
manner. All this is very likely a malicious fiction of the
zelanti. But Francis was as keenly aware of his vicar's
spiritual shortcomings as he was of his practical abilities.
Which one of the brothers of his heart could lead so great
an organisation as the brotherhood had become? And
where was the leader who could keep the great machine
in hand, and yet consent to be the humble servant of the
humblest?

For Elias, too, these days in the palace were anxious
ones. He felt himself not only the guardian of the tender
body of the dying saint, but likewise of the reputation
of the Order for sanctity. The citizens hung round the
Bishop's house, soldiers guarded it night and day, and yet
Francis and those indiscreet friends of his might have been
up at the Carceri, or among the solitudes of Greccio, for
all the heed they paid to what was expected of them
under the circumstances. Elias, like all great organisers,

was ever mindful of the *mise en scène*, and of fitting accompaniments. But hear what Leo confesses.

"While he lay ill in the episcopal palace of Assisi, and the hand of the Lord seemed to lie heavier on him than it was wont, the people of Assisi, lest he should die in the night time and the brothers should take away his holy body and carry it to another city, ordered that a diligent watch should be kept each night outside the palace wall.

"But our most holy father, for his consolation, lest his spirit should give way somewhat, for the vehemence of the pain which continually afflicted him, was wont in the day time to make Lauds to the Lord to be sung by his companions; likewise he would do the same by night to edify and console the lay folk who were keeping watch outside the palace on his account.

"Now Brother Elias, seeing that the Blessed Francis comforted himself thus in his so great sickness and rejoiced in the Lord, said to him, ' Dearest father, for all the joy which thou showest for thyself and thy companions in thy weakness, I am most glad and edified; but although the men of this town venerate thee as a saint, yet since they firmly believe thee to be nigh unto death on account of thy incurable malady, hearing these lauds sung night and day, they may say among themselves, "Why does he show such joy when he is near unto death? It is of death he should be thinking."'

"And Francis answered, ' Permit me, brother, to rejoice in the Lord, in His lauds, and in mine infirmities, for by the grace of the Holy Spirit working in me, I am united and made one with my Lord, so that, by His mercy, I may well rejoice in Him the Most High.'"

Perhaps Elias was not displeased when he asked to be taken down to the Porziuncola, " that he might end the life of the body where he had first found the light and life of the soul." When only the brothers

could see and hear, what matter though they sang loud
songs of joy round his bed, and though the Lady Jacoba
came to see him in cloistered ground?

And now we come to that vexed question of the
blessing of Elias. Thomas of Celano says Francis
blessed him with special fervour, giving thanks to him
for all he had done for the Order. "May God remember thy toil and labour, and in the day of judgment may
the heritage of the just be thy portion!" And so on.
Celano mentions no other special blessing. Leo says
Francis's chief blessing was given to Bernard, and omits
all reference to Elias. That one of them lied is not the
necessary inference. But there may have been suppres-
sions on both sides. For Celano's story there is no first
hand evidence. Could Elias have plumed himself on
being specially named, he would have said so, I think, as
a passport to favour throughout the provinces, in his
letter to Gregory of Naples. The special blessing may
have been a later invention of his or of his partisans,
when Elias saw more clearly than he did the day after
the saint's death that he had need of every kind of support to his position. But that he was fervently blessed,
and that in the blessing all his activity was put in the
best light, I do not doubt at all.

The end came. He and the other brothers were
together in their grief. Their anxieties for the future
were very different. As the Vicar of Francis, the responsibilities of the moment devolved on him, and with his
usual promptness and ability he did everything—superintended the burial in S. Giorgio, and represented the
Order to all who came to mourn or to inquire. The
day after the death of the saint he sent a letter to all the
brothers, addressed in the first place to Brother Gregory
of Naples, Provincial of France.

"To his beloved Brother in Christ, Gregory, Minister
of the Brethren who are in France, to all his Brothers and
ours, Greeting from Brother Elias, Sinner.

"I sigh before I utter word, and what wonder is it? As rushing flood is the noise of my weeping. For the thing I feared has come to pass, for me, and for you, and what I apprehended is with me, is with you. Far from us has gone the consoler, and he who carried us like lambs in his arms has set forth a pilgrim into a far country. The beloved of God and men, he who taught the law of life and discipline to Jacob and gave the testament of peace to Israel, has entered the mansions of exceeding light. Greatly should we joy for him, but grieve for ourselves : now he is away the darkness surrounds us, and the shadow of death covers us. A calamity to all, but a singular danger to me whom he has left in the very midst of night, beset by many occupations and oppressed by innumerable troubles. . . .

"Before he was taken from us he blessed all his sons, and forgave all faults of word and thought which were committed or conceived against him by any of us. . . ."

Then follow an account of the stigmata, a description of the fair appearance of the body, and yet further reasons for the grief of the brothers in their great loss and for joy in their beloved master's release, with hopes that God may raise a new leader, "a new Maccabæus going before us to battle." He ends thus : "And because it is not superfluous to pray for the dead, for his soul pray to God. Let the priest say three masses, the laics five paternosters, and let the clerks say vigil solemnly in common. Amen. BROTHER ELIAS, Sinner."

It is a rhetorical letter, not quite spontaneous in style, but there is heart in it. And well might he say, *Commune damnun, sed meum singulare periculum.*

In Elias's mind there can have been no doubt at all that he was in fact the head of the Order, though till the Chapter met he was not so in name. He took all responsibility, and did not spare himself. Every one in the farthest provinces felt his hand. He appointed ; he displaced. It was of Elias the seven gallant missionaries asked leave to set out for the death they met in Morocco. And one great plan formed in his mind, he lost not a minute in giving shape to.

Was Francis canonised less than two years after his death because the world and the Church could not ignore the radiance of his sainthood ? We would fain hope so —and, indeed, he was well loved. Yet I fear the reason of the promptness was that Ugolino, in March 1227, was Pope Gregory IX., and Elias took the matter in hand while he was ruling the Order. Francis had served the brotherhood living. Elias would see that he served it dead. With him there was no delay. Did the Congregation of Rites, or whatever answered to it in those days, want proof of saintliness ?—well, they should have it, prompt, and full, and authenticated in the most business-like way; and the Pope should come to the ceremony. If the friends of Elias had called him the St. Paul of Francis, for his vigorous publication of his name and deeds, Elias might hardly have been satisfied, even while modestly disclaiming the title. For it must have seemed a strange negligence on the part of the first friends of the Founder of Christianity that they did not immediately erect a great mausoleum or temple in Bethlehem or Nazareth, or in some more conspicuous spot. They were wanting in initiative, in the " push," which their position demanded. Early Christianity would have had a different history if they had only overawed the Jews and Pilate by some impressive step of that kind. But it was when his design of building a great convent and a basilica, to contain the remains of the *Poverello*, was published to the Brothers that he first realised the forces against him, forces represented by the most annoyingly insignificant people. Leo, a little priest, who had acted as secretary to Francis—not even in the large administration of the Order, but only for his private correspondence and for the transcription of mere devotional writings—a man whom

Rome was not aware of, with others of his quality, dared to criticise the natural, laudable, necessary work of raising such a temple as should be a sign to the world of their glory. Francis loved not great houses for the brothers, and did not wish to rival the clergy in magnificent temples or rites. But Francis was dead; and how were you going to keep his memory alive? *Fami un castello, che no abbia pietra e ferro. O bel fratello, fami una cittade che no abbia pietra e legname*, said Giles. But Elias waved off the notion of a church not made with hands, and relied on stone and lime. It was to be a great monument. The project grew as he dreamed of it. Near the great temple there must be no sordid little hovels like the Carceri, but a house worthy of the keepers of such a treasure. Money would be forthcoming: Gregory saw that authority was given him to receive money. Elias collected throughout Christendom, and for stray local offerings placed a marble pot conspicuously on the site proposed—the Hill of Hell. We know the rest of the story. Leo, as a protest against the change in the spirit and the practice of the Order, smashed the pot. When Elias struck, he struck hard. Leo was scourged and expelled from Assisi. I need not repeat what I have told elsewhere. Leo employed his exile in rallying the *zelanti*, in calling the faithful round the banner of Francis, and, probably by the manifesto of the *Speculum Perfectionis*, or some part of it, defeated the plans of Elias at the Chapter of May, 1227, when John Parenti was elected Minister General.

It must have seemed as extraordinary to Gregory as to Elias that, at a moment which demanded so much activity, the brothers should have chosen for their head a mere saintly personage. But it was not his policy to overturn the decision of a democratic assembly, though he might insinuate guidance. And Elias could ignore the decision for the time. He had not lacked power when a greater saint than John Parenti was at the head of affairs. In the great work of his life—the work that has lasted to this day—he and Gregory were close collaborators. There is a tradition that before Francis died he said, " Let me be buried on the Colle dell' Inferno," an unconsecrated place outside the town, where the bodies of criminals were laid. In his death he was fain to lie with his friends, the forsaken and the outlawed. Elias negotiated with the owner of part of the hill, one Simone Puzzarelli. " What honour for you, if you were to give up your land for the burial-place of a saint!" And Simone handed it over by a gift to Elias, March 29th, 1228. But long before that the matter had been virtually arranged, and much money collected. The grass did not grow under Elias's feet. Gregory made him Master of the Works, with full authority, which the brothers in distant provinces must have confused with that of the Minister General. John Parenti, down at the Porziuncola, had nothing to do with the affair at all, and was probably quite incapable of undertaking anything of the kind, even had he wished to. Elias, the exploiter of genius, was more than exploiter here, I believe. In his wanderings he may well have been aware of the awakenings of art. The movement he had joined was itself cause of, and co-operated in that liberating spirit which was to find its fairest manifestation in the fashioning of beautiful forms learnt from a new close reading of nature. Giunta Pisano was among his friends, and was employed early in the decoration of the Basilica. I cannot agree with Dr. Lempp that Elias was probably the architect himself. If he had been so, assuredly we should have heard the fact. If we must dismiss Jacopo Alamanni as a phantom of Vasari's brain, there is still Philip of Campello, about whom to hang some credit for the great plan. But probably the site was of Elias's choosing—for he could have easily cast aside that wish of Francis, to be buried among the outcasts, if it had been inconvenient. His artist's eye saw how a fair building to the saint's honour could command the plain, and throw a blessing through the valley

L

as once his presence had done; how the monument might grow out of the height, and give such form to it that men's eyes must turn to the hills and linger there. His later refuge in Cortona was chosen probably rather for its commanding site than because in that hill-city he first put on the habit of the Brothers Minor. But it was the opportunity of a lifetime to be architect under such a patron. Men hurried under his orders. The fabric rose as if by magic. When Gregory came in July, 1228, for the canonisation in San Giorgio, the work was going on apace. The speed was the speed of jerry-building for the two churches, the convent, and the palace which the Pope ordered for himself alongside the house of the brothers; and the result—the first flower and the fairest of Italian Gothic, a marvel of imagination in stone, a joy to all the ages ever since. Too great and splendid for the *Poverello* —whose resting-place should have been the edge of some wood where birds sing, and by a road along which pace the feet of the common men and women whom he loved —but very great. The poet in us is with Leo and with Giles; but the artist is aglow with gratitude to Frate Elias, Master of the Works.

While wandering brothers, pilgrims, and travellers were spreading the fame of the building, Elias could surely count on being one of the best-known men in Europe. But he was ever thorough, whether in directing architects and masons or in constructing his own fame. Thomas of Celano, a brother of high reputation for excellent life and for usefulness in various offices in the Order, a man of learning, too, received from Gregory IX. the command, or, at least, the encouragement to write the Life of the Founder. He brought many fine qualities to the work. He had seen something of Francis, and had loved him; but it is very doubtful if he knew anything of the first companions, save distantly. His neglect of their evidence and their personalities is probably due, not to design, but to ignorance. When you want information go to headquarters, is a rule of common sense that has sent many besides him astray. Headquarters meant, surely, the place where the Vicar of Francis was to be found, and not some hermitage or lazar-house, where a shabby brother might harangue you on the ruin of the Order. Elias was most serviceable, and Thomas was much impressed with his power. That man will make the Order go far, he thought; and he sang his praises loud in his book, the First Life of Francis, which received the approval of Gregory in February, 1229. It is counted a little masterpiece of biography even to this day, partly from its own intrinsic qualities, its whole-hearted enthusiasm for its hero, and its literary style—for Thomas of Celano, the reputed author of the *Dies Irae*, was a born man of letters. But circumstances have also greatly helped its survival and its fame. The approval of the Curia gave it a wide circulation. His Second Life—written some twenty years later, when Elias was in disgrace—which contradicted the first in many essentials, was never given the same vogue. Then came Bonaventura's sweeping edict of 1266, which ordered the destruction of all previous legends, now his definitive one had been published, an edict that more effectually caused the disappearance of the Second Life of Celano than of the First. The Bollandists included the first in the *Acta Sanctorum*, but not the second; and thus the version of 1229, which was almost officially retracted, remained for centuries the standard authority among first-hand works, not only for the life of Francis but for Elias too.

In the meanwhile the book was of infinite service to him who might be called its minor hero. He was growing tired of being so great a man without the due title. An opportunity soon occurred for pushing things on. Let me confess at once there are endless difficulties in threading one's way through the various contradictory accounts of the curious event that followed. Affò, the learned biographer of Elias in the eighteenth century, and,

Observant though he was, his eulogist for all the earlier part of his career, strives to explain matters and only talks foolishness. There was now question of the translation of the body of Francis from San Giorgio to the new church outside the town. So great an event must take place under the auspices of a Chapter General. John Parenti called the Chapter for the Day of Pentecost, 1230. On Elias, as the Master of the Works, fell naturally the burden of the arrangements for the transport and the new sepulchre. But it was time, he thought, and so did his friends, to do more than that. While he was not Minister-General he was hampered in his schemes. He knew his friends, and he sent for them to come to Assisi that he might have a clear majority. True, it was only ministers and *custodi* that had the right of voting for the Minister-General, but Elias had no pedantic adherence to any particular form of government. By his acts you can prove him democrat, revolutionary, or despot. Circumstances directed his opinions in this matter as they do those of every born politician. And, doubtless, he hoped to carry his election by a show of bluster, which might very well have been called, if successful, "a manifestation of popular opinion." John Parenti was neither weak nor meek on the occasion, and seems to have been on the alert respecting the part of Elias's plot that concerned himself. Why did not Gregory come to the Chapter which had to deal with so important a matter as the translation of the saint to whom he was so devoted ? Gregory was a prudent man. Perhaps rumours reached him of a sharp division. Perhaps Elias's attitude struck him as a little haughty. It would be difficult either to approve or to condemn his friend. He sent ambassadors and gifts instead.

But Elias's men were in the city. They could not proclaim him Minister General while John Parenti was gathering the regular assembly. But they could meet and grumble about the stupidity that hindered the election of the man of power. Elias did not grumble; he acted. The translation of the body had been fixed for May 25. The brothers gathering down at the Porziuncola were looking forward to the ceremony as something very sacred, something that should bring great good to them. Three days before, according to Eccleston, Elias called in the help of the secular powers of Assisi—the magistrates were naturally the friends of the man who had built the great church and brought fame and many people to the city—and by night the translation was carried out, so secretly that only Elias and a few others knew the chosen burial-place below the Lower Church.

What was the reason of the *coup* ? Affò, determined to justify Elias at all hazards, suggests that he hurried the affair lest the probable corruption of the body should shock the brothers or disturb the faith of simple folks. This is ingenious but quite improbable; for who so clever as Elias at arranging a *mise en scène* that should conceal the fact ? Then he makes another suggestion, and this view of the case has been taken by many, the most critical of all the biographers of Elias, Dr. Lempp, giving his support to it. The body might be stolen on its way to San Francesco by the Perugians or by the citizens of some other city greedy of relics. To the examples usually quoted in favour of such a theory more might be added. Not only was the body of Conrad d'Offida actually stolen from Bastia; not only did the Perugians diligently guard the place where lay the dying Giles, lest an enemy should take away their treasure, but Alexander IV. ordered special precautions to be taken concerning the body of Saint Rose of Viterbo. The suggestion is very plausible, and certainly the danger of the precious body being stolen would have made a very efficacious appeal to the Podestà to help in the translation by night. But there are too many difficulties in the way of accepting this theory. The ceremony of the translation could not have been arranged in defiance of Elias's wishes, since he was absolute master over the new place of sepulchre. Not only must he have been agreed, but it is almost certain the suggestion of a great ceremony came from him. John Parenti was not strong at organising things of the kind. Had Elias anticipated in a general way any danger, he had only to appeal to Gregory, with whom he was hand in glove, who would have backed him up. But Gregory, though he did not actually denounce him by name for what followed, fulminated against the laymen who assisted him. Were there sudden rumours of a plot? We do not hear of such; and if it had been so, John Parenti would have collaborated heartily in the precautions. As a matter of fact, there was no real danger in the actual translation of the body from one church to the other. Would the assembled *frati*, who were there in crowds, have let the precious body of their beloved Founder be stolen? Each peaceful brother would have been a lion in its defence. They were unarmed, it may be said. But the citizens of Assisi were not, and they had as keen a sense as the Perugians, or any others, of the commercial value of a saint's relics. The real danger, if any, would have been before or after the translation. But Francis had lain two years in San Giorgio undisturbed. And if great secrecy were needed as to the place of the new tomb in the Basilica, the crowds, even the *frati*, might have been dispersed, after an imposing ceremony, before the actual entombment. Or the place of sepulchre might have been subsequently and secretly changed, for, as I have said, Elias was sole master in San Francesco. Again, even if one were to admit the necessity of the secret burial, why were not John Parenti and some of the assembled ministers invited to take part in the midnight ceremony? Finally, is there any actual proof that the burial-place was unknown in the first years after the translation, though later ages lost the key to the spot, discovered only in our own.

A few years ago, when the high altar of the Upper Church of Assisi was being restored, there was found the wax imprint of a seal which has been declared, with some probability, to be that used by Elias during his administration of the great building scheme. Its date has been placed by authorities after 1228, the year of the canonisation, and before 1253, when the altar was consecrated. A drawing of it may be seen in an article in the *Miscellanea Francescana*, vol. vii. p. 143. Round the edge of the seal are the words, "S. Administration. Scti. Francisci." Curious observers will be struck by the fact that the design is architectural; that it seems to represent a building of three tiers or storeys; that in the lowest, immediately beneath arches that may signify the high altars in the two upper churches, is a partition—which might represent a chapel in a crypt—where reclines a single figure. Was the design meant to indicate the actual plan of the building and to be a key to the place of the saint's tomb? Or was there no secret at all in the first days?

No, the view of Eccleston and the older chroniclers generally is the only tenable one. The secret burial was a blow in the face to the Minister General and his supporters, who, according to Elias, had done nothing for the honour of Francis, and who now were taking for granted they were going to assist as principals at the ceremony. The *fautores* of Elias had not found places in the constitutional Chapter, but he and they were masters of the sacred body. The *éclat* of the Chapter General was gone. But, on the other hand, the wrath of the brothers at being tricked was terrible. The Pope was appealed to against Elias and the Podestà for their profanation. And, doubtless, Gregory was seriously shocked. He fulminated against the Podestà, and threatened excommunication unless penitence were immediate and abject. But though he did not mention Elias, hoping, perhaps, to avoid a scandal about the name of his favourite, curiously enough, the actual punishment for the affair—the interdict on the new church and convent—touched Elias and his friends much more than the secular powers who were blamed. Yet, for a moment at least, Elias had felt himself master of the situation. While the regular Chapter General was sitting, his friends stormed the doors, carried him shoulder high, and put him in the seat of the Minister General. It was a bold stroke—Cromwellianly dramatic. Had it been successful, it would have been praised as the only method of inaugurating an energetic *régime*. But the *frati* of the regular assembly were too many, and in too stern a temper. They rose in a body, and Elias and his friends were turned out. Poor Elias! He had planned a great *coup d'état*, and it had been a miserable and rather sordid failure. His reputable adherents turned up their eyes. This was hardly the conduct of a son of Francis.

Elias, it is said, now retired to a hermitage, full of vexation. Had he not worked night and day for the spread of the Order, and yet he was hindered at every step by saintly fools, who only said their prayers and gave potions to the sick? He let his beard grow, and put on the vilest habit; and, doubtless, he edified many, who said, "Poor Frate Elias, see how he repents." Perhaps he was half posing, half sulking. He was quite clever enough to exploit his own misfortunes, and, in his retirement, his friends grew. Gregory missed him, and Elias explained things. The Pentecost Chapter had been not only a sensational, but a very important one, raising, decisively, some vital questions concerning the observance of the Rule and the Testament, particularly regarding the acceptance of money and property. Delegates had been sent from it to the Pope. Before he gave his answer, at the end of September, he had had ample time to hear from Elias, or his representatives, on the subject. Had Elias framed the Bull *Quo elongati*, which was Gregory's answer to the questions raised at the Chapter, he could not have made a better reflection of his own policy than is to be found in this decree, which speaks so fairly of the memory of Francis, puts his Testament aside as not binding on the brothers, and gets over the inconvenience of not being able to receive money by a pious trickery. The hand that signed the decree is the hand of Gregory, but the voice is the voice of Elias. In his exile he saw the road clearer than ever, and the *zelanti* defeated all along the line. Perhaps his retirement did not last longer than the promulgation of the *Quo elongati*, September 28, 1230, which proclaimed the triumph of his general policy.

After all, John Parenti was no very strong rival. A good man, of beautiful nature, and, if we were to accept the view of Perè d'Alençon concerning the authorship of the *Sacrum Commercium*, of a charming fancy; but, perhaps, lacking the strong personality that would make his views growingly accepted. A little time and absence did for Elias what violence had failed to do. John Parenti had some prudence as well as saintliness, for he did not call a Chapter General for two years. When he held it, the partisans of Elias were in the ascendant. His *fautores* are said to have been there again ; and the election was afterwards declared to have been irregular. It is more likely that this time his *fautores* were in the shape of the ministers and *custodi*, with an unquestionable right to vote. The Bull *Quo elongati* had had its degenerating effect. John Parenti apparently saw in the new temper the uselessness of struggle. As a true Franciscan, he was a non-resistant. If they did not want him more, he was unworthy, and God would take care of the flock. Meekly he resigned, went out of the Chapter, and Elias was elected—as an old chronicler says, *magis tumultuose quam canonice*. It would appear that he played not the humble suppliant for their suffrages, but made conditions, said he was a man of delicate physique, that hardship would kill him. He pleaded, afterwards, that the Chapter had given him leave to take ample care of his valuable person.

The Order knew the difference of his rule at once.

It had been discovered to him that the cleft in the Order was serious, that he had irreconcilable enemies. Let them be irreconcilable; but let them, at their peril, hinder his work—which was to make the Minorite body a power, visible to potentates, clergy, and people in every land. Was he not acting in unison with Gregory, who had been the Cardinal Ugolino, the friend of Francis, and had so loved him that one day, up at the Carceri, he was nearly persuaded to leave pomp and government and Rome behind, and put on the habit of the Brothers Minor? And so, openly, Elias took his stand against the *zelanti*. One good show of strength and they would be silenced. He placed the difficulty before Gregory. "There are certain brothers," he said, "who are held in reverence by the people and by the rest of the Order, because they say they were with Francis in the first days. Their conversation is specious, but their conduct is a scandal. They are rebels. They go apart, and obey no appointed governor. Our constitution is too loose. Give me authority to curb them." And Gregory gave him leave to correct them according to the spirit and the prudence vouchsafed him. Elias's discipline was thorough. He scattered the offenders into remote provinces. For the recalcitrant there was prison; and he was not acting against the spirit of the times and the customs of religious orders in having recourse to the scourge. He was only acting in direct opposition to the commands of Francis. His chief executioner was John de Laudibus, a man whom Salimbene describes as *durus et acer et tortor et pessimus carnifex; dabat enim fratribus disciplinas sine misericordia ex praecepto Helyae.* It seems not unlikely he struck hard, for, according to the evidence of Francis himself—John was the traitor of the little band of the Companions—he was *fortis corpore super omnes homines.* Things turned out unfortunately sometimes, when Elias only meant to subject obstinate brothers to wholesome discipline. His own greatest convert had been Caesar of Spires, who had

proved an ornament to the Order, and had done wonders
in the evangelisation of Germany. He was now one of
Elias's most strenuous opponents. Elias imprisoned him,
and, by a misfortune, the brother deputed to guard him
—perhaps John de Laudibus—was a man of excitable
temperament. The door of the prison was left open one
day by mistake, and Fra Cesare stepped out to breathe the
air. The jailer, thinking he was meditating flight, struck
him, and he died. The occurrence caused no end of
annoyance to Elias. There are so many inquiries made
when you happen to kill a saint, even unintentionally.
But he did not take up an apologetic attitude. Some
days after, friends of Caesar's making themselves un-
pleasant, were scourged and chased out of the Order.
Then there was the case of the venerable Bernard of
Quintavalle; and there was much talk of Brother Andrew
of Spello, too, who died in prison. Terror was a swift
weapon, and he used it. His haughtiness was quite of
another kind from the *Poverello's*, who said his office was
spiritual, and who refused to be his brothers' executioner.

If Elias had not been pressed hard by other matters
he would have perhaps weathered this storm. But you
cannot build two great churches and an immense convent
without money. With his fiery impatience to realise
the mighty monument without delay, he clamoured for
money. The brothers must find it. His visitors went
through the whole Order. So much had to be collected
here, so much there. And they did their work like the
servants of a business-like man. Before his time visitors
had been appointed for keeping the remote convents in
touch with the centre; Francis and John Parenti had, to
a great extent, been their own visitors. Later, John of
Parma was to perform great feats of energy and devotion
in this office. But Elias increased the number, and used
them for his own ends. Elias never visited. Doubtless
he found himself in the fewer embarrassing situations.
He had picked men, wholly dependent on him. They

had full instructions and, subject to him, almost un-
limited powers. They could go where they liked, stay
as long as they liked, and answers had to be given to all
their questions. They were in constant communication
with the Minister-General. The continuance of the
custodi in their offices was made largely dependent on
their reports. They had eyes for little things and great,
and were most effective beggars. But these excellent
and devoted officers were called extortioners and spies.
Gradually they grew less prudent, and so did Elias, for
his needs were, no doubt, often desperate. Besides,
though he was wily, Elias was not by nature prudent.
Despots are not commonly prudent, but they are often
successful, and Elias was very nearly so.

There can be no doubt that he had some idea in his
head of forming the Order, and specially the head-
quarters of the Order, on the dignified Benedictine
model. He took the accustomed means of striking the
imagination of the world. Nor was he wanting in a
sense of responsibility. He encouraged learning sub-
stantially in all the provinces. Chairs of theology were
established, and he was known far and near as a patron
of learning. In fact, there was nothing he did not do to
take away the reproach from the Minorites of being a
band of poor ignorant men, careless of dignity. Patron
of art, he did more than prepare an exquisite shell for
the later pictures of Cimabue and Giotto. He invited
the great innovator of the time, Giunta Pisano, to stay
at Assisi to help in the decoration of the Basilica, and to
paint the portrait of Francis. He himself sat to Giunta
in 1236. The crucifix on which his own portrait was
painted disappeared in the seventeenth century after a
restoration of the upper church. It bore the inscription,
*Frater Helias fieri fecit Jesu Christe pie miserere precantis
Heliae. Junta Pisanus me pinxit. Anno Domini, 1236.*
From this authentic portrait may have been copied the
one that exists at Cortona in the possession of Count

Venuti and that in the *municipio* of Assisi. Elias is
represented as a small, slight man with a melancholy
face, a trim beard, and an Armenian cap.

But you cannot play the rich abbot, with power over
the life and death of your brothers and to exact money
for your great schemes, and exercise the discipline of a
general in time of war, and be a Brother Minor too.
His election as Minister-General had liberated him not
only to be the energetic leader of the Order, but to be
himself. Remember, Elias was not as Angelo Tancredi,
or Rufino, or Illuminato, nobles nursed in luxury, or like
Bernard, a rich man who had experienced all the comforts
and the pomps of life and found them wanting. He was
a very poor man's son, had striven with poverty all his
ambitious youth, and in his early manhood had been over-
powered by the personality of one who led him against
his nature into austere ways. Elias was neither a saint
nor a poet, nor did he even partake of the nature of
these. He could not find his life in singing and praying, nor in contemplation, nor in sacrificing himself.
The joy the chosen got from living in the great air and
in converse with nature did not exist for him. He
found his joy elsewhere. In his view, Rufino and
Angelo may only have been *blasés* with the good things
of life, and many of the others too stupid to have appe-
tites. But only of late years had Elias learned these
delights from the great ones with whom his office made
him consort. He was not at all tired of lying soft, and
eating fine meats, and giving an elegant turn to his
Minorite tunic. He was, or stated himself to be, of
delicate health, and he could not endanger his work by
rough usage to his body. Francis? But he did not claim
to be Francis. And for the others—you might defy the
body and still be good enough for nursing and begging,
but for administration, that was another thing. His
place at Cortona grew into something very fine. His
palfreys were famed ; his liveries were of the gayest ; he

never walked on foot; and the Cortonese were favour-
ably impressed.

Bernard of Quintavalle, the spirited old man, who was
yet to suffer for his frank opposition, was, as we have
already seen, a source of real discomfort to Elias. He
made fun of his state when he rode abroad, and the sting
of it was perhaps that Bernard had known him in his
miserable youth. It was the Minister-General's habit to
dine alone—a most ungenial habit, says Salimbene, for

> Nullius sine sotio
> Jucunda fit possessio.

His health demanded carefully-cooked food, and his
palate was delicate. His *chef* was famous, one Bartholomew of Padua. But he had no defence against the
audacious geniality of Bernard, who would enter the
private refectory, and announce his cheerful design of
sharing the good things the Lord had sent. There
were terrible inconveniences in the democratic spirit of
the Order and the communistic habits of the brothers.
Well, he did his best to change all that. The common
life was impossible to him, and he refused to live it;
and to save himself from being pestered and criticised
by ignorant ministers and *custodi* with alarming notions
of their right of free speech, he called no Chapters
General. But if he desired to live without criticism,
he did not live in idleness. We trace his hand everywhere, in little things as in great, organising missions to the heathen in the East, building the great
Basilica, and ordering certain rebellious and fastidious
brothers in England to wash their own breeches. The
English brothers meekly obeyed. The Scots refused.
Poor Elias, that such little details should be recorded
of him while he was playing a part in *la haute politique*!
As early as 1236 he seems to have been on terms of
prudent friendship with the great Emperor Frederic II.
As yet there was no intimacy, of course, else Gregory

would have known the reason why. Elias had a mind
eminently capable of comprehending both the policy and
the temper of that interesting monarch. It is possible he
may have applied to him for funds for the Basilica. He
had certainly occupied himself deeply with the differences
between the Church and the Empire, when he was sent
by Gregory IX. as ambassador to Frederic in 1238. The
Emperor's wrath had been fiercely roused against certain
Lombard cities. Could he not be appeased ? Elias consented to try. On his way to Cremona, where Frederic
was, he put up at the Convent of the *Frati Minori* at
Parma. He came there not as a mere wandering brother,
but as an ambassador of state, and he behaved as, in his
opinion, such an one should behave. Fra Salimbene, a
novice in the convent, was present when the Minister
General was received.

The Podestà of Parma at that time was Gherardo da
Correggio—called Gherardo dai Denti, because he had
big teeth ; and he came in person to the convent, with
his knights in attendance, to do honour to Brother Elias
the Minister-General, who had an apartment in that part
of the convent where is the refectory of the guests and
strangers. He found him seated near a great fire, on a
seat covered with a down cushion. On his head he wore
an Armenian cap. "And, as I saw with my eyes," says
Salimbene, "when the Podestà entered and saluted him,
he did not rise to his feet, nor move at all, which was
looked on as gross rudeness, since God Himself says in
Holy Scripture, Lev. xix. 32—" His mission at Cremona
did not succeed, but he seems to have made a good impression on Frederic, towards whom he conducted himself otherwise than to mere Podestàs. It must have been
refreshing to the Emperor to find some kind of intellectual understanding of his position in an envoy of the
Pope, who was likewise, by a strange chance, the Head
of that vexatious body, the Franciscans.

Elias's despotic plan was too wily to be all of one

piece. There is that contradictoriness about it that marks the man of policy. His multiplication of provinces looks like a democratic and decentralising measure. But its chief end was the increase of officials dependent on him. We have seen him play the patron of learning. No doubt some of the *zelanti* shook their heads over this; for Francis, with his deep sense of the futility of scholasticism, had discouraged the only learning known to him. The power of the professor grew tremendously in the first years of Elias's rule. But he was a layman himself, and probably quite ignorant of scholastic theology, in spite of his reputation. Indeed, the only science he seems to have devoted himself to in his mature years, was alchemy—though the books on the subject attributed to him are perhaps by another brother of his name. He soon found the learned theologians difficult to deal with, much set on their opinions, inclined to argument, and some of them, at least, too dominant morally and intellectually for his convenience. He saw his mistake, and he promptly rectified it. Let us return, he said, to the early simplicity. Away with intellectual pride! —did not our Father Francis warn us of the danger?— and welcome to our fold the simple and unlearned. The first signs of the new policy may have warmed the hearts of a few credulous ones. Only, Elias in his new patronage of the unlearned, sought not after saintliness but ignorance. His favour fell not on Junipers, but on such as were stupid enough to be bamboozled, or unscrupulous enough to be his creatures. Salimbene gives a lively account of Elias's laymen, who couldn't read, who had a fantastic taste in dress, and who ogled ladies out of the convent windows. Perhaps—nay, it is certain—some of them were much abler than the malicious chronicler would have us think. But their preponderance roused the wrath of the clerical brothers, the attack on whose dignity counted for a good deal in Elias's overthrow, and prepared a reaction after his fall.

A storm was muttering round Elias. Salimbene's nine counts against him contain much that is frivolous; but he had certainly roused opposition in widely different quarters. The exactions grew every day more unbearable. He wanted money for the church, and he wanted it for himself; for you cannot live like a great abbot, or on equal terms with great princes, without funds. Bernard of Quintavalle, Caesar of Spires, Angelo, Masseo, Simone dalla Contessa, and others had long protested in vain. The protests now became constant. We have a curious account of that of the Saxon brothers in 1238. First, they sent messengers; but the Minister-General ignored them. Then they went to the Pope, and by some means were admitted to his presence, where they comported themselves like the children of nature that they were. Elias did not like children of nature; but perhaps Gregory was more amused than annoyed at their behaviour. He was in bed, and when they had saluted him and received his blessing, he signified his wish that they should retire. But Brother Jordan, who was at their head, was so delighted to be in the presence of the Pope, that he was unwilling to cut the pleasure short. From the door he ran back again to Gregory's bed, and drawing out his bare foot from the bedclothes, and kissing it fervently, said to the brothers, "See! in Saxony we have not such relics." Gregory demurred to their demonstrativeness, and requested them to say what they wanted and to go. Jordan cheerfully replied for himself and the rest, "My lord, we have nothing to ask of you, for we have abundance of all good things, and we live in splendid fashion. But you are the Father, the Protector, and the Corrector of our Order, and we have come to see you."

After all, their naïve delight was something rare for Gregory. Raising himself on the bed, he said, "Come now, I know you want something. Out with it. You are here for an appeal. Frate Elias has been here before

you, saying you have been to him. I have said that
appeals made to me absorb all others." Then Jordan
laid bare the cause of their complaint.

They had not been the first to come. Gregory heard
the storm muttering round his protégé, and he would
fain have lulled it. But it was stronger than he. Rome
was full of Minorite complaints, and the protestors were
very eminent men. The great Alexander Hales was
among them. There was John of Rochelle, and, most
active of all, Aymon of Faversham. Elias represented
them as busybodies, and tried to prevent their getting
near the presence of the Pope. But they had a friend
at the Curia, an Englishman, penitentiary to Gregory,
who assured their reception there. First, a committee of
investigation was held, then a Chapter General, in Rome
at Pentecost, 1239. Elias came unbending, quite sure
of himself. Gregory wore a sad air. He was vexed his
friend should have got himself into such a scrape ; but
as Protector of the Order he could not see it defied
openly when his attention was called to the matter.
He spoke at length to the brothers of the gravity of
the occasion, and referred to Daniel's vision of the
golden image with the feet of clay. The brothers must
beware of corruption entering into the Order, said the
man who had deliberately set aside the Testament of
Francis, and just as if he had discovered five minutes
before that a breach of the Rule was possible. He was
feeling painfully for a loophole of escape for Elias.
The most articulate accuser was Aymon of Faversham.
Elias loudly protested in answer against their injustice.
He never wished to be Minister-General. Did they
think it an enviable position ? They had forced him
into it. From a sense of duty he had accepted. It
had been fully agreed he could not live the common
life of the brothers. He was a delicate man, and to
serve them he must live in decent comfort, and his
health did not permit of his taking journeys on foot.

And about the Rule—well, he had entered the Order in the early days when there was talk of a Rule indeed, enjoining poverty. But that Rule had never received the Pope's formal approval. To a *regula non bullata* no one was bound, save as his conscience dictated. This was contemptible, it may be said: it was the desperate weapon of a debater. Elias was at bay. Really, he went on, their accusations were absurd. What frivolity to call a Chapter General for them! About the money; well, had they seen the church and the convent on the side of the hill at Assisi to the memory of their beloved Founder? Did they think that could be raised without money? Here Aymon rose to answer. But Gregory thought Elias was getting on very nicely. And, *Dio mio*, these terribly severe persons might take it into their heads to level such attacks against the Curia next. He waved Aymon down. But a Cardinal and compatriot —Elias had nothing to hope from the English brothers— Robert of Sumercote, said "Hear him. He is a good man, and not tedious."

Elias sat cool, unwavering, perfectly confident, disdainful, listening to Aymon, who spoke at first timidly, but gradually waxed bolder. For want of physical strength the Rule makes provision, he said, but if a Brother Minor must ride, he had best have not so fine a stable, nor be so nice in the trappings of his horses, nor in the livery of his lackeys. He had built the church. The brothers had begged money for the purpose, but not that he might heap up treasure. Then Elias's temper rose, and he shouted in the teeth of Aymon, "You lie!" And his men shouted too, and there was a great tumult. This threatened the dignity of the assembly, and showed a want of respect to the Pontiff's person. Gregory silenced him. In this fashion is no religious assembly carried on. Would it not be better for the Minister-General to put himself in the hands of the Head of the Church? But Elias, defiant and standing on his rights, said he would not. This was more than Gregory could suffer. He told the assembly how he had chosen him—the word is significant and may refer either to his election as Vicar of Francis, or as Minister-General, or to both — because of his intimacy with their Father Francis, and because it had seemed to him that a man of such power would please them all. It had not pleased them. There was nothing to be done, therefore, but to declare that the headship of the Order was vacant. Then there was such an immense joy felt, said those who were there, as they had never felt before. They proceeded to the election of Albert of Pisa.

Elias set off in bitter disdain to Cortona. Had he been submissive he would have waited for the commands of Albert and Gregory. He waited for neither. At first he seems to have taken refuge in a house of the Poor Clares. Albert ordered him to come before him for absolution, even offered to meet him half-way. But Elias ignored the command. After all, his place at Cortona was more his than any one else's. He had friends among the Cortonese who admired him. There were a good many Ghibellines in the city. Elias entered into relations with Frederic, who welcomed any man of ability, and regarded so great a man from the Guelf side as a prize. The Emperor, who had just been excommunicated, would talk Gregory over with the ex-Minister-General, and they would be wonderfully in agreement. Really, Elias thought, there is an enormous amount of prejudice among the Guelfs. This is the most enlightened of rulers. Ah, if he had only had his eyes open in time, Sicily, not Assisi, would have been the field of his labours. Meanwhile Gregory, wroth at seeing in Elias no penitent but a disdainful rebel—for in 1240 he was with Frederic's army while it was besieging the cities of Faenza and Ravenna—excommunicated him.

At first, when he had no settled position near the person of the Emperor, Elias had his moments of doubt and bitter regret. He would have liked to have talked over Gregory as he had done before now. And, indeed, he did state his case in a letter, which he sent to Albert of Pisa, requesting him to hand it on to the Pope. The letter was found in the pocket of Albert's tunic after his death.

When not employed by Frederic, he made his home at Cortona, and he still had brothers attached to him. In his outlawry he might live as he liked. The arm of the Church could hardly touch him protected by the Emperor, and probably by the Cortonese. But at Frederic's court do not imagine him in secular dress like any other courtier. Elias testified to the power of the Order he had defied by clinging to the grey tunic. There was sentiment in this, and there was hope in it, too, the ambitious hope of doing something towards the reconcilement of the Church and the Empire. And it struck the imagination to see a grey-frocked brother doing the Emperor's work, and gave him the distinction in Frederic's court, which as a new-comer he might otherwise have lacked. But if he treated the authorities in the Order with contempt, as an old political hand he did not disdain the opinions of the simple brothers. Between his services to his Imperial master he seems to have wandered among the convents, and on the strength of his garb he would enter them. Salimbene describes him as persuading a *custode* to call the brothers of a place to a chapter, where he declared his innocence, the injustice with which he had been treated, and grieved over the growing decay of the Order in the hands of incapable men. He may have roused considerable sympathy among the rank and file just when he was earning sterner condemnation from the authorities. Innocent IV.—Gregory had died in August 1241, and there had been since then the reign of Celestine IV. and an interregnum—summoned him to a Chapter General at Genoa in 1244, called to elect a successor to Aymon, who had succeeded Albert of Pisa in the Minister-Generalship. The tale that he went with a band of followers and ruffled it at the assembly, is quite improbable. He was not foolish enough to deliver himself into Innocent's hands, and perhaps suffer in an ecclesiastical prison. But present or absent he was to be punished. His refusal to obey the summons was held to be gross rebellion. Once more he was excommunicated, and this time expelled from the Order. It was a blow he could not scoff at. Half of his ambitious projects were defeated by so emphatic a sentence. He was driven now definitely into one camp.

And had he heard rumours of the fickleness of Frederic? Was he soon to see the blinded Pier delle Vigne, to know his history, and be impressed by the likeness in their fortunes? Both men of humble birth, who had risen by their talents to be the companions and counsellors of princes, their fall Elias would certainly have attributed to the same cause, the envy of weaker men. Did he hear some anticipatory whisper of the bitterness of fate from the man who, but a few years later, died by his own hand, the noble suicide of the *Inferno*?

> " Io son colui che tenni ambo le chiavi
> Del cor di Frederico, e che le volsi
> Serrando e desserando sì soavi,
> Che dal secreto suo quasi ogni uom tolsi ;
> Fede portai al glorioso offizio,
> Tanto ch'io ne perdei i sonni e i polsi."

But whatever sinister whispers visited him, in the meanwhile Frederic was his only hope, and should have all his brains. The Emperor valued the gift, and sent him on a difficult and important embassy. Baldwin II. had appealed to him in his straits, assailed beyond his force and endurance by the Greeks under John Vatatius. Elias's task was to treat between the two, and reconcile them if possible. He did his business with

ability. A peace of a year was concluded; and he
carried through another delicate affair as well, in arranging a marriage between Vatatius and a daughter of
Frederic. As Innocent held Vatatius to be the chief
stumbling-block to the union of the Eastern and Western
Churches, Elias could have been concerned in nothing
more offensive to Rome. But he was well rewarded
by his Imperial patrons. The business was to his mind.
His persuasive tongue and ready wit fitted him for the
task. The Emperors flattered him, and sent him back
laden with gifts. A few years later there went another
Minister-General to Greece on an embassy, who also
found open-handed potentates to flatter him. He came
home with a little riding-switch as sole trophy. But
Elias was a connoisseur. It would really have been
senseless to have had scruples about accepting a few
Eastern trifles. The Church of San Francesco in Cortona preserves to this day a precious reliquary of beautiful Oriental workmanship, containing a portion of the
Holy Cross, which tradition says was part of Elias's
spoil from his embassy. Nor was Frederic ungrateful.
His ambassador might ask what he liked, and he begged
favours for the town of his adoption. The Cortonese,
recognising in him a distinguished citizen, who having
the ear of the Emperor, might be useful to them in a
dangerous time, loaded him with privileges. In 1245,
they conceded to him a valuable piece of ground called
the Bagno della Regina, and helped him in the building
of a splendid new convent. As architect, courtier,
ambassador, Elias's life was now filled to his desire.
Nor did the Cortonese regard him as outside the Church.
In consideration of his wealth and dignity and suavity to
them, they held his convent to be as good as any other
convent, and his brothers quite as regular, though what
the community might be called it would have been
difficult to say. Elias still styled himself *frate*, but he
was also my Lord Elias.

The end of his luck and his hopes came in 1250, when the Emperor died. Serving the Ghibellines as Frederic's friend, yet as a friar, he was probably suspect of the party. At his age he could serve an apprenticeship to no new master. He was old—nearly seventy, if he was born in the same year as Francis—weak in health, estranged from his early friends, at the mercy of any harsh pope. He retired definitely to Cortona, but he knew his was no real convent. The brothers might melt away from him at any moment now the Imperial favour had gone. What he had shut his ears against, or smiled at disdainfully, hurt him now, the children singing along the roads—

> " Hor attorna frate Helya
> Ke pres ha la mala via."

What had all his talents brought him? They said his name was execrated in the convents among good men. Up in his fine house in Cortona, with memories of the favour of pope and cardinals and princes, he yet felt he had missed something. To what he had missed, doubtless, he gave a pious name. But what Bombarone of Beviglia had missed was really success.

In his old age he succumbed to the terrors of excommunication. He was less of a rebel by nature to ecclesiastical domination than was Jacopone da Todi, who yet sent appeal after appeal to the despised Pope Boniface to take away from him the terrible sentence and reproach. Elias would gladly before the last have begged for absolution. But he was old. He had always been physically timid, and he feared a prison. Albert, Aymon, and Crescentius had left him severely alone. When John of Parma came, the hope of the Spirituals, the strenuous opposer of every thought and project of Elias, he did not forget the exiled rebel up in Cortona. Fain would he have brought him back to the fold, shown him the mercy Francis counselled. Now Elias, though he would have unflinchingly scourged or imprisoned John, had he crossed his will in the days of his power, had a warm admiration for him in the days of his weakness. He was a man to demand excellence, whether in administration, or in architecture, or in saintliness. John Parenti, Bernard, Leo, Albert of Pisa, and the rest, had not struck his imagination. But John was a grand figure, and at his coming there was wafted even up to Cortona a breath of the memory of Francis. When, therefore, the great Minister-General sent Fra Gerardo da Modena to ask Elias to humble himself, to confess his fault, and be one of them again, he was deeply touched. "Gladly," he said, "would I submit to Brother John. But if I come down from here, I mistrust that the Pope will imprison me, and I dare not."

The joy and the interest of life all gone, Elias crept into a corner of his house at Cortona, sad and miserable. In the streets he had the comfortless respect of its citizens, but he was not one of them. There is something strangely fitting in the place of his exile. Cortona was the right tragic setting for the outlawed Elias as it was to be, a few years later, for the clamorous penitent Margaret. It sits there on its height, strong and isolated. Even to-day many of its children rarely touch the plain. There is something sinister in its pride of place—backed by the great hills, range on range. Its foot is on the mountain side; its towers are wooed by storms. Elias walks there still, looks from the walls, nursing his proud spirit with the loneliness. I remember a cowherd, just outside one of its gates, as a wild inarticulate creature of an earlier world. The great hills menace you; and the kindly plain, and placid Trasimene, and the road to Rome and pleasant Umbria, are far below.

Pacing to and fro on his rock, or cowering in his new convent, the Napoleon of the Minorites lived three years after Frederic died, three years with a vague record of lonely regret. But his last days are reported with a painful care of detail. When he was gone, they heard

at Rome he had been given absolution by the local
clergy; and Innocent IV. sent Fra Valsco to Cortona to
find out on what grounds this had been done, and if the
authority of the Church had been rightly upheld. Fra
Valsco held an inquisition on the subject, and cross-
questioned the witnesses of Elias's last days in strictly
legal fashion. The exact evidence has come down to
us. Bencio, archpresbyter of Cortona, was a friend of
Elias. Some four or five days before his death, he sent
for Bencio and asked for absolution. He had frequently
expressed a wish to go and beg it from the Pope. Now
he confessed, and received from Bencio a promise he
would take his confession to the Pope. The absolution
was given on Easter Eve. To hear him swear loyalty
to the Church, and to abide by the mandate of the Pope
respecting every charge upon which he had been excommunicated by Gregory and Innocent, witnesses had been
called—five priests, three notaries public, and some other
laymen. Two days later he had received the Eucharist
from Diotifece in the presence of Fra Mansueto, Frate
Angelo, and Boniche, a servant. The Lady Sibilla had
been present too. Save for this proof of her charity she
is unknown to history. Next day, April 23, 1253, he
died. Fra Valsco was a man of method. On the very
number of the sighs and the depths of the groans of
the dying man he sought exactest information. Was
his sadness an effect of bodily anguish, or the mark of
a sense of sin? Did he, indeed, lament? "Yea," they
said, "he beat his breast." "He beat his breast," said
the persevering investigator, "but did his tears flow?
Who heard these laments? In what words did he show
his sorrow?" And the half articulate cries of the soul
in pain were duly recorded—*Domine, parce mihi, peccatori,
vel adjuvame peccatorem.* His manner of saying the
Miserere was inquired into. Was it before or after
absolution that he seemed submissive to the Church?
Did he know what he was saying? Yea, for his mind

was clear till the very hour of his death. Then each witness was separately examined.

The Church's dignity was vindicated. And they buried him as a son of Francis, in the grey tunic, in the new church of his new convent. His followers having no standing without him, went back to the Order. In 1255, the place became the property of the *Frati Minori*, and so his own brothers became the guardians of his bones. But a *custode* in a later age, who hated his memory, flung them out. Later Conventual occupants of the place respected him to the extent of writing an inscription, where he appears as one of the noble family of the Coppi; and an insignificant eighteenth century Vicar-General of the Conventuals being buried near the spot where once his bones had lain, the inscription attributes to them both, with a benevolent intention towards Elias, *parem famam*.

Elias was a great man wasted—unless we regard with complacency his magnificent perversion of a spiritual brotherhood into a great engine for the Church. But it is little satisfaction now to call him the Judas of the Order. I doubt if he betrayed it as consciously as did Gregory, though he defied its spirit far more openly and consistently. On the other hand, it is useless to deny, as do some of his biographers, his highhandedness, his tyranny, his defects as a spiritual guide. These accusations are perfectly authenticated. Elias had a case, but that is not it. Judged by the standard of many leaders of religious orders in his age, he can only be held guilty of imprudence. Judged by a secular standard, he was perhaps considerably above the level of the public men of his day. He loved luxury, but though already some of the *Frati Minori* had incurred the charge of immorality, in the narrower sense, even his enemies did not attack Elias on that score. Perhaps no man of his age was less fitted to be a Brother Minor. The very quickness of his intellectual comprehension of

how great was the force Francis had breathed upon the
world, blinded him to the essential purpose of his master,
which was the conquest of the Kingdom of Heaven, the
bringing of that vast territory into a little man's soul.
Elias had nothing to do with the Kingdom of Heaven,
but was nearly concerned with those of this earth.
While he was a poor ambitious lad the world was open
to him. A high bidder for his talents would soon have
appeared. Francis smiled on him, blinded him. He
lost his way, and was committed to a life of hardship,
lightened for the elect by joys he was temperamentally de-
barred from sharing. Personal attachment, employment
of a stimulating kind, responsibility, success, kept him
from seeing for long how he had lost his own path.
When he made the discovery, he turned the resources of
that alien country in which he had condemned himself
to live to his own purposes. He made his world bigger,
stronger than he found it. He ruled it, played with it,
trampled it under his foot, and paid himself for his stern,
starveling youth. But the world that he used thus
happened to be dedicate to the service of the humble
and the outcast; and then likewise it had been nursed
in liberty. If it had partly forsaken, it had not forgotten
its birthright. Surely he could defy its first intention.
But no—the spirit of the *Poverello*, betrayed often, misunderstood often, was strong yet. It rose and destroyed
him by the instrument of men far less powerful, and
some of them not much better than himself. It drove
him into his own world, the world of courts and camps,
which he entered with magnificent pluck. But too late!
Alas, for the years he had given to that alien service,
following the enthusiast in his holy madness about the
Valley of Spoleto! Poor Elias, with every quality that
makes for success, to die a failure! The martyrs of
Morocco sent out to their death by you were less
martyrs. For your sacrifice was unacceptable.

MADONNA POVERTY

" Questa, privata del primo marito,
Mille cent' anni e più dispetta e scura
Fino a costui si stette senza invito ;
Nè valse udir che la trovò sicura
Con Amiclate, al suon della sua voce,
Colui ch' a tutto il mondo fe' paura ;
Nè valse esser costante, nè feroce,
Sì che, dove Maria rimase giuso,
Ella con Cristo salse in sulla croce.
Ma perch'io non proceda troppo chiuso,
Francesco e Povertà per questi amanti
Prendi oramai nel mio parlar diffuso."
—PARADISO, xi. 64–75.

THE Mystical Marriage of Francis with Madonna
Poverty is one of the favourite themes of the early
Minorites. The image must be traced back to Francis
himself. The image—nay, I should rather say the
fact. He spoke in parables, we say; not always, even
in his most picturesque phrasing. Just as often his
parables were literal narratives of actual experiences.
He was poet and primitive dramatist; but still more
was he the actual stuff of poetry. All the main actions
of his life were impelled by great consuming love, which
forced him to adventurous and chivalrous enterprises.
Other men before him and after him have reasoned out
the for and against of the state of poverty, and many
have chosen hard living for their portion. He saw
Poverty not as a state, but as a high lady, a dethroned
queen, the chosen of the Lord who came down to earth
and was born in a manger. The Lord had gone up
again to His high heaven, and she was left despised and
comfortless. He would be her gallant, her knight, her

spouse, she his Selvaggia, his Beatrice, his Fiammetta, but without rivals. If in modern phrase we say he fell in love with her, we are far nearer the truth than if we regard the Mystical Marriage with Poverty as a mere wordy embellishment of his preference for a certain virtue and state of life. When the gilded youth of Assisi first saw him pensive and given to solitude, they said he was in love, and laughingly asked him if he was about to take to himself a wife. "Yes," he answered, "and one fairer, richer, purer than you have ever known." Then followed the thought of the dowry she would bring, freedom and the right possession of all that is good on the earth. This falling in love with and joy in possession of the neglected high lady is one of the earliest facts of his religious life. Like a true knight he wrote her name on his banner, fought for her, pledged her, sang to her. All his friends were let know her beauties and her wonders; and his talk and tales and songs of her left vivid images in the minds and memories of all the first brothers.

The thirteenth chapter of the *Fioretti* describes Francis and Masseo running to pledge themselves to her service, not merely as pious men promise to be pure and disinterested, but as lovers afire with passion. There is some trace of the images in most of the Minorite writers of the first generations, and they have of course a much earlier origin than the *Fioretti*, or the *Actus S. Francisci*, from which it was drawn. Everywhere in the first legends, in Celano I. and II., in Bonaventura, who drew from the early sources, we find some hint of high espousals, some word of Francis's Bride. Bonaventura's version is best known; but that tale of the saint's meeting with the three women in the plain between Campiglia and San Quirico, and of their salutation to him, *Ben vegna madonna la povertà*, is a very vague one. It reads as if he were alluding to something he had half-forgotten; and Giotto, who has generally followed his

versions of the Francis stories very literally, reflects this
one hardly at all in his great fresco in the Lower
Church of Assisi, though he does not follow any other
version that I know of. Bonaventura tells, indeed, how
Francis left father and mother and clave unto his Lady;
yet his words give but a far away notion of that mysterious passion, whose fruit was the brotherhood of the
Minors. Later, Jacopone made holy rhymes on the theme
of the Mystic Marriage; and in a few lines Dante gave
it eternal shape.

But long before Jacopone and Dante wrote it was
the inspiration of a curious tract, one of the most
striking and delightful things in early Franciscan literature. The *Sacrum Commercium Beati Francisci cum
Domina Paupertate* has been known by name at least
since the days of the second or third generation of the
Order. The fourteenth century chroniclers mentioned
it, and some of them gave extracts from it. Part of
it is to be found in the *Arbor Vitae* of Ubertino of
Casale, written in 1305, as also in Bartholomew of Pisa's
Book of Conformities. Later, Mark of Lisbon gave a
compendium of the tract in his Chronicle, written in
Portuguese, but translated into most of the chief
European languages except English. In spite of its
early fame it was for ages lost sight of, save by a few
rare miners in Franciscan lore. Affò, in the eighteenth
century, studied it; yet a knowledge of it was so little
spread that, in 1848, when an early, probably a thirteenth
century, Italian translation of it was published, under
the name of *Meditatione sulla povertà di Santo Francesco*,
the editors, Bindi and Fanfani, shrewdly guessed, but
did not actually know of, a Latin original. Nor do
they seem to have ever found one. Yet of the original
several codices exist. In 1894, Signor Alvisi published
the Latin text, under the title of *Nota al Canto XI. del
Paradiso*, v. 73–75; and earned much gratitude from
curious students, even though his text was faulty, though

he did not say whence he drew it, and though his edition
contained no notes at all. More recently the R. P.
Edouard d'Alençon, Archivist to the Capuchins, issued
the text of the Codex Casanatensis, carefully collated
with others. Side by side with the original he has
placed an Italian translation, which he states to be of
the fourteenth century. He has also written a preface,
and added notes, none the less valuable that some of
them raise points of controversy. Later still, in 1901,
Signor Minocchi reissued, under the title of *Le Mistiche
Nozze di San Francesco e Madonna Poverta*, a corrected
text of the Italian translation (thirteenth century, according to him), which Bindi and Fanfani, in 1848, had
printed from the MS. of Giaccherino near Pistoja.

The *Sacrum Commercium* has generally been attributed to John of Parma. The author of his life in
the " Chronicle of the XXIV. Generals" says he wrote
it. So do Mark of Lisbon and others ; but they
may have borrowed their information from one source.
In the Ravenna Codex he is expressly named as the
writer. Until lately, no one questioned his authorship
save Affò, and he, on second thoughts, was inclined to
give back the credit of it to Brother John. It certainly
dramatises the inspiration of the life of the great leader
of the Spirituals. But beyond the tradition, to which
the " XXIV. Generals" has given long life, and the
name in the Ravenna MS., there is no proof of his
authorship.

Against it are placed two facts. The first is that the
chronicler, Salimbene, does not attribute any such treatise
to John. Now, Salimbene did have a good deal of intercourse with him during his years of office ; and to that
good gossip, his fellow-townsman and kinsman, we owe
some vivid accounts of the Blessed John. But that he
knew him intimately is quite another matter. To read
the chronicle of that delightful Pepysian flibbertigibbet,
and yet to think of him as the confidant of the great

visionary is impossible. Besides, during his years of office the Minister-General was too much occupied with administration to give himself to literature. If it be John's, it is more likely to have been written after 1256, when he was in retirement at Greccio. Now Salimbene, though he was a notorious gadabout, never went to Greccio. He was so scared at the punishment dealt out to heresy, and at being the friend of a heretic, that had John written fifty treatises after his deposition, he might not have known of one, or might have pretended ignorance. The second argument is, that Ubertino da Casale—who paraphrased the allegory in his *Arbor Vitæ*—did not give the author's name, but called him a "certain holy doctor." And yet, it is said, he knew John well. Now, on what authority is it said that Ubertino knew John well? As a young man, in trouble about his soul, he paid the sage a visit in his hermitage at Greccio. The old man confirmed him in his way of life—resistance to the *mitigati* in the Order—and poured forth torrents of apocalyptic lore. Had Ubertino repeated his visit he would have mentioned it. Surely it is not necessary to believe that John must have conversed with him on his literary works. Besides, anonymity is one of the main features of Franciscan literature. On the other hand, some careful readers of the *Arbor Vitæ* hold that Ubertino clearly did know the sage to be the writer, and meant only to veil the authorship. The book may seem a harmless one now; but when Ubertino wrote (1305), the writers and speakers of far more harmless things were being hunted and imprisoned; and though John was then dead, he may well have wished to keep the name of his saintly hero out of the strife that raged round himself and his views. In this regard may be mentioned the hasty and, I think, improbable conclusion of a few, that the treatise by John of Parma which Pietro dei Nubili was imprisoned for not showing up to the inquisition of cardinals, was this very *Sacrum Commercium*.

N

Some recent writers have seen in it a tract belonging to a time anterior to John of Parma. How they have reasoned this out from internal evidence, as the Padre da Civezza seems to have done, is not clear to me. But d'Alençon has found in a MS.—the Codex Casanatensis— the date of its composition given as 1227, that is, about nine months after the death of Francis. If this date be correct, the author is not John of Parma, who did not enter the Order till 1232-33, and who, in 1227, was but nineteen years old.

Another MS. attributes it to Crescentius, John's predecessor in office. But even d'Alençon, not prejudiced in favour of the *zelanti*, whom Crescentius scattered and exiled, thinks this is out of the question, yet interesting, as pointing once more to the author being a Minister-General. Tradition is fairly firm on that point. To find, then, a Minister-General, who should be a holy doctor, and flourishing in the early days, in 1227. Why, John Parenti, of course, is his answer—the Minister-General who defeated the hopes of Elias at the Chapter of Pentecost, 1227. Little is known of Brother John Parenti, save that he was a Florentine; that he was a learned doctor of laws of Bologna, a man of great saintliness, and that, at least for a time, he stood his ground firmly against Elias. It would not be the only time, says d'Alençon, that the two names have been confounded, and acts and writings of the earlier been attributed to the better-known man.

Others have guessed the author to be the English Franciscan and celebrated mathematician, John of Peckham, Archbishop of Canterbury. He entered the Order about 1250, and is so put out of court, if the date of 1227 be the correct one. But, indeed, there does not seem to be the very slightest reason for supposing him to have been the writer. The guess is merely based on the initials of the two names by which he was known—John of Peckham and Johannes Pisanus.

The opuscule is a manifesto, without any doubt—an election manifesto it was called at once on the discovery of the codex with the early date, directed against the election of Elias. Not at all, answers d'Alençon, for it is dated July, and John Parenti was already elected in May. But Elias did not seriously consider he had been defeated, save for the moment. He and his friends were on the alert; and it was necessary for the party in power, by word and writing, to recall continually the early spirit, and hold up to shame the falling away. At all events, it is almost inconceivable that any one can read it otherwise than as a vigorous bit of polemical literature, written in acute circumstances, when fidelity to the Rule was in danger, when, indeed, the brotherhood had known many treasons. Not at all, says d'Alençon again. You see, the author praises Francis and the brothers. He hopes all from them. He is reproaching the members of the older Orders for their degeneracy, and showing the good example of the first Minorites. Why, he quotes Saint Bernard in his reproaches, and he had nothing to do with the Franciscans. Whether he quotes Saint Bernard or not, and whether any writer, in the year 1227 or later, could have wondered and lamented, as does this one wonder and lament, over the piling up of wealth by the older Orders, it would have been perfectly ridiculous for a Franciscan of that day to have complacently regarded his own Order as yet stainless, when the assaults on the rigidity of the Rule were already notorious. He may quote Saint Bernard, but he describes, in the language of an idealist of the Franciscan Order and no other, the fallings away of Franciscans and no others. We should have thought that the device of telling of the advent of Francis and his hardy brothers, in the midst of sloth and ease and riches—the degenerate Minorite sloth and ease and riches, described to the life—would not have deceived a child, if it had not deceived great scholars. But they are scholars determined at all costs, and against the evidence of history, to deny any degeneracy in the Order or in Elias during the lifetime of the Founder.

In spite of the Codex Casanatensis, with its date of 1227, I hold the weight of evidence is still in favour of the authorship of John of Parma, or of a man of his time. What was true of the degeneracy of the Order at the death of Francis, was a hundred times truer when John undertook the administration of the Minorites, in 1247. It seems most probable that it belongs to the beginning of the second half of the thirteenth century. Minnocchi's suggestion that the date MCCXXVII. is the mistake of a scribe for MCCLXVII. is plausible. In the *explicit* of the Casanatese Codex and some others, however, the date is not given in Roman numerals. *Actum est hoc opus mense Julii post obitum beatissimi Francisci, anno Millesimo ducentesimo vigesimo septimo ab Incarnatione Domini Salvatoris nostri Jesu Christi.* But this *explicit* may only be the amplification of an inaccurate copyist. If John of Parma be the author, it was probably written before 1247, or after 1256, the year of his retirement. The latter is the more likely. For had he been known to have written such a thing before, it is improbable that he should have been elected on the recommendation of Crescentius; and the years during which he held office were almost too full of activity and care to have admitted of him engaging in literature. If it be the work of John, it adds another souvenir to the holy place of Greccio.

Accepting a later date than that given in Père d'Alençon's MS., we do not need to suppose any prudent veiling of the persons on whom the reproaches fall. Some of the expressions seem to refer definitely to the abuses of Elias's government, which had not been amended under his successors. *Mutabant leges* might be said to refer to the new Rules made in the lifetime of Francis, but it has more point as touching the Bull, *Quo elongati*. *Disponebant provincias* reads like a reference to Elias's multiplication and capricious disposal of provinces, which became a scandal owing to the additional functionaries which were needed becoming his creatures. But perhaps the strongest argument for the later time, and especially for John of Parma's authorship, is to be found in the Joachimite references to the various ages of the Church (*vide* d'Alençon's edition, pp. 5, 33). At least, the ancient editor of the Vallicellian MS. interprets them as Joachimite references; and the allusions to a system of spiritual chronology can best be explained so. Now, though it was just possible for the first generation of Franciscans to be Joachimites, we have no evidence that any of them were so. Francis and the Gospels seem to have been their only sources of inspiration. But if we place the writing of the tract about the middle of the century, we come to the very time when Joachimism was rampant among the Minorites, and its traditional author was notoriously reputed to be a zealous student of the works of the Abbot of Floris. So I still prefer to call it the work of John of Parma rather than of John Parenti, till the Codex Casanatensis has been clearly proved on this point more trustworthy than that of Ravenna.

The questions of the author, the date, and of the value of the tract as a manifesto are interesting as touching Franciscan history. But these do not matter most after all. To read it is to recognise a mind saturated by the inspiration of the early time, a man who shared the adventurous joy of Francis, who had glimpses of the Promised Land, who, having cast off the burden of possessions and of self, has gained the whole world. Not all of Francis's worthy disciples understood his poetry; but this man did. He was probably more of a fanatic, perhaps wished every one to be Franciscan. But let us not for that call him narrow. A man of his time and calling had come to a place in life of wide horizons when he conceived the whole world as his cloister—though some had conceived it before him. Even now the thought has consolation not to be found in the picture of the whole world

as a factory. Surely it was looking from some great
Apennine, or maybe only from the heights above
Greccio, that he learnt that high scorn of stone and
brick, that love of the wide sky and the steep ascents,
that strong sense of universal possession by the title-
deeds of the soul. *Dico vobis quod quemcumque locum
calcaverit pes vester, vester erit.* Jacopone best understood the sensuous side of Francis, his passion of pure
flame. Leo can best tell of his exquisite morality.
But of the adventurer in life what so perfect mirror
as the *Sacrum Commercium*, though Jacopone gave its
ideas more popular expression? He knew the tract
almost certainly, used it, amplified it, and set it to his
rude rhymes. Of Dante's possible knowledge of it, his
almost evident knowledge of Ubertino's version of it,
I shall speak later. One can only wish that Giotto had
heard something of the last scene, that he might on the
walls of San Francesco have bidden us share the banquet
spread for Madonna Poverty.

Here I have roughly translated some portions of
the tract. There are many repetitions in the original,
tedious enough some of them. The writer is too often
more edifying preacher than poet. But I have cut out,
for tyrannic reasons of space, what cannot well be spared.
I do not present it as a fine piece of literature. It is
here as a morning song greeting the rise, as a lament
for the setting of the strength, of the Franciscan idea.
But it is one of the gleams in the dawning sky of the
Italian Renaissance. There is much talk in it of the
other world, but not of death. It is full of youthful
lust of living. The empty purse is filled with great
expectations. Its frugality is that of heroes of the
prime.

> " Lo secol primo quant'oro fu bello ;
>   Fe' saporose con fame le ghiande,
>   E nettare con sete ogni ruscello."

And its savour is not all of a world that has passed.

THE HOLY COMMERCE OF THE BLESSED FRANCIS WITH MADONNA POVERTY

AMONG other shining and famous virtues which make ready in men's hearts a dwelling-place for God, and show them the more excellent and the shorter road of winning to Him, Poverty is first by right divine, her title by a singular grace preferred before all others. . . . For she is the foundation of all the others and their guardian. . . . No need then for the rest to fear, though the rain descend and the floods come, and winds blow threatening ruin, if on this base they are stablished fast. And why?—because the Son of God, Lord of the virtues and King of Glory, loved her with a special love, sought her, found her, and wrought by her salvation on the earth. In the beginning of His preaching He placed her as a lamp of faith; as a door for such as would enter; laid her as a stone in the first foundation of the House. . . . Blessed, said He, are the poor in spirit, for theirs is the Kingdom of Heaven. Theirs by clear right is the kingdom of the skies, who will not possess any earthly thing. Needs be that he live by heavenly things who has no care for those of earth. In his exile he eats with relish the crumbs that fall from the table of the holy angels, who renounces all earthly things, holding them as dross, that he may taste the savoury sweetness of the Lord.

Therefore the Blessed Francis, as a true imitator and follower of the Saviour, in the beginning of his conversion, gave himself up to the search for, and the

finding, and the holding of Holy Poverty, with all
his mind and desire and purpose, doubting nor fearing
sinister and adverse things, shirking no labour, refusing
no pain of body, if only it might be given unto him
to win unto her to whom God gave the keys of the
Kingdom of Heaven.   Diligently he began, as a curious
explorer, to walk about the streets and the public places
of the town, seeking her whom his soul loved.   He
would ask the standers by, and greet all who came in
his way, saying thus, " Now then have ye seen her whom
my soul loveth ? "   But the word was dark to them and
barbarous, and not understanding, they made answer,
" O man, we do not know what thou wouldst say.
Speak to us in our tongue, and we will answer thee."
For in the speech of the sons of Adam there was neither
word nor symbol by which they might speak together
of Poverty.   They hated her vehemently, as they do
to-day, nor could they speak peaceably of her to any of
her seekers. . . . " I will go," said the Blessed Francis,
" to the great ones and the learned sages, and speak
with them ; for they know the way of the Lord and the
judgment of their God."   This did he.   But the great
ones and the sages answered him hardly, saying, " What
new doctrine is this thou bringest to our ears ?   Let the
Poverty thou seekest be thine and thy children's after
thee.   For us be the enjoyment of delight and the
overflowing of riches.   For brief and full of labour
are the days of our life, and in the end of man what
refuge ?   Nothing better have we found than to eat,
drink, and be merry while we live."   Now the Blessed
Francis hearing this, marvelled in his heart, and giving
thanks unto God, said, "Blessed art Thou, Lord God, who
hast hidden these things from the wise and prudent, and
hast revealed them unto babes." . . . And so going out
of the city with hasty step he came to a certain field ;
and there from afar off, he saw two old men, sitting
as if burdened by heavy grief.   And one spoke to the

other, "To this man will I look, even to him that is poor and of a contrite spirit and trembleth at my word." And the other answered, "For we brought nothing into this world, and it is certain we can carry nothing out. And having food and raiment let us be therewith content." And when the Blessed Francis came up to them, he said, "Tell me, I beseech you, where Madonna Poverty abides, where she feeds, and where she makes her flock rest at noonday, for I am sick' of love for her." And they answered, "Good brother, here have we sat long year after long year, and frequently have we seen her pass, for many were wont to seek her. They would keep her company for a while, but oftentimes would she come back alone and naked, stripped of her adornments and her garments, and all forlorn. Very bitterly would she weep and say, 'The sons of my mother have warred against me.' And we said to her, 'Have patience. Thou art beloved of good men.' And now, brother, go thou up to the high mountain, where God has placed her. She dwells among the holy hills, whom God loveth above all the tabernacles of Jacob. Giants may not reach to the tracks of her feet, nor eagles fly to her aery. . . . Her nest is hid from the birds of the air, but God knows her way and the place where she abideth. If then, brother, thou wouldst win to her, doff thy garments of feasting, and cast off all burdens and the sin that cumbereth thee, for unless thou art naked thou mayst not ascend to her great height. Yet, for she is kind, she is easily seen of those that love her, and found of those that seek her. O brother, the thought of her is the consummation of sense; and who has kept vigil with her may live evermore in surety. Take with thee trusty comrades, who will counsel and help, and be a staff to thee as thou climbest the hill—for woe to the lonely man who falls by the way, and has none to raise him up."

Then having taken counsel, the Blessed Francis

went and chose certain trusty comrades; and setting out together they came to the mountain.   Then said he to his brothers, "Come let us go up to the mountain of the Lord, to the house of Lady Poverty, that she may teach us her ways, and we may walk in her steps."   And when from every side they had looked at the ascent, seeing its so great height and roughness, certain of them spake among themselves and said, "Who may ascend to the holy mountain, and who may reach its summit?"   But the Blessed Francis answered, "Strait is the way and narrow is the gate that leadeth unto life, and few there be that find it.   Take comfort of the Lord, and in the power of His strength, and every hard thing shall be easy unto us.   Put down the burdens of your own wills; cast off the load of your sins, and arm ye like strong men.   Forget the things that are behind, and press forward to those things that are before.   I say unto you that every place whereon the soles of your feet shall tread shall be yours. . . . A great mystery, my brothers, is this commerce with Poverty, but easily may we win her embraces, for she has become the widow of the world; and the queen of all the virtues is miserable and forlorn.   There is none in all the land who will dare to cry out against us, none who will oppose us, none who by right may forbid this saving commerce.   All her friends have become her enemies.

Then began all to walk after Saint Francis.   And when with most easy step they neared the height, behold Madonna Poverty standing on the peak of the mountain, and looking down the steep.   And seeing the men so lustily climbing, nay rather flying, she wondered deeply and said, "Who are these who fly like clouds, and like doves to the dovecots?   Long is it since I have looked on such, or seen any so swift and so lightened of burdens.   Therefore will I speak to them those things that are in my heart, lest they, like the others, repent them of their ascent, now seeing the gaping abysses that

lie about them. For I know that they may not take hold
of me without my consent; but I shall have my reward
before my Heavenly Father if I give them counsel of salvation. And behold, a voice came to her that said, "Fear
not, daughter of Sion, for these are the seed whom the
Lord has blessed." . . . So Madonna Poverty, leaning on
her naked throne, welcomed them with sweet blessings,
and said to them, "Tell me, my brothers, the reason of
your coming, and why you hasten so from the valley of
tears to the mountain of light. An it be me ye seek, I
am as you see, very poor, stricken by storms, and all
comfort is departed from me."

And they answered, saying, "We come to thee, our
Lady, beseeching thee to receive us in peace. . . . The
King of Kings and Lord of Lords, Creator of Heaven
and Earth, desired thy face and thy beauty, as He lay in
His chamber, rich and glorious in His kingdom. He
left His house, and cast behind Him His heritage. . . .
Great, therefore, is thy dignity, and incomparable thy
height, since He left all the delights of the angels . . .
and came to seek thee in the lower parts of the earth,
where thou layest in the mire, in darkness and the shadow
of death. Not a little did all living men hate thee, and
flee thee, and chase thee away as far as they might. And
albeit they might not flee thee altogether, not the less
wert thou hateful to them. But after that the Almighty
Lord came to take thee for Himself, and exalted thy
head among the tribes of the people, and put a bride's
crown on thee, raising thee higher than the clouds.
What to thee the hate of the multitude, who know not
thy virtue and thy glory? For freely dost thou dwell in
the holy mountains, in the firm established dwelling of
the glory of Christ. Thus the Son of the Most High
Father became a lover of thy form, cleaving to thee only
in all the world, and finding thee in all things most
faithful. For ere He left His land of light for our earth,
thou preparedst a fitting place for Him, a throne on

which to sit, a bed on which to rest—the poor little
Virgin, from whose womb came this world's Light. . . .
They placed Him, as saith the Evangel, in a manger,
because there was no room in the inn. And thus ever
inseparably wert thou bound to Him, so that in all His
life when He was seen on earth, and conversed with men,
while foxes had holes and birds of the air had their nests,
He had not where to lay His head. . . . And when He
chose His witnesses, He chose not rich merchants but
poor fishermen, that by such estimation He might show
them worthy to be loved by all. . . . Alone thou
clavedst to the King of Glory when all His chosen and
loved ones left Him in fear. Most faithful bride, most
sweet lover, not for one moment didst thou part from
Him. Verily, the more thou clavedst to Him, the more
thou sawest Him despised by all. For if thou hadst not
been with Him, then never would He have been scorned
by all. Thou wert with Him in the wranglings of the
Jews, in the insults of the Pharisees, in the rebuke of
the high priests, with Him in the blows, in the spitting,
in the stripes. . . . Thou didst not forsake Him in
death, even the death of the cross. And on that cross
whereon His naked body hung, His arms stretched, His
hands and feet nailed, thou sufferedst with Him, so that
nothing about Him- seemed more glorious than thou.
Then, when He went to Heaven, He left thee as the seal
of the Kingdom, for the marking of the chosen, that
whosoever longs for the eternal kingdom should come to
thee, beg of thee, enter by thee. . . . Therefore, Lady,
have pity on us, and sign us with the sign of thy
grace. . . ."

To this Madonna Poverty answered with a joyful
heart, with a glad face, and a sweet voice, saying,
" Dearest brothers and friends, better are your words to
me than gold and precious stones, and sweeter than honey
from the comb. . . . I desire, if it weary you not to
hear, to tell you a long but not the less useful story of

my condition. . . . I am not rude and unlearned, as
many think; but ancient and full of days as I am, I know
the nature of things, the variety of creatures, and the
changes of the times. I have known the restlessness of
the human heart, learning it now in my experience of the
world, now by subtlety of nature, and now by gift of
grace. I was in the Paradise of God when man was
naked, . . . wandering through all that spacious realm,
fearing nothing, aware of nothing adverse. There I
thought to remain for ever. . . . Very joyful was I,
sporting with him all the day, having nothing of my
own, for all was God's."

[Then comes an account of Adam's sin, his shame
of nakedness, his clothing himself with the fig leaves,
which are held to be the first signs of private property.]

"Seeing, therefore, my companion become a sinner,
and covered with leaves as he had never been before,
I went away from him, and, standing a long way off,
began to wait for Him who should save me from the
weakness of the spirit and from the tempest. And suddenly from on high there came a sound shaking all
Paradise, and with it a most glorious light sent out from
Heaven. And, looking, I saw the Lord of Majesty
walking in Paradise in the cool of the day, shining with
ineffable glory." [Seeing Him and a great company of
angels, she pleads for mercy. But the apparition is not
for her, but for Adam, who is chased from Paradise and
condemned to eat his bread by the sweat of his brow
till he return to the dust from which he sprang. Then
Adam made him a mantle of skins—symbol of his mortality, now innocence was lost.

[Seeing, then, her companion clad in skins of dead
beasts, she went away from him altogether; for he gave
himself up to the multiplying of labours whereby he
might become rich. Then she went a wanderer and an
exile about the earth with weeping and bitter laments,

and from that time found no spot whereon to rest her foot till the Firstborn of the Father espoused her. But He, wishing to return to His kingdom, made known His will to His chosen through her.]

"Provide neither gold, nor silver, nor brass in your purses, nor scrip for your journey, neither two coats, neither shoes nor yet staves. And if any man will sue thee at the law, and take away thy coat, let him have thy cloak also. And whosoever shall compel thee to go a mile, go with him twain. Lay not up for yourselves treasures upon earth, where moth and rust doth corrupt, and where thieves break through and steal. Take no thought, saying, What shall we eat? or, What shall we drink? or, Wherewithal shall we be clothed? Take no thought for the morrow. Sufficient unto the day is the evil thereof. Who forsaketh not all that he hath cannot be my disciple."

[Then follows an eulogy of the Apostles, who had nothing of their own, and all things in common. Their followers were sometimes tempted to abandon so hard a life; but Madonna Poverty was able, by reminding them of their Master, to call them back to austere ways and happy endurance of persecution, and thousands were signed with the sign of the Most High King.]

"But alas, after a little time a peace was made, and that peace was harder than any war. In the beginning few had the sign on them; in the middle fewer, and in the end hardly any at all. And now, behold in this peace my most bitter bitterness, for all chase me from them; I am sought by none, forsaken by all. My peace is from my enemies, not from those of my own house; from strangers, not from my sons. . . .

"But the consummation of all the virtues, my Lady Persecution, to whom as to me the Lord gave the kingdom of Heaven, was a faithful helper and counsellor to me in all things. For when she saw any cooling of celestial love or any gradual forgetting, or placing of hearts on earthly things, at once she thundered, at once she set her army in motion, and filled the faces of my sons with shame, that they might seek the name of God. But now my sister has left me, and the light of mine eyes is no more with me; for while peace is made by the persecutors with my sons, they are lacerated by cruel wars in their own house, envying one another, provoking one another to the acquiring of riches and the heaping up of delights."

[Here follows an exultant account of a new band of disciples that came to her asking her to make with them a perpetual peace. "And I was with them as in the days of my youth, when the Omnipotent was with me, and my children were about me." With these men, "dear to the angels, gracious to men, hard to themselves, pitiful to others, pious in deed, modest of mien, cheerful of countenance," her soul was joined; and one mind and one faith were in them.

"But there arose sons of Belial working evil things, speaking evil things; calling themselves poor, though they were not poor; donning the habit of holy religion, but putting not on the new man. Madonna Poverty they soon fell out with, calling her lazy, insipid, base, rude, bloodless, and dead.]

"Their natural ally was Avarice. . . . But her they called by a holier name, lest they should seem in any way to leave me, Madonna Poverty, by grace of whom they had been raised from the dust and from the mire. To me they spoke meekly of their new friend, but craft was in their hearts." They gave Avarice fine names, such as Discretion or Providence. To Lady Poverty they said, "Thine is the power, thine the kingdom;" but she stops their flattery by naming the conditions of devotion to her. "Look not behind. Let him that is on the housetop not come down to take anything out of the house. Neither let him that is in the field return back to take his garment." Some listened unconvinced,

Others said, "Wretched is she herself, and she would that we all should be wretched too."

Farther to tempt the faithful, Avarice, under the name of Discretion, began to say to them, "Do not show yourselves so rigid towards men, nor so despise their honours, but be affable to them, and do not spit out their proffered favours in their faces. Let your scorn be inward. It is good to have the friendship of kings, the notice of princes, the familiarity of the great; for while they honour and venerate you, many seeing it, will be turned more readily to God."

This was an incitement to some to seek earthly honours with all their hearts. Still Avarice found it not a means of universal corruption, and had to seek other weapons to combat the devotion to Madonna Poverty, who continues: "Meanwhile Avarice, this barbarous enemy of mine, began to be vehemently angry, and to gnash her teeth. Full of bitterness within, she said, 'What shall I do? Behold the whole world goes after her. I will take unto me the name of Prudence, and I shall speak to their hearts so loud they must hear and acquiesce.' So did she, speaking to them humble wise. 'Why stand ye here all the day idle, providing nothing for the morrow? What boots it to have the bare necessaries of life, when the superfluities are wanting? For with all peace and quietness you can work your own salvation and others', an once your storehouse be full. While yet there is time, provide for yourselves and your children—for men withdraw their hands from those to whom aforetimes they were wont to give, and there is no surety in accustomed gifts. Good were it for you ever to remain thus; but you cannot, since every day God adds to your numbers. Will God not accept you if you have wherewith to give to the needy, and are mindful of the poor, when He says, 'It is more blessed to give than to receive'? Why do you not accept the good things that are offered to you. Beware

lest ye defraud the givers of their eternal reward. What
fear for you in the contact of riches, since ye hold them
as nothing? Evil is not in things, but in the mind—for
God saw every thing that He had made, and behold it
was very good. So to the good all things are good;
all things serve them, and for them were all things
created. Oh, how many rich men spend foolishly,
whereas, if you had wealth you would turn it to good
use; for your purpose is holy, and holy your desire.
No wish have ye to endow your own kindred, who are
rich enough. But when you have what is fitting unto
your state, more becoming and more serious will be your
walk in life.' These and other like things she said;
and some of them, whose consciences were corrupt, as-
sented at once. But others passed by with a deaf ear,
or broke into her proffered reasoning with shrewd
retorts.

"But Avarice, seeing that she could not by herself
have her will of them, changed her plan for the better
fulfilment of her desire. So she called Sloth, who puts
off the beginning of good works, nor finishes those
begun; and she made a league with her, and a pact
against them. Not too familiar was she with her, nor
too straitly joined, yet they agreed freely to work
together for evil, as once Pilate did with Herod against
the Saviour. The pact made, Sloth muttered in anger;
violently crossed their boundaries with her hordes, and
disarming them, extinguished their love, leaving them
lukewarm and torpid. And thus sunk in pusillanimity
of spirit, they became, as it were, dead at the heart.

"Then began they to sigh miserably after all the
things they had left in Egypt, and basely to seek what
they had despised when their hearts were high. Then
walked they sadly in the way of the commandments of
the Lord, and went where they were bidden with dried-
up hearts. They failed under their load, and could
hardly breathe for poor-spiritedness. [Envy of their

o

neighbours, desire for amusement, and for indulgence of their palates, followed hereupon.]

"And they began to flatter the people of the world, to make alliance with them, and to empty their purses; and they built bigger buildings, and multiplied things they had once renounced. They sold words to the rich and greetings to women. The courts of kings and princes they frequented eagerly, and joined house to house and field to field. And now are they magnified and enriched and established on the earth. From one evil they have gone to another, and they have not known God. Their fall was in their rising. They have sunk into the earth before their birth, and yet say they, 'We are thy friends.'

"In my grief grieved I bitterly, for those who were poor and despised in the world came to me and were made rich. Now fatted and cossetted, they grow more rebellious than the others, and mock me, . . . and think it no shame to spit in my face . . . and to say, 'Out with thee, miserable one! Depart from us. We will have no knowledge of thy ways.'"

[Madonna Poverty ends her lament by telling her hope of better things from Francis's followers; but warns him how common and natural are fallings away.

For answer the Blessed Francis with his brothers falls prone on the ground, giving thanks to God, and begs her to have pity on them, and is eloquent in her praise.]

"For great are thy works and beyond telling, for which cause undisciplined souls wander far from thee. Lonely thou goest and rugged. Thou art as an army arrayed in the field, and the poor-spirited cannot abide with thee. But behold we are thy servants and the sheep of thy pastures. Through eternity and from age to age we have sworn and determined to keep thy judgments."

[Lady Poverty accepts them for her servants and her lovers. Francis rejoices as at a great boon.] And coming down from the mountain they brought Madonna Poverty to the place where they dwelt, and it was the sixth hour.

And all things being got ready, they pressed her to eat with them. And she said, "Show me first your oratory, your cloister, your chapter-house, your refectory, your kitchen, your dormitory, your stable, your fine seats, your polished tables, your great houses. For nothing of these I see. Only I see you cheerful and happy, overflowing with joy, filled with consolation, and as if you expected all things to be supplied at your desire." But they answered, saying, "Our Lady and our Queen, we thy servants are tired after a long journey, and thou in our company hast laboured not a little. Let us first eat, if it pleaseth thee, and then refreshed, we shall do all things at thy command." This pleasing her well, she said, "But now bring water that we may wash our hands, and napkins with which to wipe them." Then they made haste to bring a broken earthenware vessel, for they had not a whole one, full of water. And pouring the water on her hands, they looked about for a napkin, and finding none, one of them offered her the tunic he wore, and with it she wiped her hands. Taking it with a gesture of thanks, she magnified God with all her heart who had given her the company of such men. Thereafter they led her to the place where the repast was spread. Then looked she round, and seeing nothing but three or four bits of barley bread placed on the grass, she marvelled greatly within her, and said, "Who ever saw such things in the generations of men? Blessed be Thou, O Lord, who hast care of all! Thou doest what Thou wilt, and teachest Thy people to please Thee by such works." And so they sat down together, giving thanks to God for all His gifts. Then Madonna Poverty ordered them to bring the cooked foods in the appointed vessels. And, lo, one bowl was brought to her full of cold water, that all might dip their bread in it. For there was no abundance of platters, nor were there too many cooks. She begged a few fragrant herbs might be furnished. But having no gardener, and knowing of no garden, they gathered wild herbs in the wood, and put them before her. Then said she, " Bring me a little salt that I may flavour the herbs, for they are bitter." " Wait," they said, " lady, till we go to the city and fetch some for thee, if so be we find any one who will give it to us." " Give me," she said, " a knife, and I will scrape off the foul parts of the herbs, and cut the bread, which is very hard and dry." And they answered, " Lady, we have no cutler to make us knives. For this time let thy teeth be for a knife, and afterwards we shall furnish one." Then said she, " Have you any wine by you ? " And again they answered, saying, " Our Lady, wine we have none—for the foundation of man's life is bread and water, and it is not good for thee to drink wine. The Bride of Christ should flee wine as poison." After they were satisfied, exulting more in the glory of their neediness than in the abundance of all things, they blessed the Lord, in whose sight they had found such grace ; and they led their lady to a place where she might rest, for she was tired. And when she threw herself on the bare earth, she asked for a pillow for her head, and they made haste and fetched her a stone, and placed it for her. Then after she had slept a most quiet and sober sleep, she rose quickly and begged the brothers to show her their cloister. And leading her to a certain hill, they showed her the whole world as far as she could see, saying, " This is our cloister, Madonna." Then would she have them to sit down together, and she spoke the words of life to them, saying :—

" May the Lord, who made heaven and earth, bless you, my sons, who received me with such fulness of love and pity into your house, so that to-day to be with you seems to me like being in the Paradise of God. Therefore am I replete with joy and abundant consolation. And because I have been so late in coming I ask pardon. Truly God is with you, and I knew it not. Lo, what I have desired that do I see; what I have longed for now hold I in my hands; for here on earth I am joined to them who are to me the image of Him whose bride I am in heaven. . . . Have no doubt or fear of possessing the Kingdom of Heaven, for even now ye hold the pledge of your future heritage, and have received the gage of the Spirit, signed with the sign of the glory of Christ, corresponding in all things, by His grace, to those first disciples of His, whom He gathered round Him when He came into the world. For what they did in His company, you have begun to do in His absence, and well may ye say, Lo, we have left all to follow Thee. . . . In your conversion, dearest, the citizens of heaven rejoice, applaud, and sing new songs before the Eternal King. The angels rejoice in you and for you . . . the apostles exult . . . the martyrs shout . . . and the confessors leap for joy. . . . The virgins sing aloud, following the Lamb wherever He goeth, knowing their number to grow with you every day. All the celestial is filled with rejoicing, and holdeth every day solemn feasts in honour of the new citizens; and the incense of the odour of holy prayers, rises in their nostrils from this valley continually.

" I beseech ye, therefore, my brothers, by the mercy of God, for which you have made yourselves so poor, do that for which you are here, that for which you have come up from the rivers of Babylon. Receive humbly the grace that is offered you, using it worthily in all things to the praise and glory and honour of Him who died for you, our Lord Jesus Christ, who with the Father and the Holy Spirit, lives and reigns, overcomes and governs, the eternally glorious God, world without end. Amen."

JOHN OF PARMA

" But the aforesaid Brother John was resplendent above all the rest, the which had more completely drunk the chalice of life, whereby he had the more deeply gazed into the abyss of the infinite light divine."—FIORETTI, 48.

ROUND this name there once raged a fury of contending factions—against the will of its owner, a man of peace. He refused to bear aloft the standard of a party in a movement whose differences he had been called to heal. No man ever missed a better chance of remembrance in a struggle which might have spread, with his encouragement, far beyond that movement; might have rent the Church in twain, so far as Italy and the south of France were concerned, which might, just conceivably, have lost Luther some of his later opportunities. Unsuccessful, his revolt would still have presented a spectacle to strike the world's imagination—a band of men bound to poverty and humility arrayed against the pomp and force of the Roman Church. Comrades stood waiting his call, ready for any sacrifice and hardship. He had exceptional means of sending round the fiery cross. His name was a name of power in East and West. He was personally known in almost every country in Europe. But he never gave the sign, never whispered the messenger word. He willed to be forgotten. And outside his own Order his desire has been nearly fulfilled. History has resented his neglect of unexampled opportunities of plotting.

Most writers who have spoken of John of Parma in recent times have erred in emphasising over much his

·M̄· IOHANĒS ·DEPARMA· B̄S

JOHN OF PARMA

Benozzo Gozzoli. Montefalco, S. Francesco.

connection with the Joachimite heresy. It would be at least as correct to say that the doctrines of the Abbot Joachim gained notoriety because of John's interest in them. The earlier chroniclers saw truer. His originality, as significant now as ever, does not consist in the fact that as Minister-General of the Franciscan Order he favoured a heresy. His life was his originality. He was a great practical experimenter in the field of religion and morals. Few there have been who have willed and planned on so great a scale to make the City of God a reality on the earth. He failed. And the strugglers of the world might go to school to him to learn how to fail with noble dignity.

There are living words about him in each one of the scattered and often meagre chronicles where one seeks the traces of his life. His eighteenth century biographer could add or verify a fact or two; but the man's clear personality was blunted by the ornate flourishes of Affò's pen. It does not matter. Hundreds of years before, it had been fixed by simple Minorites, who knew him as a living man, or who wrote while tradition was still warm about his memory.

John Borelli, or Buralli, was born at Parma in 1208 or 1209. His parents, according to one account, were Pietro Buralli and Antonia Bertani. Antonia, his mother, is said to have had a vision of him before his birth—"covered with sackcloth, an object of scorn, but yet a wonder to whosoever looked on him." But Salimbene, that good gossip, says John's father was called Alberto, and nicknamed *Uccellatore*, because he delighted in bird-catching, "and made it his profession." Needless to say, Affò does not mention this. Salimbene even indiscreetly tells that the future Minister-General was called "little John (Johanninus)" in the world—a statement that Affò rejects with horror. Affò is all for dignity. But Salimbene was after all John's fellow-townsman, and even acknowledges some kind of cousinship—surprising enough, seeing the chronicler is very insistent on the high standing of his own family.

Perhaps the bird-catching was not profitable. At all events, the boy owed all his training to an uncle, a priest, who presided over the *pio luogo di San Lazzaro*, a religious house outside the city of Parma, where the Knights of the Order of San Lazzaro tended, or provided attendance for the poor, the sick, and more especially for lepers. While still very young John fell gravely ill; and friends stood round watching for his last breath. But his marvellous vitality asserted itself; and the astonished bystanders heard his sudden announcement, "I shall not die. I shall live to declare the works of the Lord." Very likely he was early destined for the priesthood. But it was as a scholar he first won fame. Parma had lately been experiencing a great revival of learning by which John profited. He became a teacher of logic in his native town, perhaps before he made his religious profession. About 1232–33, in his twenty-fifth year, he entered the Franciscan Order, and probably was an inmate of the first Minorite convent in Parma, in the Prato San Stefano.

It is not likely that he had ever seen Francis—though as he was eighteen when the Saint died, it is not impossible. But if the eyes of the ascetic and spiritual youth had beheld him, he must surely have followed him at once, instead of clinging to what was always just a little suspect to the Founder, the study of worldly science. Nothing could be more unlike than the youthful days of these two men so agreed in their later ideals—Francis, the gay roisterer, singing the songs of love and war about the midnight streets of Assisi; and John, early self-dedicate to the Church and to scholarship, the sober enthusiast for Aristotle, quickening and subtilising his wits in the lecture-rooms of Parma. A man of many accomplishments was John. Later, we hear of him as a fine musician, with a good voice. His eloquence and

his powers of disputation were famed. He was much
commended for his caligraphy — in those days this
carried with it great merit — and he was reputed to
possess "a noble style."

For some time after his entry into the Order it was
still as a scholar that his powers were utilised. During the next few years he was reader in theology at
Naples and Bologna. After that his promotion was
quick. Perhaps we hardly realise the extraordinary
inter-communication in the new orders. Modern tourist
agencies seem but poor means of effacing frontiers in
comparison with the constant tramp of the brothers
through Europe on their bare feet. If a *frate* preached
well, or taught well, or begged well, or fasted well, or led
a saintlier life than his fellows, his fame could hardly be
local. Brothers from France and Germany and Hungary and Rome and England, who sojourned in his
convent, would go back and tell of him to the Ministers
of their provinces for pride in the Order. To the end of
his life John had a great reputation as a teacher. While
still young, and held fast by his duties at Naples and
Bologna, he was probably a marked man. He may have
been of the *frati* sent by Gregory IX. in 1236, to preach
the abortive crusade undertaken by the French nobles.
But this is conjecture. The University of Paris, in its
new fervour, was drawing to it young men of ability.
The Franciscans, whose settlement there was now
firmly established, could not but be affected by its keen
intellectual air. They needed among their teaching staff
the most brilliant men, the men of soundest learning the
Order could provide. In what year John went to Paris,
as successor to John of Rochelle, is uncertain ; but his
stay in that centre of learning is of great importance and
interest in view of his later history. There he was on
his mettle, living and working with the stimulus, not
only of rival intellects, but of the suspicion of the
regular clergy and of the predominant faction in the

University, who looked askance on the Franciscans and
the Dominicans, hated their asceticism, and watched for
signs of heresy in their midst.   It was John of Parma's
duty to read the *Sentences* (of Peter Lombard), and expound them, that is, to set forth, with comments, the
body of doctrine of the Roman Church.   He lectured
openly.   Scholars from all countries listened.   Not the
faintest rumour of heresy stirred about his name while he
was in Paris.   If it had been otherwise, his promotion
would have been impossible — first contested at the
Chapter, and then vetoed by the Pope.   His election
to the Head of the Order, on the contrary, was unanimous.

At Paris he was a prominent man.   Proof of the
recognition of his ability lies in the choice of him
to represent the Minister-General, Crescentius, at the
Council of Lyons, held on John the Baptist's Day,
1245.   Crescentius said he was too old, when the Pope's
invitation reached him, but he can hardly have guessed
the manner of man he had chosen as deputy.   At the
Council—called by Innocent IV. for no less a reason than
to excommunicate and depose the Emperor Frederic, the
enemy of the Church, the persecutor of the faithful—
the deputy head of the Franciscans was seen by Pope
and Cardinals, by Provincials and humble brothers, to be
no shadow.   Inside and outside the Order he was recognised as a personality.   And less than two years later,
by the Chapter General held at Avignon, in 1247, he
was recalled from Paris, and appointed Minister-General
of the Brothers Minor.

Till now he has appeared mainly as a student, a man
of reasoning, of doctrine, who might be thought to have
modelled himself on Anthony of Padua rather than on
Francis.   But there was instant proof that Francis was
his pattern.   Brother Leo, in the *Speculum Perfectionis*,
has described the ideal Minister-General as conceived by
the Founder—as realised in him.   It is a very high ideal,

and involves entire self-abnegation. The one privilege he may retain is some leisure for private prayer. After prayer he must stand in the midst of the Brethren, to be at the beck and call of each, even the obscurest, even the stupidest, to answer every question, to provide for all with charity, patience, and meekness. John accepted the whole literally, abating not a jot or tittle of it, imposing on himself even harder conditions and tasks than the Founder had indicated. Thus some of his inner life in the past is revealed : he must have lived long with Francis in the spirit ; for when the call came to fill his place so far as in him lay, the whole of him obeyed on the instant.

Why did they not know him for the man he was ? Probably for two reasons. He was never a party man. He never aspired to lead the *zelanti* only, but to guide the whole Order. Then, as a teacher of logic and theology, he had not been called on to lecture on the conduct of life. And though the gift of eloquence was his, he was in ordinary a man of few words. In later life he was wont to say he feared judgment more for his silences than for what he had spoken. The true Franciscan was a man of deeds, not of words. Associated with no party, he was hastily labelled " safe " ; and hence, with his reputation for learning, dignity, and pure living, his unanimous election in a time of bitter strife and dire confusion.

He cannot have ignored the forces arrayed against his endeavour. The Order was demoralised. The brothers accepted ecclesiastical preferment, honours, and wealth. Among them were court favourites, menials, spies. They construed the Rule according to their convenience or their weakness. Twenty years after the Founder's death the essentials of the Religion were regarded as a dream, unfit for practical men. Gregory IX. and Elias had tempted them with place and power, and they had fallen. The faithful were despised and

persecuted. Faction reigned. There were those stubbornly opposed to the literal interpretation of the Rule,
true brothers of Elias, who welcomed all alloy that would
make their Order a wide and acceptable power in the
world. There were the Moderates. The best of them
loved learning better than enthusiasm. The rest were
too chill-blooded to take any side effectually—*qui nec
pugnabant, nec fugient.* If they made feeble attempts to
stop worldly scandals, they were still more ready to op-
press and silence the third party, the zealots for the
Rule, and betrayed and forlorn, some of the zealots had
grown discontented and bitter. The regular clergy were
murmuring against the new orders and at the favour
bestowed on them by Rome. Paris was using all its wit
and vigour to attack the heretics, to undermine the
greatest heresy of all, the Franciscan ideal of life. So
destructive of all civilisation, they said. What a familiar
cry !

It was a very unhappy family, and a very large one,
scattered through every country in Christendom, and to
attempt to bring it peace was a task to shrink from.
Yet John was not content to be only peacemaker. The
root of the evil was faithlessness, worldliness. The rule
of life for Franciscans was, he held, the Rule of Francis.
He would restore the heroic age of the movement, bring
back the brothers to their own work, to preach in the
world a gospel of love, and share gladly with the poorest
all the hardships of the road. Francis knew, in agony
of soul, before he died, how laxity had crept in. The
family was larger now, the corruption greater, the difficulties more complex. But it was impossible for John,
being the man he was, to lead the Order, and not to do
all that in him lay to lead it back to Francis.

Probably only a few intimates knew his stubborn
idealism at the time of his election at Avignon. But
the *zelanti* had a quick instinct for a man after their
own hearts. Some of the old friends of Francis, those of

the inner circle, were still there. Bernard was dead, but Leo and Angelo and Rufino and Giles and Masseo were left; and their hearts warmed to this new leader, whose idea of veneration for Francis was to do his will. Said Giles to him, "Welcome, father. But, oh, you come late!"

Read in the *Fioretti* the significance of John of Parma's life. The vision of James of La Massa is his best biography. In this vision the brother saw a great tree "whose root was of gold, and its fruits were men, and they were all of them Brothers Minor." The branches were the provinces of the Order, and every single minister and brother could be seen. John of Parma, as Minister-General, was on the top. "And thereafter he saw Christ sitting on a throne exceeding great and shining, and Christ called Saint Francis up thither, and gave him a chalice full of the spirit of life, and sent him forth, saying, 'Go, visit thy brothers, and give them to drink of this chalice of the spirit of life. . . .' And Christ gave unto Saint Francis two angels to bear him company. Then came Saint Francis to give the chalice of life to his brothers; and he gave it first to Brother John of Parma, who, taking it, drank it all in haste, devoutly, and straightway he became all shining like the sun." The cup was then given to the others. Some spilled it all, and became dark and misshapen. Some drank a part and spilled a part, and became part shining and part darkened. John "was resplendent above all the rest, the which had more completely drunk the chalice of life, whereby he had the more deeply gazed into the abyss of the infinite light divine, and had learned therein of the adversity of the tempest that was to rise up against this tree and shake and toss its branches." The rest of the vision concerns a later part of the story. A partisan was Brother James of La Massa, of course. But he had seized the essential fact about John, who drank the whole chalice of the spirit of life. The draught is very bitter; he called it sweet.

It is not easy nowadays to realise the power of a Minister-General of the early Franciscans. He was subject only to the Pope and the Cardinal Protector of the Order, and they were indulgent. His authority ran in every country in Christendom. His influence was far-reaching, weighty, and subtle, over the doctrines, the morals, the studies, the daily life of thousands of men sworn to obedience. Despite the intellectual opposition of Paris and the jealousy of the secular clergy, the Order was most popular as yet in every land. Its help was sought; its leaders were flattered. The Minister-General, when a man of ability, might be ranked among the potentates of Europe. Innocent IV., whom John helped at the Council of Lyons, was his affectionate friend. Saint Louis ruled in France, and the pietistic Henry III. in England. Both demeaned themselves before him.

It was soon known to the brothers that an active force was at work in their midst. He was a skilful peacemaker. He healed quarrels, spurred the lukewarm, spoke comfort to the downhearted. The seventy-two zealots of holy life, who had been exiled by Crescentius, he first consoled by kindly letters and then recalled. "Scattered by the wolf, they were gathered again by the shepherd and led back to the fold." He was now here, now there, at every one's beck and bidding. The peace of discipline and strict justice reigned for a time at least. Nor was the political side of his office neglected. With the Pope he was in constant communication, and obtained powers from Rome that kept the Order to its own work and extended its usefulness. All looked to him for attention, and none were overlooked. He obeyed to the letter the injunction of Francis that no less heed should be paid to the simple and foolish than to the wise. He spoke, he wrote, he organised. But this he could do from the centre, though his centre may have had greater breadth than Assisi. Such work was but a small part of his plan.

John was resolved to enter into personal relations with every member of the Order, and not at the Chapters General only. In the first few years of his rule he is said to have visited every convent and hermitage of the Brothers Minor. No such complete visitation had ever been attempted before by a Minister-General since the days of Francis—and the Order was now much larger and more scattered—though John Parenti had aimed at something of the kind. Aymon had gone to England, it is true, but then Aymon was an Englishman. Through home lands and strange lands he wandered, nearly always on foot, with one or at most two companions. Now and then they had a horse; but his comrades had equal help from it on the way. He was dressed like the poorest of the brethren. There was no pomp or ceremony on the road, for he never announced his coming. At a convent he was admitted like any other wanderer, " for the love of God "; and days might pass before he was known to be the Minister-General. When his presence was known he desired to be served as the rest. His companions must fare as he did. He liked to eat of such food as was ready. If an elaborate meal was served, he ate of the first course and of no other. If he noticed that the best-favoured and the wittiest brothers were given him as neighbours, he defeated the superior's plan, and would be found at table with the humblest. Perhaps his visits were a little upsetting to the economy of a convent; for if good wine and worse were on the table, when the good was poured out to him, he served all who sat near him with the same. So far as personal privileges went, the Franciscan Order, in its early intention, was a perfect democracy; and that early intention was no pious dream to John, but a constant reality. He had need to have been a man of natural dignity. Salimbene says he has seen him cleaning the vegetables while on a visit to a convent. He did not even claim the right of bodily maintenance. During his time of office, with all kinds of business on his shoulders, he proposed to earn his keep as an amanuensis.

In these visitations it was his desire that all the brothers should freely tell him their desires and their troubles. He had come to listen and to help. And the poorest of them saw that the Minister-General was clad as miserably as himself, ate no better, bore more fatigue, more stress of weather, claimed no rights save to be a guide of souls, and let the humblest share his attention equally with the Pope. It was almost as if Francis had come again. Of course, he found much laxity, much indifference—and his eyes were very open. His reminders of the Rule by which they were bound were austere enough. Did they complain it was too hard for men of this world, he reminded them that Francis had not called the whole world, but such as desired and could earn, through their devotion to Lady Poverty, her reward of wholesome joy and freedom. He added nothing to the Rule. When additions were proposed at the Chapter of Metz he vetoed them, with "Let us observe what we have." A man of few words, he could yet utter angry ones. A reader of the province of the Marches, coming home from Rome, told his brothers of a great outburst of indignation on the part of the Minister-General against the want of hardiness in the brotherhood, the growing ambition, and the quarrels with the secular clergy. His vehemence surprised his audience, and perhaps put their backs up. Why did they not retort? it was asked. "Impossible. A river of fire gushed from his mouth."

Sternly impartial, he left many murmuring behind him. In these wanderings he had been digging the grave of his ambition, had he known any. But in the records of his visitations we meet, too, a note of passionate love. He was a man of many friends. A strange life after the quiet convent lecture-rooms, this wandering on foot to the great towns, to the obscure villages, through the waste places, and by the sunny vineyards; climbing along rocky mountain paths, threading thick forests to the lonely hermitages of Umbria, Tuscany, and the Marches; or crossing the Alps into strange lands; eating now of the bread that had been begged for him, and now sitting at the banquet of kings. At the Chapter of Sens he had much intercourse with St. Louis of France, who treated him as a dear friend. The King would have had him sit by his side at table with his royal brothers and the cardinals, but the Minister-General kept his place at the table of the poor, "which acquired splendour from his presence."

He was in England in 1247. From Eccleston we learn that he attended a Chapter at Oxford in the time of William of Nottingham; and though here also he had to urge unity, and smooth away difficulties, yet he was much pleased with the English brothers. "Oh, that such a province," he cried, "were in the middle of the world, that to all the churches it might be a pattern!" And Salimbene gives a lively description of how Henry III. welcomed him. The King rose from the table, ran to meet him, kissed him; and when his courtiers reproved him, he defended himself, saying he had done it in honour of God, of St. Francis, and of the Minister-General's saintliness; that no one could do too much honour to the servants of God; who received them received Christ. But, says the cynical chronicler, the King was reputed to be a very simple man. On his way back from England he visited France, Germany, Burgundy, perhaps Spain, besides all the houses of the Minorites in Italy.

His vigour was so untiring that, as a merciful man, he had frequently to change his companions. He was hardier than the hardiest, but evidently his austerity had the grace of natural preference and simplicity of taste, and not the painful stiffness of a too conscious overcoming of the body. When at Tarascon he is shown, with some pride, the grand bed prepared for him, he bids his guide,

P

with a laugh, take that " Pope's bed " himself, and off
he goes to sleep soundly on the hard pallet of the
humble brother. His gladsomeness, his courtesy are
constantly insisted on. In the physical picture of the
man one recognises the marks of high vitality—rather
below than above the middle height, according to Salimbene, finely made in all his limbs, well knit, sound, able
for all fatigues of the road or the study. " His face was
that of an angel, gracious and ever cheerful."

We trace his hand in many directions. Crescentius,
his predecessor, had ordered Thomas of Celano to write
a second life of St. Francis—the first with its eulogy of
Elias being now somewhat of a scandal—and had also
invited, perhaps as a sop to the *zelanti*, those who had
known the saint intimately to write their recollections
and send the same to him. The Three Companions, as
we know, responded, and probably furnished the chief
material for Brother Thomas's new work, which the
reigning Minister General still considered incomplete.
At the Chapter of Metz he asked Thomas of Celano to
compile a supplement.

All accounts seem to agree that John brought peace,
for the first few years at least. He hardly knew the
meaning of compromise, but there was some measure
in his rigour. There was no sense whatever, he held, in a
Brother Minor if he did not live a life of humble poverty ;
and he would make no terms with those who would
alter the Rule in its essentials. But he did not put back
the hands of the clock in the dark. Some changes were
accomplished facts which he could not cancel, which he
did not try to cancel so long as they did not violently
war against the essence of the Rule. There were matters,
too, he may have thought he had no knowledge of, and
he forebore meddling in their regard. Thus, he does
not seem to have stirred in any modification or confirmation of the Rule of the Clares that took place in his
time. The brothers might now hold property, not

individually, but as communities. Even Francis had
failed to stem the lust of possession. John recognised
it to some extent, for we hear of him authorising a community to take its movable property from one house to
another. He recognised another fact, too, that the
Brothers Minor accepted high office in the Church.
The Curia willed it so, and he only made some strict
regulations as to ordination.

During his term of office he was an alert man of
business. He knew, it was said, how to get through
many things in a brief space of time, how to make up
his mind quickly, and to give prompt advice. And the
matters thrust on his attention were not always high
points of doctrine and administration. We see him once
at Bologna receiving a committee in his room who
desired him to consider the wisdom of ejecting young
Guido of Massaria because he snored of nights so as
to disturb all the convent. He did not grudge his time
to simple men. His austerity was tempered by a genial
nature. No act of harshness is recorded of him. Yet
one thing he certainly lacked that makes for continued
power—a tactful partiality. The Pope took his turn of
John's attention with his poor brothers; but, to do him
justice, the Pope seems to have borne no malice. Others
were less magnanimous. You got no special favour,
might shirk no test, no duty, because you were the
Minister-General's cousin, or townsman, or old friend.
You had to be content with the privilege of his love.
And he found not a few that were so. We do not
hear of those friendships with women that sweetened
the life of Francis—the Order had stiffened into rigidity
on that point—and perhaps John was only a man for men.
But to judge him by his intimates he can have been of
no narrow nature. Among these, besides the saintly Hugo
of Montpellier, were Pietro di Spagna, the logician and
disputator, afterwards John XXI., Marco da Montefeltro
—who cannot have been too much allied to the *zelanti*,

since he acted as secretary both to Bonaventura and Crescentius; Walter the Englishman, an old pupil of John's at Naples, a man *vere anglicus*, whatever that may mean, a handsome, courtly person, and a fine musician; swarthy John of Ravenna, an honest fellow, and evidently not too ethereal—"I have never," says Salimbene, "seen a man who ate with better appetite of macaroni cooked with cheese;" Anselmo Rabuino, who in the world had been a judge; old Bonaventura da Iseo, the friend of Ezzelino, and in spite of such a friendship an excellent brother, though he did give himself the airs of a baron—*ultramodum baronizabat*—seeing his mother was only an innkeeper after all.

The first administrative duties over, his energy was still unquenched. He had the early Franciscan love for difficult and dangerous missions; and now he had a chance of realising a dream. While thinking too much prominence has been given to the heresy of his thought, and far too little to the sublimer heresy of his life, I do not, of course, deny his connection with Joachimism. The friends of his heart were Joachimites; and there was much comprised under that vague name which must have made a strong appeal to a nature like his. His next attempt is almost a proof of its influence over him. As the study of scholastic philosophy and orthodox theology had not turned him into a mere dry-as-dust student incapable of conducting affairs, so neither had his labours as a man of business and administrator, nor his constant bodily fatigue, led him to neglect that guest, his own soul. He was a mystic by natural compulsion, a man who had a sure conviction that the Kingdom of God could be realised here on this earth, that aspirations towards God were worthless without a life in correspondence, so far as human weakness allowed. The *zelanti* were the spirituals, and the spirituals were mostly tainted by the heresy of the Calabrian Abbot. John was certainly a student of Joachim's works

and, like the rest of the men of his time, may not have
very nicely distinguished between the genuine and the
spurious. Very likely it was Joachim that inspired him
with his great love for Greece, not the Greece of classic
myth and beauty, but the later Greece that had imbibed
the speculative mysticism of the East. John's devotion
to the Church of Rome is no more suspect than that
of Francis. Not only was he a submissive son but he
was a zealous one. Reverence and order in the offices
was a constant preoccupation with him. We hear of
acres litterae which he wrote to the brothers in Tuscany
who did their own will on the services. But in the
Latin genius, clear, defined, somewhat hard, which had
given the tone to the Roman Church, perhaps he missed
something which Joachim may have led him to believe
was to be found in the Eastern communion. Both
churches had something to give each other, he felt ;
and being one in their foundations, their schism was
pitiful. So now he asked leave of Innocent IV. to go on
a mission to Greece to strive to bring the two churches
together. The Pope gave leave and full credentials to
the holy enthusiast, calling him in the letters of recommendation an angel of peace. While awaiting permission he set out for Spain on one of his visiting
rounds, but he was recalled by the Pope, then at Lyons.
Innocent greeted him with a kiss, but grumbled a little
at his delay. "Why," he asked, "did you not take a
horse and come sooner?" "I came as soon as I could,"
said John simply ; "but there were brothers in the
convents I passed that said they had need of me, and
I had to do for them what I could." After Easter week
he set out from Lyons for the East, taking with him
a goodly company of brothers, and as interpreter and
guide Fra Tomaso, a Greek and a reader at Constantinople. John Vatatius the Emperor, hearing of his
coming, sent him a warm invitation. So far as Brother
John was concerned, the whole mission was a triumph.

The worth of the humble, coarsely clad men, their leader only perhaps distinguished from the rest by the *pennarolus cum calamo et pugillari et sigillum*, was not ill appraised in the East. John's manner and words, his learning and enthusiasm, his yearning for communion with their church, the evident holiness of his life, made a deep and lasting impression. Vatatius conceived a warm affection for him, and Manuel the Patriarch held him in utmost reverence. In the eyes of the clergy he was a saint already. The people hung about him and adored. All eyes turned for the moment towards Rome and the church that had bred this holy man: the mission seemed accomplished. The Emperor in his turn sent messages to Innocent to say he favoured the project, and was willing to continue negotiations. By some unexplained circumstance these Eastern legates were delayed on the way and had to turn back. Others were appointed. But then the Emperor died. Shortly after Innocent died too; and the new men in the first difficulties and preoccupations of their reign had other things to think of. The matter was shelved for the time. Yet perhaps it had been very near completion. Vatatius, with Eastern munificence, had wished to load John with presents. He would accept none of them. But one thing the Emperor forced on him, a wand (*quamdam scuriatim*) to be used when he journeyed through Greece. The legate, thinking it was a riding-switch, accepted it. But the wand was an Imperial emblem, and when the people saw it in John's hand they prostrated themselves before the humble Brother Minor, and entertained him and his company with their best, nor would accept any payment. Years later, at the Council of Lyons, in 1274, high testimony was borne to his tactful negotiations.

Many things called for immediate attention on his return. There was much irritation between the Minorites and the Preaching Order, and John did his utmost to reconcile them. Francis and Dominic had loved each other; and were they not all brothers? He and Uberto, General of the Dominicans, wrote a joint letter to the fathers of both orders urging them to peace and unity. Some Dominicans, too, had been decoying Brothers Minor into their ranks, and as a jealous shepherd the Minister-General took steps to prevent this.

But the mutterings of the greater storm that was to come were already heard. John of Parma was not overthrown by Paris. But Paris gave the impetus, provided the means of attack to his nearer enemies within the fold. The strife between the University and the Mendicant Orders was now at an acute stage. Guillaume de Saint Amour, that subtle intellect fired with white passion, had inflamed men's minds against their heresies. The old accusation of disintegrating society was flung about. There were constant recriminations between the University and the friars. John went to Paris to use his personal influence for peace. Calling the members of the University together he preached to doctors and scholars a soothing discourse. It was very humble in tone: he did not forget that he was speaking in the name of Brothers Minor. He admitted the right of the University to criticise the doctrine and science of the friars; he admitted its power to root out the plants in that "new pleasance of the Lord, the Religion of the Blessed Francis." But this full acknowledgment of the intentional subordination of the Brothers Minor in the polity of the Church was itself an appeal for fair and charitable dealing. His words were well received. It is significant that in Paris, the seat of the opposition to the Joachimite heresy, John of Parma was not only not attacked personally, but was owned as a power making for general restraint and peace. From the midst of the enemies who had come to curse his Order, one rose up to bless it, and to own what good seed had been sown by the Minorites in the field of the Church.

But the strife was only lulled. In 1255 the war over "The Eternal Gospel" burst out into a fierce flame. I need not here repeat at length what has been written so many times, the history of this bitter controversy, but only remind readers of the conclusion the most careful research has led to. The mystic Abbot of Corazzo wrote no book called *The Eternal Gospel*; but after his death, that name was given to a body of doctrine drawn from his works and from interpretations and imitations of his works made by his devoted but not very accurate students. The part of his doctrine that specially struck the imagination of the thirteenth century was his division of the history of the world into three periods, symbolised by the three persons of the Trinity. The first, that of the Father, coincided with the Old Testament era, and was the reign of Law. The second, that of the Son, coinciding with the New Testament régime, represented the active life, with the celibate priesthood, the Christian Church as it had been up to the present. The third, that of the Holy Ghost, the era of contemplation, of spiritual perfection, was not yet come; but its day was dawning. The visionary Franciscans were much attracted to this doctrine, and saw in the coming of Francis the inauguration of the new time when men should live by the spirit. It was very possible to see in this danger to the Church. Those infected with the doctrine were of many complexions. There were anarchists among them, who thought Rome had had its day, and an inner light must henceforth lead men's hearts and footsteps. That Rome took alarm is not at all surprising. It took alarm with astonishing slowness. Paris stirred it up.

In parenthesis one may say, it was not the Church alone, nor principally, that was threatened—though to connect John of Parma and his friends with any plan of social disintegration or revolution would be to go wildly astray. It is a far cry from the Joachimites to

Heine. Probably he never heard of them. Their chaotic mysticism would have made little appeal even to the most spiritual part of him. Yet perhaps, without frivolity, one may point to his second *Berg-Idyll* as a loose unconscious commentary on, or parallel to, their central idea of world-periods. He has only expressed a common experience in the progressive belief of many men who have not known themselves Joachimites, but then he has expressed it as they could not :—

> " Ach, mein Kindchen, schon als Knabe,
> Als ich sass auf Mutters Schoss,
> Glaubte ich an Gott den Vater,
> Der da waltet gut und gross ! "

(In his further description the Jehovah of the Old Testament is seen fittingly emasculated and adapted to the conception of a child.)

> " Als ich grösser wurde, Kindchen,
> Noch viel mehr begriff ich schon,
> Ich begriff und war vernünftig,
> Und ich glaubt' auch an den Sohn.
>
> .   .   .   .   .
>
> Jetzo, da ich ausgewachsen,
> Viel gelesen, viel gereist,
> Schwillt mein Herz, und ganz von Herzen
> Glaub' ich an den heil'gen Geist."

What may be called the heresy of the Holy Ghost has probably preceded or accompanied most periods of social unrest, upheaval, and revolution in Western nations. The Church was, therefore, doing political work—probably quite unconsciously—in persecuting the Joachimites and the Spiritual Franciscans touched by their doctrines. It was the Holy Ghost as the inspirer, or rather as the symbol, of freedom that drew Heine's soul.

> " Dieser that die grössten Wunder,
> Und viel grössre thut er noch ;
> Er zerbrach die Zwingherrnburgen,
> Und zerbrach des Knechtes Joch.

Alte Todeswunden heilt er,
Und erneut das alte Recht;
Alle Menschen, gleichgeboren,
Sind ein adliges Geschlecht."

None ever belonged by better right to the "noble company" of the Holy Ghost than the Knights of Francis's Table Round. But let us not disallow the claim of the valiant free lance Heine.

" Tausend Ritter, wollgewappnet,
Hat der heil'ge Geist erwählt,
Seinen Willen zu erfüllen;
Und er hat sie muthbeseelt.

Ihre theuren Schwerter blitzen,
Ihre guten Banner wehn!
Ei, du möchtest wohl, mein Kindchen,
Solche stolze Ritter sehn?

Nun, so schau mich an, mein Kindchen,
Küsse mich, und schaue dreist;
Denn ich selber bin ein solcher
Ritter von dem heil'gen Geist."

There was no such book, I have said, as *The Eternal Gospel*. But Gerard da Borgo San Donnino, an enthusiastic, hot-headed Joachimite, wrote a preface and commentaries to an abridged edition of Joachim's works. This book was known as the *Introduction to the Eternal Gospel*. No copy of it exists now. Gerard sent it out in 1255. Guillaume de Saint Amour pounced on it at once with malicious enthusiasm, and instigated the Bishop of Paris to send a copy to Pope Alexander IV. The Commission of Anagni sat to consider the production. But Guillaume, in his *Tractatus brevis de periculis novissimorum temporum*, had written things so offensive that at first he had the worst of the business. He was treated with harsh severity, and his book was publicly burned. The Pope, on the other hand, dealt tenderly with the Franciscans. By the decree of July

1255, Gerard's book was ordered to be burned too; but it was burned privately. The work had been compiled in Paris by the hot-headed zealot, who probably swallowed not only all the actual doctrines and prophecies of Joachim but likewise those to which his name had been unwarrantably attached—though here we are merely on conjectural ground. The University of Paris knew the man, and they determined to kill the evil thing that had been born at their doors. There is not the faintest reason to believe they were attacking John of Parma. The proof they were not lies in their good reception of his attempt at reconciliation just before. Also, there is not a jot of serious evidence for Daunou's assertion, repeated too often even at this hour, that John was the author of the condemned book. Would the cardinals who, two years later, were ready to imprison him for life, and who were not sparing of their accusations, have spared him this one, if they could have used it with even a show of probability? But Gerard, a man of charming nature and the purest private character, was John's friend; and the Minister-General had not hidden from his brethren that he had read the works of Joachim with edification. Gerard was probably not his initiator into the mysteries. More likely it was that holy man Hugo of Montpellier, the brother of Sainte Douceline. Salimbene, the pupil of Hugo in this new learning, says that he wrote out, in the convent of Aix, the exposition of the whole Joachimite doctrine for the use of John.

The shafts of Paris, aimed immediately at Gerard, who had openly developed his heresies under the very nose of the University, were meant to strike wider than that obscure brother. Yet assuredly they meant no special inclusion of the Minister-General. But now the price of his justice, his constant zeal for the spiritual life, was to be paid. The secret murmurs, the laying together of heads in corners, had now their visible result.

Gerard had been condemned. John, his protector, must not escape. John was a heretic. That was the cry with which they besieged the ear of the Pope—a much better cry than would have been any complaint that he had demanded strict loyalty to their profession. The Pope had to listen at last. Alexander IV. showed no distrust of John. But he was worried that a man so distinguished, who might be so useful to the Church, should have such uncomfortable ideals. He did not hasten matters. But the discontented friars did ; and when the Pope saw their temper, like a true politician, he judged the Minister impossible.

It was at the Chapter held at Ara Coeli at Rome —John himself had got the famous convent as a gift from the Benedictines—that the storm burst. But the enthusiasm for the man and the saint sent out a strong clear cry too. For there were still many spiritual brothers, still many simple ones, who had not desired, or who had not guessed their chances as Friars Minor of ecclesiastical and political intriguing. The official members, who saw in John a hindrance to the worldly advancement of the Order, chafed under his influence over these, and feared it. John had with him all the men who paid themselves for the austerity of their lives by the luxury of visions. Their recorded history is nearly all visionary. Angels and demons let and hinder them in all their comings and goings. To learn the atmosphere in which the simpler Brothers Minor lived in that age, outside the great centres and the direct influence of Rome, read the stories in the Chronicles of the time, fantastic, grotesque, poetical, childish, some-times of exceeding beauty. Here is one. Let the digression be pardoned.

Two brothers set out from Perugia on an errand late one Christmas Eve. They lost their way. They were hungry and weary. The night was cold and star-less, and they knew not where they were, save that they

stood in a dark grove of trees. Suddenly they heard
the sound of a wonderful bell, and mounting to where
the sound came from, they reached a fine convent.
There they were welcomed by the monks, were warmed,
given good food and good beds. Before they retired
they asked to be permitted to thank God by taking part
in the offices of the morrow. Ere dawn broke the bell
for matins rang, and the visitors repaired to the church.
Their Superior said the office, and preached from the
text, *Parvulus natus est nobis*, expounding to their hosts
the humility of Christ in the Incarnation. But all the
inmates of the monastery filed out one by one, save
the Abbot. And when the preacher, wondering and
fearing, asked the reason—" Brother," said the Abbot,
" you touch matter which we cannot hear. For we in
this house be all demons, who have been compelled
by the power of the Mother of God and her Gonfaloniere
Francis to minister to you in this form in this grove."
And while the brother stood trembling, lo, the monks
and the church and the monastery all vanished in smoke,
and the brothers found themselves in the bright Christmas
morning in the grove, and their way made clear before
them. This characteristic story appears with variations
in divers chronicles, and is not uncommonly told of John
of Parma himself, as happening in the " ultramontane
provinces." In these versions it is the demon Abbot
who says the office, but with such want of order, and
such terrible effect, that John commands him by the
Passion of Christ to stop and declare who he and his
monks may be. Then follow the same confession,
the same vanishing in smoke.

Had the two parties been left to fight it out at Ara
Coeli, his re-election would not have been improbable.
But Alexander held towards the Franciscans a nearer
relation than that of Pope. When John had asked him
to appoint a Protector of the Order, according to usage,
he had said he would be Protector himself. Now, as

such he was bound to concern himself very closely with their affairs. So immediately before, or during the sitting at Ara Coeli, he passed the word of order to John. "If they re-elect you, do not accept." The rumour of the Pope's command got abroad, and broke the spirit of the *zelanti*. John said to the assembled brethren they should choose a younger man—he was not fifty, and his vigour was notorious. "Choose one more worthy, one whom all will obey, and I will obey him too." It was a repetition of the scene of six-and-thirty years ago, when Francis said to the gathered brethren, "Now am I dead to you. But here is Peter of Catania whom you will all obey, and I will obey him too." A like grief took hold of the faithful, who saw one of the world's chances of holy rule vanishing from them. Leo, who was neither minister nor *custode*, was probably not present. But when some wandering *frate* brought him the news of the Chapter, he must have seemed to hear again the words of Francis echoed by John, "Lord, I commend to Thee the family which till now Thou hast committed to my care, and now on account of my infirmities, as Thou knowest, most sweet Lord, being no longer able to have that care, I recommend it to the ministers. Before Thee on the Judgment Day, O Lord, they must give an account if any brother perish by their neglect, their evil example, or by their too great rigour."

John was not a man to shuffle. His resignation was frank and decided. It is a great acknowledgment of the justice which was so salient a feature in his character, that, when some raised the cry, "Give us then, father, one to guide us," not a voice was raised in protest. They trusted any nomination by him would be in the interests of the whole body. And he named a man whose life was holy, whose learning he respected, and whose temper he thought would make for peace, Bonaventura da Bagnorea. The world has generally approved his selection. This is not the place to judge Bonaventura as a whole. He was a man of great ability, great learning, one of the loftiest religious thinkers of the Middle Ages. And he brought a certain degree of peace. He was tactful, and a politician. A follower of Francis a politician! But the incident of the persecution of John of Parma and his friends has been slurred over in the annals of his career. His motives were probably very respectable. An ascetic himself, John's extreme simplicity of life can have been no reproach to any secret weaknesses of his own. So far as Bonaventura was concerned, it was probably the heretic, and not the ascetic minister and the reformer of manners that was brought to judgment. But John's friends reproached the "seraphic Doctor" with a want of straightness. Talking together in John's cell, Bonaventura was constrained by him, listened reverently, and agreed. But in the Council he was a relentless opponent.

John would have felt he had not yet earned the right to enjoy meditation and solitude. After the decision of Ara Coeli he doubtless looked forward to following the example of Francis, to working cheerfully as a subordinate, as the minister of a province, as a teacher, or as a simple brother. But his enemies' heads were turned by their success. Having made their victims powerless, they dared now to rend them. And Bonaventura must be held responsible. First, they seized hold of the author of the *Introduction to the Eternal Gospel*, Gerard da Borgo San Donnino, with whom they associated Brother Leonard. Gerard held a bold front to his accusers. He astonished them by his clear reasoning; but their annoyance was more than their astonishment. The general feeling seems to have been that now the men were in the Church's power, they should have confessed their heresy, and had done with it. The judges demanded from Gerard and his companion this declaration: *Nos confitemur cum Petro* (*Lombardo*) *et damnamus libellum Joachimi.* And Gerard answered, Romanly, but most haughtily, *Ego confiteor cum Ecclesia et Petro Apostolo.* They had made up their minds before, and good answers availed nothing. The sentence was imprisonment for life.

The two went away rejoicing. Gerard, on the threshold of the prison, sang and cried aloud with exultation, "Into a green pasture He leadeth me." They were fettered. They ate the bread of tribulation and the water of anguish, says the old chronicler. One was released by Bonaventura eighteen years later. The other died in prison—Gerard probably: accounts differ. By that time he had become nameless. They saw no one, sent out no news to the world. The dead man was refused the rites of the Church, and was buried in an obscure corner of a garden.

John's turn came next. He was sent to the convent at Citta da Pieve in Tuscany, and there judged. The accusations were those that had been flung about at Ara Coeli. He had allowed no interpretation of the Rule, even those proposed by doctors and sanctioned by popes. John took his stand as a Franciscan. Francis had said : "I interdict, absolutely, by obedience, all the brothers, clerics, and laymen, to introduce glosses in the Rule, or in this my Testament, under pretext of explaining it. But since the Lord has given me to speak and to write the Rule and these words in a clear and simple manner, so simply and without gloss, let them be understood, and put in holy practice till the end." Well, but even if the Rule was to be strictly observed, what of the Testament ? What papal sanction had the Testament ? Had not Gregory IX., Francis's own Cardinal Ugolino, said, in his Bull, *Quo elongati*, they need not observe it ? If sanction were wanted, it was the habit of the *zelanti*, and of John, to say, the Will of Francis, composed after the impression of the stigmata, was a direct revelation from on high.

Then he had prophesied the near division of the Order. They complained loudly of this scandal while the strife was raging around them. Probably John did not deny his own shrewdness. Then he had abjured or altered the

Catholic faith in adopting the opinions of the Abbot Joachim, and sustaining them against the doctrine as affirmed by Peter Lombard. Not a murmur had risen in the alert and suspicious Paris when he lectured there on the *Sentences*. He had been in his ministry very zealous for the honour and the ritual of Rome. Standing before them now, his face turned to heaven, he began to say, *Credo in unum Deum Patrem Omnipotentem*. By the Creed of Nicæa he denied the charge of heresy. Some hearers, misunderstanding him, took it for a retractation.

I should add here that in the *Tribulations* of Angelo Clareno is mentioned a certain Fra Pietro dei Nubili, who was put in prison, where he died, for refusing to give up a treatise compiled by John of Parma. Whether he was more discreet or more unwise in his refusal we cannot tell. The rumours of a book that might not be shown to its author's adversaries must surely have done harm to John. But whatever it contained, a book that one brother could suppress definite knowledge of cannot have been greatly used for propagating heresy. John does not seem to have been questioned about it. Tocco suggests that it was the famous *Introduction*, but there is not a particle of evidence for the statement. It seems to me to limit the extent of John's Joachimism. He was the friend of Joachimite speculators. He found in the Abbot's words food and drink for his own soul in the arid places he had sometimes to dwell in while administering the Order. He lauded his doctrine with enthusiasm—*sine sale*, as said one who thought with him. But he was no fiery propagandist.

The last accusation was that Leonard and Gerard were his friends. He did not deny the friends who had gone away to prison singing. The few and gentle words in which he answered at the trial his eager, feverish accusers seem to have irritated their excited minds, and it was resolved to pass the same sentence on the ex-Minister-General as on the others. The scandalous sentence was,

Q

indeed, being pronounced, when a letter reached the judges from one too influential to be snubbed. The letter of the Cardinal Ottoboni, afterwards Pope Adrian V., was emphatic. It was almost threatening. He spoke of his sorrow at hearing of the accusation. " A holier and a more loyal man," he said, " I have never known. I do not hesitate to say that his faith is my faith. Whatever heresy you discover in him abounds in me. His person is my person. In such things as you condemn him, I also am guilty. And with him I would be counted."

This gave them pause. They could not ignore it, for they knew such words would be followed up by an agitation at Rome. Their blood cooled as they realised the might behind the meek man before them. The sentence was changed. He was allowed to choose his place of perpetual retreat. He chose Greccio, in the Roman province, " a place most apt for the spirit's peace."

Now for the remainder of James of La Massa's dream. " Brother John came down from the top of the branch whereon he stood ; and going down below all the branches hid himself in the solid root, and was all rapt in thought ; and one of the brothers that had taken part of the chalice and part had spilt, climbed up on to that branch and to that place, whence Brother John had come down." [In the *Fioretti* the name is, rather uselessly, suppressed. The other versions name, of course, Bonaventura.] " And when he was come to that place, the nails of his hands became iron, sharp and keen as razors ; whereat he left the place to which he had climbed, and with rage and fury sought to hurl himself upon the said Brother John for to do him hurt." But Christ called on St. Francis, and, giving him a sharp flint, told him to cut off the nails of Brother Bonaventura. And St. Francis did as Christ commanded.

This Tribulation made holy men in the Religion tremble. It " made lonely the hearts of many and turned their minds to a wilderness. Their mouths were dry, so that they could not utter a word. The knees of the feeble were bent, and from strong men's hands force melted away."

Perhaps, like Gerard and Leonard, he went away singing. Later historians seem to look on his resignation merely as an acknowledgment of failure. Even some of the earlier regard his exile from active life as a punishment. But to others it seemed a great opportunity. Well, simple obedience in the spirit and to the letter was his first duty as a Minorite. By his master's example he was even bidden be of good cheer for his erring flock. Had not the Lord forbidden Francis to sorrow for backsliders? "Who was it planted the Religion of the brethren? . . . Were it so that in the whole Religion there did remain three brethren only, yet even then shall it be My Religion, and I will not forsake it for ever." Now forbidden active service, the life·of meditation was sanctioned; and in spite of all his yearning to guide the brothers, John the student, the mystic, thanked the Lord for the privilege granted to him. His retrospect over ten years of constant service must have been coloured by a gentle irony.

The life contemplative is not much sought to-day; and what we neither desire nor understand we readily give bad names to. We call it egotistic, morbid, and say its day is over. The day of any great human idea and desire has always another dawn. Greccio, his retreat, is and was then a very holy place. It is situated in the valley of Rieti, about fifteen miles west of that town. To-day there is a humble Franciscan convent there. It was the birthplace of the *praesepio*. Nearly seven hundred years ago the sparse population of the neighbourhood came along the rugged paths one Christmas Eve, torches in their hands, hymns on their tongues. When they reached the place to which they had been summoned, they were ushered into a stable where were an ox, an ass, and a *bambino*.. And they adored the little Christ Child. Francis, who had arranged the spectacle with the help of the Chevalier John of Greccio, was consumed with pity. They chanted matins. Francis read the gospel, and preached, and melted his audience with his pity and love for the Babe born in a manger. In certain parts, they say—he was an Italian and a poet—his voice became like that of a little bleating lamb. From Greccio, too, the three companions, Leo, Angelo, and Rufino, sent out their legend so full of the austerity, the poetry, the beauty of the first days of the Order. And the place has many other memories of Francis and his faithful.

John, the traveller, the administrator, spent thirty-two years at Greccio. Probably his literary works belong to this time. Of most, perhaps of all, the names alone remain. Passed about from hand to hand, they were lost, and we can but guess their purport—the *De Beneficiis Creatoris*, a song of thankfulness for the peace and beauty still left to one whom the world deemed a failure ; the *De Civitate Christi*, a report of that wide country of which he was citizen while dwelling in a little obscure cell. Of the *Commercium Beati Francisci cum Domina Paupertate* I have spoken elsewhere. Whether John wrote it or not, who understood so well as he how that alliance had given his master the key to perfect liberty ? We read also of his having addressed to Roger Bacon a tract beginning "Innominato Magistro." John may have seen Roger Bacon when in England. In any case they were linked by their common friendships. His friend Hugo of Montpellier was closely intimate with Adam of Marsh and Grossetête, Bishop of Lincoln, both friends of the great Franciscan friar, the father of modern science.

John spent a good part of his time in an underground cell beneath a little church. But he was not cut off from communication with the world. Only the prison to which Gerard and Leonard had been condemned could keep a Brother Minor from his fellows, who were ubiquitous, to whom neither weather, nor distance, nor any hardships were barriers. Had he desired it, Greccio might have been an ideal place for plotting a return to power, or an overthrow of the Moderates, or the establishment of a new Order. None of the later intransigeants had so good a chance of capturing the Order for the *zelanti*. None of them had his qualities as a leader. The pilgrims to his retreat would have gone forth from him and spread his suggestions, through Italy, France, even to England. He who knew the whole Order would have known exactly where to send them. Conjuring by the name of Francis and Lady Poverty, he could, at least, have shaken some Chapter General to the heart. He had many friends at the Roman Curia. Some of them came to see him, and in their ears he might have whispered what would have injured the ruling powers in the Order. He could have laid mines against Rome itself, had he been the heretic he was said to be; for the *zelanti*, his friends, were stern enemies of the corruptions of the Church. And he could have rallied to himself the heretics outside the Church. Why did he use none of these chances? The answer seems to be a simple one. He was not the man he was supposed to be. He was no schismatic.

To none of the pilgrim brothers did he give the fiery or the insinuating message. His friends from Rome and elsewhere saw in him a prophet who vehemently denounced the calamity of the times, but also a saint, gentle towards individual men and grateful for the blessings of peace. He certainly lost his chance of a noisier fame by his restraint. Some of his partisans must have been Italian enough to despise him for not playing at the entrancing game of conspiracy. And, in the name of the stricter observance, he may have had his doubts whether resignation was best. But then Francis had given him the pattern of his conduct. He always returned to that.

He was never forgotten. During the first years some believed that by a formal declaration of past heresy he might be dragged from his hermitage back to a world that had need of him. Salimbene, that eager gadabout, got many messages for him. " Run, hasten, and rouse thy friend," they said. But Salimbene's presumption had its limits, and his prudence had none. Cardinals came to him for advice, the clear-sighted and disinterested advice of a man who knows the world and has nothing to gain or lose from it. Scholars came to be taught by the scholar who had been chosen to burn the light of knowledge in the most brilliant school in Christendom. Hugo de Digne came. But, when apart from him, Hugo seems to have known the thoughts—even inspired some of them—that visited his friend's mind. Spirituals, like Ubertino da Casale and Conrad d'Offida, went away from him comforted and instructed. Ubertino, in after years, looked back to his pilgrimage to Greccio as marking a great stage in his life. The hot-headed idealist was a young man then, and he came, on the Feast of Saint James, in great trouble and doubt. The personality of the painter counts for something in every vivid picture, and it is well to remember this in considering his portrait of John, in the *Arbor Vitae*, which represents him as even more apocalyptic than evangelic. It is that of a very old man, well nigh consumed with the fire of the spirit, pouring out prophecies and denunciations of the evils of the times, and expounding the mystic meaning of the coming of Francis. But he shed light, too, on the daily path of the anxious youth, who, looking on the sage's " angel face," flung himself at his feet, and in a passion of tears confessed his sins, and told his doubts. " Christ and Francis ordered a life for us. But the elders do not strengthen us. Nay, they even forbid our following it." John listened and advised— Ubertino well remembered all his counsels of firmness and austerity, if he forgot some others—and almost put

a date to the time when the young seeker's doubtful
path should be made all clear. Four years later, when
he was far away and much distracted, he heard of John's
death. The veil cast by alien thoughts and anxieties
was suddenly lifted, and a voice from heaven spake in
his heart the very words the sage had said to him to
confirm his faltering steps. To Ubertino John was,
indeed, that "angel which came down from heaven,
having great power; and the earth was lightened with
his glory. And he cried mightily with a strong voice,
saying, Babylon the Great is fallen, is fallen, and is
become the habitation of devils, and the hold of every
foul spirit, and a cage of every unclean and hateful bird.
For all nations have drunk of the wine of the wrath of her
fornication, and the kings of the earth have committed
fornication with her, and the merchants of the earth have
waxed rich through the abundance of her delicacies."

The pilgrims were fired by his austerity, and drank
in hope or fear from his apocalyptic visions. But one
thing they could not learn from him, his marvellous
calm. Zeal for God had eaten away all thought of
self. *Totus zelo dei corosus*, says Ubertino of him.

More than one Pope wished to make him Cardinal.
Salimbene says that death always puts a stop to their
designs. But it was a living man, himself, and the
spirit of Francis, not a dead Pope, that stood in the way
of such dignities. Although by the authorities in the
Order he was ignored, he does not seem, after some
years at least, to have been absolutely forbidden to
leave Greccio. We hear of Cardinal Pietro da Spagna
(afterwards John XXI.) sending for him. Cardinal
Jacopo Colonna, too, was his friend; and they saw each
other with mutual gladness, and rejoiced much, holding
familiar discourse of divine things.

He lived "more an angelic than a human life."
And angels served him. To this period belongs the
best known story that hangs about his name. One

morning, very early, he called a boy, his pupil and acolyte, to serve him at matins. The boy answered, but when John had gone he fell again into the heavy sleep of youth. When he woke at last, he was filled with shame. Hastening to the church, he saw that another had taken his place. Later he went to ask pardon. Brother John, meeting him on the way, put his hand on his head, blessed him, and said never before had he helped him so well and reverently. The boy said, "Forgive me, father, but I did not come at your call, for sleep overcame me. And when at last I went, another had taken my place. Yet have I asked all the brothers whether they served you at matins, and it was none of them. And there is no stranger in the house." Then John, remembering the glory on the face of the acolyte, knew that one from heaven had come to take the tired boy's place.

However diverse in character and aims were the inspired men of that age and movement, one trait they have in common—their delight in Nature. Here, as elsewhere, Francis is chief; Francis who spoke familiarly with every living thing, and found nothing dead; who loved stones and trees and flowers and water, and flame with a special delight; who would never put out a fire for reverence of its beauty. Joachim, the wild prophetic Abbot of Calabria, whom he never knew, but whose ideal of poverty was in the air and had unconsciously influenced him, and whose writings were now being devoured by the Brothers Minor, had likewise been a lover of the creatures and of the face of Nature. Folks from far and near had gathered one day to hear him preach. But the world out of doors was very fair. The sky and the trees, the hills and the valleys, were calling and singing. And Joachim dismissed his congregation that they might praise the Lord outside by delight in the world that He had made. So John of Parma, too, had Nature for his familiar friend. The wild birds of

the woods came at his call, sat by him while he wrote,
built their nests, laid their eggs, and brought up their
little ones about the table of the gentle scribe.

And so he lived his quiet life of study, meditation,
and prayer, amid the solitudes of Greccio, while pilgrims,
famous and obscure, came to him and refreshed themselves
in the presence of a man of the greater time.   The world
rolled on.   He watched from afar the struggles of the
Empire and the Papacy, the changes and chances in
his own Order.   His heart followed the strife of the
Spirituals, never triumphant, never ineffectual; trembled
for their splendid indiscretions, rejoiced in their sacri-
fices.   Like all the men of his faith he had hopes.
Some day would come "the great miracle, the stupendous reparation."   All the old friends of Francis were
dead.   Few of his own intimates survived him.   The
reign of the spirit foretold by Joachim must have seemed
long of coming on the earth.   Just all that his master
had done to wake the world he could not know.   Watching the fading and the defeat of the exquisite dream,
he could not guess that later ages should look on
Francis as the bright morning star heralding the day
of the great flowering of Italy's brain and imagination.
Dante and Giotto were born about ten years after John's
retirement.   John died but a few months before Beatrice
went to Paradise.   Ere his death Cimabue had probably
done his part in decorating the Upper Church at Assisi.
Giotto had taken up Cimabue's brush, and with clearer
eye and defter hand would, some half-dozen years later,
make the legend of Francis one of the most fascinating
painted stories in all the world.   .

And then the spirit of the wanderer woke once more
in the veteran worn with the toils and austerities of eighty
years.   The old dream of healing the breach between
the Churches of the East and West visited him again.
Greece, the land of his longings, called to him.   He
would see it before he died, fulfil his mission, and, if

God willed, he would desire to say farewell to the world beneath its skies. Nicholas IV. gave him authority to go. So, nearly forty years after his last mission, he set out once more on the long and perilous journey. First he went into Umbria, to visit the holy places of Francis and the other saints. Then his eyes turned to the Eastern road. Ancona was probably the port he aimed at. But while yet a long way off weakness came over him. This was the final call, he knew. The long journey of his life was ending. He begged his comrades to take him to the nearest convent that he might receive the sacraments, and in a little space they saw the walls and towers of Camerino. As he entered the gate he said, *Haec est requies mea in saeculum saeculi.* Daylight was failing. His coming was not known. The townsfolk saw only some poor grey-frocked friars, one very aged, and weary, and quiet. Yet the word passed round that a holy man had come to the town, and the convent where he alighted was soon full of people awaiting his blessing. A day or two later, on the 19th or 20th of March 1298, he died.

We hear of many pilgrimages to his tomb, of many miracles performed there, and of great remorse for past persecution. The Camerinians were proud of possessing his body, and when they removed it to the new monastery without the walls, they placed a fine tomb over it—*di pierra grande molto ben lavorato e accomodato.* The Camerinians could do no less. But since his bones might not rest in his dreamland, Greece, one would have liked them to lie where the wild birds might have haunted his grave, among the woods of Greccio—just as it hurts the imagination to conceive of Francis, the lover of the open road, of the face of the sky, and of his brethren, shut up in a stone vault beneath two churches.

Over his beatification there long hung much doubt. At least the Congregation of Rites thought it necessary to confirm it in 1770, and Salimbene's *Chronicle* and

Clareno's *Tribulations* were searched through by pious eyes for their testimony to his saintliness. But if before then by no formal authority of the Church, by the undoubting will and heart of the people he had always been Blessed John of Parma. They knew nothing of his heresies; knew nothing of him as theologian, logician, administrator; were not in the least affected by his dismissal from his office. In Umbria, that favoured country, the people trust their hearts and eyes, and know a saint when they see one. And for many years after the town of Camerino had got out of the way of holding great festivals on his anniversary and offering *cerii* at his tomb, it still made no difference to the people, who gathered there and found healing and consolation at his shrine.

And as in the heart of the people, so did he live in the chronicles of the Order. A murmur of regret that he was not as other men, good men too, who compromised and prospered, may now and then be heard, but it is very faint. It remained for later centuries to scorn him because he was a man of peace. Partial biographers are these old ones—the writing brothers of any note have been mainly of the Observance—but there are lives too clear effectually to defame. For the rest of the world his memory has died away, because he made no schism, no protest save by his gentle life, because he missed every chance of using princes and popes and the brothers for his own aggrandisement and the world's disturbance. Yet outside the most faithful circle of the Order, among the lovers of simplicity, the freemen of Lady Poverty, should not some fires of loving reverence still be kept alight for Blessed John of Parma?

SALIMBENE OF PARMA

" A Frere there was, a wanton and a mery.

      .   .   .   .

Until his Ordre he was a noble post,
Ful wel beloved, and familiar was he
With frankeleins over all in his countre,
And eke with worthy wimmen of the toun.

      .   .   .   .

Ful swetely herde he confession,
And pleasant was his absolution.

      .   .   .

And in his harping, when that he hadde singe,
His eyen twinkled in his hed aright,
As don the sterres on a frosty night."

AND now I come to an old friend. Here, at length, is no ecstatic, no austere reformer of manners, no scaler of the ladder of the skies. The name of Fra Salimbene of Parma may be unfamiliar. His garments and his speech may seem outlandish for the first half-minute or so; but after that, I promise you, the strangeness will wear off. Only give him the welcome his geniality deserves, and he will sit down at your hearths like a family friend. You may comfortably relax in his presence: he is very willing to take you as you are —unless you offend one of his not very numerous prejudices. In no age could he be from home; but I doubt if any age, even his own, would so have befitted his tastes and temper as would ours. As Friar Minor these had very fair chances of satisfaction. But as editor of half-a-dozen newspapers, interviewer, and diner-out he would have blossomed still more lustily.

Here some reader who has found his name in

footnotes of works dealing with Frederic II. and the
Church, may ask in a puzzled fashion — Then were
there two Salimbenes? Nay, serious reader, and again,
Yea—for there are two. There was a Salimbene who
wrote a chronicle of events stretching over the greater
part of the thirteenth century, an invaluable chronicle,
without which no historical library is complete, which has
been quoted very freely since 1857, when the work was
first printed, whose evidence makes and mars in the
eyes of to-day the reputations of the men of his own
time, and who has been given the solemnest honours
by learned German commentators. Oh, the most dignified person! The "Burnet of his time" is one of the
least of the names by which he is known. And then
there is my Salimbene—who wrote this same chronicle,
I admit, but who wrote it mainly to divert me. This
one I know so intimately that I cannot keep a perfectly
grave countenance when the other is quoted in the
footnotes of learned works as final authority for the
judgment of this man or of that. Indeed, I fear the
particular kind of interest he provides for those who
regard him first as a man is rather undermining to his
reputation as historian. The learned Quaracchi editors
propose to issue, I hear, a complete edition of his extant
works. Good news. But I cannot help thinking that
as Franciscans they will find the task embarrassing.
Evidence of appreciation of the particular brand of
humanity he displays is not, of course, altogether
wanting in his critics. M. Gebhart shakes an amused
and M. Sabatier a disappointed head over him; but
such attitudes are surprisingly rare; and I would fain
send a few more readers, curious in human nature, to
his document for what most of the grave commentators
have not troubled to gather.

One thing I would say with some emphasis at the
beginning. Salimbene is no typical Franciscan even of
the second generation. He is a familiar figure in every

age, inevitable in every movement—and some folks will
be glad therefor.   Two traits of the Minorite spirit
he reflected, its vagrancy and its fresh interest in the
world : but the latter had become a general possession
by the time he grew to man's estate.

He lived in very uneasy days ; was the actual witness
of constant war and bloodshed, did not merely hear
shuddering rumours of these from inside convent walls.
The great struggle of Frederic with the Church, the
quarrel of Frederic and the Lombard League, filled
all his earlier years, as did the fruit of these, the cease-
less strife between the Lombard towns, his later life.
His own city, turned Guelf, was in the thick of it all.
Parma was the particular aim of the Emperor's wrath,
and ever at war with its neighbours.   Between it and
utter ruin you see only the favour of its long-suffering
patroness, the Blessed Virgin.   His pages are crammed
with battles, sieges, skirmishes, with massacre and vengeance, till we in these tame days must wonder how
any other industry could be carried on save forging
spears and digging graves.   But Salimbene comfortably
informs us that, so far as his own fellow-citizens were
concerned, those who were not knocked on the head
remained mostly indifferent amid the din and confusion,
and minded their own household affairs.

He lived in an age of great religious enthusiasm.
The two mendicant Orders—and not these alone ; for the
air was full of restlessness, and bred independence, heresy,
and novelty—rousing consciences here, irritating nerves
there, had effectually waked men's souls from sleep.
They tossed uneasily, seeking hither and thither in odd
ways for salvation.   In each conflict, each disaster of
the time, a portent was read, and they cast about with
wild eagerness for escape.   Salimbene had his own safe
fold, and he looked out from it a little scornfully at
the many inferior imitations, at the *Apostoli*, *Crociati*,
Gaudenti, *Flagellanti*, *Saccati*, *Militi di Gesu Cristo*, *Britti*,

Boscaiouli, and the rest. He was not very fair to them. He despised them all; he feared a few; and his description is often caricature. But it is never mere lifeless reporting. With his own eyes he had looked on at their piety and their antics. His own Order was developing in ways that would have astonished the Founder. Salimbene, without any commanding ideals, living comfortably enough in its present, not very regretful of its past, nor very anxious about its future—for all his harangues on corruption—is not a complete chronicler of the *frati* of his day. But at least he had no temptation to be unfaithful in their regard. Once having seized his temperament and his point of view, we can gauge accurately enough the worth of his observations.

Running up and down the roads of Italy and France, with eyes and ears wide open, the rumour of awakening Europe is on his tongue. The insatiable curiosity, the impartial observation that became the Renaissance, speak through him. He is the familiar of Popes and Cardinals and humble friars, of princes and men of arms, of statesmen and crusaders, of pioneers in travel and in science, of mystics and buffoons. In his repertory there is equal room for holy hymns and drinking songs. He is alert and alive to his time and its chances, rather than beyond it—a man of the Middle Ages, but a contemporary of Roger Bacon; and Giotto and Dante were over twenty ere he died. Something of the strange incalculableness of his age is in him—an age that had begun a cold, dispassionate examination of the world; that was framing ideals of ineffable sweetness and was living them; that was racked and torn by brutal selfish strife; that was rearing the great basilicas, yet scorning all the structures of men's hands, and fleeing for refuge and joy to the City of God eternal in men's souls; an age of unnameable ferocity and of childlike freshness, of blind credulity, of dark shuddering Pagan terror, and of outspoken criticism; an age that perfected ecstasy and invented gunpowder; an age of troubadours and of torturers; the age of the *Opus Majus* and of the *Golden Legend*; the age of Francis and of Ezzelino! My Salimbene did not embody all these; but in the mirror of his chronicle something reflects from each; and his mind was large enough and keen enough for him to be a conscious observer of a goodly number of the contradictory features of his time, and muddled enough to house quite comfortably not a few. He would have listened with intelligence to Roger Bacon's dissertations on science, had they been entertainingly delivered; and though generally on the side of the powers that be, in the place of these powers would certainly have ensured the great Franciscan experimentalist his freedom. Yet Voragine's marvellous tissue of miracles and legends would have seemed to him equally worthy of credence. Let us welcome him, too, as witness of a most consoling human fact: in an age whose history, in spite of all its interest, sends most students shuddering back to the smuggest self-gratulation on their own, Salimbene enjoyed himself magnificently.

He was a born chronicler, for he would see everything, hear everything, read everything. If a king passed he must have word with him; and if the news ran of a landslip he must haste and see the damage. But I am far from saying he is a model chronicler. His book must drive a commentator crazy, and even a reader who would take stock of where he is at any particular moment grows distracted. He will suddenly dart backwards or forwards thirty years to speak of something quite irrelevant, and hardly mention he is making the leap. Of such irrelevancies he says lightly he cannot help them—"The spirit bloweth where it listeth." And a text of Scripture, the most inapt, is always the final argument and justification with Salimbene. But he had a conscience about his work neverthe-

less. We find him withholding exact particulars on the
ground that the *frati* whom he had commissioned to
gather them have not returned. He had a high notion
of his own impartiality and some instinct of his differen-
tiation from the conventional chronicler. For his style,
it is so full of the unexpected that I think it delightful.
At any rate, he is a dangerous writer to skip. Wade
patiently and steadily through some dull pages, and
when you least expect it the light will go up. All your
attention will be seized by some grotesque naïvete, some
startling revelation, some picturesque abuse. He is
artless in every sense of the word. Never witty, he is
hardly ever other than amusing. Let his talk be of
scandal, but let there be mention in it of demons, he will
suddenly pull himself up gravely, with "Now let us
return to profane history." No writer of my acquaintance can take away a man's character with such sudden,
unblushing completeness. He has been telling pleasant
stories of an acquaintance, and he continues thus : *Fuit
homo suspitiosus, qui multos libenter vituperabat et confunde-
bat ut eos posset tenere sub baculo ; quos volebat, exaltabat, et
quos volebat humiliabat; homo versipellis, callidus et malitiosus,
et subdola vulpes, vilis et abjectus hypocrita: homo pestifer
et maledictus.* So he goes on, in *crescendo*, adding "He
was my custode when I was in Tuscany." Salimbene's
adjectives are a special feature of his temper and his
style. He had a boundless store of them and he never
spared them. Out they come, chasing on each other's
heels, not all nicely chosen perhaps, but tremendous in
cumulative effect.

The Emperor is treated stingily as to epithets in
being called merely *homo pestifer et maledictus, schismaticus,
hæreticus, et epicureus, corrumpens universam terram.* This
little habit of profuseness in Salimbene must be taken
into account when we judge of men's characters by his
account of them. I am not surprised he was not always
in good odour with writers nearer his own time than we

R

are. Il Sarti, in the "Lives of famous Bologna Professors," complains loudly of his shameless way of talking of his betters. But to his style, such as it was, he evidently paid some heed. A diligent worker up of other men's chronicles, he tells of his revisions, and regrets he cannot correct everything—since vulgarisms have come so largely into use.

His education, for his time, was probably good. The fear of learning had died out of the Franciscan mind. He shows himself scornful of such upstart sects as the Apostoli, who allowed the ministrations of unlettered men, even of boys. The grammar course he had gone through before he entered the Order was followed up by lengthy studies in theology, probably in logic, certainly in music and singing. He was ever an eager learner. Writing on St. Gilbert's Day 1284, when he had been forty-six years in the Order, he says, "I have never ceased to study." With unwonted modesty he adds, "and even so, have not attained the science of my elders." But it is to be remarked that he was not chosen out, as were many of the promising young men from the Franciscan provinces, and sent to Paris to study theology. Let later ages be thankful: that, if anything, would have spoilt him for our purposes. His industry, in spite of vagrant habits, was incontestable. In his own way, and according to his opportunities, he was a real student, spending much time and trouble in copying documents for the edification or amusement of himself and friends: the works of Joachim and the Joachimites, for instance, and the sermons of Bertoldo di Lamagna, while not neglecting the topical rhymes of his day. Something of a book collector he was too; for he tells us he hid his library when Uberto Pallavicini threatened the adherents of the Church in Parma. We find his eyes fixed on the most various kinds of literature, Fra Giovanni da Pian del Carpine's travels, "The Nature of Things" of Bartholomew the Englishman, the

prophecies of the Joachimites, the book on the Art of
War by the Emperor Theodosius, the Latin Classics, and
the poet Patecchio, whom he did his very best to boom.
Perhaps his restless interest in his neighbours hindered
his book knowledge from being very profound or exact;
but such as it was he had it ready on the tip of his
tongue and used it with fine effect—as when he reproved
Robert of the Apostoli for taking a dedicate virgin to
wife, quoting the case of the King of Ithaca who married
Iphigenia, the daughter of the former king—though she
had been dedicated to the Lord by Matthew the Apostle,
and was Abbess of more than two hundred virgins—and
who incurred the most terrible penalties thereby. But in
spite of his literary curiosity and his scribbling habits, it
would be a great mistake to think of him as a bookish
man. He was too much on the roads for that, and for
all his friar's frock, too much interested in practical and
material things. He speaks contemptuously of his fellow
citizens' want of capacity, and laughs at their new canal.
If only they had given him a free hand, he knows exactly
the kind of canal he would have made for them. His
mind had a distinctly scientific bent, though he shared to
the full his neighbours' credulity and ignorance. His interest in natural phenomena is constant. The great frosts,
when wolves came howling into Parma, when horsemen
crossed the frozen Po; the eclipses, when at black midday
the stars could be seen, and men and women ran hither
and thither through Lucca, mad with fear; the wonderful comet of 1264 that disappeared with the passing of
Urban IV.; the blessed weather of 1266, May all the
year round, by the grace of God, ordained so for the
succour of the French army come to the aid of the Church
and the extermination of the host of the cursed Manfred;
the plague of birds in the autumn of 1268, when from
supper time till twilight you could hardly see the sky
over the vineyards; the lunar eclipse of 1239, when,
about matins, in the moon there appeared the sign of the

cross; the great mortality of men and hens in 1286, when one good lady of his acquaintance lost forty-eight chickens; and that year when God seemed " angry with the gardeners "—all are recorded with vivacious interest. Lest such records should be thought frivolous, he suggests them as texts for preachers.

A word as to the later history of his Chronicle. For many centuries the MS. was lost. Muratori could only speak of it at second-hand. It was found at last in the Conti Library, where it long remained, consulted now and then by a few scholars. Affò knew it and used it a little, but he was not anxious for its publication—*perciocchè racchiude cose gravi alla corte di Roma.* Bolder spirits, however, desired to bring it to light; but before the Abbate Regi, keeper of the Conti Library, gave consent, the MS. had been sold to the Vatican. The Abbate Amati had, however, already made an incomplete copy for the Duke of Marini Sermoneta, which was meant to be inserted in a new edition of Muratori, an enterprise put a stop to by the Napoleonic disturbances; and after the Duke's death the copy was sold. Finally, in 1857, it was published in Parma as the third volume of the *Momumenta Parmensia.* We cannot withhold gratitude for this edition; but it is an ill-done piece of work. Some of the omissions are of great importance, and seem regulated by caprice or indolence on the part of the copyist rather than by any weightier reason. There are many blunders of transcription. Frequently omissions are not marked, while sometimes there are marks of omissions where none exist. Clédat and Novati have done their best to fill in the gaps for those of us who cannot consult the Vatican Codex, which was first made accessible to scholars, I believe, by the present Pope when he was Cardinal Pecci. In 1882 was published an Italian version of the Parma MS., for which it is difficult to say one good word. Besides repeating all errors and omissions of the 1857 edition, it adds an incompetence of its own. With prudent indolence the 1857 editors sent their book out without a note. But the translator, feeling this rather unhandsome, has given footnotes which one critic is not unjust in describing as having their source in a railway roadbook.

Before touching further on the matter of the Chronicle, let us look at the circumstances of the writer's life. He was born at Parma on Saints Dionigi and Donnino's Day, October 9th, 1221—five years before the death of Francis—of a substantial and honourable family, known for three generations back as Di Adamo, but before that as Grenoni. His father, Guido di Adamo, was a man of wealth and position. His son describes him as a handsome and robust person, and tells us that in early life he went to the Crusades in the time of Baldwin, Count of Flanders. No other pious act is recorded of him; but he was on intimate terms with at least one Pope, Innocent IV. The family house in Parma stood near the Baptistery. Of his ancestry, of his sisters, brothers, cousins, aunts, we are given a very particular account. Not that he is vain. Oh, no. He has searched out the question of his descent and family history really on behalf of his niece Agnes, a Clare, who was desirous to know for what forefathers and relatives she should offer prayers to God! There were noted soldiers and jurists in the family; but it had also many pious members. His grandfather Oliviero was founder of the Society of Sta. Maria. His cousin Aica was a nun of St. Paul, and her sister Romagna a Clare. Another cousin, Giacomo Oltremarino, was a well-known Minorite. His elder brother, Guido di Adamo, entered the Order before him. Guido's wife became a Clare. Their child was the pious Agnes. His sister Caracosa was for a time prioress of the Clares at Reggio. His mother, Imelda da Cassio, had a brother a Minorite, and she herself in later life became a Clare.

When the earthquake at Brescia took place, Salim-

bene lay in his cradle.   His mother took his two little
sisters, one under each arm, and ran with them in terror
to her father's house, leaving him behind.   Very im-
prudently she told him the tale when he had reached the
age of consciousness.   It made a bad impression on him,
which he never got over, for inside his frock the male
creature was always lustily alive.   As if a boy were not
of far more importance than two girls !   But if he never
forgave her, he did justice to her qualities.   She was
charitable, and she never beat her maidservants.   But he
says the best influence on his childhood was that of his
grandmother Ermengarda, who lived many years in his
father's house, and gave him excellent advice.

But Salimbene was not Salimbene then.   What was
his actual baptismal name he does not tell quite clearly.
He would have liked it to be Dionigi, as he was born
on that saint's day ; but it was not.   Some called him
after his godfather, Baliano di Saetta, a great French
baron, perhaps a crusading friend of his father's, who
held the infant at the font.   But his companions
called him Ognibene, and under that name he was
received into the Order.   Doubtless, old Guido di
Adamo thought he had done enough for religion in
permitting his eldest son to be a *frate*.   When he was
aware of the determination of his second and only other
legitimate son, he was beside himself with anger.   Here
was he a man of possessions, and none of his children
would use them, or increase them, or hand them down
to their children.   It was monstrous !   But surely the
infatuation of a lad of sixteen could be checked.   Ognibene, however, was a young man of purpose ; and secretly,
or in his father's absence, took the step which was not
easy to retrace.   Perhaps the excitement of the Alle-
luia, its preaching, its processions, and its penitence,
which he watched as a boy in Parma, had something
to do with his decision.   *Jam perveneram ad bivium
pythagoricæ litteræ, et completis tribus lustris, idest uno in-*

dictionum circulo, is his unusually pedantic way of saying he was about sixteen years old when, on St. Gilbert's Day, February 4th, 1238, he put on the habit of the Order. In the convent of Parma at that moment was no less a person than Elias, the Minister-General, on his way to Cremona to negotiate between Gregory IX. and the Emperor. I think it not improbable that young Ognibene knew the fact, and rushed the reception that it should be accomplished under such dignified auspices. Yet the lad was a cool critical observer of the demeanour of the Minister-General, who received the courtesy of the Podestà so haughtily. Or he revised his impressions in later years. Not the Podestà alone did honour to the Minister-General. The Abbot of the Convent of St. Giovanni sent capons for Elias's supper, where the young postulant was present still in his secular dress. Next day, on the Eve of St. Agatha, he was received, Fra Gerardo da Modena being present as well as the Head of the Order. Afterwards the *frati* in the convent took the young novice into the infirmary, and proposed to give him a splendid supper. He had dined well at home; but a healthy boy never refuses good cheer, and he consented. Alas! then had he a foretaste of the asceticism to come. The *frati* had no capon to offer him; and the pampered youth was served with cabbage—he who had never eaten the vulgar vegetable before, and who vowed he never would again, if he could help it!

Ognibene was sent to Fano, and the place had doubtless a marked influence on him. The convents of the Marches of Ancona were faithful to the strict observance, and there the lad would be early trained in hardy ways, in strict Franciscan tradition, and to suspicion of that haughty Minister-General who had received him. Meanwhile, the boy's father was in despair. To the Emperor, passing through Parma about that time, he complained that his son had been stolen by the Minorites. Guido was a man worth pleasing, and Frederic wrote to Elias that if he valued his favour he would instantly restore the lad to his parents. Guido, with the imperial order in his hand, ran in hot haste to Assisi to find Elias. Elias evidently kept the letter among his collection of autographs of the great, for in after years his secretary, Illuminato, showed it to Salimbene. The Minister-General dealt cautiously in the matter. He must not offend the Emperor, nor one who had the ear of the Emperor ; yet the lad was of the kind that he thought valuable in the Order. So he wrote to the *custode* at Fano to let the boy go if he wished, but if his desires and vocation were clear, to keep him as the apple of his eye. From Assisi Guido ran to Fano with a company of knights to overawe the brothers. Fra Geremia, the *custode*, called for the boy, who, in the presence of his father, declared his determination final, and quoted Scripture in the promptest and pertest fashion. " You are coercing him," roars the father. " I will see him alone." Father and son are left to themselves, the *frati* meanwhile trembling like reeds in the water, or so the boy proudly imagines. Neither his Scripture nor his defiance fails him, and Guido at last throws himself on the ground, and curses him with an awful curse. " I consign thee to a thousand devils, and thy brother also who is with thee in this, for he, too, has deceived me." And Guido departs with his knights to wail over the evil fortunes of his house. " Thus I, Brother Salimbene, and Brother Guido di Adamo, entering religion, destroyed the hope of our house in sons and daughters, to build it up again in the skies."

Next night there came to him that most rewarding vision of simple, tender mediæval souls, in which the Virgin Mother gave him her child to hold and to kiss. Salimbene, looking back over a long life lightened by quite other joys, swears that never again has he felt such sweetness. Judged to be still in peril from an angry father bereft of an heir, he was sent to the house of Martino da Fano, an eminent doctor of laws; but the *custode* hearing that Guido had bribed the pirates of Ancona to kidnap him, and the Podestà to wink at the crime, despatched him to the Convent of Jesi during Lent. Here followed him a letter from the Minister-General, most flattering to a novice, complimenting him on his firmness, and offering to send him, if he willed, into another province. The young *frate* accepted; chose Tuscany because he had friends there, and set out for Lucca. On his way he passed through Citta di Castello, and there held converse with an old hermit, the last brother, he says, received into the Order by Francis himself. When he gave his name as Ognibene, the hermit said, "My son, there is none good save God alone. Let thy name be rather Salimbene, since thou tookest a good step in entering the Religion." And Salimbene he was from that day forward.

How much of all this is true, what embroideries, and what colour he put into the story of the conflict with his father, and whether the pirates were really suborned to kidnap him, I cannot tell. I think Salimbene was probably a liar about himself—a harmless liar, like some fanciful, agreeable, and quite honest children.

In the first year of his life at Lucca, Elias fell. No more special favour and notice from him any more. On all hands he heard tales of his pride, his luxury, his treason to the Franciscan ideal. Himself had witnessed his contemptuous haughtiness. Salimbene, always susceptible to the tone around him, piously shuddered now in response to it, and afterwards wrote *De Prelato*, from which the condemners of Elias have drawn so largely for their evidence. Yet if Elias had weathered the storm, Salimbene would not have been the last *frate* I can imagine in his train. Elias would have found the intelligent, news-gathering, restlessly curious, not very sensitive brother a useful hanger-on. At Lucca there happened a terrifying eclipse of the sun. The Lucchesi, maddened with fear, repented of their sins; made up their quarrels; and the Podestà, with a cross in his hand, went round the city followed by the Minorites (Salimbene and his brother Guido amongst them) and other religious bodies, and preached the Passion of Christ. At Lucca he seems first to have seen the great Joachimite Hugo of Montpellier. After two years he went for other two to Siena, where the saintly Raymond of Arezzo ordained him as sub-deacon. But the most notable personage he met there was Bernard of Quintavalle, the first companion of Francis, who stayed in the Siena convent for a whole winter. The kindly venerable old man told the boys many wonders of the Blessed Francis and other good things. Pisa was his next sojourning place; and here he went through a severe crisis, a fact we learn not by lengthy description, but by some vividly revealing anecdotes. While he and his companion—a lay brother, a light-minded fellow, and not the last of the sort, by any means, with whom Salimbene kept company—were begging through the streets, they entered a courtyard, and saw what in his account reads like a mixture of a circus, a menagerie, and a vision of Paradise. There were shady vines and fragrant flowers, and leopards and other strange beasts from over the sea; youths and damsels, too, most fair to the eye; and they played such music as entranced the soul. No one spoke to them. They spoke to none. The *frati* tore themselves away at last; but Salimbene, enervated by sensuous delight, was in no good case to withstand an encounter with the man who soon accosted him in the street, who said he knew him, and that he came from Parma. His fellow-citizen openly jeered at his way of life, not even giving him credit for saintliness—mere self-will, he called it. Whom was he benefiting? Beggary was surely a mean resort for his father's son. "How many servants in your father's house go clad in rich raiment and eat rich meats, while you are begging from door to door from those who have not enough for them-

selves! How great a giver you might be to the poor!
How much better to be caracolling on your charger
through the streets of Parma, your feats of arms bringing
gladness and spirit to the sad, the consolation of all the
ladies, and the hope of all the play-actors in your native
town! But now your father and mother are consumed
with grief on your account, miserable, blind, and naked
pauper!'" Salimbene had, of course, Scripture ready for
the occasion; and his tempter was roundly abused for his
carnality. But the incident depressed him much. The
fact was, he was tired of begging, and ashamed of it.
The words of the tempter echoed through his heart.
Wearied with struggle and regret, he fell asleep and he
dreamt. In his sleep he saw himself begging about the
streets of St. Michael, on the Visconti side—the rich Parma
merchants settled in Pisa dwelt on the other side, and
there he was always ashamed to let a son of his house be
seen on a beggar's errand. Now, in his dream he waited
at the door of a house for his companion to come out
with the bread he had begged. And, lo, the *frate* who
put the bread in Salimbene's basket was no *frate*, but the
Son of God! Oh, wonder of wonders! And His Mother
was there, too, and St. Joseph, each come out of heaven
to beg for and with the poor brothers. After that, for
the messengers who came from his still discontented
father, were they cavaliers or play-actors, he cared no more
than for "the fifth wheel of a coach." When one would
falsely say, "Hasten home, Salimbene, thy mother is
dying," he would answer, "My father is an Amorite and
my mother a Hittite." His vocation was fixed. And
he would be strengthened in his resolve by his *custode*,
Fra Lotario, the pious man to whom the shrine of Alverna
owed its restoration. The men who guarded his early
years were of the simpler, nobler order.

Having been eight years in Tuscany, he was transferred
to the province of Bologna. After a sojourn at Cremona,
he went back for a time to his native town of Parma.

He was now a man of twenty-five, and, though as yet only a deacon, had attained a certain amount of independence. Discipline, so far as coming and going went, was by no means uniform in the Order. It seems to have been very slack in Salimbene's case—probably because he was a favourite. In 1241–1243, before he left Pisa, there was no pope, and Frederic, he says, closed the ways lest any one of importance should pass to Rome. Whoever was on the roads was liable to arrest and examination. Salimbene, already a vagabond, was taken prisoner many times. It was then, he says, he learnt to write in cipher.

With his arrival in Parma ends the first part of his life. Till then he had been a good deal under tutelage. His ambitions may even have been pious. Hereafter we find him immersed in politics, in watching the strife of parties, in quite independent study, in free converse with all sorts and conditions of men and women, too—though always fulfilling the duties of a religious, and always playing the rôle of an orthodox and respectable man. I throw no doubt on his infant piety. I am sure he was no rebellious pupil of the saintly and ascetic men who trained him. A lover of the good things of the world, he gave up many of them in sticking to his profession. But I am convinced that after this date not piety alone, but all the strong instincts of a vivacious spirit very well fitted to live an active life among men, kept him fast in the ways he had chosen, and prevented a single regret. Ah, he knew something better than caracolling up and down the streets of Parma in sight of the ladies ! He had all the roads of Europe if he liked. He had all the pageantry and excitement of war, without too much of its perils, though I am sure Salimbene was no coward. He was not tied fast to camps or council rooms—could hang around both, irresponsible, yet with the ear of the great ones. No fine palazzo was his, but he was a welcome guest at a hundred tables. No one fair lady could he make his own ; but good Fra Salimbene was so amiable, so consoling, so understanding in the little difficulties of people of the world, there were scores who desired to confide in him. His Order might be abused by the secular clergy. But popes were its friends. A king belonged to it, and a margravine. Barons protected it, and begged as a special favour to be buried in its churches. Minorite guests were as fashionable in the great households as were philosophers in eighteenth century French salons. To be a soldier at this time must have seemed to the discerning eye of Salimbene a poor, provincial kind of thing. To be a Minorite was to be *dans le mouvement*. And there we have Salimbene's ruling passion.

All Romagna was at strife. Parma, where he was now stationed, was besieged. Frederic's temper was roused against it for its heated espousal of the cause of the Church. Salimbene found himself in a whirl of excitement. He was doubtless in the thick of it all, catching a word with the leader of this faction or of that, discussing the whole business with the man in the street. But whether subsistence was difficult, or whether the siege made him restless for adventure, or whether, as he afterwards said, he had the direct orders of his provincial, he suddenly left the city, and made his way to Lyons, where the Pope was. Innocent had been a canon of Parma and a friend of his father ; and Salimbene evidently counted on a good reception ; but his best passport to favour was the news he brought of the besieged city suffering for its defence of the Church. The Pope sent for him on All Saints' Day, 1247, spoke with him alone in his chamber, bestowed on him the faculty of preaching, and gave him also a permit for his mother, now probably a widow, to enter the Clares. At Innocent's court one day he was asked by Cardinal Fieschi what was thought in Parma of the papal legate in Lombardy, Cardinal Ottaviano, and Salimbene spoke out frankly : " They think him a traitor who will betray them as he did Faenza." " Oh—oh—oh ! " came in shocked tones. But Salimbene stood his ground. "So they say. I know not." They all crowded round him, the man out of the besieged city on which so much depended. He enjoyed the sensation he made—men standing on each other's shoulders to watch his audacious face, and saying with admiration, "Never in our lives have we heard a *frate* speak with so much frankness and assurance." "But they said this," he goes on, "because they saw me sitting between the Patriarch of Constantinople and the Cardinal who had invited me to that place, an honour which I did not think seemly for me to refuse." Nevertheless, in later years Salimbene was on good dining terms with Ottaviano. He would sit with him at table, only one *frate* between—and the wine was exquisite! In such circumstances he took as his guide the Scripture counsel as contained in Proverbs xxiii. 1—"When thou sittest to eat with a ruler consider diligently what is before thee!" He had a standing invitation, indeed, but he recalled Ecclesiasticus xiii. (The copyist gives no exacter indication of the text that limited his acceptances; but Salimbene's intimates are hardly left in doubt in a chapter which contains, "If a mighty man invite thee, be retiring, and so much the more will he invite thee.")

Yet he never pretends the legate was a good man; and frankly tells stories against him. A jester mocked the Cardinal one day aloud, as a traitor to Rome; and Ottaviano in a whisper ordered an attendant to give him money—"for everything yields to gold." "And so was he rid of that vexation," adds our friend.

But to return to Lyons. Salimbene was always at the Pope's side, he assures us. Indeed, according to his own account, he enjoyed such favour that why he never became a Cardinal, at least, remains a mystery. Preferment of a kind, of course, he might have had. What he would have accepted was evidently not offered; and with that winning preference of his for freedom over

tame honours, he used such favour as was given him
to go a-wandering.

France was his field. So after All Saints' Day, 1247,
he set out, and his travels were entertaining from the
first. In his earliest stopping-place he found Fra Giovanni da Pian del Carpine, just returned from a
mission given him by Innocent IV. to the Great Khan
of Tartary. The brothers sat round him to hear of his
struggles to reach the palace, of his life amongst the
strange Tartars, who eat horse and drink asses' milk, of
how he saw men of every nation under heaven, save two,
and how he might not enter the Great Khan's presence
except clad in purple. Then they heard how the Lord
of Tartary asked Fra Giovanni of the West and its
rulers, and how he answered as a good Guelf, and delivered the Pope's letter; and how the Fortitude of God,
the King of all men, sent one in reply to the Great
Pontiff, proud, dignified, piously ferocious in words and
tone. Were the Christians the only lovers of God?
Nay. And for those slaughtered Moravians, Hungarians,
and Poles, had they not disobeyed God and the Great
Khan? And since they had been delivered into Tartar
hands, had not the Lord 'so willed it? Is it peace the
Christians want? Then let them lay down their arms.
If not, we shall know it is war they desire. And what
is to come, only God knows. Salimbene, eager and curious as usual, copied the letter ere he parted from Fra
Giovanni. Briançon was his next stopping-place, then
Troyes, where he stayed fifteen days, for it was the time
of the two months' fair, and there was much chattering
to be done with the Lombard and Tuscan merchants.
Then on to Provins, and a halt there from St. Lucy's
Day to the Purification, when he reached Paris. Concerning Paris, where he stayed eight days, he is dis-
appointingly silent, saying only he saw many things that
pleased him. His visit to Clugny impressed him much,
and at the Benedictine magnificence he was in no wise

shocked. Then he went on to Sens, in response to a hearty invitation. "The French brothers liked my company, for I was peaceable and young and gay; and I used to say nice things about their doings." There, while laid up with a cold, came the news of the flight of Frederic from his own city of Vittoria, the destruction of Vittoria, and the loot of the Imperial treasure. At the news the impressionable Salimbene threw off his illness altogether; and to amuse him, there was Fra Giovanni again, returning from a mission to the King of France. He had his book about the Tartars with him, and the brothers read it greedily, the author commenting and explaining where necessary. Salimbene says he was the special companion of the traveller and diplomat, his neighbour at table in the convent and when he dined out, as he often did, in the monasteries and abbeys of the district. Our *frate* saw much life in his company ere he passed on to Auxerre, to which convent the French provincial had allotted him. And Auxerre was only a fresh chance of making friends, for there he frequented the house of the great logician and disputator, Master William, who wrote the *Summa* on the offices of the Church—though he was such a poor hand at a sermon! There was nothing at all monotonous in the life. Three times did he go through the whole diocese, first with a brother who was preaching St. Louis's Crusade, again with another who preached on Holy Thursday in a magnificent Cistercian monastery. These two spent Easter with a countess, who gave them twelve courses at dinner—and if the count, her husband, had been at home there would have been even better cheer. Pontigny, the asylum of the exiled Thomas à Beckett, that most honoured Guelfic saint, was pointed out to him as a special place of interest on this tour. Then came a third round with Brother Stephen, during which he made several secular observations—in which convents, for instance, beer was drunk, and in which wine. On

the white wine of Auxerre he is eloquent.   Who drinks
it grows gay and frank.   And in this gay mood, he
trolls out—

> " El vin bon et bel sel dance
> Forte et fer et fin et france,
> Freits et fras et fromijant."

But he shakes his head over the thirsty French and
English, though, as is his wont, he is more kindly to our
nation than to the French.   After all, the poor English
have so little wine at home that a little excess when an
opportunity comes is pardonable.

After Pentecost, 1248, from Auxerre he went back
to Sens, to attend the Provincial Chapter, a very notable
one, for St. Louis was present.   The *frati* went out to meet
him, and lined the streets, all eager to have the first glance
of the king.   Salimbene, of course, was not merely one
of the crowd.   Fra Rigaldo, Archbishop of Rouen, had
taken so long to put on his full canonicals that he
was late for the procession.   Salimbene saw him, a mitre
on his head and a crozier in his hand, running hither
and thither, asking, "Where's the king, where's the
king?"   He couldn't let a poor dressed-up archbishop
run about like that and lose himself.   So he followed
him close, and no doubt guided the prelate and himself
to a place of honour and vantage in the spectacle.   Salimbene was impressed with the pageant; but, really, the
Sens ladies might have been more attractive.   *Pedissequæ
esse videntur.*   Of the king we have a charming picture.
He was *subtilis et gracilis, macilentus, convenienter et longus,
habens vultum angelicum et faciem gratiosam.*   He came
not in royal pomp, but on foot, in pilgrim's dress, *habens
capsellam et burdonem peregrinationis ad collum, qui optime
scapulas regias decorabat ;* and his brothers were in as lowly
guise as himself.   But Salimbene's admiration for so
very monklike a king is not complete.   As Louis came
out of the church of the *frati*, where he had been pray-

s

ing, the chronicler was at his elbow. In the house of the Chapter the king spoke of his Crusade—only the knights and the *frati* being present—amid floods of tears from the French brothers. And when the Minister General, John of Parma, had spoken and blessed the enterprise, the king and the nobles dined with all the company. Salimbene gives us the menu of this comfortable fast day fare—cherries and fine white bread and good wine fit for a king, then wafers, beans cooked in milk, fish and lobster, eel pies, rice with milk of almonds powdered with cinnamon, eels browned in exquisite sauce, tarts, junkets and fruits without stint and of the best, and all served with daintiness.

Next day Louis went on his way, and somehow Salimbene felt a burning desire to go that very instant to Provence. Having got leave for this from the Minister-General, he followed in the king's track, and as Louis only went off the high road here and there to pray in some Minorite hermitage, it was easy to keep him in sight. Indeed, our eager note-taker dogged the royal devotions with something very like indiscretion. At Vezelay, for instance, we learn that the king sat on the unpaved floor of the church, called the *frati* around him, and again begged their prayers, and waited patiently till his brother Charles, Count of Provence, should have finished his. Salimbene is careful to tell us he stationed himself so as to watch, impartially, the king waiting on the threshold and the count on his knees at the altar. And of this description of Louis at the Chapter of Sens, and of his journey to the coast, nothing is to be found in his own special chronicler; for the Sire de Joinville did not join the royal party till it had reached Cyprus.

The king embarked soon after; and Salimbene, paying his respects to the Pope at Lyons in passing, went on to Arles, to Marseilles by sea, and then to Hyères to visit the famous Hugo de Digne.

It would be a mistake to look on our pleasant Salim-

bene as merely a vulgar button-holer, a hanger-on of rich
and powerful folks. He was a quick-witted man, who
took impartially the whole of life for his sphere of interest. Whatever was in the air, whether a good dinner
or a heresy, he would nose it; and he would never grow
besotted with good cheer, nor endanger his safety by his
light coquetting with heterodoxy. A new book, a pretty
face, a bit of news, a savoury dish, a new sect—if this
last did not interfere with Minorite sources of maintenance—he would run hither and thither in search of each
and all. He had met Hugo before at Lucca and Siena,
but since then had heard more of his opinions and his
fame. At Pisa he had seen an abbot of the Order of
Floris, who had brought there all the copies of the works
of Joachim, for fear the emperor should burn his own
convent. At Provins he had found two zealous Italian
Joachimites, who would fain have converted him. One
of these was the famous Gerard da Borgo San Donnino,
whom the French brothers hated for his dismal prophecies concerning St. Louis's Crusade. Salimbene listened
out of sympathy, and then was much impressed, notwith-
standing the expostulations of Brother Maurice, who
advised him rather to help in the compilation of a book
of precepts for preachers.

Joachimism was in the air. It was *dans le mouvement*
to be a Joachimite, still rather distinguished, delightfully
secret, yet not very dangerous. Four years would pass
before Gerardino should write the notorious *Introduction;*
and no taint of heresy clung as yet to the Minister-
General. To Salimbene's curiosity we owe some remarkable pictures of mediæval intellectual and religious
coteries. Hugo, a man of real learning, a great preacher,
"this other Paul, this second Elisha, with a voice like
the sound of many waters," the great disputator, the
friend of Hales and Grossetête, who had refused the
cardinal's hat, did not disdain to instruct any inquirers
who came to seek for truth. Salimbene and others found

him an eager teacher. Hugo's community is vividly
described. His office in the Order he had by this time
resigned, and he lived at Hyères very poorly. A great
master of the spoken word, he wielded a paramount
influence in the neighbourhood. Many of his adherents
were lawyers, judges, doctors, and men of letters, who
met together in Hugo's cell to hear him speak of the
kingdom of God that was coming on the earth, expound
the mysteries of Scripture, and foretell the future. Some
visitors were scoffers. Hugo was ready to challenge
them; and one disputation between him and the Dominican Peter of Apulia, in which Peter appeals impartially
to Merlin and the Hebrew prophets, is described with
spirit. Hugo was too much for him, and Peter left a
beaten man, his vanquisher remarking of him and his
Order, "Those good fellows always pride themselves on
their science, and say that the fount of all wisdom is in
them, and that they come amongst idiots when they
come to Minorite houses, where, nevertheless, they receive
nothing but kindness." But Peter came back to sit at
Hugo's feet.

Joachimism may have been for Salimbene only *le
dernier cri;* but he always took trouble in feeding his
interests and fancies, and retiring from Hyères to the
convent at Aix, he devoted himself to the writing of an
exposition of what he had learned from Hugo of the new
doctrines, for the Minister-General, John of Parma. He
spent seven months over this laborious work, and at the
end of that time Hugo and he were invited by Raymond
the Provincial of Provence to go and meet the Minister-
General at Tarascon. Here he was on very intimate
terms with Brother John, it would appear—as fellow-
townsman, distant relative, as one who had just been toiling in his service, and as the always agreeable Salimbene.
Together they went to see the body of St. Martha. When
John stayed out late in the cloister, it was Salimbene sat
up for him to show him to the state bed, which the sub-

ordinate had after all to lie on himself. From Tarascon
he and his friend Giovannino dalle Olle went down the
Rhone in the minister's company to Arles, and so genial
had John been on the road that Giovannino begged
for himself and his companion the *aureola*, that is, the
faculty of preaching. But the austere one made answer,
"Were you indeed my own brothers in the flesh, you
would not have it without test of fitness." Whereupon
Salimbene, a little puffed up with all the favours of the
great, burst out, "A fig for the aureole! Pope Innocent
himself gave it me a year ago at Lyons; and should I
receive it again from Brother Little John of San Lazzaro?" Wise John of Parma did not quarrel with a spoilt
child. Salimbene's companion was more flattering. He
would rather receive it, he declared, from their Minister-
General than from any Pope; and here was the illustrious
Hugo who would be examiner. Nay, said John, no
intimate friend shall examine you, but the reader and
repetitore of the convent. Salimbene, in spite of his sauci-
ness, appears to have undergone the test also, perhaps
voluntarily, to score a triumph in the eyes of the General,
perhaps compulsorily, for John was quite equal to ignor-
ing a faculty given without a test even by the Pope
himself. He conferred the faculty on Salimbene; but
put out a mild hand of authority to check the vaga-
bondage of the garrulous busybody. "Choose a convent," he said to him, "any you like save Paris. Tell
me to-morrow which you have chosen before I set out
for Spain." But a born vagrant has few local preferences,
and this one said sweetly, "Where you will, my father."
"To Genoa, then," was the answer. "I commend you
to the minister there, to make you priest, and your
companion deacon. When I come there, if I find you
content, I shall rejoice. If not, I shall send you elsewhere." And they accompanied the minister to his
boat on the Rhone, and said adieu, going by sea themselves to Marseilles, where they kept the feast of their

father Francis. Again by sea they went once more to
Hyères, lingering a while in the company of Hugo till All
Saints, Fra Giovannino ill and unwilling to move—though
Salimbene urged him to go ere the storms of winter
came on, and because Hyères was so unhealthy at that
season. By dint of coaxing and scolding, the timid man
was shoved, grumbling, on board at last, and saved, ir
roughly, from death, for the mortality after they left
was great. A hearty reception awaited them at Genoa.
The guardian gave them two tunics, one fine and one
coarse. Salimbene was ordained priest, and given lessons
in saying mass and singing. At Genoa, as elsewhere,
he knew everybody, and kept his eyes and ears open.
Next year, 1249, he was sent by the Provincial to John
of Parma concerning the affairs of the province. He
took Hyères on the way, and the ascetic Hugo made
good lenten cheer for him. The Minister-General was
at Avignon, and Salimbene journeyed on with him to
Lyons, where John went to see the Pope about the
mission to Greece. There our vagrant met with another
reproof, this time from Rufino, the minister at Bologna,
who had evidently lost sight of him. But Salimbene's
reproofs from his superiors were always so flattering.
"Did I not send you into France to study for my province? And yet you have been to Genoa. Most annoying, this kind of behaviour, when I take so much trouble
to get studious brothers for Bologna!" And Rufino
was peremptory as to his return. So off Salimbene set,
by way of Vienne, to deliver his message in Genoa and
do his superior's will. But he took time, as he passed
Grenoble, to go and see the great landslip of the year
before. He stopped, too, at Embrun, though he refused to dine with the archbishop—who had such a liking for the *frati Minori* that he had no pleasure in
life when he had none of them at his table. But then
a reception fit for one who had come lately from the
Curia would delay his journey. The Genoese brothers

received him back with open arms, and feasted him, because he had come from far and had brought good news. On his way back to his own province Salimbene and his companion travelled through countries racked and torn by strife. It was the moment of Enzo's capture. But he was always a sight-seer. At Bobbio they were shown one of the water-pots which had held the miraculous wine of Cana—at least, so they were told. Whether it was so, he remarks, God knows, to whom all is clear and open. After that to Parma. But now there was confusion. For the Minister-General had visited Genoa after they were gone, and he knew not of Rufino's order. Vagabonds again! He met them at Parma, and with a merry face, he said, " Ah, boys, how you run about! Now in France, now in Burgundy, now in Provence. Yesterday Genoa. To-day Parma. Oh, if I could but rest like you, you wouldn't see me always on the roads." And the genial humbugs answered, " But indeed, father, we never wander save in obedience to our superiors." And John, because he loved them, uttered no hard reproaches. But after that Salimbene was sent to Ferrara, where he says he stopped seven years. His wandering life was not over, but henceforth his journeys were mostly between the various convents of Romagna. Yet it would be a mistake to think of him at any time as closely immured within convent walls.

Gradually he seems to have become a professional chronicler, revising and continuing the work of other men, as well as composing on his own initiative. Much of his work exists no longer. In fact, all we have is the Chronicle of which there is question here, and of which the book *De Prelato*, printed separately in the Parma edition, forms a part, though it is a digression. The *De Prelato* deals chiefly with the generalship of Elias and the evils he wrought in the Order. The Parma edition starts with the year 1212, where Salimbene's original work begins. This part he probably began to write about 1283. The question of the sources of the Chronicle is an interesting one, but it is outside my scope, as well as beyond my scholarship, to discuss it here. Enough to say that he used the matter of the Chronicle of Sicard, Bishop of Cremona, though not in the state in which that Chronicle is to be found in Muratori. He probably drew also from the Monteferrati History of the Crusade, by the same author. For this question I will refer my readers to two learned German authorities, Dove and Michael, who, by the way, have taken away from Salimbene the credit of the *Memoriale potestatum Regiensium* attributed to him by Affò.

Salimbene speaks of other works of his,—a history of Pope Gregory X.—the loss of which, touching as it would on years when his existing Chronicle is somewhat meagre, is much to be regretted—and a moral work modelled on his favourite Patecchio, the *Liber Tædiorum*, written at Borgo San Donnino in 1259, when he was in low spirits on account of the plague.

To give an exact account of his movements in the later half of his life, after his seven years at Ferrara, is impossible. He evidently meant to give full particulars, but his chronology is a muddle. He left Ferrara in or about 1256. In 1259 he was at Parma and Borgo San Donnino, and the next year in Modena, during the *Flagellanti* excitement, when he says he was taken out of his convent by men and women who loved him, and sent to Reggio and to Parma to take part in the strange demonstrations. All the citizens, great and little, men and women, went in procession through the city, headed by the bishop and the religious, and flogged their naked bodies. Quarrels were made up, ill-gotten goods restored, and sins confessed, so that the priests had hardly time for food. And who would not flog himself was thought worse than the devil. Only Pallavicini and his Cremonesi mocked at the thing. He set up a gallows near the Po, to hang any Flagellants that should enter his territory. Salimbene, the impressionable, was full of the revival. The Flagellants were newer than the Joachimites, and much more exciting, and almost orthodox. Then perhaps Joachim had predicted the thing. 1260 was the great year when the world's third, most glorious period should begin. Strange beginning for the reign of the spirit, with fanatics thronging the streets, and war all round! In the same year he was at Bologna. He spent five years at Faenza, and was there when the city was besieged by the Bolognese; five at Imola, at Bagnacavallo near Ravenna one year, and another at Montereale near Forli. From Faenza he made a pilgrimage to Assisi and Alverna. His latest years were mostly spent in the neighbourhood of Reggio, with some excursions to Bibbianella and Montefalcone, where his brother Guido lay buried. But from his convent there, in the wood at the foot of the hill, he made frequent excursions into Reggio. The world called to him, and he must look on at the troublous excitement; and all day long he would be about the streets in quest of news and conversation. During these years he is a student of books and character, a busy chronicler, a centre of news; to whom the wandering *frati* bring rumours and information, hail-fellow-well-met with every one, good and bad, once at least a formal mediator between the cities of Modena and Sassuolo, and ever a sturdy defender of his Order. The year of his death is uncertain; but in 1288 he was still alive.

So much for his life and the events he watched. Now for the chronicler himself. For a wonder he does not give us a picture of his outer man. But I conceive him as a solid, lusty fellow, breathing health and energy, neither big nor little—for even in jest he says nothing derogatory of himself, and had he been very short or very long and lanky, or, by the way, red haired, he would not have quoted the rhyme—

"Vix humilis parvus, Vix longus cum ratione,
Vix reperitur homo ruffus sine proditione."

When Guido da Tripoli came to the aid of the brothers when their convent of Reggio was attacked, and bludgeoned off the rascals, it was to Salimbene he turned as he said, "Eh, *frati*, have you no cudgels to avenge yourselves on your spoilers?" Assuredly it was not poor health that kept the tireless, vivacious fellow out of all the fighting of his time.

His testimony to his own popularity may be accepted without reserve. The proof is our own feelings at the end of his book. The man of high moral sense seen by Tabarrini, who has read him so carefully and missed all his savour, you look for in vain. I do not ignore his eloquent invective against the corruption of the clergy, nor his praise of asceticism, and I am aware that much that he wrote in this regard has been omitted from the Parma edition. A vigorous indicter of the Church of his day he certainly was—among the first, by the way, to transcribe one of those grim letters from Lucifer to his friends the clergy, which later became a favourite form of satire. In looking at these attacks as professional rather than personal, I am not calling him insincere. He was untouched by the greater evils himself. He probably never went farther in his acquiescence than by dining with great churchmen for whose character he had less than no esteem. He was of the ascetic party, not himself an ascetic. And no number of moral discourses can convince us to the contrary against the general atmosphere of his book, and his naïf revelation of his own character when he is not in the pulpit.

A quick-witted, comfortable, vivacious creature, he is excellent company—a gossip of genius, not interested in humanity at all, but very much in his neighbours, which is a deal more important for a chronicler. Welcome at folks' tables, of course, was this man who had always "been there," seen with his own eyes, heard with his own ears. Did he know anybody very well? This is open to doubt; but *he* never doubted he was in the inner confidence of those who liked his company. A lover of great folks, he was no snob, for he is just as hearty about his friend Ugolino the shearer as if he had been a great baron. And no exclusive prig. He certainly consorted with better men than himself, and, quite impartially, with many who were a great deal worse. The solemnity with which his judgments on men are received, is absurd ; but he had a marvellous eye for detail, and is therefore excellent as corroborator, supplementer, vivifier of what we know from other sources of the men whose portraits appear in his long gallery. He had the faults and the virtues of the gregarious. He could hurl down abusive epithets like a hundred of bricks on a man's memory ; but he was not censorious in common life. His self-complacency kept him good-tempered. The climax of his eulogy of a dead man is that he had been a devoted friend of his own, and that he had been generous to the *frati minori*. He had many social gifts, and among the lesser ones his power of mimicry, of which he gives instances, was found very entertaining. But then his interest in ladies and his tact with them, counted for much. He thinks it wonderful virtue in the Count of Verona that he, no cleric even, but a great lord, should go through the town and not once lift his eyes to look at them. The favours which the sex bestowed on Salimbene, were, I am sure, very innocent, and quite deserved. He was such a comfortable, understanding confessor, and such a lively guest. He introduces us to Donna Fior d'Oliva, pretty and plump, and his familiar and devoted friend. There were Diana and Galla Placidia, wife and sister of Pietro Pagano, both on the very best of terms with him, Imperialists though they were. There was the charitable and perhaps elderly Mabilia, who distilled excellent rose water for the sick, to the vexation of all the apothecaries. She was his near neighbour at Ferrara. Then there was the unhappy Beatrice, beautiful and rich, and a famous player of chess and dice. A strange visitor this for the convent—but often she would come there with other ladies for a walk and to talk with the *frati*. Salimbene she picked out as her confidant, and she had a sad story to tell. Perhaps the kindly brother regretted for once he was only a *frate*, and, instead of ridding the earth of her dangerous kindred, could only bid her confess and hold herself ready for death. He was a safe confidant. Indeed, when ladies forced their attentions on him, he could even be ungallant—for his good and their own. There was that daughter of the Cardinal Ottaviano, a nun, who felt lonely, and begged Salimbene would be her friend, as she would be his. But he said, with a line from his favourite Patecchio, he didn't want her for a friend. What was the use of a friend shut up in a monastery, to whom he might not speak? The romantic lady was to be content with a less than Platonic attachment. "Let us love each other with our hearts, and pray for each other's salvation," she said, and would fain have quenched his cynical Patecchio with the last chapter of the Epistle to St. James.

He was humane. The horrors and miseries of war round him did not leave him untouched, and the tale of Ezzelino's atrocities wrung his heart. Only on two other subjects does he speak out with almost as fierce indignation—on the slander of his Order, and on the iniquities of the French. There are many unkindly and unjust references to French folk and French *frati*— though he loved French wine—and his book breaks off with a wild invective of the nation. But he wrote it towards the end of his life, when he had realised the disastrous consequences of the entry of Charles of Anjou into Italy. This vitiated his view of the nation. His mention of the Silician Vespers is surprisingly cool. Salimbene was, indeed, a patriot, with that great sense of the unity of his country and the wrong done to *Italia infelix* by her invaders, possessed by many men of his time, and lost in later ages. Always a Guelf, though with relations in the other camp, he remained true to the better kind of Guelfism that lamented the Angevin aberration of the Pope.

But he never spends his indignation on the fate of his friends. Was it the effect of the obedience taught him in the Order, or from a prudent desire to dissociate himself with heterodoxy, or the contempt of a practical man for enthusiasts, I cannot say; but he accepts the martyrdom and disgrace of John of Parma and Gerard da Borgo San Donnino with complacency. Yet of Gerard he thought highly, and to John's lofty character he is an eloquent witness. Indeed, his pages were searched to justify John's beatification. Not only does he acquiesce coldly in their destiny, but he attributes John's consistency to his being ashamed to confess he had been in the wrong, and thus betrays his common mind. Very likely the process against Gerard roused him to a sense that he had been dabbling in dangerous matters. It was all very well to be reputed learned in prophecy, to sit under a fig-tree expounding it to the Marchese d'Este at Ferrara, or listen to Gerardino under the vine at Modena. The Joachimite coteries had been fashionable and exclusive. But, lo, the hand of authority was down on them. A decree was issued that no book should be published by any brother until it had been approved by his minister and the *definitori* in the provincial chapter. Disobedience to this order meant three days' bread and water and the vanishing of your book. Salimbene dabbled no more in prophecies. At Imola he burnt a copy of Gerardino's treatise—for which posterity owes him a grudge—out of sheer terror evidently. "But you, too, were a Joachimite," says a brother to him, when he had been lamenting John of Parma's obstinacy. "That's true," he answers. "But after Frederic died and the year 1260 went by, I gave up the doctrine entirely, and made up my mind to believe no more than I see." To describe Salimbene as a Joachimite is to misread him entirely. Granting that his curiosity had something intellectual in it, you have done all that is possible. The world as it existed, in spite of a few drawbacks, was very dear to him, and very amusing. He would not have been at home at all in Joachim's spiritual kingdom. There were many like him, to whom Hugo had preached in vain. When 1260 had not proved the Year of Destiny, when there were no signs of a literal, wholesale, and quite material triumph of the *frati*, they cried out they had been deceived. And, besides, the bread of anguish and the water of sorrow that fell to Gerard's portion were not to his mind at all.

And Salimbene as Franciscan? I have said he was no ascetic. He loved eating and drinking, though one gathers he was more *gourmet* than *gourmand*, and he was hard on drunkenness. But to smell good cheer and not to share it was a pain he remembered with some bitterness ; and he consigns to a place of infamy those prelates who drink good wine in the presence of their inferiors to whom they offer none, "as if all men's throats were not sisters." Inspired by the wine of Chiavari, he trolls out with gusto a drinking song of Trutanno. In his earlier years he begged his bread, it is true ; but in reading of his later doings we seem very far from the days of devotion to the lepers and the outcasts of the world. Formally he belonged to the party of the strict observance. But there is a curious silence in his pages concerning the divisions in the Order. As a supplementer or corroborator to Angelo Clareno, he is of no use at all. Now and then he quotes, as if by rote, some one's praise of simplicity. But he thinks it quite natural that preferment should be given to Minorites, even though it was on the cards that Innocent, as his father's friend, might offer him a bishopric. Why did he get no office? I give him the credit of liking his liberty better than place with its responsibilities. But I doubt if any of his contemporaries took him so seriously as students of his Chronicle are inclined to do to-day. Like all the Boswells of the world, he was somewhat lacking in personal dignity; and he aspired to be not one but every man's Boswell.

Francis plays a small part in his book, yet he was dead only a little while. He quotes one of his sayings; and says that as Jesus Christ chose Francis for His own particular friend, so the devil did Ezzelino. He made the pilgrimage to Assisi, and was fiercely loyal to his Order, according to his lights. But the Founder was a far-away and not very much regarded model.

Of the *frati* we have many glimpses, though no general picture. He shows them at Parma burying Frederic's victims, when he had fled to Vittoria, and striving to keep the wolves from the dead. We see them vigorous in the Crusade against Ezzelino. One, a lay brother—a friend of Salimbene's, it need hardly be said—made himself standard-bearer, mounted a horse, took a pole for a lance, and rode hither and thither crying, "On with you, soldiers of Christ. Courage, soldiers of the Blessed Peter!" And they followed where he would. Another, who had been in the world an engineer, by the order of the legate put on a white garment over his habit, and made an engine which threw out fire in front, and behind was full of armed men, to break down the walls of Ezzelino's city—and so was Padua taken. He shows us Fra Rainoldo d'Arezzo scorning preferment, and almost defying the Pope in his determination to remain a simple *frate*, humble, and unregarded, and faithful—like those two Germans who went to Rome to see the Holy Father, but, being refused admittance, never got a glimpse of him till he was dead. Then, "Holy Father," they said, "those who have refused us entry these many months have little care of you now. We will wash your body." We see the brothers coming out of their obscurity in response to their dreams, like the unknown humble one, to whom the devil (this is Salimbene's suggestion) promised the papacy. He only wished for it to pacify the world, and seems really to have been disappointed when he was not chosen on Martin's death. He tells of Buoncompagno whom he had known at Pisa, who when the brothers received two tunics, would only accept one, and could never give thanks enough to God for His mercies.

On the other hand, Salimbene, in no vein of satire, but with perfect complacency, reveals a state of things far removed from the early ideal. The brothers have servants. We see the growth of the large and magnificent convents, and the brothers' pride in them. We see them favourites in the houses of great churchmen, of barons and princes. He tells with pride how the Cardinal Protectors of the Order became Popes, Gregory IX., Alexander IV., and Nicholas III.; and for this he thanks not only God and the virtue of their lives, but, strangely enough, the intercession of the Blessed Francis, the *Poverello*, who refused all preferment for his followers. Of the rights and wrongs of the quarrel between the secular clergy and the Minorites at the Council of Ravenna, it is not easy to judge amidst such mutual recriminations as he reports. He, of course, defends the Order lustily. "You do not preach the duty of tithe paying," say the clergy. "No," he answers. "Persons of less consideration can do that—those who benefit by tithes. Our sermons are on a higher level. Preach the duty of tithe-giving, indeed, seeing to what uses the secular clergy put the money!" And as for the *frati* burying in their churches the dead of other parishes, or poaching on the priests' preserves in the matter of confession, or being so given to preaching that there are no audiences left for any others, he can only see envy, malice, and all uncharitableness in the charges.

Salimbene seems to have been on excellent terms with many Clares. Several women of his family had joined the Order. But, alas, he gives no particular account of any save a few bad ones—the violent Badessa of

Chiavari, and the turbulent Badessa of Gattaiola, near
Lucca, the Genoese baker's daughter, who feasted men
and women of the world to make her place secure, and
stirred up all Lucca against the *frati*.

The echo from the early days is very faint; yet
Salimbene did not grow up in ignorance of the heroic
times and of the saintly companions of St. Francis.   He
knew Leo, or at least had spoken with him concerning
the Stigmata.   He knew Bernard of Quintavalle when he
was himself a young *frate* at Siena.   He knew Illuminato,
and had met Giles.   He records the writing of Celano's
Second Life, which he had probably read.   He calls it
Memoriale beati Francisci in desiderio animæ, and states
what use Bonaventura made of it in his fine book—which
does not contain everything, nevertheless.   He, Salimbene, could have added many tales of miracles.

So much for the general character of the work.
There is a curious divergence of opinion regarding
Salimbene and his Chronicle, but modern critics are mostly
complimentary, not to say fulsome about it.   The Germans have done him the honour of examining it with
great closeness and erudition; but the man Salimbene
has mostly escaped them.   Gebhart's study, slight, and
inaccurate in detail, has more psychological value.   His
appreciators have been fantastic in the comparison of his
work to that of other writers.   Another Boccaccio, says
one.   Well, we feel he is a fellow-countryman.   Another
Rabelais.   It is to do him too much, and too little, credit.
Salimbene is no conscious humorist, no inventor; and
he does not gloat unduly over strong-odoured stories.
Montaigne!   They were both autobiographical.   But
who goes looking for the fine wit, the sober and sophisticated philosophy of the great Frenchman in the *frate's*
book will be disappointed.   The Sire de Joinville.   Well,
a comparison of two almost contemporary chronicles
is not a waste of time, and Salimbene's description of
Saint Louis's start for the Crusade, which the king's

T

biographer did not witness, is an interesting supplement. But their purposes were entirely different. The one aimed merely at picturing in orderly fashion the doings of one man, a hero and a saint, the other of giving posterity some idea of the whole of a rough-and-tumble time. Salimbene is infinitely the more amusing. Joinville has the greater delicacy and the finer art. And one unfathomable critic says Salimbene's pages remind him of the *Fioretti*! The *Decameron* and the *Fioretti*! Our good *frate* was pretty universal, but not quite so universal as all that.

Where he really excels is in his story-telling. His Chronicle, disorderly, topsy-turvy, all out of proportion, and by no means to be depended on, is alive all through with stories. There is the tale of Fra Leone, the militant Archbishop of Milan. Once he confessed the dying administrator of the hospital at Milan, and made him promise to return from the Shades and say how it was with him. Leone and two *frati* watch from a garden hut for the fulfilment of the promise. Suddenly a desperate howling is heard, and looking up they see him wheel down from the sky like a hawk on its prey. The brothers nudge the sleeping Leone, who wakes up and asks the "thing" how it is with him. "Ah, I am damned, for I have caused the death of some unbaptized infants to whom I wouldn't give shelter in the hospital."—"Why didn't you confess this?" asks the indignant priest. "Well, I forgot, or I didn't think it worth confessing." And Leone, his professional instincts outraged, is filled with disgust, and pitilessly bids him depart and go to his own place.

There is the story of the pope who kept company with the magician. It is just as moral, though the Parma edition omits it. Innocent draws the wise man to a secret place outside Rome, and desires him by his spells to raise a friend from the dead for a time, that he may know how it fares with him beyond. And the pope's friend appears with much fantastic circumstance,

and wails of the lot that has come upon him for his
haughtiness and luxury. There is the story of Fra
Vita of Lucca and the nun. Vita was a marvellous
singer, who not only delighted cardinals and popes, but
whose music was respected even by the nightingales.
They would stop their songs to hear his, or would take
up his melody, and sing alternately with him. So
courteous was he, that if he were asked to sing he never
said he had a cold—nor, probably, that he had left his
notes at home. Vita was a great favourite, and he used
his favour to indulge the vagaries of his artistic temperament. Every now and then he would leave the Order,
thinking the Rule of Benedict suited him better.
Then he would seek readmission, and the Pope never
refused him. Nobody ever refused him anything.
His singing so drew the susceptible heart of a nun
that she jumped out of a window to follow him
over the world. But she couldn't follow him after all,
for she broke her leg. Here is one of the stories
of the saintly preacher, Fra Bertoldo di Lamagna, more
commonly called of Ratisbon. A certain noble lady
with her companions followed all his wanderings for
years, to hang on his words and teachings. At the end
of six years all her money was gone. She and her ladies
had nothing to eat, and at last on the Eve of the Assump-
tion she went to Fra Bertoldo and told him their misery.
He sent her to a banker, bidding him give her as much
money as would buy a day of indulgence, for which
privilege she had followed him all the time. The banker
smiled and said, "How should I know the price of a
day of indulgence?" And she answered, "Put money
in one scale, and I shall blow into the other. When the
scales are balanced, the money will be exact." So he
did; but still her scale was always the heavier. He
heaped and heaped, and still his seemed as if of feather-
weight. For the Holy Spirit was blowing through her
mouth. The awestruck banker gave the lady and her

company all they wanted, scattered his wealth to the poor, and became a religious man. And, I suppose, the lady followed Fra Bertoldo six years more.

Fra Bertoldo had some of the savour of Francis. He was attacked and imprisoned by a Castellano and his bravos, and was to be hanged. But when the chief discovered him to be the famous preacher, he gave orders to stop the ill-treatment, threw himself at his feet, and begged him to speak of holy things to him. Fra Bertoldo moved him and his desperate company to tears. They promised to lead a new life, and the chief begged to be received into the Order. The brothers departed to preach in the town, and the Castellano, forgetting in his new zeal for God his usual precautions in a city that hated him, and that had just heard rumours of his ill-treatment of holy men, walked meditatively by himself towards the preaching place. He was seized on the way by the citizens, and hoisted on to a gallows. Suddenly Fra Bertoldo saw his audience melting away. Never had this happened before. But it was explained to him. "No wonder they run, for our worst enemy, the Castellano, is caught, and they are hanging him." "Ah," cried Fra Bertoldo. "Stop! He is a changed man. He has repented, and confessed. He is entering our Order. He was coming to hear me preach. Set him free! Set him free!" But ere the liberators reached him he was dead. When his body was lowered, they found round his neck a paper, and on it in letters of gold, "Being made perfect in a little while, he fulfilled long years; for his soul was pleasing unto the Lord: Therefore hasted he out of the midst of wickedness." And, at least, the robber chief was buried in the convent of the Brothers Minor, and in the habit of the Order.

Among the most vivid accounts of historical events is that of the women of Pisa after the war between the Genoese and the Pisans. About thirty or forty rich and

noble ladies went on foot from Pisa to Genoa, to see
their men-folk in prison.   But the jailer refused them
entrance.   Yesterday thirty died, they were told, to-day
forty, and their bodies are now in the sea.   And that
happens to the Pisans.   When the women heard that
they fell as if dead.   But recovering consciousness they
fell on the jailer ; they tore their hair, and wept aloud
till they had no tears left, for the men who had died
of hunger and hardship and grief.   And when the ladies
reached home again, they found others dead whom they
had left sound and safe, for God had struck the city with
a pestilence.   Pisa deserved punishment, thinks Salimbene, for its rebellion against the Church, but inasmuch
as he had lived in the convent there four years, forty
years ago, he cannot help sorrowing with its sorrows.

Salimbene's gallery of portraits is also long, rich,
and varied.   Perhaps they are not the final presentments
of the men and women who crossed his path ; but one
is glad enough at this distance to get these popular
pictures of the great churchmen, preachers, men and
women of the world, saints, princes, soldiers, burghers.
It is impossible to indicate a tenth.   There is a vigorous
sketch of Obizzo, Bishop of Parma, the worldly prelate,
clerical with the clergy, religious with the religious, a
soldier among soldiers, a baron among barons, great
ruffler, prodigal in spending, open-handed, courtly, who
played with the lands of the bishopric, giving them
to *truffatori*.   But he got them back again, and his see
was all the more prosperous for his reign.   Strong in
canon law was he, and a skilful chess-player.   The many
clergy of his diocese were in excellent order, and there
was preferment for those who did well towards him.
Salimbene makes us realise vividly the wily, strong-
willed, able priest.   Of his portraits of Elias and of
John of Parma I have spoken elsewhere.   Then there
is Philip, Archbishop of Ravenna, legate in Lombardy,
whose history is a romance.   Born near Pistoia, when

young and poor he set off for Spain to study necromancy, as a means of pushing his fortunes. A soldier found him sitting disconsolate on a doorstep in Toledo, and recommended him to a magician of great fame. The magician, a man of horrible aspect, gave the young aspirant a book, and shut him up in a room to study it. But when left alone there appeared to Philip armies of demons in the shape of rats, mice, dogs, cats, pigs— the room was full of them. Terror closed his lips, and suddenly he found himself outside the house, where he met the old magician, who told him to try again. Once more he was shut up with the book, and this time the demons took the shape of young men and maidens dancing about the room. Not a spell could he utter, and again he found himself in the street. "Ah," said his master, with scorn, "you Lombards are not made for the art. Leave it to us Spaniards, who are proud and like unto demons ourselves. As for you, my son, go to Paris and study the Scriptures. You may yet become a great man in the Church." The disciple humbly accepted this rôle in the lower ranks of intellectual enterprise; and the magician's words were fulfilled—though never enough for Philip's ambition. Step by step he rose, became a great prelate, kept a large household, was feared only less than Ezzelino, against whom he preached a crusade. Fiendishly cruel to his servants, he would drag one through the water like a fish, and hold another on a spit above the fire. Fierce was the great archbishop, unchaste, yet with strong affections, melancholy, disappointed, a proud uncontrollable son of Belial. "But to me," adds Salimbene complacently, "and to all the *frati*, ever benevolent, familiar, and generous."

Hardly more agreeable, according to our chronicler's account, yet less sinister, is the other Lombard legate, the Dominican Cardinal Latino. The ladies loathed him for his meddlesomeness. It was the fashion to wear

trains an arm's length and a half long; and he ordered
the skirts only to touch the ground, or to lie on it no
more than a palm's length. He had this preached in
the churches, and ordered priests to withhold absolution
from the disobedient. One lady confided to her dear
sympathetic Salimbene that her train was more precious to
her than all the rest of her dress together. Oh, the ordin-
ance was bitterer than death to women's hearts! And as
if that wasn't enough, he would have them all, old and
young, wear veils on their heads out of doors—"which
was to them horribly grievous." But for that tribulation
they found a remedy, for they had the veils woven of
silk and gold, and so they were only the more seductive
in the eyes of the beholders. No mere meddler, however, does he appear even in the pages of Salimbene, but
a statesman, incessantly labouring for peace among the
Lombard cities. Yet his grim temper casts a shadow on
his path. He plays the inquisitor; brings down an interdict on Parma, and the expulsion of the Preaching
Friars for their burning of the heretic Alina.

There is Saint Douceline, Hugo of Montpellier's
sister, a worker of miracles, who entered no monastery,
but lived virtuously in the world, girding herself with
the cord of Francis, and spending her days in the
churches of the Minorites. No one spoke ill of her.
All, worldly and unworldly, held her in reverence; and
she obtained from God the special grace of ecstasy. It is
well known in Marseilles, he records, that she would be
suspended from morning to night an arm's length from
the ground, so all absorbed was she in God. And ladies
of the city followed her counsel and rule. But this is,
I think, a second-hand portrait. When he lived with her
brother, the *béguine* was probably not visible. I miss the
familiar " as I have seen with mine own eyes!"

Then there is a great gallery of wonderful revivalists,
preachers who foretold disasters, who preached penitence
and peace, who added to the agitation of the stormy time,

and opened havens of refuge and vistas of reconciliation. Salimbene had seen them all, had stood in the crowd of each. There was Fra Benedetto da Cornetta, the hero of the Halleluia, in 1233, when all the men laid down their arms, when joy and gladness reigned in every heart, when fighting men joined with women and children and priests in signing lauds, and went in procession with their parish banners, and branches of trees, and lighted candles, and could hardly stop singing, so drunk were they with love divine. Fra Benedetto was a simple unlettered man from saintly Umbria, belonging to no religious order. He lived by himself, and strove to please God. Like another John the Baptist was he, who prepared for God a perfect people. He wore an Armenian cap, a long beard, a black robe to his feet, a hairy girdle about his loins, and before and behind a long and spreading red cross from his neck to his feet. The boy Salimbene, from the walls of the half-finished episcopal palace in Parma, saw him surrounded by the crowd with the green branches and the candles. He sounded a trumpet to announce his coming in church or piazza, and again before he preached; and ever ended with the salutation to the Virgin, *Ave Maria, clemens et pia.*

Salimbene's jealousy of other Orders, that might become rivals of the Minorites, renders certain of his portraits suspect. But if his account of the great Dominican preacher, Giovanni da Vicenza, and of Seghalello, the founder of the Apostoli, are caricatures, they are, at least, amusing, and doubtless only emphasise what was popularly associated with their names in quarters where they were not admired. The energy of the former is freely acknowledged by Salimbene, who owns that he brought about the canonisation of St. Dominic. But he goes on to tell how success turned his head, how he thirsted for recognition of his saintly eminence, till once when he was being shaved he was offended the brothers of the convent did not pick up portions of his beard as relics.

Seghalello and his apostles—"that congregation of ribald men, pigs, fools, and low wretches, who call themselves apostles, and are not, but Satan's own synagogue"—are his favourite butts. Gerardino Seghalello he describes as a low-born, ignorant, idle young man, who hung round the *frati minori* with lazy admiration, and would fain have been one of them. Rejected, he loafed about their church, till finally he conceived the idea of outrivalling them in dress, in manner of life, and popular favour. On the lamp in the church were pictures of the apostles, sandal-shod, their shoulders picturesquely wrapped about with mantles. These he would stand and gaze at for hours. The outer habit, if we are to believe our chronicler, was his first care. So he let his hair and beard grow, put on a grey tunic, a white mantle round his shoulders, sandals, and the Minorite cord. Then he felt quite the apostle. His next step was to sell his little house, all his property in the world. Having been paid the price of it, he stood on a stone slab in the middle of Parma, scattering the cash, not among the poor, but among the idle crowd, crying, " Who wants money? Here's money for all who want it." And fast enough was it picked up ; and off they went to play dice with it, laughs and blasphemies on their lips. Disciples did not come at once, but ere long he had a goodly number of followers—all rustics and idiots, says Salimbene—who were not ashamed to beg for their living from those whom the Minorites and the Preachers had taught, with long trouble and good service, to give to the servants of God. There were attractions in an Order whose members had no duties, not even towards each other, and whose chief employment was to gad about the streets and ogle the ladies. Gerardino was a fantastic. He wished to simulate the Son of God, and thought he had best begin at the beginning, for he lay in a cradle wrapped in swaddling clothes, and sucked the breasts of an accommodating lady. Proceeding in his career, he went out to the country on the road from Parma to Fornaro, where the hills begin, and standing in the middle of the road, he said to all the passers-by, " Go ye likewise into my vineyard." Now he hadn't any vineyard ; but the simple hill folk followed the direction of his pointing hand, and seeing a fruitful vineyard, feasted handsomely on the grapes, which were not his to give away. Sometimes Seghalello would take on an impressive air of dignity, and would speak to no one, save to say aloud, *Penitenzagite*, his illiterate rendering of *Poenitentiam agite*. He played the prophet with antics to make the angels smile ; and if he were asked to dinner, would say with the manner of an oracle, " I shall come, or I shall not come." With numbers came dissensions in his ranks. There was a split in his army, and the founder seems to have fallen to the place of mere prophet, while Guido Putagio led one section and Matteo of the Marches led another. At Faenza the two parties came to blows, and there was a great scandal. But, indeed, scandal was with them always, and of a sensational kind. Robert, an old servant of the Minorites, who had gone over to the new sect, apostatised once again. They always did things dramatically, and on Good Friday, at the time when the Son of God was crucified, he cut his hair, shaved his beard, and married an *eremetessa*. Seghalello's order, all the same, spread over Italy, went on pilgrimages, and joined with them lady apostles, who are blamed for bringing about the ruin of the Order, which seems a trifle unjust. In his later days, the founder seems to have consented to be a kind of jester at the episcopal court of Parma, glad to have tit-bits thrown him in return for playing the antic fool. But without his leadership the Order grew ; and even after its formal suppression by Gregory X., new apostles were enrolled. We should do well not to accept Salimbene's spiced account as the final one of this strange anarchic movement which prejudiced his own Order.

But Seghalello, Roberto, and Guido Putagio were known to him ; for he was never one to hold aside the skirt of his tunic when human nature was manifesting itself in any new and entertaining fashion.

Through all the first part of the Chronicle there is one haunting figure, that of Frederic, the evil genius of the time, according to good Guelfs. And Salimbene strongly disapproved of him not only as an enemy of the Church, but as the ravager of his own neighbour-hood. Parma felt the weight of his vengeful hand. To the emperor's personal character he is not compli-mentary. He describes him as cruel, faithless to his friends, avaricious ; and there is triumph in his tone when he tells of his defeat, and how the Parmigians looted his treasure, even to his imperial crown, all of gold, studded with precious stones, chased and embossed, and big as a cooking-pot. Salimbene knows, for he had it in his hand. A little man, Passacorto, found it, and carried it about the streets, till the city bought it of him for two hundred lire and a little house. They put it as a trophy in the Duomo. But it is not all scorn and hatred that he feels towards Frederic. His interest in him is infinite ; the gossip and scandal about him and his mother, and his birth and his relations with his sons, are endless. Frederic overawes him. He tells breathlessly of his bold experi-mentalism, how he had children brought up without hearing any human speech at all, to see whether, when they found utterance, they would speak Hebrew or Greek or Latin, or their own mother tongue ; and how the children, hearing no caressing word, never grew up at all, or uttered anything more articulate than wailing cries ; how he brought outlandish animals, elephants, camels, and leopards into Lombardy — Salimbene saw them with wonder on their way from Parma to Cre-mona. An uncanny personage, this emperor, our *frate* thinks. But the good Guelf had a sneaking admiration for him all the same. If only he had been a good

Catholic! At times he could forget his wrath against this imposing personality. "And yet truly have I never seen any man with more of the bearing of the great prince than he; he had the appearance, the qualities, and the substance of it. When he brandished his sword hither and thither in battle, the enemy turned aside and fled as if from the face of a demon. And when I would conceive of his person in my mind, the picture of Charlemagne comes before me." It was no tame heart that beat inside his friar's frock.

And now for one more figure detached from Salimbene's gallery, and no great prince this time. Parma was in terrible straits, trembling at the coming of Pallavicini's tyranny, and helpless against it. A man was needed, and a man arose, a humble tailor, of peasant parentage, Giovanni Barisello by name. With the Cross and the Evangel in his hand, he went through the streets, inspiriting the Guelfs, persuading the Imperialists not to give their city over to the tyrant. Five hundred men-at-arms followed him, and obeyed him as if he had been a great *condottiere*. By his persuasion and threats, by the force of his character, Parma's heart beat strong again, and Pallavicino delayed his coming. The city was not ungrateful. It cast gifts at the leader's feet, gave him a *nobil donzella* to wife, and named him perpetual counsellor, with the power of assembling men-at-arms. And Barisello's head was never turned. When Manfredino da Rosa pointed out how undignified it was to have a tailor in such a place of power, he knew his work was done. He gave up his state, returned to his own house, and the same day took up his needle and thread, and under the eyes of his fellow citizens whom he had saved, sat cross-legged at his old work. And Parma was noble enough not to forget him.

Such is Fra Salimbene, such his Chronicle. A history

of the Order, or a history of the century, is very incomplete without his notes, his records, his stories, his
scandals, his own vivacious, complacent personality. If
his book were of no other use, it would still present
one more striking instance of the fact, which is not
without consolation, that the other side of an age of
terrible unrest, of varied interest and misery, of sore
awakenings, is an abiding interest in little things. It
is a far journey from Dante to the vagabond friar. But
there is a road leading directly from one to the other,
and students of the great poet would do well to tread
Salimbene's galleries. They will find not a little of the
stuff out of which Dante dug to find the matter for his
invective and his praise. It is seen here, of course,
through commoner eyes. We have always to take
account of the man in judging his worth as a biographer
and historian. We are on our guard against him, but
we leave him in most friendly humour. A more disorderly work than his was never penned; but if to put
your personality into your writing is to write a book,
then Salimbene wrote one of the books of the world.
We feel in him a tremendous fall from the heights of
Leo and Bernard and Giles. He breathes a grosser air.
We are far from the fierce idealism of Cæsar of Spires,
and we hear in his voice no wailing sorrow for the
persecution of the sons of God, as in Angelo Clareno's.
He longs for no city of God upon the earth. But
neither is he a coarse friar of the later type. The
vivacity, the ardour, and the strenuousness of his Order
and his time are in him, though he is ardent and strenuous not for holy things, but in his curiosity about the
world around him. And so is he the more at home among
us, this eager, chattering buttonholer, this indefatigable
scribbler, this comfortable, yet not wholly self-interested,
maker of the best of two worlds, this diarist, diner-out,
and ladies' man, this all men's Boswell without the hero-

worship, this complacent, candid, cheerful Friar Pepys. He loved life, and it was towards the end of it he wrote down in his Chronicle—

> " Heu! heu! mundi vita,
> Quare me dilectas ita?
> Cum non possis mecum stare
> Quid me cogis te amare?"

CONRAD D'OFFIDA

" Man is a tree that hath no top in cares,
No root in comforts."—BUSSY D'AMBOIS, v. I.

OVER Conrad d'Offida the guardian angel of Francis
kept watch. So says the legend ; so speaks his life. In
the midst of the strifes of the Order, from which he did
not keep apart, with which his name is, indeed, closely
linked, he retains the gentleness, and breathes the open-
air fragrance of the early time. One of the favourites
of the *Fioretti*, the tales of him there record his piety,
the grace bestowed on him by visions, and something
of his genius for friendship. From elsewhere we learn
the individual lines of his nature, and how to colour
his picture. He was allied with Angelo Clareno, and
the friends of Angelo were fighters. Live hard and
free your soul, they said. Conrad early wrested that
prize from life, and he had a soul worth freeing.

The year of his birth was probably 1241, and the
place Offida, a little town in the Marches, to the north-
east of Ascoli. At fourteen or fifteen he girt on the
cord of Francis in the Convent of Ascoli. In his mature
years he had a reputation for learning ; and he continued
his theological studies at least as far as to qualify for the
priesthood ; but there came a time, early in life, when
the pursuit of secular letters seemed to him a poor vain
thing, puffing up the mind, and affording no nourishment
to the soul. He gave it up, at least for years ; and was
content to serve and love his brethren. The crisis probably
took place at Forano, where he spent ten years, begging
the bread for the convent from door to door, and cooking

for the community. His spare time was passed by
himself in a cell in the woods. The wild things grew
tame in his neighbourhood, and chief among his friends
was a bird that perched on his shoulders, or hopped before
him on his path through garden and wood, singing the
while. Such songs were not merely to be taken for granted:
to a soul like Conrad's they were great joys, too great
for days commemorative of the sufferings of Christ.
They say that on Holy Thursday he asked God that
he might not see or hear his friend for three days. But
on Easter morning there it was, its voice sweeter and
more jubilant than ever. In the woods Conrad did not
regret his lapsed studies. This bird revealed to him "great
things"; and heaven as he watched and listened came
down. But he was no morose hermit. At Forano he
had his beloved friend Peter of Monticello. Says the
Fioretti of their friendship: they "were two shining
stars in the province of the March, and like denizens
of heaven; for between them was such love as seemed
to spring from one and the self-same soul; they bound
themselves each to each by this agreement, that every
consolation that the mercy of God might vouchsafe
them, they would reveal the one unto the other in love."
Each shared the other's spiritual experiences; but Conrad, in the delicate awe of his soul, would fain have
hidden even from his friend the great honour done him
by the Virgin that day—the Feast of the Purification—
when among the trees she put her Son in his arms, when
he was "melted altogether and dissolved in the love
Divine and consolation unspeakable." But Peter, too,
had been in the woods, had seen the favour, and greeted
his brother as a triumphant hero, "O heavenly one,
to-day what comfort has been thine!" When Peter
had his vision of the Virgin and St. John, with St. Francis
in a glory more resplendent than theirs, it was on Conrad
that he called—"Quick, help me. Come and see things
wonderful!"

ST. FRANCIS PREACHING TO THE BIRDS

GIOTTO. Assisi, S. Francesco.

One day when he was in his cell in the woods, the hunt was out. The shouts of the hunters broke in on his leafy quiet. Through a thicket tore a harassed, desperate wolf. Conrad's cell gave it welcome refuge, and it knew a friend. The hunt went by, and he led it by the neck to the convent as if it had been a pet lamb.

These were Conrad's forming years. He served humbly, and he had leisure and space under the sky and among the trees he loved for friendship with man and beast, and for the company of his own soul. Probably he was ordained priest before he left Forano. Later he looked back with regret on these days. To serve at the altar was not holier, and was to his nature somewhat hampering.

His wanderings were not very extensive for a Minorite. He sojourned at Sirolo on the coast, south of Ancona. But the effusive gratitude of a mother, out of whose daughter he had cast an evil spirit, threatened to make him notorious, and he fled away hastily. One return, at least, he made to his native place. The brothers at Offida entreated him to turn one of their number, a careless, dissolute young fellow, from his evil courses. Good seemed a goodly thing in the person of the gentle Conrad, and by his side the reckless boy grew in grace and gravity. But he died. After death, out of Purgatory, it was on Conrad he cried. "Say a paternoster for me, father. Thy prayers are strong with God." And Conrad said the paternoster and the *requiem æternam*, and the troubled soul responded, "That does me good. Go on, go on." And Conrad said them not once but many times, for each time the poor soul cried out what refreshment it brought him. Conrad said a hundred paternosters, till he prayed away the earthly stain, and opened the gates of heaven. And the soul of that youth went to Paradise through the merits of Conrad.

A little before the death of Leo, a message was

brought to Conrad to repair to Assisi, to drink the words and wisdom of the Founder from Leo, their special guardian. The old man told him "great things"; and not only spoke, but wrote for Conrad, who, intimately bound to all the spirituals and even the intransigeants, became hereafter the chief medium between them and the men of the early time. Leo handed the torch on to Conrad. These memories and messages may be read, indirectly, in the *Arbor Vitæ* of Ubertino. Their substance is in the *Speculum Perfectionis*. Some of the actual texts given to Conrad were deposited with the Clares at Assisi, where they went astray. Ubertino, who quoted them, perhaps from memory, was called liar and scoundrel because he did not produce the scripts. They related to Francis's exact will and words respecting the observance of the Rule, and his grief for the degeneracy of the Order, "which Fra Bonaventura took pains to omit, not wishing to write of such calamities in a Legend to be read by all . . . or the brothers to be defamed to outsiders while he could help it." But he would have done much better to have published them, thought Ubertino. It might have prevented worse calamities.

In the *Speculum Perfectionis* is an interpolation claiming to be the words of one of these messages of Leo. It was probably written by a disciple of Conrad.

"St. Francis stood behind the tribunal of the Church of St. Mary of the Angels, in prayer, raising his hand on high and crying to Christ to have mercy on the people for the many tribulations which must come on them. And the Lord said, 'Francis, if thou desirest I should have mercy on the Christian people, then let thine Order stand, for it is all that is left to Me in the world. And I promise thee that for love of thee and thy Order I will permit no tribulation to come upon the world. But I tell thee that they will fall away from that life I ordained for them. And they will provoke Me to such anger that I will rise against them, and I will call on demons and give them what power they desire, and they shall cause such scandal between the brothers and the world that none of the brothers will dare wear thy habit, save in the woods. And when the world shall lose faith in thy Order, there will remain no other light, for I stablished them as a light to the world.'

"And St. Francis said, 'On what shall my brothers live who shall dwell in the woods?' And Christ said, 'I shall feed them as I fed the children of Israel with manna in the desert.'"

For some years Conrad lived in or near Ancona, and his stay there is marked by his friendship with Benevenuta. She was not of the Clares, being a married woman with the cares of a household and a family on her shoulders. But charity towards the Brothers Minor and intercourse with them were the refreshments of her life; and the spiritual experiences and consolations which they brought filled her with wondering gratitude. "Good Lord," she would say, "visit holy virgins who dwell in monasteries, for I am not worthy." She, too, had a vision of the Blessed Virgin and her Child, and longed to hold Him in her arms. This grace was not granted, but the Blessed Virgin said, "I will show thee dearest sons of mine that I would fain have thee take for sons of thine." And suddenly the place was full of grey frocks. From that day she valued her worldly goods for what help they could bring to the Sons of Francis. A table was always spread for them in her house at Ancona. Her daughter-in-law would say, "For whom are all those things?"—"Wait a bit, and you will see," answered Benevenuta. And ere long the brothers would troop in from their begging, or their nursing, or their preaching. Nothing was spread in vain. So many loaves, so many brothers. It was not always easy to keep the balance between her domestic interests and her works of charity, but as her desires were pure and generous, a miracle came to her aid. Her husband and one of the brothers were both ill at the same time of the same malady. They made a dish of good wine to strengthen the rich citizen of Ancona, and the poor brother in his bare convent should not fare less well, said Benevenuta. But the wine was a favourite brand of her husband's. When he sent the handmaid to fetch more, there was none left; and in his wrath he cursed the pampered Minorites. Benevenuta strove to soothe him, and taking the vessel from the girl's hand, said with some guile, "If you went for water the well would be dry. Give the thing to me." She went to the cellar. Wine? There was wine enough to flood the place. But the same wine? It seemed so; and yet the sick man had no sooner tasted it than his health came back. Of course the ailing brother had his share, with a like result. This was the kind of event to appeal to the rich citizen. Never must an alms be refused to a friar any more, he ordered. Preaching was not in his way, but for the ordinary things of life it was worth while being on good terms with saints. He had a cargo of oil on board a ship one day. A great storm rose; all their lives were in danger, and he recommended the sailors to call on St. Francis. The sea went down. Next day he said to the men, "Seek my vessels, and I'll pay you well for your trouble." They searched and searched, and perhaps it was well for Benevenuta's peace and future charities that the vessels were found heaped up undamaged on the shore.

The link between Benevenuta and Conrad was strong. Afterwards he told Brother Andrew at Alverna wonderful things of her, and it is said he wrote her life. But in their friendship was always the pang of parting. A Brother Minor had no home, and her lot was fixed in Ancona. "I know the Lord will take you away soon, Brother Conrad. It has been revealed to me. And I shall no longer be able to see you as I am used."—"Perhaps," said Conrad, "it means I am going to die." A few days later he got the summons from the Minister-

General, probably the Spiritual Raymond Gaufridi, only
sent to such as shone by the sanctity of their lives, to
repair to Alverna. Brothers called thither lived near
the cell of the Stigmata, and were exempt for the time
from begging. Their duties were confined to religious
ceremonies, and they were given abundant time for
meditation. This Alverna prize was a great honour, and
much sought after. Conrad was probably alone in
shunning it. His sensitive heart was filled with sorrow
and some fear. It was to leave his friends. The holy
place was too holy for him. From Alverna he wrote to
Benevenuta to plead with the Minister-General that he
might return. She answered, " For three or four days
after you left Ancona I was very sad ; but then it was
revealed to me that it was the will of God you should
go. So as your works are pleasing to God, do not be slow
to ask of Him a favour, for He will give you what you
desire. And I was with you in the spirit on St. John's
Day and on the Feast of Holy Innocents. And I saw
you and learnt that your state was pleasing to God.
And so pray for me."

Afterwards he showed this letter to his friend, Brother
Andrew, who had joined him on Alverna. Andrew fell
on his knees before him, and he, too, said, " Pray for me."
—" But I was praying for you, Andrew, before you came
here," answered Conrad, shamefaced at favours asked so
humbly.

It was about this time that an angel of God appeared
to him while he prayed. " Who art thou ? " asked
Conrad. " I am the angel whom God gave to the Blessed
Francis for his aid. And the Lord hath sent me to thee."

Conrad was not dependent on times and places for his
spiritual experiences. Divine things were not more with
him up in lonely Alverna, with the memory of Francis
and other holy men, than elsewhere. So he confided to
Andrew his friend, who had been puzzled by Conrad's
attitude to such a privilege, also by his want of eagerness

in saying the sacred office. "Know, Brother Andrew," he said, "that before I was a priest, for seven years it was with me so that in all creatures, in trees, in stones, in everything, I looked at God by a certain heavenly and sweet light; and Paradise was everywhere. Then it was hard for me to serve at the office, for I was withdrawn from this consolation. Why then should I now celebrate the Mass? Yet I receive the Body of the Lord on Sundays and feast days, for reverence and the efficacy of the sacraments. But it seems to me that before I was priest, the Blessed Francis was with me oftener than he is now. Sometimes he would rest his head on my breast, and he would speak to me longer than he speaks now."

Benevenuta had not been one to encourage solitary communion at the hour of the office. In the church of the convent at Ancona one day they were burying a dead brother, and Conrad decided not to take the sacrament lest he should be distracted by the mourners and the funeral rites. His good friend, who had been in the church of the *frati*, reproached him next day. Conrad gave his reasons. They had no weight with her. "Yesterday morning I saw Christ over the altar, and the Blessed Virgin was in one corner of the altar, and you sat in the other. And Christ turned now to you and now to His Mother. You did ill, Brother Conrad, to make Christ and His Mother wait for you. If you had gone to the burying, what harm would it have done you?" Benevenuta did good service, doubtless, to a man fearful of all formalism, thirsty for solitude. But that guardian angel of his did better, giving him experience of visions in the midst of active, humble work. He had his doubts—what man of his temperament has not?—as to the best life to lead. One day he was nursing a sick brother who was in great pain. He could do nothing to relieve him but stroke his head and his neck with a soothing hand. And as time went by in this patient lowly ministration, Conrad, tired, doubtful, and maybe having other calls, asked, "Is this indeed the service that the Lord would desire?" Echoes of promise came, and a voice, saying, "Inasmuch as ye did it unto the least of these, ye did it unto Me." But he was not at all assured. "And straightway appeared the Lord Jesus, delectable and serene, and saying, 'Brother Conrad, for answer I do unto thee as thou hast done to thy brother.' Then the Lord Jesus put His hand on Conrad's head and neck, and the consolation was unspeakable. And He said, 'Now mayst thou know how the service pleased Me which thou didest to thy ailing brother.'"

At what period of his life he gained his reputation as a great preacher is uncertain, but probably it was under the robust influence of Benevenuta, and with the encouragement of the Spiritual Minister-General, Raymond Gaufridi. His preaching mission doubtless gave a wider chance to that generous capacity for intimate friendships which was his. We know something of his friends, Peter of Monticello, in his younger days, Benevenuta in Ancona, and up in the winter solitudes of Alverna, Andrew and the great austere John of La Penna. Angelo Clareno and his band of wandering protesters were among his intimates. John of Parma in the solitudes of Greccio loved him. When he and Pier Jean d'Olivi were with Conrad they only desired to listen. Margaret the penitent saint up in Cortona concerned herself with his welfare. To Margaret, it would seem, he went not as the counsellor but the seeker of counsel, and in some anguish of mind. Her court was a court of abstinence, and penance, and self-abuse. But she was queen, nevertheless, as in the time of her earthly lovers. Her counsel, her prayers, were sought by holy men, who hung on her words as they might not have done on those of one who had not sinned as she, and, therefore, had not shown her great miracle of repentance. Her self-abasement, her penances were real. None the less did she accept her position of sovereign pentitent and efficacious intercessor, with full confidence. And so, when Conrad, " that brother beloved of God, came from a remote province " to see the handmaid of God, and to commend himself to her prayers, Margaret gave her mind to his case with thoroughness. It is significant that the message delivered to him through the medium of her prayers was not unlike the advice of his friend Benevenuta. His mind was troubled on the question of ritual. Perhaps he had been reproached that he, a priest, found his spiritual consolation outside the prescribed ceremonies. Well, he was not to trouble too much. He might let some of his priestly functions go. She prescribed a minimum. Conrad had evidently expanded with Margaret, which gave her the occasion to warn him shrewdly against pouring out the flavour of his spirit indiscriminately. Then follows a counsel of general resignation rather than particular commands. She promises special graces for his reward ; but he was to know, for his present pain and future bliss, he would never buy these favours at so dear a price as now. Margaret, stricken with pity, also, maybe, with some envy, asks on her own account : " Lord, why dost Thou not correct me as thou dost him ? " And the answer comes, " I correct thee now by separating thee from the worldly desires of all men. I correct thee by denying thee the surety of promises." But to Conrad was given assurance of her state. He prayed for her, and by night he saw her in the spirit, all burning with Divine love. And a voice came, saying, "This is that Margaret who desires nothing, needs nothing, save Christ."

But Conrad was no mere hermit shunning the world, now happy in the woodlands, now nursing his spiritual maladies. He was one of Angelo Clareno's men, one of the band of protesters—chief among the others were Peter of Monticello, Jacopone da Todi, Thomas of Trevi, and Conrad of Spoleto—who sent ambassadors to Celestine V. to beg his protection. On him the

burden of the Fifth Tribulation fell, says Angelo, who
cries aloud on the injustice to one who lived all for
Christ, and so heartily followed the footsteps of his
master that the brothers seeing him, seemed to see
another Francis. Accusations showered on his head.
He was disloyal, it was said. He preached and taught
that the Rule could not be observed within the Order;
that the good and the wise must come outside. He
was summoned before the Minister-General, Giovanni
da Murro, who read him all the slanderous talk of the
friars. The Minister could hardly contain himself.
But Conrad soothed him with his gentle words and
simple ways, and even at last obtained leave to go with
Jacopo da Monte and Thomas of Tollentino and twelve
of their disciples on a mission to the heathen. They
had heard of the trouble of those brothers who had
gone to the region of Achaia and Thessaly after the
renunciation of Celestine. They intended therefore to
go where they might work and obey the Rule as they
wished. But Conrad stayed behind, after all, warned,
it is said, by an oracle.

Towards the end of his life he lived at the Convent
of Santa Croce at Bastia, near Assisi. There he was
probably left in peace. At least he attained to peace,
and a life spent in service and struggle had its desired
crown in an increasing gift of visions. Brother Giles,
dead forty years ago, was his master in this divine art.
Conrad called on him, and Giles came. "How did you
win, my glorious father, in this low life to such high
grace of contemplation?"—"Three wings were mine,"
said Giles, "to mount to God—faith, hope, and charity.
On them I flew and reached this grace."—"Ah! if I
but knew thy rapture!"—"Open thy mouth." The
spirit of Giles blew into the soul of Conrad, and Conrad
knew that rapture. Giles was often with his kinsman.
"Thou art made like unto me, Brother Conrad," he
said.

In 1303, three years before his death, as he was praying in the Porziuncola on the night of the Indulgence,
a brother came to him, and said, "Father, even now
there was a great noise among the watching people.
We know not why, only that we saw a dove, radiantly
white, circling swiftly round the church." And Conrad
answered, "Hear, my brother, but keep the secret I tell
thee, at least to the hour of my death. Know that I
saw the Queen of Heaven come down from the heights
in her great love, with her Son in her arms; and her
Son blessed all those watching people, and filling all their
hearts with special devotion, stirred them to loud wails
and to shouts of joy."

Conrad died in 1306, and was buried in Bastia. A
great concourse of people assembled at his funeral. In
his life he had asked that he might not work miracles
after his death; but we hear of five dead men being
raised by the power in his relics. And the legend runs
that on every anniversary of his death, he goes to
Purgatory and gains the remittance of all the pains
of his erring and loving sons, and leads them up to life
eternal. The Bastians, proud of having a saint, did
him honour. They built a chapel to his memory, with
his picture in it. But bold Perugia was on the watch.
The body had rested sixteen years in its grave when
the Perugian marauders stole it and took it to San
Francesco in their own city. They gave it a very fine
housing, and, doubtless, it was a keen disappointment
that he worked no wonders in his new home, while
he still granted favours asked at Bastia. But the
Perugians, magnanimous rascals, still esteemed him great
and themselves fortunate.

They say Conrad was learned, that he preached finely,
that he wrote books. Wadding gives a letter of his,
containing good advice to a friend. All these rumours
mean very little to us. Contemporaries like Angelo
Clareno boasted the hard life he led, and say he wore

the same tunic for fifty years and more. This seems to tell more of the durability of the stuff from which the brothers made their garments than about Conrad. We are drawn for other things to him who walked in the midst of troubles and harassments and persecution, gentle, and with a sweet voice; to the lover of Nature and of all creatures, who hid not from the strife but bore arms on the harder, poorer side; the priest to whom Francis and all the holy dead ones came more often in the woods than at the altar; the spiritual son of Giles, who crowned his life at the end with the special grace of vision; the man over whom there watched the guardian angel of the Blessed Francis.

CELESTINE V

" *Quod illud solatium . . . sperare . . . pro paucis lachrymis intermina-
bilem risum . . . pro incolatu sylvarû jus civitatis etheree, pro fumoso tugurio
stellantia Christi palatia, pro agresti silentio cantus angelicos.*"—PETRARCH,
" DE VITA SOLITARIA," Lib. I. c. vii.

POOR Celestine's story has been told over and over again,
contemptuously, affectionately, pityingly, apologetically.
The Church canonised him ; his virtues have been counted
and named ; his tragic fate has given him a melancholy
interest. But who has stood up frankly to admire him ?
Ecclesiastical biographers and critics, even those who have
sung his virtues the loudest, have mostly been ashamed of
him. They shove him up to a shining corner of heaven;
but he wasn't the man wanted down here, they seem to
say—not in Rome, at any rate. Dante meets him in hell,
among those

> " ill spirits both to God displeasing
> And to his foes, these wretches who never lived."

Yet Dante's hard judgment is more favourable to Celestine's manhood than that of his soft-spoken eulogists.
If the poet denounced his "great abjuration," surely he
meant he would have had him keep the gate of the
Church citadel at all hazards against the robber Boniface.
They, if they denounced it, did so out of reverence for
a fantastic tradition, which said God's vicegerents might
only be released from their office by death. But they
heave a sigh of relief over *lo gran rifiuto*, being mostly
convinced of his want of capacity ; and is not an incapable
saint much less tolerable in a high estate than an incapable
rascal ? There have been rascally popes a deal more incap-

able than was Celestine, even at the lowest estimate of him ; but good men have been less ashamed of them than of him.

He has no clear right to a place among my Franciscan portraits. He was not a Minorite, and I see very little trace of Minorite influence upon him. Later in point of time than Francis, he is yet of an earlier age. He represents the spirit of monasticism, and is of the ascetics who neglect or maltreat the body, because the body is vile and must be chastened—with an eye, too, on heavenly gain as the price of such corporeal sacrifice—not of those who would drive the body relentlessly to make it the servant of a free spirit. But for a brief moment he was the hope of the Franciscan Spirituals, some of whom took refuge under his wing, calling themselves Celestine Hermits, giving up the dear name of Francis that they might the better do his will. Moreover, by his election to the papacy was flashed on the world the idea of a return to days when the head of the Church was one who shone by his Christian graces rather than as a high-handed administrator, an idea shared by the Franciscans with all the spiritual thinkers of the time. And yet again in him we have the spectacle, so maliciously fascinating to the cynic, so burningly interesting to the enthusiast, of mere goodness set in a high, conspicuous place amid a world of intrigue, greed, and violence, a spectacle from which a clear and certain moral is drawn by all common-sensible men, but which presents a problem unsolved to the minds of an obstinate remnant of idealists. It was the continual problem of the thinkers among the first Franciscans. Only such light-hearted, short-visioned souls as Brother Juniper were untroubled by it.

The world is full of devil worshippers to this day. We fawn before what can destroy. The real slave does not flatter the master exercising over him the arbitrary power of life and death. In his heart he sincerely admires him ; and he is only obeying a universal instinct in saluting power where it is manifest to him. The

Napoleons fascinate the gentlest. Even monsters are given the meed of respect due to strength. Only when the butcher's hand trembles, from lack of nerve, or from some wind-blown impulse of pity, is the respect withdrawn. Success consecrates ambition in the eyes of those who would not hurt a fly. Their instinct is right—their vision faulty. Theirs is the crude limitation of acknowledging power in the loud tempest, and the tearing beast of prey, and the great steam-engine, and missing it in the seed that makes a flower, in the still small voice, the two or three notes, the faintly struggling thought that makes a mood, or lifts a heart, that germinates long in darkness before it persuades a nation. As rare as to hear the grass growing is it to feel the slow moulding of that solidest of all things, an ideal, and salute the power.

The election of Celestine is not only a tragically picturesque incident in the annals of the papacy. It had important consequences. The Church canonised him, but never gave him a successor of his kindred. The experiment was closed, and the moral drawn. Meanwhile, even at this hour, it is worth inquiring whether Celestine was the heavenly fool he is said to have been. Was he conquered by his innate powerlessness, or by a combination of abnormal rascality and intrigue? The ragged, haggard, trembling hermit, fleeing in terror from the proffered honour, then bowing to what he held to be a celestial command, descending from Mount Morrone, his ass's bridle held by a king and a king's son, while cardinals followed in his train down to the coronation pomp at Aquila, is a memorable picture. One would not willingly destroy the dramatic effect, nor deny the real significance of the scene. But it was not the first time that the old man had faced the world.

Pietro da Morrone, born about 1215, was the son of peasant parents in Iserna. His father, Angelerio dei Angelerii, dying, left his wife, Maria dei Leoni, to bring up seven sons. She was pious, and vowed one of them to the priesthood.   But the chosen one did not live to reward her efforts, and Peter, the youngest, was set to theological studies in his place, to the envy and indignation of the others, whose lot was the harder that he might have time for his book.   At about seventeen he entered the Benedictine monastery of Santa Maria di Faifolla, where he remained three years.   But with his mother's death a crisis in his life seems to have occurred.   He longed for more solitude than could be his in the community, and with one companion he left to seek a place where no worldly noise or cares or comforts could come between him and the contemplation of God.   They took the road for Rome, but ere long the companion repented and went back to the monastery.   Peter went on alone, and in January 1235 found himself at Castel di Sangro.   There, hindered from crossing the river by a strong wind, he went into the little church of Saint Nicholas, where he heard of a hermit living near.   He was about to seek his cell, but was warned the hermit led no holy life ; and it would seem that during his sojourn in the neighbourhood for twenty days he endured the rigours of mid-winter with no shelter.   The cold did not hinder a temptation of the senses.   Though Peter was not of those hermits who continually pay themselves for their austerities by shining pictures of pleasures in the world, alternating to and fro between voluptuous excess and voluptuous deprivation, yet in wild January weather, up in the mountains of the Abruzzi, he was visited by two beautiful ladies, who seized his hands while they said sweet things to him, and begged him not to leave them.   He was a tall, lusty young fellow in those days. But the enchantresses did not lead him down the hill again.   He sought among the heights till in Mount Palena he found the place that fitted his purpose.   There were few enough distractions.   His house was a cave, his food just what he could produce himself by the cultivation of the poor land around.   He was very happy.   His life seemed grand and spacious; an awestruck guest saw him hang his cowl on a sunbeam. Every morning the bell of no visible church, echoing among the hills, called him to a new day and its prayers. But a pious woman gave him a cock. She said it would wake him in the morning, and be cheerful company. It waked him, but he heard no more that mysterious bell echoing in the mountains.

After three years of this life, in 1238, he was persuaded to go to Rome to be ordained priest. How long he stopped there is uncertain, but there is no proof of his being back in the Abruzzi before 1240. He had had time enough to see Rome, to mix with the clergy, to realise the pride and splendour of the papacy.

Solitude claimed him again. Among the woods of Mount Morrone, with which his name is particularly associated, he found a place to suit his wild and lonely fantasy, where Rome and all the kingdoms of the world seemed but as the dream of a past night. Others joined him. One by one they came to build their poor cells near him, their elder brother in the spirit, their shining example in the contempt of earthly prizes. But the peasant's son knew how to use his hands. The band of hermits made an oasis up in rugged Mount Morrone. Celestine as practical farmer has been hardly enough regarded. But work was to him more than fruition, and it was not to his mind to dwell on a well-tilled farm. He left the crops and the gardens to the few inhabitants and to such brothers as liked to stay there, while he retired to a higher, wilder place at the top of Mount Majella. Here his followers grew quickly. The fame of his austerities and of his saintliness was helped, astonishing as it may seem, by his undoubted practical qualities, and by his capacity for dealing with men— hermit men, it is true; but there was presumably diversity of character amongst them. Substantial offerings came to him, which were transmuted into stone and lime for the service of God. But not a hermit slept the softer, or ate

finer meats because of these gifts.   They lived under the
Benedictine Rule, made more rigid by Peter for himself
and them.   In an age when the worldly pretensions of
the church were at their height, there was yet a pathetic
eagerness on the part of the faithful to give towards the
support of such as genuinely despised the world.   And so
arose the walls of the Badia of San Spirito in Majella.
Peter was an excellent man of business, and he was not
without his ambition to found an Order that should lead
in sanctity and austerity.   He had not the preference of
the Franciscan Spirituals for the house of God not made
with hands.   After the old monastic fashion, he insisted
on coarse raiment, hard fare, and all the rigours of the
weather for his brothers.   But there should be splendour
in the temple ; and so he dreamed of a great abbey
church in Morrone.   The rich monasteries helped him,
spurred to generosity by the thoroughgoing character of
his plan of life.   In 1248 Innocent IV. conceded full
indulgences to Peter's oratories in the Abruzzi ; and his
adherents obeyed the Benedictine Rule of the Reform of
Saint Damian and the Dove.   Urban IV. approved the
new Order in 1264, and his successor, Clement IV.,
protected it actively.   In the eyes of the Church there
was nothing dangerous in Peter's Order, nothing of the
suspect social influence of the spiritual Franciscans ; and
so in its first days it had no struggle for success.

But the mere fact that it was a new Order was soon
seen by its shrewd founder to be a danger.   It might be
confounded with the Apostoli or other newfangled,
troublesome bodies that had sprung up in imitation of
the Minorites, and were looked on as unruly, eccentric
breeders of heresy and loose manners.   Peter did not live
out of the world even at the top of Majella.   In 1273
he heard that Gregory X. was suppressing all the new
congregations.   No notice had reached him, but he would
not wait meekly for the blow to fall.   Resolutely the
sturdy mountaineer of fifty-eight set out on foot for

Lyons. He reached Lyons, pleaded his case before the Council, and won it. The decree had not been directed against him and his sons; and his Order was confirmed by a Bull in 1274. Having said his say, seen the Pope and cardinals, and done his business, he set off for home, still on foot, through Tuscany and Umbria, back to the Abruzzi. In his time the hermit pope had seen many cities and much people. On his return he called a chapter to tell the brothers the good news, and then, with quiet, patient obstinacy, set about recovering the property of the Order, which had slipped out of its hands during those months of doubt concerning its legal existence.

Peter was by this time no obscure hermit, but the famed head of a growing Order. His old monastery of Faifolla, which he had entered as a lad, was proud of him, and invited him back as abbot. He consented in order that he might win over the brothers there to his own austerer rule. Indeed, one of the principal aims of his life, it seems, was the reform of the Benedictines. Even in those terribly harassing days when he was Pope, he went to the head-quarters at Monte Cassino, and pressed the stricter yoke. Famous now in all circles where austerity was revered, and even outside them, he had already received the favour of Charles II. of Naples. We need not judge Charles's later, interested favours by his earlier, which perhaps had no other motive than sincere admiration. In 1280 Peter was persuaded by his brothers to go to Rome, and this time he arrived as no mere humble deacon but as the head of an Order. Hermit by personal predilection, and chief of a brotherhood of hermits, he was yet never a hermit for his Order, but faced the world that it might rest on a solid foundation. The two monasteries of San Eusebio and San Pietro in Montorio were given him for his brethren, and he had for his friends some among the great churchmen, notably the Colonnas. From Rome he visited

Tuscany, probably on business of the Order, and found his path lined by people eager to see and touch the holy man. Thus the hermit pope had known reverence and adulation long before they came to fetch him down from his rocky solitude to sit in Peter's chair. Every day he saw his monasteries growing in number and power, his brothers models of austerity, and always the pioneers of agriculture in their solitary places, irrigators, vine-growers, tree-planters. It must have seemed the climax of his career. He had done his active work, and was growing old. The rest of the time should be his own to give to God. A solemn council was held, where he gave up office, and named his successor quite definitely. Peter's was no democratic body; and he was not so lost in contemplation as to let business go wrong for want of due care.

It was to Morrone, the cradle of his Order, that he retired in 1293, an old man of seventy-eight. His hermitage of S. Onofrio was built on the side of a steep cleft rock, about two miles from the Badia of S. Spirito at Sulmona. But the Sulmonese would not let him alone. He must farther away. Yet in his four months there the happy touch of his rough hand had made the place green, and he left an impulse of farming industry behind him. One more chapter he held, to order—for he ordered still, though he had given up office—that the Badia of Sulmona should be the head-quarters. The men and women of the place came out, singing in procession, with crosses and torches and banners, begging the saint to stop with them. He blessed them, but said he must away. Taking Robert of Salle, a much-loved disciple, with him, he mounted the hill, doubtless thinking he would never be so near the world again. Leave him there to his peace, while it lasts—an old man rounding his life, who had gone through the natural stages of every perfected career.

But his prayers up in his mountain solitude were not

all for himself. The papacy was vacant, and the delay
in the election was growing a scandal. Peter, in his
hermitage, was sad for the shadow on the fame and the
welfare of the Church. Nicholas IV. had died in April
1292, but the Sacred College was all divided about his
successor. Jealousies, interests to be guarded, spites,
and timidities produced the longest conclave in the
history of the Church. To the College belonged
eminent men—Matteo and Napoleone Orsini, Latino
Malabranca, Matteo d' Acquasparta, Jacopo Colonna,
the great patron of the Spirituals, Peter Colonna, his
nephew, and the ablest, the most formidable, the most
unscrupulous of all, Benedetto Gaetani. To the shrewd
Gaetani it was soon clear that he was not to be chosen.
He was looked on as too dangerous. All the Angevin
force was ranged against him. Five-sixths of the cardinals
were adherents of Charles II. of Naples, who watched the
Conclave jealously, and insinuated his influence. Its first
sittings ended in strife. The place of meeting was
changed, with no effect. Two hot, unhealthy Roman
summers came, and twice the members were scattered.
Only the Colonnas and one other stayed in Rome, and
sent threatening messages that, unless the rest assembled,
they would by themselves elect a pope. In a moment
of agreement it was arranged to hold the meetings at
Perugia ; but there the old spirit prevailed. The evil
genius of the Conclave was Gaetani, a prince of ob-
structionists. In March 1294 they were still sitting
when Charles took Perugia on his way back from
Provence, and tried to interfere. Their choice was
everything to him. Gaetani's protests against his intervention were loud and angry, and a hot altercation
ensued between him and the king, who left at the end
of March for Aquila. Was Charles working for the
election of Peter ? It has been said so ; and at least
he paid a visit to the solitary about this time. There
may have been rumours of the probable election of an

outsider as safer for the interests of all parties, and Charles may have gone to sound him and capture his alliance. But if so, Peter seems not to have understood the visit.

Soon after this the cardinal Latino Malabranca in Perugia received a letter from the hermit, whom he had known and reverenced in Rome. It was not the first time Peter had written to him; but this had a special significance, for it depicted the evils that would come to pass, and prophesied the vengeance of God on such as hindered the choice of a vicegerent of the Almighty. Malabranca kept Peter's letter on him as an amulet, but delayed using it. At last one day, when sickness and other circumstances had reduced their number to eight, a desperate spirit, a pricking of consciences, roused the Conclave, that is, all the members of it present save Gaetani, who sat there cynically confident. He could always prevent the election of a Colonna or an Orsini; and the delay worked well for his interests. But, said the others, we must now proceed to the election. Yes, said Malabranca, or evil will befall us. Hear what a saintly man says of us. And the letter, with its highly coloured pictures of coming judgment, was read amid the silence and the stinging of consciences. In their susceptible condition it was like a direct message from Heaven —to all save the cool, shrewd Gaetani, who said quietly, at the end of the reading, "One of Peter Morrone's visions —no doubt about that." There was a silence, and then a cry—from all save Gaetani—"Peter shall be Pope. Who better than Peter of Morrone?" Gaetani shrugged his shoulders, and smiled inwardly. If they would not elect himself, it was just as well they should elect an idiot. He saw a very satisfactory prospect.

The formal election was proceeded with on July 5, 1294. Legates were chosen to carry the announcement up to Mount Morrone, and the news travelled quick to Charles. Whether it was the consummation of his hopes or not, he determined to make use of the event without delay. More open and less astute than Gaetani—who adopted, for the moment, the attitude of washing his hands of the whole affair—the King of Naples, with his son Charles Martel, was at the Badia of Sulmona about the same time as the legates from Perugia; and the younger prince was of the company that went up the hill with them. Cardinal Peter Colonna had come too. All the pomp of the Abbey of Sulmona as well as a concourse of excited people followed fast. Stefaneschi, afterwards cardinal, Boniface's biographer and eulogist, was with them, and he described the scene in his rhymed chronicle. Climbing to the top they found a poor little hermitage of two cells, divided by a rough low wall. In front on a narrow flat place on the steep mountain-side grew some wild flowers. There was a barred opening for a window. From the door, an old man, blear-eyed with long watching and weeping, clad in a rough and dirty tunic, looked out with a startled face. Rumour had been before them. Fra Roberto, wandering about the mountain, had brought it. Peter's first thought had been of flight, and indeed, he had been brought back by the excited people just before the deputation arrived. "Evviva il papa!" they cried. "Evviva il papa!" Ah, to have a pope of their very own at last!

The Archbishop of Lyons advanced, prostrated, and made the announcement. Peter shook his head. "I am the least of God's servants. And I am old."—"It is the will of God," said Cardinal Peter Colonna; and the hermit asked for time to pray for guidance. King and cardinals and bishops and people waited at the door of the little cell till the old man came out with meek consent on his lips. The people shouted again. The archbishop read the letter of the Conclave. Splendour and rank fell down before the rugged old hermit. The Kingdom of God had surely come upon the earth; and its coming was inaugurated in the high pure air of the hills; and great worldlings had been drawn up along a rocky path to greet it.

There is dramatic rapidity of effect in the changing of the scenes. Peter had no affairs to set in order. The *cortège* was formed at once. The old man, in his ragged tunic, with his pale, haggard face, his unkempt beard, seated on an ass, with Charles Martel, King of Hungary, on one side, and a cardinal on the other, looked back through the shouting, singing crowd at his beloved mountain-top, and at the cell where he had known peace. Then he took his way down the familiar rocky path into the unknown. The ways of God were past finding out. But he could obey.

For several days he stayed at Sulmona, and from there wrote to the cardinals that he was an old man, used to the cold of the mountains, that for a midsummer journey to Perugia he was unfit, and that he chose Aquila for his coronation place. This was Charles's doing, of course. " You will be freer there," he said, " away from the tyranny of the Pontifical State." Peter set out for Aquila towards the end of July, his procession further swelled and still more splendid, for in it were all the Angevin courtiers as well as the chanting churchmen in their splendid vestments. He rode still on his ass, but its bridle was held by two kings. Strange sight for the Aquilese, who came out to meet them at the Badia of Collemaggio, and were filled with awe ! Into the town meanwhile flocked crowds from all parts, drawn by the court, still more by the new hermit pope, who was to bring back the peace and virtue of the early Church. Charles levied contributions on Apulia and the Abruzzi for the maintenance of the concourse of people. In vain the cardinals sent envoys begging him to go to Perugia. Peter remained firm to stay in Aquila, trusting Charles more than them.

The account given by Gregorovius of Celestine's character and actions is not quite accurate. Probably he relied too much on the rhymed chronicle of Stefaneschi, who was more the creature of Boniface than Celestine ever was of Charles. The new Pope was not, as we have seen, merely a hermit " who had spent his life in the solitude of the mountain." The sensible historian has only contempt for the " simple anchorite." But one need make no undue pretensions for him. His capacity for ruling anything more complex or more disorganised than his own Order, from this time known as the Celestines, is simply unproved by his five months' office. It is probable that he had no very large mind. He could not have grasped all at once the vastness of his task, first blinded, then tortured as he was by the intrigues around him. He had always the air of being a little too much occupied with the advancement of his own Order, on which Charles heaped favours and property to please and flatter him. He was caught in a trap ; but he was creditably restive in the trap, and he kept his conscience there and a quick enough mind. If he had been a better tool he would have been longer pope. His five months' record contains mistakes, but no very serious ones, no vileness, and a groping but very serious endeavour to use the high influence of his office for good. To clear the Church of corruption would have overtaxed the powers of a man in the prime of life ; and he has been sneered at because he did little in five months, with a politician king—not a very able one, I admit—on one side, and, on the other, a divided cardinalate, each party in it, almost each member of each party, bent on tricking him.

In spite of his humility he had a notion it was for the cardinals to come where he desired, and, of course, Charles encouraged him, and made such preparations as forced them. Even Gaetani came to Aquila. It was agreeable to disdain, but a little dangerous. The coronation of the hermit, now Pope Celestine V., took place on the 29th August 1294, in front of the church of Santa Maria of Collemaggio. He did not resist the

traditional splendour of the occasion. On the great
raised stage he was seen in white and gold robes, and
about Aquila that day there were said to have been
two hundred thousand persons to look at him. They
came from Tuscany, Apulia, the Marches, Umbria, from
all parts of Italy ; and some have guessed Dante to have
been amongst them—but then they would have him
everywhere. Mounted on a white horse, two kings
holding the bridle, Celestine went in triumphant procession from the Badia of Collemaggio to the Palace of
Aquila, where he sat in state with his cardinals. Gaetani
the scorner was now watchful. From that day his presence was needful to undermine the influence of Charles
—though a moment came when he saw the more useful
device was to divert the favour of the king to himself.

Celestine's time passed in a whirl of petty business.
There are thirty decrees of his between the 1st and
17th of September ; and though they were of little
importance, his habit of not consulting the Sacred
College gave great offence. Ignorance of etiquette
may have had much to do with this ; but a distrust of
the cardinals, and the old habit of independence in the
founder and the ruler of an Order probably had more.
Says an old historian, he did not depart from the
innocence of his first state, but kept the same humility
and purity. Yet though his mode of living was un-
changed, he was deceived by his officers, who gave favours
in his name without his knowledge. Too trustful, he
could be induced by plausible tongues to sign documents
giving unstated favours to unnamed persons. These
were the mistakes of a bewildered man. Among the
cardinals there were only three whom he trusted : Matteo
Orsini, Hugo of San Sabina (a Frenchman), and Giacomo
Colonna. It was through the mouth of one of these
that he was wont to speak in the Consistory or elsewhere.
He is shy of speaking Latin, which he hardly knows at
all, said the cardinals. As a matter of fact Celestine

could read it, but it did not come readily to his tongue. So they spoke to him in the vulgar, which Stefaneschi thought a most undignified proceeding. But he spoke little, wise man, and he never answered in public.

To his monks, of course, it was a great thing that their founder should be Pope. Their privileges and wealth increased, and many Benedictine abbeys flatteringly placed themselves under the Celestine rule. His election of new cardinals was a bold stroke, a suggestion of Charles's, no doubt, but acquiesced in very heartily by him as a means of making harmless certain dangerous cabals. They were not a bad choice. The fact that seven out of the twelve were French suggests Charles's compulsion; but there is no evidence they were unknown to Celestine during his sojourn at Rome and Lyons.

Meanwhile, amid petty business, constant suspicions, under the vigilant eyes of king and cardinals, especially the cynical Gaetani, Celestine lived in discomfort, feeling his ignorance, his difficulties, his bonds, struggling for freedom that he might serve the Church, keeping up pomp before the world, but in private living as in his poorest days. Some one describes him walking about his room gnawing a crust of bread and drinking from a rough pitcher of water. "I eat and drink as my mother taught me," he would say, "as a wise man should." Then, turning to the monks, he would add, "Ah, my brothers, if it were not for you, I would not be Pope. It is as wearisome to me as it was delightful to live up there in my solitude." Poor man, he knew the needs of his Church, yet at every moment he was hindered when he stretched out a helping hand; and his one interested thought concerned the monks of his Order.

Yet the hopes of some were high because he sat on the throne. The Spirituals among the Franciscans had been going through a hard time of tribulation. The little band led by Fra Liberato and Angelo Clareno looked to the new pope as to their true father. He would not tell them, surely, to tamper with their Rule and dishonour Francis, as did their superiors. Towards the end of September they came to Aquila with their demand. Celestine listened, and granted their request, giving them his supreme authority for their mode of life. It was for their convenience, and to save confusion, rather than from vanity, that he gave them the name of the Poor Hermits of Pope Celestine. This act, at least, was done on his own initiative. So also perhaps was his very important ratification of the Bull of Gregory X., which had been annulled, respecting the duty of a speedy decision in the Conclaves. Disagreeable penalties were to attend all delays : the scandal after the death of Nicholas IV. should not happen again, he had resolved. His plan is practically the same which holds good to-day.

Indeed, the poor harassed old man's mind was busy ; and perhaps Charles was not quite so convinced as he had been of the certainty of his influence. Celestine was meditating a crusade, and he appealed for help to Philip le Bel. Besides, he had a great, if vague idea of promoting the peace of Europe. A treaty between Charles and the King of Aragon, a dear desire of his, was only hindered by his own abdication. And he sent Bertrand de Gout to England to discuss the differences between England and France. Up in Morrone and Majella he and his brothers had lived in peace, and the soil had blossomed under them; and abbeys had grown up for the shelter of holy men and the encouragement of good work. But below here in the great world each man mistrusted, and obstructed, and malinged the other. To bring some measure of peace to the struggling nations and to the divided Church before he died, was his one desire. Death was often in his thoughts. He never hoped to see Rome, and hardly wished it; for Rome, he knew, was the centre of all the bewildering, useless, weary intrigue he saw too much of in Aquila.

Perhaps Charles enticed him to Naples by telling him

that the treaty with James of Aragon demanded his presence there. Celestine was easily persuaded, for he knew by instinct that in Rome he would be bound still more by the weight of tradition, and more harassed by the clamour of interests. He was a most submissive son of the Church, one whom heresy never touched, yet he feared Rome. But the cardinals would certainly have protested against his going elsewhere, and there was something secret in the departure of the king and the pope in the early morning. Charles kept by his side all the time, terrified lest he should be persuaded, in the name of duty and the welfare of the Church, to turn back and go to the City. He arrived at Naples in the beginning of November. He was lodged in the Castel Nuovo, where he made a cell as like his own in Morrone as possible. This was not according to Charles's wishes, who had not imagined the asceticism of his *protégé* would last so long. He was an ascetic, the king doubtless thought, because a hermit has to be so for professional reasons, or because he has few temptations. But now it was absurd, even dangerous. Charles had the fear that possesses all the orthodox in every age, of poverty and austerity, save when forced, or when exercised in a hermit's cell. It was inconvenient that he could not lull his mind to sleep by the opiates of unaccustomed luxuries.

While the more sanguine Spirituals were looking towards him with hope, the shrewder ones knew the terrible task before him, and waited doubtful. It was probably at this moment that Jacopone sent him his outspoken warning and exhortation :—

> " What will the end of thy testing be,
> Peter Morrone ? We're watching thee.
>   Now at last we can judge right well
> What thou dreamdst of in thy cell.
>   If thy falling away the story must tell,
> There is deep damnation for thee.

See thy name on high ascend,
See thy saintly fame extend.
If thou soilst it ere the end,
Good men will 'wildered be.

As to the mark the arrow flies,
So to thy throne turn the world's eyes.
If thou'rt shifty, bitter cries
Shall mount to God against thee.

Labourer, art thou worth thy hire?
The court of Rome's a testing fire.
Soon we'll know to our heart's desire,
What's gold, what's dross in thee.

Art thou swelled with pride of place?
Then thou'rt sickening apace.
A poor end 'twould be for thy race,
To lose God for Peter's key.

In my heart there boded ill
That day thou utteredst ' I will.'
Thou darest the world thy soul to kill,
Taking this yoke upon thee.

.   .   .   .   .   .

Of sly designing cheats beware,
Who say, ' Lo, white,' when black is there.
If to fend thyself thou dost not dare,
A poor song we'll get from thee."

Poor Celestine did not need such exhortations: he knew his case too well. He needed encouragement rather. And things grew worse. Gaetani was much about court, most civil to his old enemy Charles, gracious and insinuating to Celestine in his presence, and giving him much advice which, however, was at first entirely distrusted. But then he seemed to be omniscient; and Celestine, longing for his mountain-tops, finding little practical help in books, and divided councils among the men about him, at last consulted him. The visionary heard voices. Were they from Heaven? They were all discouraging, sometimes denunciatory and terrifying.

Ancient legend said Gaetani's voice through a speaking-tube accounted for some of these messages, infernal or Divine. Could he resign? the poor hermit asked. Was it best? With mock gravity, Gaetani said, yes, if the reasons were very serious. His intention was whispered about, and it reached the people outside the palace. They besieged Castel Nuovo. Celestine appeared, and talked them into calmness; but he could not be persuaded to change his mind. Meanwhile Gaetani had worked on the not very able or far-seeing Charles. A saint pope with no personal interests to serve had seemed an excellent tool for the king. But the saint had been restive in his hands, and his evident unhappiness in dependence was a bad augury. He could be deceived; but he was the poorest partner in an intrigue. It had been clever to checkmate Gaetani. But Gaetani was not checkmated after all. And if Gaetani with all his learning in law, his man of the world training and experience, his total unscrupulousness, were to throw in his lot with him! The cardinal and the king whispered together. Then Charles said Celestine deserved a rest. His duties were too much for him.

Celestine's last acts as pope were done in order, and with great dignity. The Consistory convoked, he read his renunciation—" I, Pope Celestine V., moved by lawful reasons, to wit, by humility, a desire for a better life and an unharmed conscience, likewise, because of my weakness of body, my want of knowledge, the malignity of the people, the infirmity of my person, and that I may regain the peace of my aforetime consolation, of my own will give up the papacy, and definitely renounce the place, the dignity, the burden, and the honour, giving full and free faculty to the sacred College of Cardinals to elect and provide, in accordance with canonical law, a Pastor for the universal Church." If Gaetani dictated this resolution, Celestine read it very willingly. Previously he had subscribed to a declaration that it was lawful for popes to renounce. Putting off the papal insignia in the Consistory, he put on his monkish cowl. Men were moved to tears at the sight who had not helped Celestine much in his task.

His Order was in despair. A groan rose from the more spiritual part of the Church. The Angevins complained bitterly; for Charles did not convince all his party that Gaetani was the pope they needed. The Conclave had to meet at once, in accordance with Celestine's ratification of the Gregorian law. There could be no delay; and Gaetani was elected as Boniface VIII., to the chagrin of the Colonnas and their partisans.

Poor Celestine was now mocked by a great calm. Back to Morrone was his one desire. But Boniface willed otherwise. Leave an ex-pope free to be set up as a rival at any moment? No, he would have him under his eye. He can hardly have thought of keeping a tame saint in his household at Rome; yet the order to his predecessor was given peremptorily to proceed thither. Angelerio, Abbot of Monte Cassino, was appointed his guardian. But the abbot, who did not take his position to be that of jailer, and who let Peter have his own will about the direction of his journey, was thrown into the prison of Santa Cristina on the Lake of Bolsena, a prison only used for those under accusation of grave religious offences. Theodoric of Orvieto was next sent after the fugitive. But Peter had the power of melting the hearts of men of less tough fibre than Boniface; and the messenger finding a quiet old man in his cell at Morrone, left him there, and went back to tell of his guilelessness to the Pope, who had in the meanwhile called in the aid of Charles, and induced him to send Guillaume d'Estendart to secure the hermit. Peter, however slow to think evil, was no fool. It is probable that his flight took place even before he heard that Boniface, with gratuitous insolence, had formally revoked all his acts and privileges. Apart from that, it seemed to him that all these guardians and messengers augured ill for his peace and safety; and with some of his faithful brothers he took flight, aiming beyond the seas. For two months he wandered about desert places of the Abruzzi. In the forests of Apulia, whither he hastened, saying wearily, "It may be I shall rest here," he was recognised. To his cell people flocked to venerate him. For more than a month he was hidden in the monastery of San Giovanni in Piano, below Monte Gargano. Then hearing that Boniface had procured the aid of a civil officer of Charles, as less likely to be over-awed in the presence of a saint, and feeling the near pursuit, Peter, weary and unhappy, set out to sea in a poor little boat bound for Greece. Once on the great waters, his peace returned. It was as when he was up in Morrone and Majella, amid the eternal hills. But a storm arose; the little boat ran aground near Viesti in Apulia, and while the hermit waited for the calming of the tempest, he was caught. In vain the people resisted. While he was going away in custody they fought for pieces of his robe. D'Estendart delivered him over to Boniface's chamberlain, Theodoric, and he was brought first to Capua, then to Anagni to the Pope, who received the old man with mock courtesy, and informed him of the necessity of saving him from his friends—for the good of the Church, of course, to which, they all knew, Celestine was so deeply attached.

Boniface had to fight hard for his place. The Colonnas were heading those who said a pope might not renounce. To have that old imbecile hermit about, a centre of faction, while people palavered about his saintliness, Boniface would not endure. In vain Peter protested he only wished to be alone with his God up in the mountains, that he had no desire to speak with any save his brothers. In vain the meeker cardinals said, "Let the old man go to his cell." Boniface insisted that Celestine was a formidable rival. For the place of the ex-pope's confinement he chose the Castle of Fumone, between Alatri and Anagni, built threateningly on the top of a hill, frowning down on the whole Campagna. The hill was a place of beacons. *Si Fummo fumet, tota Campanea tremet,* used to be said. It was a place of ill omen.   Many popes' prisoners had languished there. There the anti-pope Clement III. had died.   And it was a prison in very truth.   The two Celestine brothers, his first companions, were taken very ill in the unwhole-some air.   They were replaced once, with the same result ; and then he was guarded by seven knights and thirty soldiers, whom no one checked for their want of respect, even for their ill-treatment of him.   Here was solitude, but not as in the pure air of Morrone amongst his friends the birds and the flowers he tended.   No hanging of his cowl on a sunbeam here.   He lived in a fetid atmosphere, amid suspicion, gibes, the terror of death, and the sense of failure.   It was his misfortune that he had not crossed Gaetani's path and purposes during his years at Rome, and earlier tasted some of the vengeance that the grim cardinal meted out swiftly to all who were not his creatures.   In his five months as pontiff he could at least have shunned him more insistently, and inspired James Colonna to a prompter resistance to Gaetani's election, which might have saved the Church from Boniface's rule.   He knew him now all too late. Boniface, it is said, paid one visit to him in Fumone, and with specious words told him his infinite regrets for this compulsory seclusion.   There were intrigues—he would understand.   There were persons who would delight in a schism.   It has been said that Peter rounded on him with, "You crept into the papacy like a fox ; you will reign like a lion, and die like a dog."   But the saying is more accurately attributed to Boniface's other prisoner, Jacopone da Todi.   The feeble old man lingered for ten weary months.   Death freed him on the day of Pente-cost, May 19, 1296.

His obsequies were splendid !   Boniface ordered two

solemn masses to be said in Rome, and his representative superintended the removal of the body from Fumone to the church of S. Antonio in Ferentino, where the Celestine brothers laid him lovingly in the earth.

His critics are divided, but very unevenly, between those—by far the greater number—who think his mistake was in accepting the papacy at all, and those who, like Dante, hold that he had a sacred trust to keep the villain Boniface out of Peter's chair, and that he betrayed it. Dante has not a word of pity for the old, frail, innocent creature, set about by evil councillors and intriguers, all of them bent on using him as a tool, and ready to desert him because he was no tool, who lauded his virtues as an electioneering bait, and counted them foolishness when they obstructed their purposes—a poor old man, lonely for the solitude of his mountain-tops, and weary after a hard and active life, which had surely paid for rest. He consigns him to hell, among the cowards. But, as I have already said, his judgment is more honourable to Celestine than that of some other critics. It is the attitude of one who believed not that he failed because of his impotence, but for want of perseverance. Petrarch gives Celestine his due, and lauds the dignity of his retirement—but shirks the interesting problem. Granted Celestine's feeble powers —though these are belied by his earlier records; and though his five months' rule, when he was nearly eighty years old, proves bewilderment rather than incapacity— was it worse for the Church that he happened to be a saint? The general answer seems to be, Yes. No rascal of mediocre abilities was ever so despised. But the problem was solved for ever for the Church fatally endowed by Constantine, in the tragic episode of Peter Morrone. The Spirituals saw one glimpse of the light of the Kingdom, and again the door shut fast. They waited in vain. They wait. For them the problem is never solved. Its statement in the Celestine episode was, they feel, not perfect.

ANGELO CLARENO

Her nis non hoom, her nis but wildernesse :
Forth, pilgrim, forth !   Forth, beste, out of thy stal !
Know thy countree, look up, thank God of al ;
Hold the hye wey, and let thy gost thee lede ;
And truthe shal delivere, hit is no drede.
                                    —BALADE DE BON CONSEYL.

THE second chapter of Franciscan history is interspersed with lauds as jubilant as those to which the first companions tuned their march. But satires, foreign to the early times, are heard likewise ; and more than one Jeremiah arose to tell a bitter tale of persecution, and to lament aloud the evils of the age. The Spirituals flashed their inciting torch, and many followed; but the path was perforce towards the wilderness rather than to the teeming world of men. The *Chronicle of the Tribulations* has several authors, but of these the name of Angelo Clareno alone remains. His story is so full of significance for his own and other movements that I choose to tell it rather than the more stirring tale of Ubertino da Casale, his contemporary and fighting ally. The career of no other marks so clearly the forced change in the plan of life of the true-born sons of Francis. He should have been one of the first twelve. It was his sole desire to be like them. In his youth he sought intercourse with all who could tell of them. The will of Francis was his law. But his life is a wholesome test of some glib assertions on the value of persecution. Its fires may purify—but they change. Something more than the dross is apt to be consumed, or scattered in the fumes. Angelo and his

339

friends made no compromise respecting the will of the Founder ; and for their staunchness they were driven hither and thither on the winds and the waters of the world. Faithful to the end, they were yet at the end something other than sons of Francis. Not merely had been quenched the overbrimming joy, but the ideal had suffered.

The *Chronicle of the Tribulations*, which has never all been published, is a record of the persecution of the Spirituals from the time of Elias. Strongly partisan in portions, it is, on the whole, wonderfully moderate in its judgments and language, and entirely undeserving of the abuse and neglect which it has suffered. The MS. is in the *Magliabecchiana* at Florence. Ehrle has published most of it in the *Archiv für Kirchen und Litteraturgeschichte des Mittelalters*, and a good part of the rest, that is, the earlier portion, is to be found, but inaccurately, in Döllinger's *Beiträge zur Sektengeschichte des Mittelalters*. The "Tribulations" are seven, of which only five concern us. The First part deals with some results of Francis's absence in the East, and the discontent of the relaxed brothers ; the Second with the generalship of Elias, his high-handed interpretation of the Rule, and his harsh treatment of the faithful ; the Third with the generalship of Crescentius, and his scattering of the protesting *zelanti* into distant provinces. The Fourth relates the persecution of John of Parma and his deposition ; the Fifth, the trials of Pier Jean d'Olivi and his companions, and the sufferings of Fra Liberato's band, of which Angelo was a prominent member. The early portion is probably by some comtemporary of Francis. But Angelo had a principal part in the compilation of the book. That he speaks in his own person only in later portions is no proof against this, for certain passages which, from their mention of him, might be thought to be the work of another, bear a strong likeness to the *Epistola excusatoria*, most certainly written by him

in justification of himself and his brothers, and addressed
to John XXII. From these two sources, and what
remains of his personal correspondence, we get nearly
all we know of Angelo and his group.

Angelo da Cingoli, generally called Angelo Clareno,
is said to have become a Minorite not long after 1260,
perhaps at Cingoli in the Marches. His fervent spirit
lived in the first days of the Order, and the Companions
of Francis, whom he knew through the tales of their
comrades, were his natural exemplars. The high rule
of John of Parma was just over, but he lived with men
who had been the faithful adherents of the spiritual
Minister-General. His Chronicle contains a magnificent
eulogy of John, and was, indeed, the principal source
from which were drawn, in the eighteenth century, the
materials to justify his beatification. It is probable
Angelo was the writer of this portion, and, doubtless,
he had been a pilgrim to the hermitage at Greccio.
That other John—the often named but, for us, shadowy
companion of the Blessed Giles—was his friend, and,
following his counsel, he sought intercourse with the
great visionary, James of La Massa. John, quoting
the testimony of Giles, Marco da Mentino, Juniper,
and Lucido, had said, " If thou wouldst have learning
in spiritual things, haste and hold speech with James
of La Massa." And James did not disappoint him,
but told him things " truly stupendous." Another
brother of his province, and his strong ally, Conrad
d'Offida, had known Leo. Thus, he was probably ac-
quainted with a good many more of the Franciscan
writings of the first days than the edict of 1266
considered good for the brothers.

Angelo had some claim to learning. The *Conformities*,
on the authority of Fra Simone da Cassia, one of Angelo's
pupils, declares him to be the translator of the Greek
Grammar of Johannes Climacus, of a dialogue of the
Blessed Macharius, and a devout treatise of St. John

Chrysostom. He received his knowledge of Greek direct from Heaven, says Bartholomew of Pisa, who forgot to take into account his long wanderings in Greek countries.

But the Marches, the refuge of the Spirituals, were going through a hard time under the generalship of Jerome of Ascoli, of Bonagratia, and of Arlotto. Angelo's mode of life was to the authorities intolerable, because disturbing to the interpretation of the Rule which they imagined to have been arrived at by universal consent. He came to close conflict with the Ministers. But in this he was not the first, nor even the leader. Gregory X. was suspected by the Spirituals of wishing to make a certain amount of common property obligatory on the brothers ; and, in 1274, before the Council of Lyons, where it was presumed the law would be enacted, certain Spirituals of the Marches began a hot agitation against the proposal. The Council enacted no such law ; but the agitation was not overlooked, and some of the most outspoken protesters—among whom were Liberato and Thomas of Tolentino—were severely brought to task, and separated from each other in scattered hermitages. But the conduct of their superiors convinced them their suspicions were well founded, and they did not cease their protests. They had many followers, and the strife grew. Certain provincial ministers met secretly and discussed the dangerous example of Liberato and his friends, and at the next provincial Chapter of the Marches, they were condemned unheard to perpetual, solitary, and silent imprisonment, without the consolation of the sacraments. Angelo was among them. The better to overawe brothers who might presume to have opinions of their own on the ideals and conduct of the Order, the sentence was read aloud every week in every convent ; and woe to him who said a word in protest !

But when Raymond Gaufridi became Minister-General in 1289, he examined the imprisoned men's offence, found it none, and quashed the sentence. The same hostility, however, met them again when they came out of prison ; and it was doubtless from prudence that Liberato, Angelo Clareno, Thomas of Tollentino, and some others, were sent, in 1290, on a mission to Armenia. King Aiton II. desired for himself and his subjects the ministrations of faithful Franciscans. So impressed was he with the simplicity and purity of the brothers sent him, that in spite of persecution from his family, some years later he counted it great joy to lose his kingdom and become the Minorite Brother John. Aiton described with enthusiasm their work and their lives in a letter which was read at the Chapter General of Paris, in 1292. But they were not the first Franciscans in his kingdom. A Minorite colony had long existed there, and in the course of time had become demoralised. The king's favour of the newcomers was doubtless the first cause of the fierce hostility encountered by Liberato and his companions. But they introduced a more active, more ascetic standard of life, and brought a breath of the first ardour it was irksome to be reminded of. The old gang tried to make mischief between the new men and the king, and spread scandals about them. The king did not listen, but in the end, by petty and constant tyranny, their life and work were made impossible. For three years they struggled on, and then returned to Italy. But libellous letters had reached home before them, and their old offences were not forgotten. In the Marches they could find no resting-place. Raymond Gaufridi, for all his good-will, had not made his authority on this point supreme. Worn out, ill, and depressed, Angelo and Liberato wandered from place to place, Fra Monaldo, vicar of the province, making it impossible for them to rest anywhere till they should have a chance of seeing the Minister-General. He would rather receive and keep fornicators in his province, said Monaldo.

But that year a light had arisen on the Spirituals'
horizon. Peter of Morrone of holy fame had come
down from his moutains to sit on the throne of the
Church, not in pomp and pride, but as the Vicegerent of
the humble and pitiful Christ, to spread the reign of the
spirit on the earth.   Peter was known to the pious
throughout Central Italy, his cell a place of pilgrimage
and refuge.   Surely the day of tribulation was over.
Surely the worldly provincials would not persecute when
Celestine sat on the papal throne.   Liberato, Peter of
Macerata, Angelo, Jacopone, Conrad d'Offida, and some
others held counsel together, and with the Minister-
General's encouragement, the three first made their
way, in the autumn of 1294, to the papal Curia, then
at Aquila.   The interview was important for several
reasons.   Perhaps it was the only occasion when poor
Celestine was allowed to act on his own initiative.   But
to Charles and to the Cardinal Gaetani, this receiving
delegates from a few discontented friars doubtless seemed
a thing of. no moment.   The petitioners' demand was
pathetically humble—leave to obey the Rule of their
Order as Francis had planned it, to live according to the
commanding of his Testament.   It might seem an obvious
thing for Celestine to have issued a general order to
the Franciscan provincials to put no hindrance in the
way of a strict and faithful following of their Rule—
thus strengthening the hands of the benevolent Minister-
General.   It corroborates our idea of his knowledge of
the events of the time, and of his general shrewdness,
when he was not hustled and frightened and deceived by
Charles or the cardinals, that he did nothing of the sort.
Such an order to be efficacious could only be issued at a
Chapter General, which would have once more reopened,
and with violence, the question of the interpretation of
the Rule.   What chance had the poor prisoner of Aquila
of supporting the Spirituals by his presence at such a
Council ?   Even had he done so, he would only have

brought down on himself the wrath of the *mitigati* at a moment when his position could stand no more hostility. Then Celestine was no Franciscan. His ideal was like that of Francis only so far as purity of life and poverty were concerned. Probably he thought, like most other people, that the *mitigati* had permanently triumphed, and that for the faithful remnant shelter could only be found outside the Order. But he made no attempt to tamper with their loyalty to the Rule. Francis should still be their father, to whom their love and obedience were due ; but as the world was evil, and they needed a protector, he, Celestine, would be their foster-father. They should wear the tunic of his brothers—there is a tradition among the white-robed Celestines that in the early times their robe was very like the Minorites'—and in his habit follow their own rule of life. But it is characteristic of Celestine, whose weakness was a spiritual pride in asceticism, that he recommended them to add to the rigours of the Rule—*et superaddere, si possemus, ad regulam et testamentum*. He absolved them from all obedience to the Minorite authorities. Him, Celestine, should they obey, and Fra Liberato under him, to whom he gave full power of absolution and of receiving others into the fraternity. He looked round the cardinals to see whom he might trust to give a helping hand to the little flock, and his choice fell on Napoleon Orsini. If in the world they were asked who they were, they should answer, " We are poor hermit brothers of Lord Celestine, keeping our rule of life and poverty in desert places." The last words are very significant. Then the Pope sent messages to the abbots of his own Order that they should have a care of Liberato and his companions.

The step was a revolutionary one for Celestine to take. But the need of the moment seemed to dictate it, and Angelo and the rest showed no reluctance to obey his suggestion. Doubtless, they had in their minds the answer of Francis to Cæsar of Spires, giving him leave to keep the Rule outside the Order, against the command of the superiors, rather than fail to keep it inside. But perhaps they did not realise all it meant. Tocco, with some show of justice, traces the rise of the *fraticelli*, who had not yet been heard of, to this interview with Celestine at Aquila. The statement cannot be accepted without modification. Angelo and his brothers remained directly inspired by Francis. Only faintly in them is heard the beginning of the later pedantic clamour for a particular form of asceticism at any price. They were schismatics against their will, and, probably, those that actually took the Celestine name and the habit were few. If Conrad d'Offida did so, it was but for a short time. Perhaps Pier Jean d'Olivi, who strongly disapproved of the step, and who wrote to expostulate with him, may have brought him back. Jacopone da Todi has been named as one, I think inaccurately. The mere fact that Boniface annulled all his predecessor had done may, to the minds of all save the leading protesters, have involved their reinstatement as Minorites. The desire for rest and freedom deceived the Poor Hermits of Pope Celestine. Henceforward they were banished from the social life of the communities of Francis, and driven to the care of their own souls in solitude. The hermit life — in Francis's scheme the refreshment of workers in the world — became their common habit. To Celestine this seemed the natural way for holy men. But it was a great step back from the plan of Francis.

The event redoubled the fury of their enemies. They had escaped, and by a means that insulted their foes. Raymond Gaufridi was not strong enough to make their stay in the Marches a happy one. Then followed Celestine's "great renunciation," December 13, 1294. With the coming of Boniface their protection was gone. Raymond was even replaced by John of Murro, not inclined to favour them. Angelo and his friends, marked men, again sought a home across the seas, this

time on the island of Trixonia, in the Gulf of Corinth.
After some months of comparative peace, their lives
became once more a pitiful story of petty intolerance.
They ate no meat because they were poor, and this
was put down to their holding some dangerous tenet.
Careful not to interfere with the priests there established,
who were always suspicious on the count of dues, they
did not celebrate the sacraments. For this they were
declared infidels or Manichæans. When they did preach
or say mass, their large following made the prejudiced
enemies still more furious, and the leader, a certain
Fra Hieronimo, from Catalonia, a man to whose dis-
reputable life their goodness was a foil, slandered them
everywhere. An apostate Order has sprung up in
Achaia, said envoys to Pope Boniface ; and, to the
credit of the arrogant Pope be it said, his first reply
was, "Leave them alone. They are better men than
you." But the slanders persisted, and news came to
the hermits they were to be suppressed. In fact they
had now no standing, seeing that Boniface had annulled
Celestine's decrees. Appeals to the Patriarchs of Athens
and of Patras helped them not at all. Taking refuge in
Thessaly, they were excommunicated on a vague charge
of heresy. From isle to isle they wandered, having no
money or friends to help them to cross the sea. Liberato
found means at last to send messengers to assure Boniface
of their loyalty to the Roman Church. But Boniface
succumbed to the violence of Anagni ; and in October
1303 Liberato himself was on his way to Perugia to
see the milder Benedict. They were not the only little
band in trouble. It was a time of terrible suffering and
unrest for all their Spiritual brethren. Ubertino had
been summoned to Rome, and was writing the Apologia
of the Spirituals, threatened by the agents of the Inquisition of Italy and the south of France. Liberato's
business received scant attention. Benedict died in July
1304. Then, with Fra Paolo his friend, Liberato girt up

his loins once more to go to the new pope, Clement V.,
but he took ill on the way, and the rest of his life was a
misery of physical suffering. Meanwhile Angelo had
been working hard to ship the rest of them home. He
was the last to come. On his arrival he was hustled
and captured, released and captured, and released again.
(Charles of Naples had been stirred up against them by
Gonsalvo, the Minister-General.) And when at last he
was a free man, he found his chief ill and in trouble.
Under Clement the persecutions were stricter. In the
kingdom of Naples Liberato had been called with his
companions before the Inquisitor, Thomas of Adversa.
The result of the examination was, as usual, a pro-
nouncement of strict orthodoxy. Indeed the inquisitor
had pity on him, and revealed the machinations of his
enemies. "Fra Liberato, Fra Liberato, I swear by Him
that created me, that never was any poor man's flesh sold
so dear as I could sell thine. The brothers would drink
thy blood an they could." At Perugia Angelo found
Cardinal Napoleon Orsini, who had not forgotten his
promise to Celestine, though in the struggle with Boniface, when he had been an ally of the Colonnas, the
affairs of the little wandering band of hermits had had
small chance of his attention. "Come," he said to
Angelo, "to Avignon, and watch the interests of your
brothers in the Curia there. In my household you will
be safe, and ready to speak and bear witness for them."
But he was ill, and besides, when Liberato died at
S. Angelo della Vina, in 1307, he became head of the
fraternity. They were mostly divided into three groups,
one in the kingdom of Naples and Sicily, another in the
Marches, and yet another, in which were the special
brothers of his heart, near Rome. For four years he
seems to have wandered among these last, instructing
them, stimulating them, leading in their midst an austere
and simple life, inwardly peaceful, but liable to sudden
disturbances from without. Again and again he was

examined on his faith. With stupid persistence the judges returned ever to the charge of heresy, and ever vindicated him. The curious position of Angelo and his friends brought on them the double accusation of interpreting the Rule of Francis against the papal decree and of being apostates to the Order. The inquisitors were ever baffled, never satisfied.

At last Angelo, in 1311, came to Avignon, very unwillingly. He hated the atmosphere of courts, perhaps even of towns. "Although I have always hated, with all my heart," he wrote later, "to be in the Curia more than any other pain I have ever suffered till now in the world—and there I was but a *poverello*, with none familiar, to all a stranger—nevertheless, God willing that our affairs should come to a clear issue, I made no haste to return to my companions." But their position never was made clear. During the years he spent at Avignon he lived in the household of Cardinal Colonna, yet in spite of protection his life was one battle against secret and public accusations, and to obtain permission for his brethren to lead their inoffensive lives in peace. The days were dark. Clement put down the Tuscan Spirituals with a high hand. John XXII. was their determined enemy. In the beginning of 1317 the sixty-four Spirituals of Narbonne and Beziers were brought to Avignon. Twenty-six were formally charged with heresy, and the Inquisition was given full power over them. Four were burnt to death in May 1317. Ubertino the fighter was called up for examination along with the heads of the Spirituals, Angelo Clareno and Raymond of Cernona. The exasperated Ubertino went over to the Benedictines. Angelo found himself confronted with exactly the same accusations he had met twenty-one years ago in the time of Celestine and Boniface. It was a weary thing to stand and say continually, "And we do not acknowledge that we are, or have been, apostates, or heretics, or excommunicate, unless it be heresy worthy of excommunication to believe, confess, and love and work . . . that which St. Francis believed concerning the observance of his Rule . . . what he taught living, and loved dying. . . . This heresy I have always held, and now confess I hold." Angelo was ordered to be detained after the examination, suffered again a short imprisonment, had many cautions given him, and was released without being satisfied that the matter was cleared up.

He had had his fill of the vexations of prison. In a letter written from Avignon he tells the tale of his more than thirty years of vexed and harassed life. " Only for confessing and loving the Rule I was imprisoned as a notorious heretic in the various prisons of Ancona, Forano, Rome, Viterbo, Assisi, and in all the places of the brothers from Rome to Ancona, for two or three days at a time. With my companions I was bound captive and brought again to prison in Ancona." In Holy Week he was led captive in Rome. Two years after, at the same holy time, he was captured once more, in Terra Nova with his companions, and vilely imprisoned. For several days they were under the custody of violent men, " bound one by one in separate houses as if we were dangerous. We came to Messina on the sixth hour of the sixth day in Holy Week, where after unseemly treatment, clamour, tumult, and threats, we were kept shut up with condemned criminals in a dark and fetid prison." Ejected from the island, they were thrown on the desert shore of Calabria—and on all that they endured after that, he says, it is better to keep silence.

His stay in Avignon ended in disappointment. True, he had his personal liberty, save for a short time. But in vain had he written his *Epistola excusatoria* to John XXII. He had not won his case. His patron, Jacopo Colonna, died in 1318. He was old. His brethren needed him. Perhaps he might be left in peace to guide them, and in this hope he went away, leaving many allies fighting in Avignon, but mainly on grounds which were not his. Their fight was to defy the Pope. Politics mingled with it, and it concerned itself with such matters as the length of the brothers' tunics and the precise meaning of the *povero uso*. Clareno cared nothing for these things. He was not puzzled as to how far he might use the goods of the world. And in sentiment he was loyal to the papacy.

Even from this time to his death he was practically in hiding, in hermitages and various religious houses, protected by Celestines and Augustinians and some of the more advanced Franciscans. But the frail old man was still fervent in spirit, with burning words of counsel to his younger brothers and sisters. His longest rest was at Subiaco, where the Abbot of the Sacro Speco sheltered him longer than was prudent. When it was unsafe to trust himself in the world, or when he was too ill to travel, he carried on his mission by correspondence. His letters to the brothers, addressed to " lovers of the poverty and humility of Christ, serving Him far from the world," and the explanatory one to John XXII., reveal better than the *Tribulations* his temper and his aims. Most of the letters written at the end of his life are to Augustinian hermits, principally to Simone da Cassia and Gentile da Foligno.

Leaving the Sacro Speco, in consideration for his friend the abbot, he wandered about the Basilicate and near Rome, and found his long rest at last in the Celestine hermitage of S. Maria de Aspro in the diocese of Marsico, June 15, 1337. Crowds came to see him when he lay dying. The prior, Thomas the Englishman, fittingly described the dead man as " pilgrim and stranger." Simon of Cassia wrote of him to John of Salerno, " Angel in name but more in nature, and he followed the life of the angels as much as men may on this earth."

He is not one of the shining or burning poets of the Order. There is no reflection in him of the charm of Francis, nor even of Conrad d'Offida, and none of the verve of Jacopone. He was driven by evil times to a goal not that of the Founder's. His road led to the desert, the

calm of the mountain-tops, away from the kindly ways
of men. But he had been driven there. His precepts
were not made for hermits. A wonderful consistency,
an unconsumed determination were in him. Only Leo is
his equal in these. But he was no tactless, insensitive,
narrow fanatic. There is a wistful patience, a shining
purity about his words. His feet found no rest, but his
spirit was the pole star of many anxious souls. Yet his
temper varies. Now he is a proud fighter, now a
quietist. Here he calls, " Resist, resist," and there,
" Leave all to Christ. Let evil men do what they may,
and see ye do well." He has waverings in policy, too, if
his simple modes of warfare can be called by such a name.
This heretic is consumed by a burning love for the
Roman Church. In his wanderings in Greece he is never
tempted to enter the Greek communion. He is tender of
the fame of the priests. " Honour the Lord Archbishop
and all the other clergy, and do not consider their sins."
Did he not appeal to the arrogant Boniface and the
tyrannical John? His warnings against schism are profound. " Let there be no division; the time appointed
by Divine power will come not by man but by the
workings of the holy spirit." They called him apostate,
"but Francis," he said, "is not in the name of an Order,
nor in walls, nor roof, nor in anything outward whatsoever, but in his obedient sons and his lovers." It is the
same voice that rises in proud counsel to his disciples to
make their stand when any one, be he king or pope, orders
what is contrary to their faith and confession, and against
charity and the fruit of charity. " They will coerce you
in the name of Francis to do as they do. But there is no
authority in the Rule against the Rule, as there is none in
the Church against the Church." And he flashes the terrors
of a higher excommunication against such as condemn
holy Poverty, the Bride of Christ. He wastes no time
whining over his own sufferings and those of his brethren.
Their part is to fight and to think not of their numbers,

BROTHERS BEHOLDING THE VISION OF ST. FRANCIS :
THE CHAPTER OF ARLES

GIOTTO. Assisi, S. Francesco.

To

however small they may appear, nor say as did Elijah, in the cave on Horeb, "I, even I only am left, and they seek my life to take it away." There are others who have fought and will fight. He has the true Franciscan sense of great possessions, owned by none, owned by each. The way to the treasure was the same for all—"to seek heavenly things, desire spiritual things, despise the things of time, reach out to those that are before and forget those that are behind." He has likewise the Franciscan sense of the abiding country. Customs change, much knowledge is often vain, but in every place upon the earth rise the walls of the kingdom of Heaven.

The story of the ever hustled, homeless Angelo is, as I have said, significant for other movements. Guilty of one heresy, he was persecuted by insincere foes, and tried by puzzled, baffled judges, for another. The saying that not the Church but the world is the persecutor is corroborated by such a history even more than by John of Parma's. The world knows instinctively and well how dangerous are men contemptuous of the good things of life. As mere visionaries they may be exploited. But visionaries are apt at unforeseen moments to turn terribly sharp eyes on the things about them; and when they do, with what can you bribe them to complacency? Angelo and his brothers never woke out of their celestial dream to plot against the secular power, or to plan a juster social contract. But the prudent world, lest revolutionary thinkers should arise among them, soiled their fame in advance. The *frati* were but its instrument. Heretic, schismatic, anarchist, they called him who yearned after peace, whose rallying cry was meant to reach through all the troubled Order, and to reconcile—*Totum igitur studium esse debet quod unum inseparabiliter simus per Franciscum in Christo.*—"And so let us have no other care but to be one inseparably in Christ through our father Francis."

z

JACOPONE DA TODI

" Quid enim sunt servi Dei nisi quidam joculatores ejus qui corda hominum erigere debent et movere ad lætitiam spiritualem ?"—SPEC. PERF. 100.

THE story of the first Franciscan century that omits Jacopone is, as it were, blind and dumb—something insincere too. He points the goal of the dim gropings, and gives voice to the vague yearnings. Many of his brothers never did more than whisper or stammer their desires, and so lead their admirers to, and leave them in, undefined places, uncommitted to anything very alien to their usual Sunday frame of mind. But though there were grave defects in Jacopone's style and expression, he could excellently utter the final meaning of the Franciscan Spirituals, and he did it with frank audacity. You may call him their summit, or, if you will, their *reductio ad absurdum.* There is no shilly-shallying in Jacopone. The big world of his day condemned his plan of life just as much as the world of six centuries later would do. What cared he? He spread his rough banquet, and invited all with confidence. There were more to savour it than we perhaps imagine; but it tasted not a whit less good that most men turned away to fatter tables. Poets are credited, often quite mistakenly, with a special interest in an immaterial world. In all the six hundred years that have gone by since Jacopone died, I can think of no other who has been so joyfully, triumphantly assured that the world of sense and all that in it is, cannot be compared with the world beyond it, yet not beyond a mortal's quick experience. It is a great claim to make for an obscure, neglected poet. I shall make all others in strict moderation.

A mad fellow, an "awful warning," a bringer into disrepute of spiritual aspirations—quite estimable when decorously controlled—these names and worse he has been called. Perfect sanity cannot be claimed for him. But the madman had long intervals of shrewdness, when he planned his folly. Every wise man who hungers after strength and light, learns how these best come to him. Jacopone had learnt that Lady Folly was the surest guide to where he wished to go ; so he praised her and sang to her, that she might the more willingly give him her strange wild company on the road to his goal. He sang of other things besides, but I am quite content to introduce him as the Laureate of Folly.

> " Senno me pare e cortesia
> Empazir per lo bel messia,"

he sings.

> "A wise and courteous choice he'd make
> Who'd be a fool for the dear Lord's sake. . . .
>
> The Paris doctors search to win
> In vain this high doctrine.
>
> Who is a scholar in this school
> Will learn great things by a new rule.
> Who's never learnt to be a fool
> Knows naught of all the best."

The life and the poetry of this high-hearted and convinced fool are closely intertwined. Who speaks of one must speak of both ; but my object is not literary criticism. His name was Jacopo dei Benedetti ; he was the eldest son of Benedettone dei Benedetti ; and his family were noble in the town of Todi, where he was born in, or about, 1228. Early in life he studied law at Bologna, where he got himself much secular learning and a knowledge of those ancient classics he held after-

wards in such light esteem. Let it be well grasped that
he spent full half his life in the world. His youth seems
to have been a wild and spendthrift one, if we are to
accept as literally true the black accusations he hurls
against himself in his autobiographic poem, *O vita penosa
e gran battaglia*. Gaming brought him into such straits
that he resorted to worse methods for obtaining money.
But once his wild days over, his secular affairs were
presumably conducted with seriousness; and he earned
repute and a substantial income as a *procuratore* in Todi—
a dangerous profession for the soul this, thinks one of his
old biographers: "la quale e de tanto periculo che chinon
a la conssienzia molto limata tira lomo nela damnatione
eterna." There he lived extravagantly and ostentatiously,
to judge from his laments, in the aforementioned poem,
on the vanity of all the fine meats and drinks wasted
on a body that the worms would feed on ere long.
This poem, by the way, represents the lowest ebb of
Jacopone's spirits. The lawyer seems to have been as
lusty as the later singer, one who might be trusted to
carry through a client's case with energy, perhaps with
a high hand. Much he gave up, but he kept to the end
the lawyer's gift of ready wit and quick perception of an
opponent's weakness. We must conceive of him as a
vigorous, full-blooded man, well able to speak and fend
for himself. The fool had an experience behind him
that taught him the cost of folly.

Was he a poet in those days? No one seems to
know, but to me the thing hardly needs proving. A
student of literature he was by his own scornful confession of what pleased him when he followed the light
of this world's wisdom. But apart from that, I think so
skilled and fervent a singer of love-songs to the Virgin
must have learnt his *métier* in praise of earthly ladies.
He was forty before he thought of giving himself up
to the pursuit of his high folly. We have not a scrap
of his verse dating before that time; yet in his later holy

romances you may read he was but a troubadour who had changed his lady. Surely he wrote songs to his Vanna while he wooed her. After she died, all he wrote and all his life were dedicate to her, unnamed, whose loss unhinged his reason and released his soul. Vanna was the daughter of Bernardino di Guidone of a noble Ghibelline family of Umbria, and probably much younger than Jacopo, who did not marry her till 1267, when he was thirty-nine. He had long been looking for the fitting woman, his ideal being exactly that of the conventional man of the world in search of a wife. She was, for his pleasure, to be beautiful and of good health, nor given to vanity. Her dowry was to be large, and her temper gentle and accommodating. She must not show herself haughty, and should have a light and amusing tongue. But he adds, " Compito desire non è sotto 'l cielo." Where the real woman fell short is not stated— perhaps only in the matter of the dowry. At any rate he was the ardent lover of his meek and beautiful wife, though he did not know much about her. When he sang to her eyes, she smiled ; and he did not know the thoughts and desires of her quiet nature. He was very proud to show her decked out, and she was his gentle, willing consort at Todi's feasts. Then one day at a great spectacle, all the ladies were gathered on a raised platform to watch. From below Jacopo looked at his Vanna, the fairest of them all. Suddenly the platform fell. When they extricated Vanna she was still breathing, alive enough to strive vainly to hide from her husband bending over her what was discovered when they loosed her dress to find her injuries, the hair shirt she had long worn next her soft skin, under her silken gala raiment. She had never thought it necessary to quench Jacopo's lust of life by a knowledge of her own pious austerities.

Her death closed the whole past volume of his life. There was no use for it any more. Life meant something else than he had ever dreamed. Vanna had had a secret from him, a great secret. The hair shirt had hinted its meaning. " Oime una fenmena ma engannato conssider- ando la vita vana che quella mostrava ennapparenzia defore." He would learn Vanna's secret ; and he went far beyond the journey of her gentle timorous spirit on the road to that learning. His manner of life now became an outrage to his highly respectable family. His work was all given up, and his wealth distributed among the poor. He went unkempt, uncared for. He took up with religious fanatics. In his hermit's frock he was as a wild beggar-man in the streets of Todi. He cried his sorrow and his penitence aloud, mocked at by the boys. The learned Bologna doctor, the pride and power of Todi, Ser Jacopo dei Benedetti, was now Jacopone. It is not difficult to pity his relatives. Not only was he a byword in the town, but he was an active nuisance to them. On a great festa he was seen among the people, naked save for a rough loincloth, ambling on all fours, saddled and bridled like an ass, and playing his part with such dramatic earnestness that the specta- tors did not laugh, but went away shuddering and de- pressed. There was a marriage in the family, and they were naturally nervous concerning Jacopone's conduct. His brother sent a grave relative to beg him to come, but to be on his good behaviour. " Tell my brother," was the answer, " that as he will strive to bring honour on our house by his wisdom, so will I by my folly." He surpassed himself in his bizarre appearance, entering the dance tarred and feathered from top to toe. Another day, one of the citizens, an old friend, seeing him hang about the streets, said, " Jacopone, here are two chickens I have bought. Will you take them home for me ? " There was no haughtiness left in Jacopone, and he said, " Yes, right willingly." But when the friend had left him, he took them straight to the church of San Fortunato, and put them in the citizen's family tomb ! It is said the citizen was much edified by the grim reminder Jacopone had given him. How much of this was sardonic jesting, and how much pure madness, it is impossible to determine nicely—and I do not mean to enter on another Hamlet controversy—but madness played the lesser part, of a surety. Consider the reasonings, the expostulations of his friends in his sorrow. "A sore blow has fallen on you, Jacopo. But time is a great healer—and work. You will find much consolation in your old work. Do not give way to despair. You have a great career before you." Their understanding and his were not meeting. So he forced them by his wild pranks to see that a new Jacopo had been born, on whom they could not count, to whom all the delights and interests of his old life had lost every force of appeal. He had found a new mirror of Truth, and looking into it saw his old prudence as mere foolishness. Besides, if he was not already a Tertiary, he was looking to the Rule of Francis to guide him into the new country, and holy Folly was one of the mistresses that the true sons of Francis were all eager to woo. She released them from the fear of men, and in the degradation of her service were their souls exalted. Jacopone was the warmest of all her lovers ; and so his townsmen, according to their tempers, found him a continual source of uneasy shame or of entertainment.

But already the penitent was finding audiences. He sought no hermitage or convent yet, save by moments. He was not good enough to be a Brother Minor. For ten years, during the greater part of which he probably belonged to the Third Order, he led a wandering homeless life, but a life that kept him a citizen of the world. Jacopone was not of the hermit breed. Later in prison his most piteous cry to Boniface was to give him back to his brothers. He had deep regrets that his original nature did not lead him to solitary contemplation—

" Son legato a vita attiva
E vorrei contemplativa :
Molto mal de qui deriva ;
Non so Marta nè Maria."

In the great air he recovered his former power of speech
and laughter. He loved men, and was at ease with them,
because he felt the great freedom of having nothing
to lose by them. And he was likewise their keen, cool
observer, their rough-tongued satirist. The news of the
market-place was his, of the convent, of the hamlet, and
the roadside ; and he had more than forty years of the life
of a man of the world behind him. He called up people
where he would, on the road or in the piazza ; and
it was never dull work listening to Jacopone. He lashed
the vices of the people ; but he seemed in truth to be
one of themselves. Indeed, if his noble origin were not
well authenticated, one would feel assured he sprang from
the common people. Their emotions, their needs, their
tongue, their accent were his. What great preacher in a
vast church had a chance with Jacopone, who heard the
songs of the fair, of the workers among the corn and
the vines, or by the winter fireside ; and echoed them
back lustier and more singable than ever, but tuned to
holy things ? Probably he as often sang to his audience
as preached. He was a great improvisatore. Imagine
him stopping in a village street, lifting up his voice
perhaps to the tune of a familiar love-song. "Ah,
Jacopone!" they would cry, and gather quickly. He
sang what came uppermost—a hymn to the Virgin, a
carol of the little Jesus, or a ballad of my Lady Poverty.
His rough dialogues were acted by him with fit voice
and gesture ; and these, from an Italian to Italians, were
doubtless the most telling of all. Jacopone's place is
a high one in the history of primitive Italian drama ;
but our concern is not with that here. Perhaps no one
wrote down his rhymes at the time ; and the wandering
man did not carry manuscripts about him. They passed

from mouth to mouth, and travelled up and down Italy. Very likely they were never all gathered ; and, on the other hand, he has got the credit of many that are not his, for he was not the only wandering singing *frate* of the time.

During these ten years of vagabond life he lived as hard as mortal man may, and was undoubtedly very happy. Tertiary or not, he had already begun to taste and know *la liberta francischina*. At night he lay where he could, sleeping or waking in a hermit's cell, or in a peasant's hut, or in a cave in the woods, or by the roadside in the snow. It was all in the adventure. On a crust of bread or green stuff from the fields he feasted royally, and took no credit for bearing hardships well. He denied the hardship. Search the world of singers over, and you will scarcely find a happier, in spite of his satiric and his penitential moods. Francis joined himself to Lady Poverty in high mysterious espousals. John of Parma and many another felt her releasing hand, and knew her sweetness to spirited lovers. But Jacopone frolicked with her. Of his many songs in her praise it is hard to know which to give, but the following is at least eminently characteristic. I make no apology for the roughness of my version. The original is even rougher—but its vigour oozes sadly away in modern tongue.

> " Hear, sweetest Poverty,
> All our love is due to thee.
>
> Little Poverty, tender thing,
> Humility's own sisterling,
> For eating and drinking and everything
> One bowl contenteth thee.
>
> At her table she eats of the best,
> Bread and water and herbs, with zest.
> If there comes from without a guest,
> A pinch of salt adds she.

Poverty's a hardy maid ;
With no care her mind is weighed.
No lurking thief makes her afraid,
For never a plack has she.

Poverty knocks at the door ;
Has no scrip nor purse nor store ;
Never will carry away any more
Than will bid her hunger flee.

Poverty has no bed,
Nor ever a roof over her head,
Nor with linen fine is her table spread :
Content on the ground sits she.

Quiet leave of life can take :
Never a will has she to make ;
Nor for her lands' and riches' sake
Need any quarrelling be.

Joy of my soul, thy mind is high
Above the world ; may'st quiet die,
With never a friend to plot and pry
To be the heir of thee.

Little Poverty, pitied of men,
But in heaven citizen.
The earth offers its treasures again :
Not one of them tempteth thee.

Poverty, how sad he goes
Who the lust of riches knows !
Hear him groan ; the man of woes
Can ne'er consoléd be. . . .

Poverty has no pay,
But free of hand gives all away ;
Makes no hoarding for to-day,
Nor for the days to be.

Light her footstep by the way,
Never frowning, ever gay ;
To stranger land she fares away,
Lacking all and free. . . .

Poverty thou name of power,
Great queen, the whole world is thy dower.
O'er all thou scornest from thy tower
Thou hold'st high signory.

Poverty thou wisdom deep,
Holding all possession cheap,
Thy will that thou fast bound dost keep
Springs up in liberty. . . .

Poverty, great wisdom's height,
Each day more clearly shows thy might;
And here below thou walkst in sight
Of the high life to be.

Gracious is the maid and fair,
Open-handed, debonnair;
Her livery is no base wear.
Let's follow Poverty! "

Let one thing be borne in mind: it is never the mere
bareness of Poverty he would sing, but of her riches. It
is to Lady Poverty he cries in another song—

" God does not lodge in narrow heart;
Love claims the whole and spurns the part.
Greathearted one, where'er thou art,
Thou shelterest Deity! "

If true-born, high-spirited Bohemians want a laureate,
Jacopone is their man—in certain moods. And here is
a song of their calling for them to troll out. Their
swinging steps on the open road will compel a rhythm
into it :—

" France and England are my dower,
Between the seas I wield great power;
Yet no cruel wars me devour,
Nor nations envy me.

Mine is all the Saxon land;
Mine is all the Gascon land;
Burgundy I hold in my hand,
And all of Normandy. . . .

Tuscany's within my pale,
And the fair Spoletan vale.
In the Marches I prevail,
Likewise in Slavonie.

Lord in Sicily I roam ;
In Calabria I have my home ;
Lord in th' Campagna, Lord of Rome
And the plain of Lombardy. . . .

My vassals wait upon my will ;
All my vast lands for me they till.
My crops and fruits their garners fill—
So great my courtesy.

Corn that grows on fields of mine,
Crops and fruits so rich and fine,
My yokéd oxen and my kine,
What are they all to me ?

River and lake and sea and spring,
Fish in the water clear swimming,
Hurrying winds and birds on the wing,
I have in my treasury.

Sun, moon, sky, and stars of night
Are mine, all mine, dear delight.
Hearken there up in the height
My singers sing for me.

Now since it's pleased the King of kings
To make me lord o'er many things,
To heaven I mount on lusty wings,
My path is straight and free. . . ."

That is the kind of song Jacopone walked the roads to,
and singable yet, have we but the right gait.

It is impossible correctly to apportion his lauds to
their various periods. An ancient biography has this
pretension ; but the writer, not a contemporary, was
probably only guessing. He was ever a wanderer—save
when he was in prison ; ever a fervent devotee of
Madonna Poverty ; ever liable to hours of ecstatic emotion,

and to moods of satiric observation. If the *Detti sentiosi* in the Venice edition of his works (ii. 33) be his, I should say they belonged to these years of special freedom, when he was the peasant's missionary, who took their own modes of speech and rough wisdom out of their mouths, and gave it them back with edification. Some of the *detti* are excellent common sense—

> "Vediamo bella imagine
> Fatta con vili deta."

Fine pictures are sometimes made with dirty fingers—

> "Non ti sforzar d'apprendere
> Piu che non puoi con braccia :
> Che nulla porta a casa
> Chi la montagna abraccia."

"Don't strain yourself to seize more than you can carry. For who takes the mountain in his arms carries nothing home with him." (An inelegant but expressive saying of American origin sums this up more aptly.)

> "Il muro tu non rompere
> Se aperte son le porte"—

a counsel not to break down the walls if the doors are still open.

> "Non sicurar la nave
> Fin che non giunta in porto.
> Santo non adorare
> Innanti che sia morto."—

Wherein he advises us not to make sure of our ship till it has reached port, and not to adore a saint till he is dead. They are too common-sensible, I fear, to be Jacopone's— he was always embracing the mountain—though I can imagine him cooling the morbid fervour of some band of intransigeant *frati* with a discourse from such texts. The peasants and townsfolk could produce that kind of thing for themselves. To understand how he worked on them we must read the *Lamento della Vergine*, a wonderfully dramatic dialogue in verse, between the *Nuncio, Vergine Turba* and *Christo*, where the whole scene of the Passion is gone through. Who would not have wept to stand and hear Mary's heartrending outburst of grief? It was Jacopone wrote the *Stabat Mater*—later, in a cell, probably—but that great Latin hymn, with its full dignity of rhythm, though it has been sung by the Church for six hundred years, and has inspired fine music, cannot have produced such intimate reality of sorrow as did his laments in the vulgar made for listening peasants. His vogue was immense among them. What to them if he were a fool? They could be the more at their ease with him—and to this day in country places in Italy they treat very tenderly those of wandering intellect. But perhaps they shrewdly guessed he was no fool. It was not with poor simple folk he needed to hoist ostentatiously the banner of sacred Folly. That was for sophisticated men of the world, and for *frati* demoralised by the subtleties of the schools. There is no evidence that he led or encouraged any political movement among the people. Oppressed in turn by feudal lords and the tyranny of the cities, they had no articulate desires or ambitions at all. They needed one who lived with them, felt with them, and had a voice. The fine troubadours were of no use. Nor were the learned churchmen's works and homilies. Jacopone was all their own. He stirred their hearts and imaginations—may be said to have proved their own existence to themselves; and in the dawning consciousness of the people in Central Italy he counts for much. He was no parish poet, but to be found here one day, there the next; he had no ties, no calls, save of the spirit. Strange it seems to us that, a popular poet, he yet never sang woefully of their trials of hunger and fatigue and neglect. He sang to them instead of the sorrows of Christ, sang to mothers of the sorrow of Mary over the pain and anguish of her Son. He was singing to a happy-natured people. And then, for the toil and

trouble of everyday men, he bore it with them—it was
all in the bargain—and the world, if only people were
not so desperately wicked and ungrateful, was a delightful place. There is a constant recurrence of *maggiolate* in
his work. He loved the open air, and watched the
seasons ; but it is mostly the spring-time, a rich southern
spring, that he flashes on us in his song. Not amongst
the most exquisite poets of nature, nor amongst the
most definite, yet he can tell excellently of the joyous
incitement that comes from sun and sky and flowing
water and the flower-lined roads.

> " Quanto è nel mondo m'invita ad amare,
> Bestie e uccelli e pesci dentro il mare ;
> Cio ch'è sotto all' abisso e sopra all' are,
> Tutti fan' versi davanti al mio Amore. . . .
>
> Voglio invitar tutto 'l mondo ad amare,
> Le valli e i monti e le genti a cantare,
> L'abisso e i cieli e tutt' acque del mare,
> Che faccian' versi davanti al mio Amore."

This was a very fine life. It had a zest for the vagabond minstrel of fifty that the comfortable can hardly
dream of. Yet, when he had wandered for ten un-
trammelled years, he sought, in 1278, the cloister. He
was not tired of the road—indeed, he returned to it
over and over again—but, like Giles, he feared for his
soul undisciplined by obedience. It was not enough to
make himself despised of the world : he must know the
yoke of daily duty. But when he proposed to enter the
First Order, the *frati* demurred at receiving the mad
vagabond, fearing by some freak he might bring discredit
on them. He seems to have taken their doubt in good
part, and as a test of his sanity wrote a laud, *Or odete
nova pazia*, which they accepted as proof enough. Among
the *frati* he was of the most austere. Did his body cry
out for a little indulgence, he found ingenious and
sometimes what we should call disgusting means of

punishing it. He never would be other than a lay brother, doing all menial services willingly. But though humble and obedient, he was far from meek. From first to last he was ever an outspoken man, as ready to speak his mind to a feeble or faulty superior as he was to drudge for the youngest brother in the place. In his wanderings from convent to convent he looked at his brethren with frankly open eyes; swelled with hot indignation, and broke into biting sarcasms, or into sore laments over their falling away from the perfection of the early time; and he scourged the evils in verses that reached every convent of the Order, and were quite as effectual as any decrees of any Chapter General.

> " Impregnable were they in their prime,
> High forts built on a proud rock.
> But floods have mounted with the passing time,
> And wasting waters mock
> Walls that may not endure the shock.
> Feebly the ruins float, unbuoyed, since they
> Have all forgotten how to pray."

He was quite as indignant over their growing desire for vain philosophy as over their indulgence in soft living.

> " The *frati* flock to Paris schools,
> And all Assisi's ardour cools. . . .
>
> With learning stuff who'd muddle his head,
> He must off and be Paris bred.
> And the rest who stay behind
> Good fat meats in the larder find."

(Here I have, for lack of wit, left an effective pun untranslated.)

> " The convent reader's pale ; therefore
> We feed him like an emperor.
> The cook is sick ; but how he fares,
> Nobody asks, and nobody cares.

The Chapter meets so solemn wise,
Brand new rules for to devise ;
And he that is the quickest to make 'em
Is for sure the first to break 'em."

There is more of the kind, including some biting illustrations of Christians' love for each other, and concerning
the pleasure the *frati* found in the conversation of fair
ladies ; and it ends by making mock of that favourite
butt of the satirists of the Order, the low-born brother
who found his membership an excellent means of worldly
advantage.   Maybe it's not very subtle wit ; but it
served its turn, and while the *frati* laughed at Jacopone's
gibes, many felt the pricking point of them in their own
consciences.

His observation of the ambitious friars made another
occasion for singing the praise of Folly :—

" Science is a thing divine,
    Where good gold we may refine,
    But sorely doth God's truth pine
    Neath all our sophistry.

Now, my brothers, hear my plan—
    To be thought as mad as ever I can,
    An ignorant and a clownish man,
    And full of bizarrerie.

And so away with syllogisms,
    Your reasoning chains and your sophisms,
    Your tiring puzzles and aphorisms
    And all your subtlety.

Plato and Socrates may contend,
    And all the breath in their bodies spend,
    Arguing without an end—
    What's it all to me ? . . .

Only a pure and simple mind
    Straight to heaven its way doth find ;
    Greets the King—while, far behind,
    Lags the world's philosophy.

2 A

Let's of the ancients make an end
(Among them I had many a friend);
E'en Cicero I'll not defend—
Though he once made music for me. . . .

Away with canzons and rondels,
Dainty ladies and damosels,
Their fatal glances and their spells,
And all their trickery.

And so now say whatever you please,
The wise man still will hold his peace.
Your power, false world, 's at the end of its lease.
Now—only God for me! . . .

Lord of my heart, give me to know
Thy will, and how to do it, show.
That done, what care I whether or no
Damn'd or sav'd I be."

Yet for all that Jacopone probably went back to
his books, though not to his old Bologna learning.
His verse seems to be fed by more than popular
poetry and the legends and literature of his Order.
His German editors think they have found traces in
him of the mystical writings of Augustine, Dionysius
the Areopagite, Saint Bernard, and of Richard Saint
Victor. Such wide studies are not at all improbable ; but
he was himself of the true mystical breed, not merely
one who set other men's soarings to his verse. His
ecstatic poems cannot be set down to any special period,
though towards the end of his life these moods increased.
Over the terrible sufferings of Boniface's prison he
triumphed by forcing quick escapes from the body.
Yet even had he had no such escapes in middle life,
his mind was then not all engaged in singing of
austerity or in satirising his Order.

In the world Jacopone had been a lover. Only in
the tenderest heart could have been born his songs to
the Christ-child—*Dio fatto piccino*. The holy childhood
had been a special Franciscan theme ever since Francis

had inaugurated the *presepio* at Greccio. The rough poet melted at the thought of "God made a little thing"; and he depicted the Bethlehem scenes that haunted his fancy with the warmest human love. It is never as a past event he conceives the Nativity. It is a present joy, and he is the inciter of the people to come now, now, without delay, to greet the little wonder in the stable. I could fill many pages with examples of these carollings, rough in form but going very straight to the heart.

> " The little angels join their hands
> And dance in holy ring.
> Love songs they're whispering,
> The little angel bands.
>
> Good men and bad they call and greet :—
> High Glory doffs its crown,
> And has come down,
> Low lies there at your feet.
>
> Now, shamefaced boors, why keep
> Ye back ? Show courtesie.
> Hasten and ye will see
> The little Jesus sleep.
>
> The earth and all the skiey space
> Break into flowery smiles.
> So draws and so beguiles
> The sweetness of His face. . . ."

In gratitude he cries in another :—

> " Sure, ne'er hath been
> Such court'sy seen
> 'Mong mortal men. To-day
> The Omnipotent
> His only Son hath sent,
> Our ransom for to pay.
> Now since He's here,
> Show your heart's cheer
> And high content.
> Feasting is meet
> The little King to greet
> That's come with us to stay.

Give now your thought and care.
Prepare, prepare ;
Make ready for your guest.
With finest bread
His table must be spread,
And all your best.
Sweep hearth and floor ;
Be all your vessels' store
Shining and clean.
Then bring the little guest
And give Him of your best
Of meat and drink.   Yet more
Ye owe than meat.
One gift at your King's feet
Lay now.   I mean
A heart full to the brim
Of love, and all for Him,
And from all envy clean."

This is one of his favourite themes, and the loving humanity with which he touched it did not all escape when he wrote of it in Latin, in his *Stabat Mater Speciosa* :—

" Nato Christo in presepe
Coeli cives canunt laete
    Cum immenso gaudio ;
Stabat senex cum puella
Non cum verbo nec loquela
    Stupescentes cordibus. . . .

Fac me vere congaudere,
Jesulino cohaerere
    Donec ego vivero.
In me sistat ardor tui ;
Puerino fac me frui
    Dum sum in exilio. . . ."

Perhaps his deepest human note is the sorrow of Mary for her suffering Son.   All the world knows his *Stabat Mater Dolorosa*, and how in its sonorous Latin he utters his pity for the Mother of God enduring her human pains :—

" O quam tristis et afflicta,
Fuit illa benedicta
　　Mater Unigeniti !
Quae moerebat et dolebat,
Pia mater, dum videbat
　　Nati poenas inclyti.

.　　.　　.　　.　　.　　.　　.

Eia mater, fons amoris,
Me sentire vim doloris
　　Fac, ut tecum lugeam.
Fac ut ardeat cor meum,
In amando Christum Deum
　　Ut illi complaceam."

Here he is far from rough popular models; his Latinity, considering the time and the low standard of hymn-writers, is polished and dignified. But in the vulgar he makes the laments of Mary come home with greater intenseness to our hearts. She is a very human mother, full of caressing ways and dear extravagance of speech. The great God is her child still as when He lay on her bosom. As He hangs on the Cross she pleads with Him to speak to her, calls Him by all lovely, fondling names, rails on the cruel world, and fain would mount to die by His side.

" O figlio caro figlio,
Figlio amoroso giglio,
Figlio chi da consiglio
　　Al cor mio angustiato ?

Figlio occhi giocondi,
Perche non mi rispondi ?
Figlio perche t'ascondi
　　Dal petto v' se' lattato ?

.　　.　　.　　.　　.　　.　　.

Figlio bianco e biondo,
Figlio volto giocondo,
Dhe per qual causa il mondo
　　T'ha si anciso e sprezato.

.　　.　　.　　.　　.　　.　　.

O Joanne figlio novello
Morto è il tuo fratello ;
Sentito haggio 'l coltello,
    Che mi fu profetato.

Percosso ha figlio e matre,
E in un colpo atterrate.
Troveransi abbracciate
    Matre e Figlio annegato."

Jacopone's friend, Pier Jean d'Olivi, was excommunicated for the fervour of his book on the Virgin. Jacopone shared his heresy. To northern ears at least the warmth of a few of his songs is astounding, even offensive. Yet at times he neither offends nor surprises, but is only the most tender, most courteous, most chivalric of her knights. She and the Bambino lent grace even to the rugged, fiery rhymer, as they had brought beauty into his bare life.

" Mary, maiden of pity,
    All pity is thine.   Have pity on me.

Gracious and fair in our sight,
Mother and maid—our light,
Full moon new risen in our night,
Sweet Lady, hearken to me.

O lily of fragrant breath,
Thy sweetness whispereth
Our law ; Christ beckoneth
Us, for His love of thee.

Thou dost not turn away
Thy face, our hope, our stay,
Our fountain at midday,
Our fruitful olive tree.

Mother and bride of the King,
Men not disdaining,
In heaven is holy dancing,
We will tread a measure with thee. . . .

O Mary, path to the skies,
Gateway of Paradise,
Let love be strong as our cries
That we may come unto thee.

Up thy high stair we wind.
Grant now that heaven we find.
Lady gentle and kind,
Call us now unto thee."

He sings to many Marys—to his spouse, his partner in the dance divine, his celestial guide, and to his serviceable aid in everyday needs, as here :—

" Go, ballad, out from me,
And humbly greet
Her, rose of all roses sweet,
Queen and mother and maid.
Our Lady everywhere is she.
Hail her with duty meet.
So, all men may entreat
Her potent royal aid.
Lost on the sea, or in the dark road strayed,
Long be the way or short,
She the safe guide, and she the friendly port.
Mary, now pray we for thy comfort
    In our so anxious day."

But he cannot long think of her apart from her Child. He is all afire as he wonders over the human portion of her—

" Fine rose in flower,
Thy womb was sheltering bower
For the Pilgrim Divine.

Wert beyond bearing blest,
When He chose thee for His nest,
And fed upon thy breast,
Thy Son Divine ?

Didst thou near pass away
As near thy heart He lay,
Taking thy kisses ? Say,
O heart so fond and fine ! "

There is little evidence of doubt of any kind in
Jacopone. He loved not by fits and starts, but with
an ever-increasing fervour. He accepted his rôle so
lustily, knew his own mind so clearly on the events of
his time and the fortunes of his Order, was so reticent
respecting any inward struggles for self-mastery or for
belief, that the poem entitled " Diversity of Contemplation " is almost unique. It might be a dialogue between
two *frati*, one of the courageous breed, the other relaxed.
It is more likely to be a contest between two overpowering moods of one soul, and that soul Jacopone's.
Is it likely indeed that a man, who had lived so full a
life in the world, should have won in the battle with his
old self at once, or ever won with absolute decision ?

" Far let me flee from the Cross that devours me ;
Relentless and cruel, its heat overpowers me.
The fire of its breath I may not abide.
Out of its scorching range who will me guide ?
Nay, hurrying heart, but where shalt thou hide ?
The memory burns in thee still.

Nay, frate, flee not delight so dear.
Frate, thou fleest, I fain would come near.
For the high grace of the world's cheer
Methinketh thou payest ill.

Frate, I flee, for my hurt is sore,
My wounded soul may endure no more.
Ne'er hast thou borne what long I bore,
And thy words are void unto me.

Nay, see, the Cross with flowers is ablow ;
Decked with its silken pansies I go.
Naught of its wounding, its burning, I know ;
It useth me tenderly.

Nay, 'tis a quiver of arrows of flame.
From ev'ry side piercing my heart they came.
The bowman marked me as his aim :
No armour covered me."

And so goes on the contest. The one declares his darkened eyes have seen the day since he looked on the Cross; the other that he has been blinded by its wondrous eyes. To one it has given the gift of tongues; the other it has stricken dumb.

He had been *frate minore* fourteen years when the long papal interlude took place. Jacopone was already closely leagued with the struggling Spirituals of the Order, with Fra Liberato, Angelo Clareno, Conrad d'Offida, Pietro da Macerata, and the other protesters of the Marches. That he had not been forced over seas with Clareno's band, was perhaps due to the licence that had to be given to a man of his bizarre temper, with his poet's articulateness, if he were to remain friar minor at all. During his wandering years he may have been a frequent visitor to Rome. At least he was there in 1288, at which time he may have made the acquaintance of the Colonnas. The long delays of the conclave at Rome and Perugia he watched with keen interest, probably with much irony. The kind of pope elected mattered a great deal to a man of his way of thinking; but then was there any likelihood of the fit man being chosen? When the choice of the conclave fell suddenly on the hermit Peter, Jacopone's allies were inclined to hope for a near millennium. They all knew the ascetic saint of Morrone. But the wild vagrant minstrel was more a man of the world than his friends; and he knew not only the hermit, but he knew Rome, its intrigues, its corruption, all the fatal barriers in the Curia between a right intentioned man and the desire of his soul. I do not think there is any proof he distrusted him. He was of the little band that sent ambassadors to Aquila to demand from Celestine leave to keep the Rule of Francis according to the intention of the Founder; and, for a time at least, he seems to have been counted among the Poor Hermits of Pope Celestine. But to his shrewd mind, practical for all its mysticism, it was not enough to have a holy hermit Head of the Church. He wanted to know how he would rule it. And Jacopone had ever a mordant tongue. Hence the warning verses I have already given, *Che farai Pietro Morrone*, which the poor prisoner pope doubtless thought a very harsh greeting from an old friend.

He might give him warnings, and utter his doubts ; but, like Dante, he evidently meant Celestine to stick on —though, being nearer the scene, he may not, like Dante, have blamed him afterwards for his forced abjuration. But of Boniface's fraud and villainy he had no doubt at all ; and of the growing indignation he was one of the most articulate spokesmen. Naturally enough he rallied to the revolting Colonnesi, who defied Boniface in their fortress of Palestrina. Jacopone was hard by in a house of the Celestines, and probably in daily communication with the rebels. For all his friar's frock, they found him full of the spirit of fight, a most effective defender of their cause, and a vigorous lampooner of Boniface. The history of the revolt is well known. Palestrina was razed to the ground. The Colonnas were deprived of the purple ; and the satirist, Jacopone, was excommunicated and thrown into a dungeon. Whether or not he held, with many others, that Boniface was not really pope, since Celestine might not lawfully resign, the dark terrors of excommunication seized on him with terrible force. He evidently did not question the power of the pope *de facto* to endanger his eternal safety as well as deprive him of Christian privileges. For once the sturdy Jacopone flinched, and appealed in a mild and ingenuous rhymed letter to Boniface. If only he may have absolution—he cares for nothing besides. It is a winning letter, not servile, though prudent, and it ends :—

> " And now, adieu, adieu.
> God keep all ill from you.
> But say the words of grace
> Will light with joy my face.
> My treatise end I here
> In this place most drear."

Boniface took no notice of it, and Jacopone sent him
another, this time heartrending in its appeal.   The shepherd for his sin has put him out of the fold.   He does
not defend himself.   If imprisonment be not enough,
then punish him more.   Only absolve him.   He has
called and called in vain.   Give him some hope.   He is
the centurion's paralytic servant, not worthy that his lord
should come to his house.   But will his lord send the
word that his sin is forgiven ?—

> " Hard by the pool too long I lie,
>   At Solomon's porch all the long day.
>   The saving waters move, and I
>   Look on—my helper still doth stay—
>   And see the favouring season pass away.
>   And yet I wait to hear it said,
>   ' Rise now, sick man, take up thy bed.
>   Fare thee back whole.' "

Like a leper is he banished from the way of healthy
men, and from the table of the Church.   He is lying
dead like Jairus's daughter.   Will not his father reach
out his hand and give him back to Saint Francis, who
will set him down once more at the board with his
brothers ?   At the very gate of Hell he has been.   His
Religion is making bitter wail for his fate ; yet his
brothers still hope to hear the high voice say, " Old
man, arise."   Then he ends with an appeal that his intercessor, Fra Gentile, may prevail.   The year 1300 was
the great year of jubilee, when prisoners were pardoned,
sins forgiven, and when Rome rejoiced.   The second
letter had been written in expectation of his benefiting
by a general release.   But Boniface took no notice of it,
nor sent any hope to the wretched man in the Palestrina
dungeon.   Jacopone never wrote in the same humble
tone again.   Perhaps before he wrote his third letter he
had had the famous interview with Boniface, when they
spoke to each other through the grating of the prison.
The pope walking above mocked his victim below,

saying, " Jacopone, when are you coming out ?" " The day you go in," was the prophetic reply. Perhaps already the pope knew the *frate's* words of him, wrongfully put into Celestine's mouth, that he had entered the fold as a fox, would reign there like a lion, and go out like a dog.

The fear of excommunication had left Jacopone, and he had no other fear. His spiritual joy in the dungeon when bereft of the sacraments had taught him at last his soul was not in Boniface's hands. Besides, he had returned to his earlier haughty indifference on the matter of salvation. The third letter is, indeed, a bitter attack, a fierce indictment, not only of the pope's treatment of himself, but of his whole conduct in the Church. He thought by craft to master the world ; but the world is no horse to be caught by guile and then bridled and spurred. The whole career of Boniface is cursed. A darkness came over the land when his first mass was sung. Each word of his is harmful. Oh, butcher's tongue, he says, that spitteth evil !

Of Jacopone's prison days we have in another poem a curious and terrible account, one of the few records of his own history that he has written, and one of the most haunting bits of autobiography extant. In his rough ballad form he tells the tale, now with dry sarcasm, now with touches of fierce realism, and again with outbursts of magnificent pride. Captured in Palestrina, he is thrown into the dungeon. His capuchon stripped from him, he is chained like a lion in an underground hole, amid nameless horrors. The place doesn't smell like musk. No man may speak to him save him who brings his meat. Every word he says is carried by his jailer to the authorities. He wears jesses like a falcon, and they ring as he moves. If you stand near his prison you can hear the sound of a fine new dance. At night he lies down and is entangled in his chains. A little basket is hung from the wall above the reach of the mice. It holds his bits of bread and an onion for a savoury — a most noble beggar's wallet. While his teeth grate on the hard crust he stamps up and down his shivering cell.

Then what the gain to any one from his captivity? He has within him what makes it useless as a penalty. And his great pride bursts out, triumphantly based— or so he thinks—on tried humility.

> " For the pain cannot prevail
> While my champion fights for me.
>
> See my champion stand and wait ;
> He wears my scorn for breastplate,
> Invulnerable mid the blows of fate,
> My scorn his safety.
>
> O wondrous scorn of mine !
> Lordship of every woe is thine.
> For thee nor pain nor pine—
> Shame but exalteth thee.''

He has had a long apprenticeship to this kind of shame. What is it but a *vento di vessica di garzone?* They can bring up no forces that may defeat him. Shame and fame —he gives them both into the keeping of a braying ass ! In prison, more than half frozen and starved, crying to deaf ears, living in the odour of a cesspool, he had his most triumphant visions of beauty and gracious sweetness. This is a wondrous fact, rather than a wonder to stare at. Visions do not come generally in comfortable armchairs, nor, I think, are they invariably associated with the odour of roses. But it is a fact consoling and exciting, one to make some hearts wild for Jacopone's scorn of self and circumstances—*o mirabil mio odio*—that had such rewards.

In 1303 came the seizure of Boniface by the Colonnesi and the violence of Anagni. At the death of his jailer, Jacopone, an old man of seventy-eight, was released. The long waited for words, *Vecchio, surge!* were said at last. After this time in prison the world had little hold on him. The visionary moods that had ever been wont to come on him so increased, that "at times, going outside the commerce of the people and the *frati*, he ran in a fury of love, and imagining to himself that he was embracing Christ and straining Him to his heart, he embraced a tree, crying aloud, calling Him by diverse names—Sweet Jesus, my Jesus !—like a lover."

In some of the visions he recorded we have little hope to follow him. He mounts to a rarefied air where we cannot breath—

> ". . . contemplando
> Bellezza senza colore."

He mounts to a region where there is no form, but only light—where he is not, where no one is, where nothing is save God, yet where all are, for all are in God ; strives to utter his idea of the sublime Nothingness, where all humanity is absorbed in the radiance of Deity. No Eastern seer has gone beyond Jacopone in his negation of human desire and sentience. There are infinite gradations in his Heaven, from the fair field where angels sport and dance in celestial glee, to the space about the Throne, whose light man may not face till he has cast himself into its sea, and there drowned, absorbed, has known the great reconciliation. Hĕ was not always the ballad-monger Jacopone, singing the people's own fairy tales of Christ and the angels to the people's own tunes.

It is not only to-day that heads have been shaken over his mysticism, his yearnings after Nirvâna. We read in the *Antica Vita*, published by Tobler, that the *frati* complained of him, saying, "Era uno fantastico e tuto quello che aviva dito erano fantassie fondate en paglia et che figiurava la divinitade quando per un modo e quando per un altro et quassi volendo dire che lui avese fantasteca hopinione e erase en qualche cosa." For answer to this accusation he is said to have written the laud, *Sopr' ogni lingua amore*. I can hardly imagine a less popular refutation than this strange poem, this sublime attempt to express the sinking of the soul into the sea of universal being, the annihilation of self in the contemplation of the Divine Light :—

"Love beyond telling, Good unimagined, Light without measure, shine now in my heart.

> Vast, ineffable Light !
> Great Sun—and undiscoverèd
> Save by the lone souls darkly led
> Through night's obscurity.

> Mock'd by a rush his sight,
> Who, ' Lo 'tis here ' doth certain call,
> And claims to measure all
> Its height and mystery.

> This know I only, night
> Is day resplendent ; but no strength
> Have I to prove its breadth and length,
> Its shining verity. . . .

> In midst of this great vast
> Abyss, thou findest never more
> Or landing-place or shore,
> Or any path or clue."

> Self has forgot its past.
> Thou art—but say, what meaneth ' thou ' ?—
> Reborn and all transforméd now,
> And clad in raiment new."

Again and again did Jacopone try to utter the unutterable, to tell the *magnalia* of his visions, which are less pictorial than those generally reported of the *frati*, or than might be expected from an Italian of his time, and seem directly inspired by Eastern dreamers. D'Ancona and others of his critics regard these efforts to sing of the *alta nichilitade* as mere fruitless experiments, and hold that they have not even the stuff of poetry in them. "Crediamo fermamente che le dottrine del misticismo ed i suoi andamenti non sieno avviamento buono a poetare, perchè la poesia vuole il concreto, e le immagini della fantasia tramuta in forme reali, nè perciò paion fatte per lei sifatte vaporose sottigliezze." There are debatable assertions here; but, nevertheless, we must admit that Jacopone was defying the Latin genius. Northern critics may be permitted to plead his cause—though none will venture to follow or interpret each step of his wanderings in the abyss or in the empyrean. He dared greatly, and with obstinate frequency, in themes which even Dante falteringly approached. Success in such an attempt is impossible, if success be held to mean a clear demonstration of what lies beyond the world of sense. But Jacopone's rhapsodies about drinking of the wine of self-forgetfulness, of dreaming outside himself, drowning in the great sea of light, of absorption in universal being, are not all presumptuous failures. They even do more than darkly suggest the "greater things" of Giles—who sees not which "believes everything poor and small." And the something more is what Western readers find hard to forgive, that is, his representation of the unending end of Man as quiescence in Deity, where the individual is all lost. The Western dreamer of celestial things would fain be himself as he stands about the Throne, and note all his new circumstances with the keenness of a sightseeer. If he be, indeed, resigned to absorption in the Whole, he would first like to know exactly what is the function of the little atom he contributes. And Jacopone wakes no echo in such with his—

> " O rapture then to find
> The Nothing vast and deep—
> Appeas'd the craving mind,
> The crying heart asleep ! "

They suspect it to be the aspiration of a sluggish nature. But that, at least, they may not hold with reason.

Jacopone was all fire. He dared all love, all pain, all joy, beyond human daring. Rather might it be said, the *alta nichilitade* is but the swoon that releases from unbearable excess of sentient life — though that, too, is far short of what he meant.

Yet there is ever a return to the more homely air of human love. Love was the answer to every human problem. Others have said so, sentimentally, wistfully, despairingly. You cannot read Jacopone without feeling that he said so from a conviction twined about the very roots of his being. He would fain have suffered for the demons in hell, and have seen them go before him into Paradise. Asked once why he wept so sore, he said, "I weep because love is not loved." Each song of his later days is an experience of his own consuming commerce with love. It was such an experience he put into the untranslatable—

> "In fuoco l'amor mi mise,"

which, with some other of Jacopone's mystical songs, has generally been attributed to Saint Francis.

> "In fuoco l'amor mi mise ;
> In fuoco l'amor mi mise ;
> In fuoco d'amor mi mise
> Il mio sposo novello,
> Quando l'agnel mi mise :
> L'agnello amorosello,
> Poichè in prigion mi mise
> Ferimmi d'un coltello,
> Tutto il cor mi devise.
> In fuoco, &c."

The fire of love wore him out at last. Up at Collazone, in 1306, he was very ill. On Christmas Eve the *frati* were going to give him the sacraments, but he said, "Not yet." "Nay, Jacopone, but you may die. Would you die unblessed?" He shouted aloud his belief in a new laud. Belief is not everything, they told him. The sacraments are a necessary grace.

2 B

"I will wait," he said. "Peradventure my friend, brother John of Alverna, will come. From his hand would I fain take this grace." "John will not come," they answered anxiously. Yet Jacopone waited in patience, passing the time and stifling his weakness with canticles. Hardly had he made an end when the watchers saw two moving figures in the plain, and soon after two brothers arrived without warning at the convent. One of them was John. The joy of meeting was surpassing great. John gave him the sacraments. The dying man sang once more a song of love and triumph, and his spirit passed. "It was believed by those standing near that he died, not so much conquered by his malady, though that was grave, as from an extraordinary excess of love."

And so farewell, Fra Jacopone—good fighter, most excellent lover, mad vagabond, and one of the wise men of the earth. Other sons of Francis were gentler, none more companionable, despite thy journeying away from us in visions. Too keen a fighter and protester to be all poet: too much poet to be all saint; but, his best minstrel, thou hast a seat of honour at Francis's Table Round.

·

ST. FRANCIS WITH OTHER SAINTS

FRA ANGELICO. Florence, S. Marco.

To face p. 3

DANTE AND THE FRANCISCANS

" Io aveva una corda intorno cinta,
E con essa pensai alcuna volta
Prender la lonza alla pelle dipinta."
—INFERNO, xvi. 106–108.

THE story that Dante girt himself with the cord of Francis—as a Tertiary, according to the tradition of the Order, as a regular, though he did not complete his novitiate, according to Buti, who wrote about fifty years after the poet's death—has had less doubt thrown upon it than many legends of his life better authenticated so far as external evidence goes. Some of the commentators have even put a date to his experience in the cloister, placing it between the death of Beatrice and his marriage or the episode of the *gentil donna*. That place where he sat apart, remembering his lost beloved (*V.N.* xxxv.), and drew the likeness of an angel upon certain tablets, was, one of them says, the Minorite convent; while the men who looked on, while he sat unconscious of their presence, and to whom it " behoved him to do honour," were the *frati*. This is interestingly imaginative, but not very convincing. He refers in the *Convito* (ii. 13) to youthful studies *nelle scuole de' religiosi ;* but the schools were not necessarily those of the Minorites. Scartazzini suggests that his entering the Order would explain more if it could be looked on as an episode of his later years, and his suggestion is interesting inasmuch as it points to a close connection between Franciscanism and the climax of Dante's work. The able commentator appeals for a more thorough investigation of all the documentary evidence on the question. "Up till now," he says, "the matter has been too lightly passed over, as though it were a side issue of quite subordinate importance; there has been no suspicion that a final solution of the problem would be of decisive importance in explaining the leading passages of the poem." But I doubt if the examination of such documentary evidence as we have will yield us much more. Buti was not always careful of his statements; and the assertion of Fra Mariano, quoted by Tognocchi, concerning Dante's connection with the Franciscan Order, was written nearly two hundred years after the poet's death.

The well-known lines—

> " Io aveva una corda intorno cinta,
> E con essa pensai alcuna volta
> Prender la lonza alla pelle dipinta "—

it is difficult to interpret otherwise than as a reference to his wearing the Minorite cord. His deep understanding love for Francis would, in his time, have been strong inducement to attach himself to his Order, to model his life to some extent after the Poverello's pattern, and to seek burial in or near the *frati's* church in Ravenna. That he did join it, in the looser bonds of the Third Order, I think any one who so desires may take for granted. The cord worn as a Tertiary would have committed him to no cloister, only to an austerer life than his fellows. Whatever value may be attached to the assertion of the famous Franciscan chronicler Fra Mariano, it means distinctly that Dante became a Tertiary at Ravenna. " *Amissa omni spe reditus sui [Dantes] Ravennam profectus, ibidem sub principe Guidone Polentano amico suo, sub ea norma quam beatus Franciscus fratribus dedit de poenitentia vixit; denique in articulo mortis constitutus, eodem habitu fratrum minorum indutus migravit a saeculo aetatis suae anno 56, salutis vero 1321, in templo sancti Francisci sepultus.*" After all these centuries one may well despair of testing such assertions, or earlier ones, by external evidence.   But too little effort has been made to compute their value by internal evidence.   The Franciscan researches of the last twenty years have rendered Mestica's interesting study of the question out of date.   Recent Italian writers have examined separate points connected with the matter with thoroughness ; but English commentators have for the most part completely neglected it.   This is my excuse for adding a few notes to some episodes of the *Paradiso*, which must seem to many to have been already annotated only too abundantly.

That he was a cloistered regular, save perhaps in his very early youth and for a short time, is highly improbable.   It is almost impossible to conceive of Dante, in his maturity, attaching himself very closely to a body of which he did not become the most learned member. And an examination of the matter leads me to believe that, while he cherished a special devotion to Francis, while the *Commedia* is, indeed, a reflection of the sublimer Franciscanism, he was, nevertheless, singularly indifferent to the interests and the struggles of the Order, and of its history and personnel his knowledge did not exceed that of any very moderately informed outsider.

Apart from the famous eleventh and twelfth cantos of the *Paradiso*, to which I shall return, the references to Francis and the Order are not many.   There is the praise of St. Clara (*Par*. iii. 98, 99).   There are the tales of Piccarda, rent from the shelter of the Clares to a worldly marriage (*Par*. iii.) ; and of Guido da Montefeltro, retiring after his battling life to the cloister, and being forced out again to help the schemes of Boniface.   For Guido's soul, after death, Francis and the black cherub are seen struggling (*Inf*. xxvii.). Then also there is the reference to the holy hermit and honest comb-maker, Pier Pettignano, a Franciscan Tertiary, whose prayers released Sapia from her worst pains (*Purg*. xiii. 128).

There is no evidence in Dante's life of close friendships with the noted Franciscans of his day. Great Minorites of the past generation, like Roger Bacon and Alexander Hales, have left no trace on him. Only in Bonaventura did he dig deep. It was to a Camaldolese monastery, Santa Croce of Fonte Avellana, he retired, after the death of Henry. In his last years he lived next door to the Franciscan convent at Ravenna. Yet the popular accounts of his stay there—and perhaps the tale of the composition of Dante's Creed has some basis in fact—suggest an intercourse very scanty and not very civil between the friars and himself, though this need not be used as an argument against the probability of his having been a Tertiary in that city. It will be remembered that his daughter entered the convent of San Stefano degli Olivi, not a monastery of the Clares. Here I should mention a not very successful attempt by Signora Sajani to prove that Beatrice Alighieri did, indeed, belong to the Second Order of the Minorites.

Francis had been dead forty years when Dante was born. The forty years had brought the Order through various periods of extension, modification, degradation, struggle, revival, vicissitude, and distortion. Before he grew to man's estate the great majority of the Friars Minor were hardly to be distinguished from the members of other Orders in their standard of life and morality. Only they were more ubiquitous, more influential, and on occasion more mischievous. The Spirituals were broken and scattered and somewhat diverted from their right way by persecution and misunderstanding. The free spirit inherent in Franciscanism had led some to heresy, some to rebellion; and a good many loyal sons of the Church among them were branded with accusations of these. Dante was not naturally inclined to favour either. In the later years of his life their protests had become complicated by politics. The sun of the Minorite idea was still shining; but an idealist of

Dante's day was ill placed for seeing it, save when he looked behind.   Of course, in his wandering life he may have met humble, obscure brothers living according to the spirit of the early days, that made known to him the reality which Franciscan cardinals hid.   All along the roads he would come upon the vagrant Minorites—

> " Taciti, soli, e senza compagnia,
>   N'andavam l'un dinanzi e l'altro dopo,
>   Come frati minor vanno per via."
>   —*Inf.* xxiii. 1-3.

So went the *frati* of his day.   So went not Francis and his brothers singing lauds.   But Dante, too, was wont to go, *tacito, solo, e senza compagnia;* and, I think, he did not often break the silence of the wandering brothers.

One Franciscan exercised notoriously a baleful influence on his fortunes.   The Cardinal Matteo d'Acquasparta, envoy of Boniface VIII. to Florence in 1300, during the Priorate of Dante, marked the poet as the obstinate enemy of the pope.   The cardinal's embassy, specially on behalf of the Neri, failed, and he was perhaps not wrong in thinking Dante mainly responsible. But the Neri, helped by Charles of Valois, triumphed ere long in spite of the Signoria, and Dante's sentence of exile came about a year and a half later.   He never saw Florence any more.   He sent his blame to the fountain head, to the high Boniface, him who was selling Christ every day.   His only reference to the envoy who had denounced him is in respect of his conduct when Minister-General of the Franciscans as slackener of the Rule.   The mention of him in this regard is the sole proof that he paid the least attention to the dissensions in the Order.

In judging these dissensions he steers a middle course between d'Acquasparta and the men whom d'Acquasparta persecuted.   Here, as elsewhere, the spirit of Bonaventura is his guide.   The irreconcilable idealist in every strife

admires the calm follower of the Middle Way. Now in the
Seraphic Doctor's mouth these words are quite fitting—

> " Ben dico, chi cercasse a foglio a foglio
> Nostro volume, ancor troveria carta
> U' leggerebbe : ' Io mi son quel ch'io soglio,'
> Ma non fia da Casal, nè d'Acquasparta,
> Là onde vegnon tali alla scrittura,
> Che l'un la fugge, e l'altro la coarta."
> —*Par.* xii. 121–126.

But whether Dante would himself have kept the careful
middle path, if he had been a little nearer the fray, is
another matter. It is significant that d'Acquasparta's
notorious opposition to the Spirituals in their strict adherence to the Rule was an old story when Dante wrote.
He may have chosen him as the most notorious of the
persecuting Generals—stronger and harsher than Giovanni
da Murro or Alessandro d'Alessandria, and more consis-
tent in his policy than Michele da Cesena, all nearer the
time when Dante was writing. It is just as probable that
he learnt this passage of Franciscan history because of his
painful interest in a cardinal who had played so grievous a
part in his own history and that of Florence. I cannot
find any special reference to the struggles of the *fraticelli*
in Dante, since the mention of Ubertino da Casale, even
if he be counted among them, probably refers only to his
earlier career, when he was feeling the weight of d'Acquasparta's authority. Did Dante know Ubertino? It is
almost certain, as I shall prove later, he knew his *Arbor
Vitæ*, written in 1305. But had he met the man himself
I think his reference would have been more explicit, if
not more kindly. One cannot but link together in
thought the two fiery, pertinacious idealists, ever fighting,
ever maligned, ever arraigned, ever exiled, each with some
years of disdainful peace at the end—Dante torn from
his Florence, which he would not enter on humiliating
terms, and Ubertino from the fold of Francis, preferring
a Benedictine refuge to an Order that had denied its

Founder.   Perhaps they were too much of the same
temper to have been friends.   Nor might they have
recognised they were fighting the same battle.   But
they could not have passed each other by unnoticed.
And thus, I judge, both from what he says and what
he does not say, that Dante lived entirely outside the
Minorite circles in his mature years, either because of
absorption in his own form of the common struggle, or
from distrust of a movement that had become associated
with heresy and schism.   His Franciscan inspiration came
from an earlier time.

The famous doctor Bonaventura, with his Paris
learning, his literary style, his suavity, his sanctity,
would naturally draw the admiration of the fastidious
Dante, apart from his great gift of high mystic speculation.   His reputation as it had been handed down—
he died in 1274—would be more sympathetic to the
poet than, say, the reputation of his own contemporary,
Ubertino da Casale, as it might not improbably be reported to him.   He says himself he was needle to the
seraphic Doctor's star (*Par.* xii. 29–30).   He owed him
much.   Yet so far as Dante's particular knowledge of
early Franciscan history is imperfect, Bonaventura is
the cause.   That he knew Bonaventura's Legend well
is a certainty.   Now you do not go to that life for
the most vivid history of the first days of the Order,
though he tells some tales of the Founder charmingly.
Consider the circumstances in which, the purpose for
which the Legend was written.   The Order had gone
through a tremendous crisis.   On one side had been
ranged those who wished to reconcile the Rule with
the comfortable traditions of religious life, to make it
a reasonable yoke for average men : on the other those
who wished to keep it as Francis had made it, who
had no thought of reasonable average men at all, but
of spiritual athletes.   The champions of the Rule, *sine
glosa, sine glosa, sine glosa*, were the survivors of the early

companions of Francis. Round this little aristocracy of very humble men, with their "This did Francis say," "Thus wrote he," "So did he live," the strife waged fiercely, and with varying fortunes. The Companions won in John of Parma's election, 1247, and under his administration. The others, seeing the Rule now not a theory but an actual reality, rallied for a fresh struggle, appealed to the Pope, and overthrew John on the insincere ground of heresy. Bonaventura, his successor, said, "Now I will walk between. I will reconcile all parties. There must be no great relaxation, save what the Pope has granted, but the Spirituals must not defy the head of the Church in the name of obedience to Francis." There was outward peace in his time, for he was a man of will and an able administrator—though the questions at issue were only delayed. But he shrewdly saw that the fomenters of strife could always feed the flame by the Franciscan legends already in existence. So he put out his smooth, strong hand, and effaced the earlier legends. All copies were to be destroyed was his order at the Chapter General of Paris, 1266. He had previously written his own, which summed up all a good Minorite need know. The compilation has lasted as the standard Life of Francis all these centuries, helped to the retention of its sure position by its own intrinsic qualities. There are passages of real beauty in it, and the writer's devotion to his master is undoubted. But the vividness, the intimacy, the circumstance that give life to the pages of Thomas of Celano, to the "*Legend of the Three Companions*," to the *Speculum Perfectionis*, are not in it. Much detail is fearfully suppressed. In the earlier legends Francis was a man. In Bonaventura's he is seldom other than the saint in the niche, and sometimes only the hero of a string of nauseous wonders. The first biographers have the freshness of Giotto. He, better Latinist, and with a pretty power over his pen, is among the conventional hagiologists, though first among these.

It was his legend Dante knew. What scattered copies of the earlier ones remained were hidden away in friars' libraries and cells. Bonaventura, the politician, was specially careful not to dwell long on the virtues or the stories of the first Companions. The purpose of his book is clearly illustrated by the fact that neither Leo on the one hand nor Elias, the notorious, on the other is ever mentioned by name. Not that he objected to names —of quite safe people. All the brothers who brought gaping tales of wonders are named. But of calling up the memories of those round whom the late battle had waged, he was chary. The brothers actually mentioned by him, apart from those cited as witnesses of miracles, are Bernard of Quintavalle, Giles — courteously but curtly referred to—Silvester, Morico, Pacifico, Antony (of Padua), Monaldo, Illuminato, Leonardo and Agostino. Of these, so far as we learn from the early documents and traditions, only Bernard, Giles, Illuminato, and Silvester were of the intimate circle. Morico was probably one of the first twelve, but he, Monaldo, Leonardo, and Agostino have left only faint traces in Franciscan history. That Leo, Angelo Tancredi, Rufino, and perhaps Masseo, were alive when he wrote, seems hardly a reason for silence respecting them. Illuminato was also alive, and he is referred to with special honour. But he was a man of high position, not dangerous, and a personal friend of Bonaventura's, in whose reign he was made Minister of Umbria and Bishop of Assisi.

Dante omits all reference to the little-known Morico, Monaldo, and Leonardo, also to Pacifico, the poet— which is remarkable—also to Antony of Padua—remarkable, too, for he must have been witness of his cult in Padua. He names none that the seraphic Doctor does not mention, and only Bernard, Giles, Silvester, Illuminato, and Agostino. Concerning the two last he falls into a mistake from Bonaventura's partial mention of them. Dante makes him say—

> " Illuminato ed Augustin son quici,
>   Che fur dei primi scalzi poverelli,
>   Che nel capestro a Dio si fero amici."
> —*Par.*, xii. 130–132.

Agostino is only known from Bonaventura's legend as the brother, who dying far away, in Francis's passing hour, broke the speechless stupor of death with, "Wait for me, father. Behold, I come with thee;" also as a miracle worker, curing the sight of Brother Robert of Naples. Neither he nor Illuminato was of the first brothers. But, of course, an assertion of Dante is treated like a text of Scripture, and thus we have Mr. Gardner picking out these two men, "the bare-footed *poverelli*, Illuminato and Agostino, who did indeed follow in the steps of St. Francis as he willed, and so, although they had no doctrine to teach but that of their own good example and renunciation, have illumined the world as much as if they had been among the greatest teachers of the schools." This is a natural surmise. I have said what is known of Fra Agostino, not one of the first, nor of the most intimate circle. But of Illuminato we know a great deal more. And I regret to say that Illuminato's Franciscanism, in the stricter sense of the word, meaning the special virtues for which he is praised by Dante and Mr. Gardner, is at least suspect, far more suspect than that of any other of the men of the Founder's intimate circle, to which, nevertheless, he did at one time belong. Illuminato was in the world a nobleman, lord of the Rocca Accarina. He must have been of man's estate when he entered the Order, as he had a son. This fact and another, namely, that he was acting as Bishop of Assisi in 1282—the last survivor of the early companions—make it difficult to think of him as enlisting under Francis in 1209 or

1210, the first recruiting years. And his name appears in none of the early lists. We hear nothing of him till he goes with Francis to the East in 1219, which may well have been his first enterprise. It was a custom of Francis to demand great efforts from his new recruits, and let them taste of adventure. When he entered the Order he seems to have provided for his son by bestowing on him his lands and castle. I do not suggest for a moment that Illuminato did not renounce the world and its goods, but from peculiar circumstances the intention of the Founder—that relatives should not benefit by property renounced, but only the poor—was in his case waived, and no doubt reasonably, for the son was perhaps an infant. That he was of Francis's intimate circle at one time is proved if Masseo's account of the saint's farewell to Alverna be an authentic document. He is credited with combating Francis's *Secretum meum mihi*, holding that to men, for their conversion, was due the wondrous tale of the Stigmata. Later, in 1246, he is quoted as a witness by the Three Companions, in the prefatory letter to their Legend, certain proof that he was of the inner circle at one time, and testimony also to his high character. But that he was of the stricter, humbler party in the Order, those that Mr. Gardner, in the passage I have quoted, points to as the true Franciscans, is disproved by the fact that he was secretary to the notorious Frate Elias, and that, too, in the last and most tyrannical years of his Minister-Generalship. He was so in 1238, the year before Elias's deposition. Illuminato need not be closely associated with the policy of Elias, therefore; but he must be clearly dissociated from all the strict and humble sons of Francis, who followed close in the footsteps of their Father. There exists a legal document, dated 15th October 1238, by which Elias gives power to Illuminato to do what he likes with the Rocca Accarina and all its dependencies, which has fallen to him by the death of his son Henry.

There was, of course, no necessity under Elias's régime for his giving it to the poor. As a matter of fact he gave it to the city of Spoleto. We lose trace of him for years, save when he is quoted as witness by the Three Companions. But he was appointed by Bonaventura Provincial of Umbria, and later, in 1273, Bishop of Assisi. He is the only one of the early intimate companions who became an official, save Peter of Catania and Elias—and he must always be treated apart from the rest; the only one who accepted promotion; the only one who disposed of his own property; the only one who had friendly dealings with the renegade Elias in the days of his power. Doubtless, a very good man, but without the special Franciscan flavour. Of the external facts of his life we know a good deal, but we have no mental picture of him. He did not touch the imagination of his time. Dante named him because Bonaventura did; and Bonaventura named him because he was a friend of his, a man of standing, and one who had never troubled the Order by inconvenient idealism.

Even now there is something to be done for the annotation of the eleventh canto of the *Paradiso*. In Mr. Toynbee's admirable dictionary I find he says of Bernard of Quintavalle that " after the death of his master he became the head of the Order ! " Is this some half recollection of the tale of Francis's blessing him as the first-born son ? Not only did Bernard not become head of the Order, but he never held any office at all. He lived his life mostly in obscure convents and hermitages, and during the reign of Elias had to flee to the mountains out of the reach of persecution. Again, Silvester is called St. Silvester. No Congregation of Rites ever considered that good man's claims. Egidio is called St. Giles of Assisi. This is to mock poor Giles. The story should be better known of him dying up in Perugia. The citizens and men-at-arms watched without the convent walls lest his body should be stolen, and the dying man sent out a message, a little sad, quite resigned, and prophetic, that the bells would never ring for his canonisation. And they never did—though the Church, after many years, named him Blessed. They were all *Beati*, of course, but mostly by the popular voice. The Bollandists were wise enough sometimes to listen to the popular voice, and justify the popular cult.

Ozanam has a pleasing picture of Dante sitting at the feet of the good *frati* in the portico of Santa Croce, and listening to the tales and legends of the early time which were afterwards collected into the *Actus S. Francisci et Sociorum ejus*, known to us in its Italian version as the *Fioretti*. Now whether Dante ever sat in the cloisters of Santa Croce or not I do not know ; but that the *frati* ever told him a single one of their wonderful and charming stories there is not a jot of evidence. Had he known them, or been aware of the personalities of the first Companions, he would not have drawn so exclusively on Bonaventura.

But for one thing, and a notable one, in the magnificent eulogy of Francis, he found no suggestion in Bonaventura—the marvellous image of Mary (*Par.*, xi. 70–72) at the foot of the Cross, while Poverty, clinging closer than a mother, mounts with Christ. I suppose it is generally held to be Dante's. It is not his, but he gave it immortal shape. There is no trace of it in Bonaventura, neither in the " Life of Francis," nor in his treatise on Poverty. Of the Mystical Marriage with Madonna Poverty we have faint traces in all the earlier Franciscan works. I have no doubt that the legend or allegory derives from Francis himself. It is like one of his pictures. Flashed by him into the minds of his companions, it would be repeated till it became the possession of all Franciscan writers with imagination enough to see its force. But when did it take definite shape, not merely in allusions to a chosen spouse, but as a detailed story? Two erroneous statements are constantly repeated. The first is that Giotto painted his fresco of Poverty on the ceiling of the Lower Church at Assisi after Dante's words. But Giotto had painted his fresco long ere Dante wrote the *Paradiso*. The other is that Giotto painted it from Bonaventura's version of the allegory. Giotto did nothing of the kind—though it is about the one instance in the Francis frescoes where he did not follow the Seraphic Doctor. And if you read Bonaventura you will know why. He is a good story-teller, but here he evidently does not know the story, or has forgotten it; and his tale of Francis meeting three ladies in the plain of San Quirico, and their greeting him with *Ben vegna Madonna Poverta*, is quite incoherent. No painter could use it. Giotto either held a clearer story from the *frati*, or he imagined the thing for himself, and painted three separate pictures symbolical of Poverty, Chastity, and Obedience, which owed nothing to Bonaventura at all.

Probably the earliest literary form of the legend of the Mystical Marriage is the celebrated, but too little known, treatise, the *Sacrum Commercium Beati Francisci cum Domina Paupertate*, which is dated in one codex, 1227, that is, about nine months after the death of Francis, and which Père Edouard d'Alencon, accepting this date as correct, assumes, against tradition, to be the work of John Parenti, first Minister-General after Francis. I am not convinced enough of the correctness of the date to share his opinion; and hold that the ancient tradition which assigns it to John of Parma, Minister-General, 1247-1256, is more probable. At least, it seems from internal evidence to be the work of a man of his time. But the date is not of importance here. Now in that treatise there occur these words, " *Tu sola sociabaris ei. Non reliquisti eum usque ad mortem, mortem autem crucis. Et in ipsa cruce, denudato jam corpore, extensis brachiis, manibus et pedibus confixis, secum patiebaris, ita ut nihil in eo te gloriosius appareret.*"

Here we are on the track of Dante's great image. Poverty, faithful indeed unto death, is alone with Christ upon the Cross, suffering with Him, the most glorious thing about Him. Did Dante know the *Sacrum Commercium?* It is not necessary to conclude that he did. Jacopone da Todi knew it, and set it to his rough music. In his *Della Santa Poverta* he tells how Lady Poverty and her sister would not leave Christ even in death :—

> " Amistà non mai più udita
> Con nui ebbe in questa vita ;
> Anzi en croce alla partita
> Volse unito a nui passare."

That would have been enough to have suggested to Dante half his famous picture. He might even have got a further suggestion from the *Lamento della Vergine,* where—according, at least, to the Venetian edition— Mary cries to her Son, already on the Cross :—

> " Figlio questo non dire ;
> Voglio teco morire ;
> Vo costà su salire
> Et morirmiti a lato."
> —(*l.* iii. 12.)

But the question arises—Did he know Jacopone or his work ? Crescimbeni says, indeed, the rhyming *frate* was *molto amico di Dante ;* but of his authority for the statement we know nothing. A sentimental imagination rushes to the thought that the two victims of Boniface's vengeance, poets both, satirists both, would have met and poured out their souls to each other. But is it so likely after all ? Jacopone lived in hermit cells, in prison, or on the highroad — a mixture of vagrant, fanatic, high poet, and fool. He had thrown over all his Bolognese learning, and affected the roughest Umbrian. Of such were not Dante's friends. Even in exile he lived in great houses. Even in

2 C

would not have where to lay his head. It was surely his sacrifice of this greatest gift of fortune, that made story-tellers link the tale of the King of Heaven coming down to share the lot of men, and save them, with the tale of the happy-natured Umbrian, voluntarily taking on himself all human pains, waging a great battle with himself, leading his chosen to become wrestlers too, and knowing all suffering because he linked himself to universal love. Yet the stern Florentine and the Seraphic Francis are akin. And Francis is the spiritual father of the poet perhaps even more than Dante was aware of. It is not easy to compare their attitudes towards the Church. That of Francis seems, at first sight, of the meekest. He held neither the infallibility of the pope nor of the clergy; but to him they were the representatives of God, and as such deserving of respect. Of the humble secular clergy he says, in his Testament, " I have no wish to consider their sins, for in them I see the Son of God, and they are my lords, . . . and because I see nothing here below of the Most High Son of God save His most holy Body and His blood which they receive, and which they alone distribute to others." He was never in conflict with Rome. The Curia quickly saw the use to which his army might be put, and flattered it and its leader. They tried to cajole him into modification of his purposes, but he was humbly staunch. The changes brought about in his lifetime in the Order were so subtly, insinuatingly wrought that, though he was aware his spiritual idea was being tampered with, it was almost impossible to a man of his temper to resist them forcibly. He never had to confront a Boniface VIII. or a John XXII., and we have no guide as to what would have been his attitude in such a case. He was submissive, but his spirit was essentially free; and much as he loved the Roman Church, I cannot say that he loved it more than Dante. He had to face no evil living, and no notoriously avaricious pope. He

knew the general corruption of the Church, and he said,
"Let us, my brothers, live otherwise; waste no time in
recriminations, but look to ourselves.   The life we mean
to live is so glorious that we shall attract multitudes,
and the Kingdom of God shall be seen upon earth."
At least he raised for his own age and the age after him
the spiritual ideal of the Church, so that Dante was no
voice crying in the wilderness; and made a corrupt and
avaricious papacy seem a monstrosity in the eyes of simple
men who did not speculate and dream.   What appears
in Dante as an ecclesiastical policy had already been
shown in the daily rule of life of the simple Minorite.

But it is elsewhere we find them very nearly drawn
together.   Had Francis never lived, Dante would have
been other; and he needed all his Franciscanism.   He
took life hardly and bitterly, and if he escaped the condemnation of those who deprive themselves of life and
light, who confess among the tortures, they were sad
amid the sweet air made gladsome by the sun, it was
because he was taught by a master whose followers had
to wear a gallant mien in the warfare and the dungeons
of the world, and who held it was deep discourtesy to
the Most High to banish the good guest of joy from
one's heart and house.   When from his soul, as he was
journeying through Purgatory, the sin of pride fell off
first of all—"*A che guardando il mio Duca sorrise*" (*Purg.*,
xii. 136)—Francis might have been directing the heavenly
way of his soul.   And when his leader explains to him the
communism in all real possessions (*Purg.*, xv. 49 *et seq.*), he
is but turning the daily economy of the Franciscans into
philosophy.   The joy of doing without for the better
possession, none of the Minorites have sung so exquisitely.
Who has painted the angel of abstinence like Dante, or
the beauty of his path ?—

> Quinci si va chi vuole andar per pace.
> —*Purg.*, xxiv. 141.

His picture of the light-hearted wayfarer with the empty pockets (*Conv.*, iv. 13) might be from the pen of Jacopone.

As to the question of poverty, we gather that Dante curbed his luxurious instincts in obedience to an adopted code, the Franciscan. But he had lived through troublous times respecting that virtue. The *fraticelli*, growing pedantic, were forgetting that, in espousing this Bride, they should but take her as a close companion and fellow pilgrim on the way to love. They forgot their goal sometimes in their stern joy in the Bride. Her name was a battle-cry in Dante's time. That the question was at least discussed in the circles he frequented is proved by the verses of his two friends, Guido Cavalcanti and Giotto. Giotto's, probably a retort to some taunt that the painter of the *Poverello* was yet no disciple, is the merest commonplace doggerel, but not a whit more conventional than that of the courtly poet's, who may, as they say, have once set out as pilgrim to Compostella, but certainly never to Assisi.

Bonaventura was Dante's teacher in Franciscanism. He borrowed from him in essential matters, adopted his classification of sins, his special homage to the Virgin, and the plan of illustrating the seven capital virtues by incidents in her life, as Dr. Moore has pointed out. He and others have shown the poet's close acquaintance with the Seraphic Doctor's *Speculum Beatæ Virginis Mariæ*. I speak under the correction of the learned when I say there is infinitely more of Bonaventura than of Thomas Aquinas in the "Divine Comedy." Bonaventura's mingled Platonism and Christianity is illustrated again and again, and ever increasingly, as the poet rises towards the highest heavens. Only, the seraphic mysticism is put into more syllogistic form by the keen Tuscan intellect. The soft, vague glow is turned to fiery line and star.

But Bonaventura's philosophy was nothing save a commentary drawn from Plato and the New Testament,

on the life of his master Francis, who lived it all.   The
Franciscan theme, the union of the soul with God, is the
theme of the *Paradiso*, and but the theorising on a fact
extraordinary in its literal truth in the lives of Francis
and his brothers, who attained to it in the flesh.   Mr.
Gardner, in his "Dante's Ten Heavens," says, "In one
of the poems ascribed to St. Francis there occurs a passage
concerning love and order, in which may be seen the basis
of the whole moral structure of the *Purgatorio*, the soul's
purgation from disordered love: *Ordina quest' amore, o tu
che m'ami.*"   And he amply proves his thesis.   That the
hymn is probably not by Francis, but by Jacopone, does
not matter: it is Franciscan none the less.   Thus we
have the *Purgatorio* and the *Paradiso* based on ideas which
the Minorites did not originate, but which their thinkers
emphasised and made the foundation of their system,
because their Founder lived them.   And so Francis and
Dante are drawn together.   Throughout the dark vision
of the *Commedia* we feel the soul of the poet lighten
suddenly, as if a soft wing flapped and fanned his face.
By different roads, by different means, they saw the same
vision in the end.   Francis in his love for men and women,
beasts and birds and trees and fire and water, had been
learning all his life the oneness of things.   Without
philosophy, or speculation, by love alone he realised the
unity of the universe.   He flung himself, a burning
sacrifice, into the whole, knew in his body the pain of
all the world, and learned the price of love.   He lived
from day to day a humble struggling life, its tale
wonderful, yet plain to the least of us.   But into an
hour of agony on a mountain, was gathered one day all
his sublimated faculty and experience, a mystery to the
highest.   Alverna was his poem, apart from the human
Francis only so far as his scattered lights and fires were
there concentred.   Dante led his life of struggle and
exile, loved a few souls well, and found many hateful—a
hard battling life, where he was wounded many times.

But his great eye searched throughout created things, his mind brooded, till he, too, conceived the universe as a whole, found the centre, and, despite his own world-experience, proved it law and harmony. Beatrice taught him to call it Love, and linked his *Paradiso* with all the dark behind.

> " Nel suo profondo vidi che s'interna,
> Legato con amore in un volume,
> Ciò che per l'universo si squaderna."
> —*Par.*, xxxiii. 85-87.

The reconcilement with him took place likewise in a moment of mystery apart. He cannot tell it clearly, he who can tell all things with such accuracy of circumstance and order. From his Alverna night he flashes the truth down on a world dull and incredulous. Like the shepherds of the Casentino we see a light up there spreading over the earth, and are afraid ; or like the mule-drivers we rise from our beds in the inn, and saddle and load our beasts, saying the sun has arisen, and feel light-hearted for the day has come. But the glory fades, and the night is yet with us. Each, guided by the star of Francis or of Dante, must tread the road by himself of perfect sacrifice, or endless search, if he would have abide with him the vision of which the *frati* babbled in wondering awe and Dante stammered gloriously.

> " All' alta fantasia qui mancò possa ;
> Ma già volgeva il mio disiro e il *velle*,
> Sì come rota ch' egualmente è mossa,
> L'amor che move il sole e l'altre stelle."
> —*Par.*, xxxiii. 142-145.

GENERAL BIBLIOGRAPHY

Under the different chapter headings will be found particular references to the chief sources of information. But important works are constantly being added by eminent scholars in Italy, France, and Germany. My bibliographical notes are merely intended to give readers a start on the long but most fascinating road of Franciscan study.

The reader misses much who does not drink at the early sources, and most of these are now accessible. Among the most important are :—

> *B. P. Francisci Assisiatis Opusc.* Ed. Wadding, Antwerp, 1623.
>
> *Speculum Perfectionis*, ed. Paul Sabatier, Paris, 1898.
>
> (English translation, of the text only, by Sebastian Evans, Nutt, 1899.)
>
> Celano, *Vita Prima S. Francisci, A.SS.*, Oct. 4, p. 683.
>
>   ,,   ,, *Secunda*   ,,   ed. Amoni, Rome, 1880.
>
> *Legenda trium Sociorum, A.SS.*, Oct. 4, p. 723.
>
>   ,,   ,,   ,, ed. Faloci-Pulignani.
>
> (French translation by A. Barine, 1901.)
>
> For other versions of the Legend, see note to p. 109.
>
> Bonaventuræ *Legenda S. Francisci, A.SS.*, Oct. 4, p. 742.
>
>   ,,   ,,   ,, ed. PP. Collegii S. Bonav. Quaracchi, 1898.

For general information respecting the first ages of the Order—besides the biographies of St. Francis named below—the following may be consulted :—

> *Monumenta Franciscana*, vol. i., ed. Brewer, Eccleston, *De Adventu Minorum in Angliam*, 1858 ;

the numerous, weighty, but most readable tomes of

> Wadding, *Annales Minorum ;*

the *Chronica XXIV. Generalium O.M.*, and other early chronicles collected in

> *Analecta Franciscana*, 3 vols. in progress. Quaracchi, 1885, &c.

Till a modern editor has taken in hand the chaotic work of Bartholomew of Pisa, only the most persevering students will tackle the

> *Liber Conformitatum*, Mediolani, 1510,

which, in the form of parallels between the lives of Christ and St. Francis, contains a great treasury of Franciscan lore.

More orderly, and more readable—but in England at least, less accessible, is

> Mark of Lisbon's *Chronicle of the Minors.*

Reference to this work in Portuguese and in translations will be found in the British Museum catalogue under *Silva (Marcos da) Bishop of Oporto.*

Then there is the ever delightful and invaluable *Fioretti.*

> *I Fioretti di San Francesco,* ed. Amoni, Rome, 1889.
> „　　　„　　　„　　ed. Manzoni, Rome, 1900.

Wherever I have quoted from it I have used the admirable English translation—

> *The Little Flowers of St. Francis,* translated by T. Arnold. Temple Classics.

The original Latin has recently been published by M. Sabatier—

> *Actus S. Francisci et Sociorum ejus,* ed. Paul Sabatier, Paris, 1902, and *Floretum S. Francisci Assisiensis,* ed. Paul Sabatier, Paris, 1902.

Of modern lives of St. Francis that of M. Sabatier stands highest—

> *Vie de S. François d'Assise,* Paris, Fischbacher.
> (English translation by L. Houghton : Hodder & Stoughton.)

Other lives that may be consulted are those by Le Monnier, Thode, Hase, Chavin de Malan, Chalippe, Papini, Knox Little, and Herkless.

What may be called the temperament of the Franciscan movement will be found reflected in

> Tocco, *L'Eresia nel Medio Evo,* Florence, 1884.
> Gebhart, *L'Italie Mystique,* Paris, 1887.
> Ozanam, *Les Poétes franciscains,* Paris, 1852.

For the general history of the time the most convenient authority is—

> Gregorovius, *Geschichte der Stadt Rom im Mittelalter.*
> (English translation by A. Hamilton, Bell.)

Fleury's *Histoire Ecclésiastique* is by no means out of date. He is at least as accurate in dealing with this particular subject as Milman, and is more sympathetic to the mediæval mind.

Abundant information respecting the topography of Assisi and the neighbourhood will be found in Miss Duff Gordon's *Story of Assisi* (Mediæval Towns : Dent, 1901).

NOTES

CONTENTS

A word is necessary as to the intentional limitations of the book. Had I searched outside Italy, in England, France, and Germany, I should have found many worthy Sons of Francis, but I was minded to trace the spirit of the Father among his own countrymen. Possibly in my aim at consistency in this respect I may have hindered a proper understanding of the Spiritual struggles of the latter half of the thirteenth century, by looking at Pier Jean d'Olivi not directly, but only through men inspired by him, like Conrad d'Offida and Angelo Clareno. The fiery Ubertino da Casale would have had a place, had he not seemed, though not one of the *fraticelli*, to fit in better with a history of that sect. Politics, the protection of Louis of Bavaria, and the rasped temper which was the fruit of constant harrying persecution, complicated in time the history of the Spirituals; and so I have found the beginning of the fourteenth century a convenient stopping-place. The inclusion of Pope Celestine V., who was not of the Order, may be justified by the fact that he was for a few short weeks the hope of the spiritual Franciscans, and, besides, his career raises a question closely connected with the whole subject. I have included one daughter of Francis — but she was called "Brother Jacoba." Though she was not a very important person, though little is known of her—far less than of Saint Margaret of Cortona, Saint Rose of Viterbo, and the Blessed Angela of Foligno—yet that little is distinctly Franciscan, and much we learn of them is not. The Clares and women Tertiaries mostly need treatment apart. And so a study I had made of the strange disordered soul of Saint Margaret, so alluring, so repellent, so fruitful and fascinating a subject for the romantic psychologist, I have omitted. None of my personages, save Brother Elias — and he in a limited way—illustrates what Franciscanism did for Art. But its influence in this direction has been elsewhere done ample justice to, though hardly, I think, exaggerated. Herr Thode's book, "Franz von Assisi," remains of great value.

INTRODUCTION.

P. 2, l. 11. For the questions of the history and authorship of the *Fioretti*, see Manzoni: *Studi sui Fioretti* (*Miscellanea Francescana*, vols. iii.

and iv., Foligno, 1889); and *Actus Beati Francisci et Sociorum Ejus*, ed. Paul Sabatier, Paris, 1902, preface.

P. 7, l. 28. Walter de Brienne.—See Sabatier, *Vie di S. François*, p. 19.

P. 9, l. 7. "did not war against rich men."—Admonebat . . . fratres ut . . . non dispicerent illos qui delicate vivunt ac superflue induuntur ; nam Deus est noster et ipsorum Dominus. *Leg.* 3, *Soc.* xiv.

P. 9, l. 23. For reproofs of depression, see *Speculum Perfectionis*, ch. 96 ; II. Celano, 3, 68.

P. 11, l. 17. For Juniper, see his life in the *Fioretti ;* and *XXIV. Gen.* (*Anal. Fran.*, iii. 54–64).

P. 12, l. 10. "perfect joy." See *Fioretti*, viii.

P. 15, l. 15 *et seq.* Love of fire and water. See *Spec. Perf.* ch. 115–118.

P. 16, ll. 21–22. A whole controversial literature has grown about Francis's *Song of the Creatures.* Lists of the more important studies on it will be found in M. Sabatier's edition of the *Speculum Perfectionis*, p. 289 ; also in Gaspary's *Italian Literature to the Death of Dante*, transl. Oelsner (Bohn.), p. 358. Matthew Arnold's version of the laud is the best English one.

P. 17, l. 6. "Jongleurs of the Lord." See *Spec. Perf.* ch. 100. l. 14. "Knights of the Round Table." See *Spec. Perf.* ch. 72.

P. 17, l. 19. "reluctant leave to Anthony of Padua." For letter see *Opus. B. Fran.* Epist. iii. p. 16. Sabatier (*Vie de S. François*, p. 322) casts doubt on its authenticity.

P. 20, l. 32. For the vexed question of early Franciscan Rules, see K. Müller, *Die Anfänge des Minoritenordens*, Friburg, 1885.

P. 22, l. 32. *Nos qui cum eo fuimus*—a phrase reiterated by the author of the *Speculum Perfectionis*.

NOS QUI CUM EO FUIMUS.

Main Sources.

Legenda Trium Sociorum.
Celano, *Vita Prima.*
    ,,   ,, *Secunda.*
(For references to particular editions, see General Bibliography.)
Wadding, *Annales*, vol. i.

P. 28, l. 5. "loved each other." Casti amplexus, suaves affectus, osculum sanctum, dulce colloquium, risus modestus, animus simplex, lingua placabilis, responsio mollis, idem propositum, promptum obsequiem, &c., I. Cel. *A.SS.*, Oct. 4, p. 694.

P. 29, l. 14. At Rivo Torto, near Assisi, on the road from Sta.

Maria degli Angeli to Spello, stands a church commemorative of the early settlement. But M. Sabatier—see Italian translation of his *Vie de S. François*—holds that the real site is near the chapel of S. Rufino d'Arce.

P. 29, l. 15. The Porziuncola may be called the birthplace of the Franciscan Order. Built, according to tradition, by pilgrims from Jerusalem, restored by St. Benedict, it was ministered to by Benedictines till the Abbot of Monte Subasio gave it to Francis. Cells were built round it for himself and his brothers. What remains of these holy places is now enclosed in the great church of Santa Maria degli Angeli.

P. 30, l. 4. "the traditional first twelve." These were, according to some texts of the *Legend of the Three Companions*, Francis, Bernard, Peter of Catania, Giles, Sabbatino, Morico, John of Cappella, Philip, John of San Constantio, Barbaro, Bernard of Vita, Angelo Tancredi. But see *Miscell. Francesc.* vol. viii. p. 57, and Sabatier, *Vie de S.F.*, p. 102.

BERNARD OF QUINTAVALLE.

Main Sources.

Chronica XXIV. General (*Anal. Fran.*, vol. iii. p. 35).
I. Celano, *A.SS.*, Oct. 4, p. 691. II. Cel., 1, 10; 2, 17; 3, 52.
Legenda Trium Sociorum, ch. 8, 9, 10, 12.
Speculum Perfectionis, ch. 107.
Actus S. Francisci, ch. 1–5, 30.
Fioretti, ch. 1–5, 28.
Papini, *Storia di San Francesco*, I. pp. 44, 45, 78, 81, 194.
Jacobilli, *Vite de' Santi e Beati dell' Umbria*, ii., July 10.
Wadding, *Annales*, is a mine of information on all the prominent early Minorites, including the First Companions.

P. 32, l. 11. The church of St. Nicholas, Assisi, no longer exists.

P. 32, l. 31. Peter of Catania, Canon of the Cathedral of Assisi; went with Francis to the East; made Vicar General, 1220. Died 1220. A disturbing number of miracles was wrought by his relics at the Porziuncola, till Francis begged his spirit to cease its activity in our world.

P. 35, l. 3. Erant viri poenitentiales de civitate Assisii oriundi. *Leg.* 3, *Soc.* x.

P. 35, l. 5. Silvester. See *Fioretti*, 1, 2, 16.

P. 36, l. 19. This pilgrimage is probably only an incident in Francis's mission to Spain.

P. 36, l. 36 "sick had to turn out." See *Spec. Perf.* 6.

P. 40, l. 1. See Clareno's *Tribulations* in Döllinger's *Beiträge*, ii. p. 464.

P. 41, l. 23. This story is also told of S. Francis.

RUFINO OF THE SCIFI.

Main Sources.

Actus S. Francisci, 31–35.
Fioretti, 1, 29–31.
XXIV. Gen. (*Anal. Fran.*, iii. p. 46).
Papini, *Storia*, ii. p. 201.
Jacobilli, *Vite de' Santi*, iii., Nov. 14.

GILES THE ECSTATIC.

Main Sources.

Leg. 3, *Soc.*, c. 9.
A.SS., April 23, p. 222.
XXIV. Gen. (*Anal. Fran.*, iii. p. 74).
(The short life of Giles in the *Fioretti* is extracted from the longer lives in the *A.SS.* and *XXIV. Gen.*)
Jacobilli, *Vite de' Santi*, i., Ap. 23.
Papini, *Storia di San. F.*, I. 46, 53, 83, 195, ii. 213.

P. 56, l. 26. Brother Lucido. See *Spec. Perf.*, ch. 85.

P. 61, l. 24. "His scorn for the idle prayerful man," &c. On another like occasion he says : "Si homo esset tanta devotione et gratia elevatus, quod cum Angelis loqueretur, et a suo praelato vocaretur, statim deberet colloquium Angelorum dimittere et praelato promptius obedire."

P. 65, l. 27. Gerard da Borgo San Donnino. See p. 234.

P. 69, l. 28. It is a pity to have to acknowledge the fact that Saint Louis did not pass through Italy on his way to the Crusade, and probably never visited Perugia at all.

P. 78, l. 36. "His sayings." Sbaralea (*Supplementum ad Scriptores 3, Ord. S. Franc.*, p. 4) gives a list of editions.

ANGELO TANCREDI.

Main Sources.

Spec. Perf., 67.
Actus S. Francisci, 9.
Fioretti, 16.
Papini, *Storia di S.F.*, ii. p. 202.
Jacobilli, *Vite de' Santi*, i., Feb. 13.

P. 80, l. 13. "Knight of Christ." *Cf.* a story told in the *Actus*, ch. 66, of another great soldier who entered the Order.

P. 83, l. 2. Angelo is, however, mentioned in the *Tribulations* as suffering for his protests against the exactions for the Basilica.

MASSEO DA MARIGNANO.

Main Sources.

Actus S. Francisci, 10–13, 41.
Fioretti, 10–13, 32.
XXIV. Gen. (*Anal. Fran.*, iii. p. 115).
Tractatus de Indulgentia S. Mariae de Portiuncula, ed. Sabatier, 1900, ch. 5 and 8.
Jacobilli, *Vite de' Santi*, iii., Nov. 17.
Papini, *Storia*, ii. p. 198.

P. 91, l. 9. The original of the letter is to be found in Amoni's edition of the *Fioretti* and Sabatier's *Spec. Perf.*, p. 305. Discussions of its authenticity in *Misc. Fran.* viii. p. 75, and Minocchi, *Studi francescani*, vol. i., Florence.

P. 91, l. 20. Here St. Mary of the Angels on Alverna, but on p. 92, l. 16, the church at Assisi is meant.

P. 92, l. 18. For Francis and the falcon, see *Fioretti*, Second Reflection on the Stigmata.

P. 93, l. 3. See p. 191.

P. 94, l. 14. See Sabatier's *Spec. Perf.*, p. 168.

LEO.

Main Sources.

Spec. Perf., lxii–lxxxv.
Actus S. Francisci, 7–9, 38, 39, 59, 64.
Fioretti, 8, 9, 36, also Reflections on the Stigmata.
XXIV. Gen. (*Anal. Fran.*, iii. p. 65).
Angelo Clareno, *Tribulations*. Döllinger, *Beiträge für Sektengeschichte*, ii. p. 445 *et seq.*, p. 510.
Jacobilli, *Vite de' Santi*, Nov. 6.
Papini, *Storia*, i. pp. 130, 153; ii. p. 203.

P. 98, l. 26. For the Blessing of Leo, see Sabatier, *Spec. Perf.*, lxvii.–lxx.; Montgomery Carmichael, *La Benedizione di San Francesco*, Livorno, 1900; the same writer's, *In Tuscany*, p. 231; also Faloci-Pulignani, *Tre Autografi di S. Francesco*.

P. 99, ll. 3–4. "Only one other." See Wadding, *Op. S. Francis.*, Epist. vi.; *Spec. Perf.* lxxiii–lxxv; Sabatier's *Vie de S. François*, p. 300; Faloci-Pulignani, *op. cit.*

P. 103, l. 21. Aymon of Faversham, fifth Minister-General of the Order; native of Faversham, Kent; received into the Order at Paris; sent by the Pope as an envoy to Greece; one of the most prominent opponents of Elias; author of several theological works; died at Anagni, 1244.

P. 104, l. 18. How Clara reconciled her strict observance with her evident high respect for Elias is a question worth investigation.

P. 104, l. 25. This breviary is still at San Damiano.

P. 105, l. 2. Leo recedentis lectulum osculatur. *A.SS.*, Aug. 12, p. 764, *Vita S. Clarae Virginis.*

P. 106, l. 28. For M. Sabatier's arguments, see his edition of the *Speculum Perfectionis.* For the other side, see Faloci-Pulignani in *Miscellanea Francescana*, vii. 1 and 2 (1898), and *Analecta Bollandiana*, vol. xix. p. 58. The contest is hot and keen.

P. 107, l. 11. Documenta Antiqua Franciscana, pt. 2, ed. Lemmens, Quaracchi, 1901.

P. 108, l. 11. Documenta Antiqua Franciscana, pt. 1, ed. Lemmens, Quaracchi, 1901.

P. 109, l. 1 *et seq.* "non contenti narrare solum miracula, quae sanctitatem non facuint, sed ostendunt, sed etiam sanctae conversationis ejus insignia, et pii beneplaciti voluntatem ostendere cupientes. . . . Quae tamen per modum legendae non scribimus, cum dudum de vita sua et miraculis, quae per eum Dominus operatus est, sint confectae legendae. Sed velut de amoeno prato quosdam flores, qui arbitrio nostro sunt pulchriores, excerpimus, continuantem historiam non sequentes, sed multa seriose relinquentes, quae in praedictis legendis sunt posita." From Prefatory Letter, *Leg.* 3 *Soc.*

P. 109, ll. 16, 17. *La Leggenda di San Francesco scritta da tre suoi Compagni* (legenda trium sociorum) pubblicata per la prima volta nella vera sua integrità dai Padri Marcellino da Civezza e Teofilo Domenichelli. Roma, 1899.

Those interested in the subject of the *Legend of the Three Companions* may consult besides the above work, M. Sabatier's *Vie de S. François* and *Spec. Perf.*, the *Analecta Bollandiana*, vol. xix. 1900; Minocchi, *Legenda* 3 *Soc.* Nuovi Studi in *Archivio storico italiano*, 1899–1900, and Faloci-Pulignani in *Miscellanea Franc.* vii. ff. 3, 4.

BROTHER JACOBA.

Main Sources.

Spec. Perf. c. 112; pp. 273–277.
Bonaventura, c. 8.
Bernard. de Bessa, *Chron.* (*Anal. Fran.*, iii. p. 687).

Actus S. Fran. c. 18; 44.
Fioretti, Fourth Reflection on the Stigmata.
A.SS., Oct. 4, p. 664.
Jacobilli, *Vite de' Sanct.* i. Feb. 8.
Wadding, *Annales*, an. 1226.
Papini, *Storia*, i. p. 157; ii. pp. 16, 207.
Fratini, *Storia della Basilica*, p. 48.
Miscellanea Francescana, vi. p. 168.   Article by P. D'Alençon.

P. 114, ll. 10, 11.   pannum griseum illius coloris, quem gestant Fratres Cistercienses ultramontani.   Colorem alaudarum imitabatur in habitu; qualis illis in plumis, talem volebat in vestibus fratrum, nativum terrenum; ut meminerint communis originis terrae de qua sumpti. Wadding, vol. ii. pp. 139 and 146.

A KING OF VERSES.

MAIN SOURCES.

Spec. Perf. c. 59, 60.
A.SS., July 10, p. 162.
Monumenta Germaniæ, v. 22, p. 492.
Sbaralea, *Supplementum*, p. 571.
Affò, Dizionario della Poesia Volgare, Parma, 1777.
Papini, *Notizie Sicure*, p. 132.
De Angelis, *Dell' Albero di S. Francesco*, Siena, 1827.
Lancetti, *Memorie intorno ai poeti Laureati, Milan*, 1839.
Carboni, *Memorie intorno i letterati della Città di Ascoli*, Ascoli, 1830.
Miscellanea Francescana, ii. 1887, p. 158.

P. 127, l. 30.   The tendency now is to attribute all early Franciscan poems to Jacopone; but probably Pacifico should get the credit of some of them.

P. 130, l. 15.   Hales. See note to p. 178.   Scot. Johannes Duns Scotus (1265?–1308), called *Doctor Subtilis*, traditionally held to have been regent of the University of Paris.

P. 133, l. 6.   See Bull, *Magna sicut*, 1227.

,,   l. 15.   Papini says he was alive in 1261.   I do not insist on the identity of the King of Verses with the Pacifico of the *Fioretti*. Papini seems to give some support to the idea, but the question has hardly been discussed.

P. 135, l. 19.   See Salimbene. Chron. p. 83.

FRATE ELIAS.

Main Sources.

Sabatier's *Spec. Perf.* and *Vie de S François.*
I. Celano (*A.SS.*, Oct. 4, p. 709, *et seq.*).
Eccleston, *De Adventu Minorum in Angliam*, ed. Brewer, p. 44–48.
Chronica Fratris Jordani di Giano (*Analect. Fran.* i.).
Glassberger, *Chron.*, (*Anal. Fran.* ii.).
XXIV. Gen. (*Anal. Fran.* iii. p. 216).
Angelo Clareno, *Tribulations.* Döllinger, "Beiträge für Sektengeschichte des Mittelalters," ii. *Prima et Secunda Tribulationes.*
Affò, *Vita di frate Elia.* 2nd. ed. Parma, 1819.
Azzoguidi, *S. Antonii Ulyssiponensis Sermones*, vol. i. xci. *et seq.* Nota xxvi. Bologna, 1757.
Rybka, *Élias von Cortona*, Leipzig, 1874.
Studi Storici, vol. iv. i. p. 41, Turin, 1895.
Lempp, *Frère Élie de Cortone*, Paris, 1901.

P. 144, l. 36. "the sick turned out." See *Spec. Perf.* 6.
P. 148, l. 23. "a great extension and increase." In II. Celano there is an echo of Francis's fear of the too quick growth of the Order. "O si fieri posset ut mundus perraro fratres minores aspiciens de paucitate miretur!" *Cf.* the often-quoted words of Salimbene—"Ah! domine Helya, multiplicasti gentem, non magnificasti laetitiam," Chron. p. 404.
P. 151, l. 21. For the letters of Francis to Elias, see *Opus. B. Franc.* Epist. vi.–viii.
P. 153, l. 15. "at Foligno." See Faloci-Pulignani, *Le Relazioni tra S. Francesco et la città di Foligno.* Foligno, 1893.
P. 157, l. 5. Celano's version is as follows—"'Te, inquit, fili, in omnibus, et per omnia benedico, et sicut in manibus tuis fratres meos et filios augmentavit Altissimus, super te et in te omnibus benedico. In caelo et in terra benedicat te omnium Dominus Deus. Benedico, sicut possum, et plus quam possum; et quod non possum ego, possit in te, qui omnia potest. Recordetur Deus operis ac laboris tui, et in tribulatione justorum sors tua servetur. Omnem benedictionem, quam cupis, invenias, et quod digne postulas, impleatur." I Cel. *A.SS.*, Oct. 4, p. 713.
P. 157, l. 31. "letter to all the brothers." The original letter—or letters, for it may be two run into one—will be found, *A.SS.*, Oct. 4, p. 668-69.
P. 159, l. 1. "seven gallant missionaries." Brothers Daniele, Agnello, Samuel, Donulo, Leo, Nicolo, Ugolino, See *XXIV. Gen.* (*Anal. Fran.* iii. pp. 32 and 613).

P. 160, l. 27. For John Parenti, see his life in *XXIV. Gen.* (*Anal. Fran.* iii. p. 210).

P. 161, l. 9. The deed of gift is to be found in Azzoguidi, *op. cit.*, and in Lempp's *Frère Élie*, p. 170.

P. 161, l. 29. Jacopo Alamanni. For the building and art of the Basilica see Thode, *Franz von Assisi* and *The Story of Assisi* (Mediæval towns).

P. 163, l. 20. "sweeping edict." Bonaventura ordered the destruction of all legends anterior to his own, which was written in 1263. His object was, of course, to stop controversy. See p. 425.

P. 166, l. 37. discovered only in our own, *i.e.* 1818. See Papini, *Notizie Sicure.* Foligno, 1824.

P. 173, l. 26. "learned these delights." It is interesting, in connection with Elias's love of luxury, to remember that he had early been reproached for his attempts to exaggerate the asceticism of the brothers.

P. 177, l. 11. the Saxon brothers. See Chron. Jordani de Giano (*Anal. Fr.* i. p. 19).

P. 178, l. 7. "the protesters." Some of the chroniclers give the name of St. Anthony of Padua among these, even ascribing to him the rôle of Aymon at the Chapter of 1239. Anthony, who was probably a moderate supporter of Elias, died 1231.

P. 178, l. 8. Alexander Hales, called the *Doctor irrefragabilis*, born at Hales, Gloucestershire; entered the Franciscan Order at Paris, 1222; lectured there till 1238; died 1245.

P. 181, l. 37. Dr. Lempp seems to think it possible that it is to this Chapter Salimbene refers (ll. 27–29). It does not seem likely. Salimbene says only, "Postquam erat depositus, et ibat cum Imperatore vagabundus, quadam die venit ad *quemdam locum fratrum Minorum, et congregatis fratribus in capitulo,* coepit velle ostendere innocentiam suam." Chron. p. 412.

MADONNA POVERTY.

Main Sources.

Sacrum Commercium Beati Francisci cum Domina Paupertate, edidit P. Eduardus Alinconiensis O.M.C., Romae, 1900.

English translation of D'Alençon's text. *The Lady Poverty,* by Montgomery Carmichael. Murray, 1901.

(Mr. Carmichael supports D'Alençon's views concerning the authorship of the treatise.)

Nota al Canto XI. "*del Paradiso,*" v. 73–75, ed. Edoardo Alvisi. Lapi, Citta di Castello, 1894.

Le Mistiche Nozze di San Francesco e Madonna Povertà, ed. Salvatore Minocchi. Firenze, 1901.

Meditatione sulla Povertà di San Francesco, ed. Fanfani and Bindi, Pistoja, 1847.

P. 193, l. 12. For Ubertino's paraphrase see *Arbor Vitae crucifixae Jesu*, lib. v. c. iii. For the remarkable figure which he added, and for the whole subject, see chapter on *Dante and the Franciscans*, p. 400 *et seq*.

P. 193, l. 35. See *Tribulations*. Döllinger, ii. p. 479.

P. 194, ll. 29–30. John of Peckham. See Sbaralea, *Supplementum*, p. 447.

P. 201, l. 11. "long year after long year," literally, " a time and time and half a time."

P. 204, l. 21. " Thou didst not forsake." See p. 400.

JOHN OF PARMA.

MAIN SOURCES.

Tribulations, ed. Ehrle. *Archiv für Litteratur-und-kirchenges-chichte des Mittelalters*, ii. pp. 280–82, 270–286; Döllinger, *Beiträge*, ii., Tertia Tribulatio, Quarta Tribulatio.

Eccleston, *De Adventu Minorum.*

XXIV. Gen. (*Anal. Fran.*, iii. p. 270).

Fioretti, 48.

Salimbene, *Chronicle.*

Ubertino da Casale, *Arbor Vitae*, l. v. c. iii.

A.SS., March 19, p. 58.

Affò, *Vita del beato Giovanni da Parma*, Parma, 1777.

Daunou in *Hist. Litter. de la France*, 20, p. 23.

Gebhart, *L'Italie Mystique*, Paris, 1887.

For the strife between the University of Paris and the Mendicant Orders, see Rashdall's *Universities of Europe*, vol. i. pp. 369–390.

For the questions of Joachimism and the *Eternal Gospel*, see Denifle, *Archiv für Litt.*, i. pt. 1, 1885; Renan's *Nouvelles Études d'histoire réligieuse*, p. 217; and Tocco, *L'Eresia nel Medio Evo.*

P. 226, l. 21. For this supplement see *Analecta Bollandiana*, xviii. p. 81; *Trattato dei Miracoli di S. Francesco di Assisi.*

P. 227, ll. 34–35. Better known as Hugues de Digne. See Sbaralea, *Supplementum*, p. 360. An interesting account of him is given by Salimbene. Joinville describes his preaching before St. Louis.

For these notes respecting John's friends Salimbene is, I need hardly say, the authority.

P. 241, l. 12. Pietro dei Nubili. Döllinger, *Beiträge*, ii. p. 479.

P. 242, l. 3. " letter of Cardinal Ottoboni." Let Adrian's generous intervention be put against his avarice condemned by Dante, *Purg.* xix.

P. 250, l. 22. "many pilgrimages." Of his cult at Camerino some interesting details are given in an otherwise worthless book—written to urge the acknowledgment of his beatification by Rome—*Vita del B. Giovanni da Parma*, by P. Filippi Camerini.

SALIMBENE OF PARMA.

MAIN SOURCES.

Chronica Fr. Salimbene Parmensis O.M., Parmæ, 1857.
Affò, *Scrittori Parmigiani*, vol. i. p. 208, 1789, &c.
Gebhart, *Études Méridionales*, Paris, 1887.
Clédat, *De fratre Salimbene et de ejus Chronicae auctoritate*, Paris, 1878.
Novati, *La cronaca di Salimbene* (*Giorn. Stor. della letterat. ital.*, 1883).
Dove, *Die Doppelchronik von Reggio und die Quellen Salimbene's*, Leipzig, 1889.
Michael, *Salimbene und seine Chronik*, Innsbrück, 1889.
Tabarrini, *Studi di Critica Storica*, Firenze, 1876.

P. 258, l. 36. Fra Giovanni da Pian del Carpine, Minorite, one of the most notable of mediæval travellers ; sent on a papal mission to the Great Khan ; died Archbishop of Antivari in Dalmatia. His book, *Liber Tartorum*, was abridged by Vincent de Beauvais, and quoted by Hakluyt and other writers ; but the complete text was only published in 1839 in the *Recueil de Voyages* of the Geographical Society of Paris, vol. iv.

P. 258, l. 37. Bartholomæus Anglicus, fl. 1230–1250, an English Minorite, sent from Paris to the Saxon province in 1231. His book, *De Proprietatibus Rerum*, was the encyclopædia of the Middle Ages.

P. 259, l. 3. Gerardo Patecchio (Girard Pateg), author of *De Taediis*, favourite poet and contemporary of Salimbene, is the earliest known poet of N. Italy.

P. 269, ll. 4–5. "A king . . . a margravine." St. Louis and St. Elizabeth of Hungary.

P. 291, l. 20. Fra Bertoldo da Ratisbon. d. 1272. One of the greatest preachers of the thirteenth century. His mission in Bavaria, Bohemia, and Moravia was a revival on a great scale. The Pope gave him the power of granting an Indulgence of several days after his sermons.

P. 293, l. 23. For another account of Obizzo, see Affò, *Scrittori parmigiani*, vol. i. p. 195.

P. 294, l. 36. Cardinal Latino Malabranca. See *Histoire des Hommes Illustres de l'Ordre de S. Dominique*, t. i., l. 6, p. 542.

P. 295, l. 21. See *Vie de Sainte Douceline*, Marseilles, 1879.

P. 296, l. 27. Giovanni da Vicenza. For a corrective account of this great Dominican, see *Scriptores Ord. Praedic.*, i. 150.

P. 302, l. 4. The rest of the poem seems to come from a man to whom life had no value at all. Bartoli, *Storia della Letter*, i. p. 194, gives part of it. So does Trench, *Sacred Latin Poetry*. But the cheerful Salimbene did not quote the rest.

CONRAD D'OFFIDA.

Main Sources.

Ehrle, *Tribulations* (*Archiv.*, ii. p. 311 *et seq.*).
Döllinger, *Beiträge*, ii. p. 494 *et seq.*
Actus S. Franc., 50, 53.
Fioretti, 42–44.
XXIV. Gen. (*Anal. Fran.*, iii. p. 422).
Spec. Perf. Sabatier's preface, cxl–cxlv.
Jacobilli, *Vite de' Santi*, iii., Dec. 12.
Giunta Bevegnati. *Antica Leggenda di Sta. Margarita di Cortona*, ed. 1793, pp. 243, 289.
Bartholi, *Tractatus de Indulgentiâ*, ed. Sabatier, 1900.
Salvatore Vitalis, *Monte Serafico della Verna*, p. 258.

P. 306, l. 6. "chief medium." For words of Leo quoted by Conrad, see *Miscellanea Francescana*, t. vii. p. 131.

CELESTINE V.

Main Sources.

A.SS., May 19, p. 418.
Stefaneschi, *Opus metricum* in *A.SS.*, p. 443.
Petrarch, *De Vitâ Solitaria*.
Analecta Bollandiana, vols. ix. and x. ; *Vita et miracula Scti. Petri Coelestini*.
D'Ailly (Card.), *Vita B. patris D. Petri Coelestini*, Paris, 1539.
Marino, *Vita et Miracoli di S. Pietro del Morrone*, Milan, 1637.
Tosti, *Storia di Bonifazio VIII.*, Milan, 1848.
Celestino V. ed il VI. centenario della sua incoronazione, Aquila, 1894.

P. 316, l. 3. "Church canonised him," under Clement V., 1313.

P. 320, l. 2. "hang his cowl on a sunbeam." Amid much nauseous stuff there are many curious and picturesque legends to be dug out of the old lives of Celestine. My limited purpose only permits a passing reference to these.

P. 321, l. 7. "Badia del San Spirito." The legend says that while he was looking for a site a wild dove flew round and round him and his brothers. This was looked on as a good augury and a direct message. Hence the dedication to the Holy Spirit.

P. 326, l. 14. "a poor little hermitage." "Domus et facies habitus gestusque beatum demonstrant." Stefaneschi.

P. 337, l. 7. "a prison in very truth." When Peter first saw his quarters in Fumone he is said to have exclaimed : "Cellam desideravi, cellam habeo, sicut tuae placuit pietati, Domine Deus meus." This has encouraged a curious complacency on the part of some of his biographers, even of those who confess that the cell was so narrow that where he put his feet when he said mass he laid his head when he slept.

P. 337, l. 35. "Death freed him." In the hour of his death Robert, his beloved disciple, far away on Majella, saw him on the mountain side as if he were seeking a still higher, lonelier resting-place. He would have gone with him, but he was bidden wait ; and Peter went on alone.

ANGELO CLARENO.

MAIN SOURCES.

A.SS., June 15, p. 566.

Ehrle, *Die Spiritualen* in *Archiv für Litteratur-und-kirchen-geschichte des Mittelalters*, vol. i.–iv.

Döllinger, *Beiträge zur Sektengeschichte des Mittelalters*, Theil 2, p. 417. Munich, 1890.

Wadding, an. 1289, &c.

Tocco, *L'Eresia nel medio evo.*

P. 340, ll. 8–9. "never all been published." A complete edition is promised by Tocco, who has changed his mind about the *Tribulations* in some respects since he wrote *L'Eresia nel medio evo.*

For the after history of Angelo's brotherhood, see Wadding ; also *A.SS.*, June 15, p. 572.

JACOPONE DA TODI.

MAIN SOURCES.

I Cantici del Beato Jacopone da Todi—con la vita sua (life by Modio), Roma, 1588.

Poesie inedite del B. Jacopone da Todi, ed. de Mortara, Lucca, 1819.

Le Poesie Spirituali del B. Jacopone da Todi, ed. Tresatti, Venetia, 1617.

Ausgewählte Gedichte von J. da Todi. Deutsch von C. Schlüter and W. Storck, Münster, 1864.

Antica Vita, ed. Tobler, in *Zeitschrift für romanische Philologie*, ii. p. 26.

Wadding, *Annales*, v. vi.

D'Ancona, *Studi sulla Letteratura ital. de' primi secoli*, Ancona, 1884.

D'Ancona, *Origini del Teatro in Italia*, Firenze, 1877.

Gaspary, *Italian Literature to the Death of Dante*, trs. Oelsner, Bell, 1901.

Ozanam, *Les poétes franciscains.*

Mohnike, *Studien.* Stralsund, 1825.

P. 356, l. 12. "lo quale," *Antica Vita*, ed. Tobler.

P. 360, ll. 33–34. "Jacopone's place . . . in primitive drama." See d'Ancona, *Origini del Teatro.*

P. 361, l. 3. "has got the credit of many that are not his." There is no critical edition of Jacopone, and one is wanted. Criticism may take away from him many poems I have referred to here—may even give some of them back to S. Francis.

P. 361, l. 9. "la liberta francischino," *Antica Vita*, ed. Tobler.

P. 366, l. 5. On the one hand some critics have taken the *Stabat Mater* from him and given it to Innocent III. On the other he has been given the credit of *Cur mundus militat.* See Wadding.

P. 366, l. 30. "no parish poet." *Cf.* the conclusion of the Jesuit poet Balde's fine eulogy of Jacopone. See Trench's *Sacred Latin Poetry*, p. 245.

P. 386, l. 12. "It was believed," &c. Life by Modio, preface to *I Cantici*, Rome, 1588.

DANTE AND THE FRANCISCANS.

Main Sources.

Commento di F. Buti sopra la Divina Commedia, ed. Giannini, Pisa, 1858.

Bonaventura, *Legenda S. Francisci.*

Sacrum Commercium (see p. 191 *et seq.*).

Arbor Vitæ, v. c. iii.

Scartazzini, *Dante, Manuali Hoepli*, 42.

    ,,   *A Companion to Dante*, ed. A. J. Butler, Macmillan, 1893.

E. G. Gardner, *Dante's Ten Heavens*, Constable, 1900.

E. Moore, *Studies in Dante.* Second series.

P. Toynbee, *Dante Dictionary*, Clarendon Press.

Thode, *Franz von Assisi.*

Savini, F., *I papi . . . i chierici . . . i frati a giudizio di Dante*, Ravenna, 1889.

Kraus, *Dante, sein Leben*, 1897.

Ozanam, *Dante et la Philosophie Catholique au XIIIème siècle*, 1845.

Di Bisogno, *S. Bonaventura e Dante*, Milan, 1899.

Giornale Dantesco, 1899, *Noterelle Francescane.*

U. Cosmo, *Le mistiche nozze di frate Francesco*, Florence, 1898.

P. 389, l. 4. " Mestica's interesting study," *Nuova Antologia*, 1881, xxvii. xxviii.

P. 394, l. 19. "effaced the earlier legends." "Praecipit generale Capitulum per obedientiam quod omnes legendae de beato Francisco olim factae deleantur et ubi inveniri poterant extra ordinem ipsas fratres studeant amovere, cum illa legenda quae facta est per generalem sit compilata prout ipse habuit ab ore illorum qui cum beato Francisco quasi semper fuerunt et cuncta certitudinaliter scriverint et probata ibi sint posita diligenter." Edict of Chapter of Paris, 1266.

P. 395, l. 15. Morico. For two early brothers of this name, see Le Monnier's *Histoire de Saint François*, i. pp. 117–18.

P. 397, l. 15. Masseo's account of the saint's farewell. See p. 91.

„ l. 34. "a legal document." The text of it is given in Lempp's " Frère Elie," p. 173.

P. 400, l. 21. Sacrum Commercium. See p. 191 *et seq.*

P. 402, l. 6. Nannucci, *Letterat. del primo secolo*, p. 385.

P. 406, ll. 14, 15. " verses of . . . Guido Cavalcanti and Giotto." Translations of both will be found in D. G. Rossetti's *Dante and his Circle.*

P. 406, l. 25. Dr. Moore, *Studies in Dante*, second series, pp. 63, 65, 194, 258 *et seq.*

P. 407, l. 10. Ordina quest' amore. See *Amor di Caritate.* Ven. ed. vi. 16. Rossetti has translated part of the poem in *Dante and his Circle*, ascribing it to S. Francis.

P. 408, ll. 15, 16. "shepherds of the Casentino." *Fioretti*, Third Reflection on the Stigmata.

INDEX

THE END

Printed by BALLANTYNE, HANSON & Co.
Edinburgh & London

Lightning Source UK Ltd.
Milton Keynes UK
UKHW022355191219
355711UK00007B/226/P

9 781342 125439